Ukraine Crisis

ANDREW WILSON is a Senior Policy Fellow at the European Council on Foreign Relations, and Reader in Ukrainian Studies at the School of Slavonic and East European Studies, University College London. He has published widely on the politics of Eastern Europe, including *The Ukrainians* (now in its third edition), *Ukraine's Orange Revolution*, *Virtual Politics: Faking Democracy in the Post-Soviet World* (the latter two joint winners of the Alexander Nove Prize in 2007) and *Belarus: The Last European Dictatorship*, all four books published by Yale University Press. His publications at the European Council on Foreign Relations (www.ecfr.eu) include *The Limits of Enlargement-Lite: European and Russian Power in the Troubled Neighbourhood* and *Meeting Medvedev: The Politics of the Putin Succession.*

D0916766

Ukraine Crisis

Crisis

WHAT IT MEANS FOR THE WEST

Andrew Wilson

YALE UNIVERSITY PRESS
NEW HAVEN AND LONDON

For information about this and other Yale University Press publications, please contact:
U.S. Office: sales.press@yale.edu   www.yalebooks.com
Europe Office: sales@yaleup.co.uk   www.yalebooks.co.uk

Typeset in Minion Pro by IDSUK (DataConnection) Ltd
Printed in the United States of America

Library of Congress Control Number: 2014950580

ISBN 978-0-300-21159-7

A catalogue record for this book is available from the British Library.

10 9 8 7 6 5 4 3 2 1

Contents

Introduction   *vi*

1   Unfinished Europe   1

2   Russia Putinesca   19

3   Yanukovych's Ukraine   38

4   Maidan 2.0   66

5   The Uprising   86

6   Crimea   99

7   The Eastern Imbroglio   118

8   Ukraine's Unfinished Revolution, or a Revolution Barely Begun?   144

9   Other Hotspots   161

10 Russia versus the West   183

    Conclusions   205

    Notes   *208*

    Index   *233*

Introduction

I was in Kiev in February 2014, the week of the Uprising. The protests that had begun the previous November looked like they were heading for some kind of dénouement, but I was actually travelling because it was university half term – it seemed like a good idea at the time. When the bloodshed began, I kept my promise to my wife to stay out of obvious danger, and I know the city quite well; but that meant I needed to think just where the by now notorious 'Berkut' militia was on the attack, and where the snipers' bullets were coming from – and then go in the opposite direction. I was actually more worried about the gangs of government thugs – the so-called *titushki* – who were randomly roaming the streets and who, by that point, were out of control and prone to simple theft and violence. Ducking down back streets was not a good option either, as that was where the militia's vans were parked (horrific stories were later to emerge of beatings and killings inside them). There were more Ukrainians who disappeared than were confirmed dead during the Uprising.

Ukraine was in turmoil, as men in masks carried out a coup d'état at gunpoint. Except that the coup was not in Kiev, as Russian propaganda claimed, but in Crimea a week later. Russia would annex Crimea, after little more than two dozen heavily armed militia took over the Crimean parliament and installed a pro-Russian puppet government. Many belonged to the Berkut, and had just been killing people in Kiev. They were therefore on the run, their main motive being to avoid arrest. They were still wearing their balaclava masks as if in a Quentin Tarantino movie, with a trail of disaster unfolding after a bungled heist.

But they got away with it. Russia's Crimean adventure brought about the first formal annexation of territory in Europe since 1945 – other states have collapsed and new ones been born, but this was the first formal land grab.

Russia's misadventure in the Donbas region of east Ukraine, however, then left it embroiled in a seemingly unwinnable proxy war. In March, Putin looked clever, fiendish and unstoppable. In July, the Malaysia Airline's flight MH17 was shot down over the Donbas with the loss of 298 lives.

This book is about the 'Ukraine crisis', but the label is somewhat misleading. The crisis was also of Russia's making and was about Russia's future. Norman Stone is fond of reducing the complex causality of the twentieth century's two world wars to the claim that 'the Germans went ape'.[1] This is not an anti-Russian book, but the story of the twenty-first century has pretty much been the same: the Russians went ape. Russia's action was really Putin's action, but it was also the product of Russia's addiction to dangerous myths – myths which, at some point in the 1990s, the world stopped correcting: that Russia had been 'humiliated'; that the former USSR was the 'lost territory' of historical Russia; that Russia's historic fear of encirclement was replaying itself because of NATO expansion.

Russia has the world's biggest persecution complex. Maybe Russia had been humiliated, but if so it is by other Russians – both the oligarchs who dominated the Yeltsin era and those who rule it now (known in Russia simply as 'Putin's friends'), who happen to be much richer than their predecessors in the 1990s. Even if true, metaphors like 'humiliation' or 'encirclement' are not a programme of action or a guide for policy. They could generate many responses, both good and bad: aside from invading your neighbours, making friends and alliances is another way of breaking the fear of encirclement.

The crisis was also international. Russia's annexation of Crimea and its undermining of Ukrainian sovereignty were direct challenges to the whole post-Cold War security order, which Russia had previously stoutly defended. That order was never entirely satisfactory, and it had failed to defend Ukraine; but the challenge from Russia was not merely local or short term. Russia was undergoing a major change in its attitudes, its worldview and its level of assertiveness, and there would be no return to 'business as usual' after the immediate challenges in Ukraine. Nationalism based on Russian ethnicity and language had come together with the imperial notion of 'Eurasia' and the 'conservative values' agenda launched by Putin in 2012 to replace the vague hope of Soviet restoration that dominated the 1990s and 2000s. Or so it seemed. Putin's Russia was as cynical as ever. The new ideological mix was also just the latest cover story for a kleptocratic regime. This particular mix was just more dangerous. Ukraine was not the only state under threat.

Russia had many tactical advantages to push this agenda in the short term, but in the longer term it was clearly overextended. The economic boom of the original Putin years (2000–08) was ending. It seems likely that the whole adventure will eventually cost Russia dear, but the collateral damage might be huge.

This was also a major crisis for Europe. The worrying thing was that there were so many in Europe who did *not* think that this was a major crisis of the EU's credibility, powers of attraction and entire modus operandi, and therefore carried on with business as usual. Putin thought he could exploit this way of doing business, and he was right. The EU's initial response was weak and inept. It constantly sought to 'stabilise' a situation that Putin kept redefining, and was prepared to equate the unequal by arguing for the same restraint from Ukraine's legitimate authorities on its own sovereign territory as from the men in masks – often Russians from Russia – who were challenging that authority. Putin thought that Europe was too comfortable and too prosperous, even after the Great Recession, and was so unused to sacrifice that it was incapable of addressing (or even understanding) old-fashioned hard power. And, at least until the wake-up call of the Malaysia Airlines disaster, it seemed he was right. There was still something impressive about the way European incomprehension predominated over anger: why would anybody do such a thing? But there were also dangers: what would stop anybody doing the same again?

The crisis was also a test for the United States. Obama's entire foreign policy was about prioritisation, and his administration duly de-emphasised the whole of Eastern Europe after 2009. Ending the Bush wars in Iraq and Afghanistan came first. America's voice in Eastern Europe was barely audible off-stage before the Ukraine crisis broke in November 2013; it then woke up and began playing a more active role, but the long-term assumption that the US could lead from behind in the EU's backyard had clearly been proved wrong. More generally, global prioritisation would produce few net gains if regional powers simply made trouble in any region left behind, and if Washington had to return to fire-fighting mode.

The crisis was also about the future prospects for the entire region, and about Russian pressure on other exposed states in Eastern Europe, the Caucasus and Central Asia – and on some badly-run EU countries, like Bulgaria, or even some well-run ones, like the Baltic States. The crisis was also about Russia's influence at the heart of Europe, in Germany, Italy, the UK and France. Because Europe had failed for so long to address problems on the periphery, Russian money, Russian business and Russian media were now corrupting public life in London, Berlin and Brussels.

Even within Ukraine, the crisis was about challenging the entire post-Soviet order, not just ending the corrupt regime of President Viktor Yanukovych. According to Freedom House, which likes to rank these things, only three out of fifteen post-Soviet states were 'consolidated democracies' in 2014 (the three Baltic States). Another three (Ukraine, Georgia and Moldova) were classed as 'transitional' or 'hybrid' regimes. The Uprising was, in one sense, an attempt at the anti-Soviet revolution that Ukraine never had in 1991. It was a curious concoction of a revolution, though. Statues of Lenin were pulled down, protestors hurled cobblestones and Molotov cocktails, but then wandered peacefully around Yanukovych's abandoned villa. To some extent, the Uprising was on behalf of everybody in the former Soviet Union; but whether or not its effects would spread was another question. Russia intervened because it wanted to see the Uprising fail, because Putin argued that Ukraine was not a real country, and because he contended that Ukraine was a 'failed state' anyway. Ironically, Ukraine seemed likely to emerge from the crisis with a stronger sense of national identity, born out of struggle with Russia. But Russian intervention looked as though it would succeed in making it very difficult to transform Ukrainian politics, society and economy in the way the Maidan protestors had hoped. If Ukraine remained a weak state, it would be no role model for its neighbours, or for the submerged Russian opposition.

Finally, the Ukraine events were part of a cycle of global protest, but marked a change in that cycle. The February Uprising was a combination of old-style passive resistance, an Occupy Wall Street movement and a Cossack rebellion. It had much in common with the wave of protests, from the Indignants Movement in Spain to Tahrir Square in Egypt; but it was also uniquely Ukrainian. Unlike many other social network-based, leaderless, non-violent protests, it ended up rather old-fashioned, with protestors hurling cobblestones and Molotov cocktails at the police. Other protest movements, and other nervous autocrats, would take note. But the fact that rebellion has a tradition in Ukrainian history going back to the medieval Cossack era was not necessarily a good thing. According to a former adviser to Viktor Yushchenko (the president before Yanukovych), 'Ukrainians are good at uprisings, but not at revolutions; we are good at *bunt* ['rebellion' or 'anarchic revolt'], but not at using the results; better at putting people in place, but then it is always a problem when those people have to deliver.'[2]

Time will tell. I have written this book in the knowledge that events are still changing fast on the ground. By the time you read it, many things may seem out of date; but I have tried to focus on general trends, albeit with lots of local detail. Thanks are due to all my contacts in Ukraine – specifically to Alex Andreyev and Anton Shekhovtsov – to Stanislav Secrieru and to all at University College London and the European Council on Foreign Relations, to Daryl Joseph, to Dimitar Bechev, and to Robert Baldock, Rachael Lonsdale and Clive Liddiard at Yale University Press, plus my anonymous reviewers. Some of my research was financed by the European Union: ANTICORRP (Grant agreement no. 290529). I have translated rather than transliterated the footnotes to make them a little more accessible.

CHAPTER 1

Unfinished Europe

In March 2014, Herman Van Rompuy, then one of the two presidents that oversee the Byzantine politics of the EU, said of the Ukraine crisis that 'the world will never be as before'.[1] This was deeply ironic, because the EU was the one institution most likely to carry on as if nothing had happened. But Van Rompuy was right: real Europe had changed, even as institutional Europe stood still. A neat quarter of a century after the fall of the Berlin Wall in 1989, the post-Cold War order faced fundamental challenges. Russia's annexation of Crimea was an affront to assumed rigid rules of international security; Ukraine's willingness to rebel against a corrupt president and fight for its territorial integrity were reminders of an older and more vigorous Europe beneath the malaise of a Euro crisis and decaying public politics. The demonstrators in Kiev began the crisis by massing in the streets when their president rejected a key deal with the EU, but ended up convinced that they had sacrificed blood for 'European values', while EU states would not sacrifice treasure for the same cause. The European Union's version of Europe had not just sheltered, but actively touted for, the money of Ukrainian and Russian oligarchs, and constantly shied away from sanctions that would harm its own banking or business interests.

But it would be a mistake – albeit a tempting one – to begin this story in 1989, when the Berlin Wall came down, or in 1991, when the Soviet Union's bricks and mortar collapsed. Especially because Russian President Vladimir Putin claimed that his actions had flowed from the illegitimate way in which the USSR came to an ignominious end twenty-three years before. This was a false reading of events. Russian politics has not been driven ever since 1991 by a burning desire to 'recover' territories like Crimea. Ukraine has not been oppressing its minorities and failing as a state all that time. Most of the other post-Soviet states have moved on from whatever happened in 1991: they do not even like being called 'post-Soviet' anymore.

But it would also be misleading to start the story in early 2014, only weeks or days before the Russian annexation of Crimea. Clearly, Putin's moves against Ukraine were in large part opportunistic. He also felt threatened by the Uprising in Kiev – though the threat was mainly to his own political system, rather than to his fellow Russians in Crimea or the Donbas. Only one Russian was killed in the February crisis – Igor Tkachuk, a father of three – and he was shot by one of President Yanukovych's snipers in Kiev. Putin's calculations were indeed mainly short term. The takeover of Crimea was so smooth that it appeared to have been prepared in advance; but everything might have been different if Ukrainian President Yanukovych had not fled Kiev, or if Ukrainian armed forces had put up a fight in Crimea.

2008: The New Year Zero

I would choose to start the story somewhere in the middle: to be precise, in 2008, the year when everything changed globally – in Europe, at least, super-seding 1989 as a reference point. In fact, so many things happened in 2008 that it is often impossible to distinguish cause and effect. Events segued into one another, and the dust was still settling in 2014. Putin ceded the Russian presidency to Dmitriy Medvedev in May 2008; Russia and Georgia went to war in August. The collapse of Lehman Brothers in September was followed by the onset of global economic crisis and, in November, by the election as American president of Barack Obama, who organised massive financial bailouts even before he took office the following January. War fatigue and intervention fatigue set in for the West as the Iraq 'surge' in 2007 was followed by Obama's Afghanistan surge in 2009. Increasingly introspective Western public opinion would also be austerity-weary by the time Russia annexed Crimea in 2014. The EU responded to the war in Georgia by fast-forwarding its new 'Eastern Partnership' for the six states in Eastern Europe and the Caucasus, Georgia included (the others being Ukraine, Belarus and Moldova, plus Armenia and Azerbaijan); but its formal launch at a summit in Prague in May 2009 could not have been more badly timed, as the global economic crisis soon became the euro crisis.

More generally, European politics became more nationalistic, more populist and more zero-sum. The 'renationalisation' of foreign policies and a new harder-edged emphasis on geo-economics and national business interests killed off such grand projects as maintaining the expansion of NATO and the EU to Eastern Europe. Domestic politics was more volatile and politicians

competed to be the most ardent defenders of 'national interests'. Politics in
Russia and Eastern Europe beyond the EU became more of a local affair, more
subject to toxic local rivalries.

Putin Returns

The second proximate cause of the events of 2014 was Putin's return to the
Russian presidency in 2012. The process was supposed to be a coronation
rather than an election, but Putin briefly let the crown slip on his way back to
the throne. After initially seeming disoriented as mass protests broke out in
Moscow, Putin II chose to discredit those who rallied against him as the 'metro-
politan' vanguard of the decadent West, unrepresentative of his Russia, the 'real
Russia', the guardian of older and truer European values, the Holy Trinity of
God, authority and family. Armed with this 'conservative values project',
the new Putin was a different man from the Putin who had been president
from 2000 to 2008 – and, of course, from Dmitriy Medvedev, his stop-gap
predecessor, even though most observers had assumed that Putin had been
pulling the real strings of power all along.

The explosion in Ukraine in 2014 was not an inevitable result of all these
factors, but nor was it either complete chance or preordained back in 1991.
There was also a law of variable consequences after 2008. Anything could
happen after so much had happened. Economic crisis could have caused Russia
to retrench, but it chose to expand. Or in fact it did both. Immediately after
2008, many Russians were talking about wanting a zone of influence but not a
zone of responsibility, or selective influence without picking up all the bills. In
2014 they invaded Crimea at great long-term cost.

Institutional Europe Enlarges

When the Berlin Wall fell in 1989, people looked forward to a Europe whole
and free. The definition of the ultimate borders of Europe, however, was not
clear; nor was it even much thought about at the time. It was simpler to start by
rejecting the idea of two distinct Cold War Europes, there being no historical
reality behind the idea of a politically distinct Socialist Camp. *Mitteleuropisch*
intellectuals like Milan Kundera liked to argue that Prague or Budapest or
Warsaw were in reality 'the kidnapped West' behind an artificial Iron Curtain.

Then the Soviet Union first opened up, and then collapsed in 1991. It was
less clear just how much of the former USSR was made up of other parts of
captured Europe: a reasonable proposition might have been everywhere west
of Russia, plus the two ancient Christian southern Caucasus nations of Georgia

and Armenia; meanwhile the status of Russia itself would be up for debate, as always.

By 2004, most of the USSR's satellite states in Central Europe and the Balkans were in the institutional EU version of Europe, with the big but declining exception of the former Yugoslavia. Most of the former USSR was not, with the exception of the three Baltic States. None of this was preordained. The new post-communist Member States of the EU and NATO had to work much harder to get in than the original members or earlier applicants, like Greece, and were constantly being told that their aspirations were 'unrealistic'. Then, ironically, in 2007 Bulgaria and Romania were let in, before they were ready. Ukraine and Georgia looked like they might catch up after their 'coloured revolutions' in 2003–04; but while Georgia made a success of its anti-corruption reforms, Ukraine was unable to make much of a fist of anything. Meanwhile, the EU talked of 'enlargement fatigue' or 'digestion fatigue'. Unfortunate Eastern Europe was left in the waiting room – although Croatia joined in 2013.

The EU sleepwalked through another twenty-year boom from 1989 to 2008 (after the original thirty years, the Trente Glorieuses in France and elsewhere from 1945 to the mid-1970s). But it did not use the good years well. Some internal barriers came down, but not all; harmonisation and the expansion of common standards was a route to ever-increasing unity, but not to the cheaper costs and dynamic markets that were driving the rise of other global powers. Long-term relative decline accelerated: in 1980 the European bloc accounted for an estimated 31 per cent of world GDP (though it was still two blocs back then); by 2013 the figure was less than 19 per cent.[2] Germany reformed under Gerhard Schröder, and under Tony Blair the UK looked for an elusive 'third way'. But most of the 2000 'Lisbon agenda' to increase European competitiveness remained on the shelf.

Post-modern Europe

But the EU that expanded in the 2000s was also different from the institution that was founded in the 1950s. And not just because it kept changing its name. This story could also begin in 1968, the year that divided Cold War Europe more or less neatly in two. Talk of a new Cold War beginning in 2014 rather neglected the fact that the original Cold War went through many phases and changes: the level of confrontation rose and fell, and it was actually back on 'hot' in the early 1980s, not long before it ended. The West also changed with the cultural, intellectual and technological revolutions that we can conveniently date from around 1968. Western Europe at least became less martial and more post-modern, whatever that meant. Its economic model stalled in the 1970s and was rethought in the 1980s. The West was therefore not so much rising as reorienting and recovering when it 'won' the Cold War.

In 2000, the leading EU foreign policy thinker Robert Cooper published a hugely influential book called *The Post-Modern State and the World Order*, in which he traced some of the foreign policy implications of these changes. He argued that nineteenth-century shibboleths like the state, sovereignty and hard power were being succeeded by a new era of smart interaction, the rise of non-state actors, and security gains and greater strength through sovereignty sharing.[3] On the other side of the fence, Robert Kagan made a similar point less generously: 'Europe is turning away from power . . . it is moving beyond power into a self-contained world of laws and rules and transnational negotiation and cooperation. It is entering a post-historical paradise of peace and relative prosperity, the realization of Immanuel Kant's "perpetual peace".'[4]

This made some sense as a vanguardist description of the priorities of Western European elites, though large parts of their publics remained stuck in the 'old' ways of thinking about the importance of old-fashioned nation states – as, ironically (given Western myths about 'Polish plumbers'), did many of the former communist Member States that joined the EU from 2004.

But, apart from Poland, the large and capable states were still in Western and Southern Europe. The head of the Moscow Carnegie Centre Dmitri Trenin inverted Cooper's perspective, arguing that 'most European countries have long ago ceased to be modern states provided with the complete toolkit of classical statecraft and the will for using it. The few states that still possess elements of both, such as the United Kingdom and France, are no longer big enough to play in the world's premier league.' So, argued Trenin, Cooper's 'notion of a "21st-century world" in which Europe supposedly lives is misleading. The real world, including all of Europe's neighbours, contains large chunks of the legacy of previous epochs.'[5]

Among major nations, only France and the UK passed the NATO target of spending 2 per cent of GDP on defence, though Poland was close. Tiny Estonia also passed (with more moral than practical effect) because it believed in the policy. Most Member States were free-riding on the US until 2008. Then they introduced even deeper defence cuts because of the economic crisis – rather than spending more because of the Georgia war. Now they were free-riding on the assumed provision of some kind of collective security from the EU (alongside NATO); but that assumption was challenged in 2014.

The EU's few foreign policy triumphs have depended on effective partnerships with other players, including the EU's own Member States. The old security paradigm rested on NATO, which bombed Yugoslavia once the US was on board, saving Europe from its embarrassing inaction earlier in the 1990s. In the first big Ukraine crisis in 2004, Poland dragged the EU in. During the Russia–Georgia war of 2008, French President Nicolas Sarkozy took the initiative. On its own, the EU is nowhere near as effective as a security provider. It has some minor successful initiatives, like the border-monitoring mission in Moldova, but it cannot cope with the big stuff like Russia or old-fashioned war at the edge of Europe.

The renegotiation of EU architecture, leading to the Treaty of Lisbon, which came into force in December 2009, did little to help. If anything, it created new institutional rivalries both within and around the new European Commission. Eastern Europe was the responsibility of the new high representative (the 'EU foreign minister'), Cathy Ashton from the UK, but also of Štefan Füle from the Czech Republic, the commissioner for enlargement and the neighbourhood, and to a lesser extent Germany's Günther Oettinger, responsible for energy. The new Commission to be elected in 2014 was due to be formed in much the same way, after most European leaders complacently assumed that the European parliamentary elections in May had not actually been the disaster they were forecast to be.

Post-modern Russia

Russia did not experience 1968 directly: the USSR was too busy invading Czechoslovakia. However, it caught up quickly (albeit selectively) after 1991.

The EU version of Europe is, in reality, a mixture of post-modern factors and old nation-state traditions, reflected in the most complex constitutional and decision-making arrangements imaginable. Russia also mixes up the traditional and the post-modern, but in a different way. It is often said that Russia adopted the communist propaganda version of capitalism; but it also adopted a distorted view of how post-modern societies and political systems work. Russia's post-Soviet politics leap-frogged into an ultra-cynical world of manipulation (explored in Chapter 2), where everything is permissible and where there is no higher truth. But Russia took the opposite journey from the EU in international politics. The USSR was a multi-national state that was something like an empire; modern Russia is on its way towards becoming an ethnic nation state, arguably for the first time in its history – though its journey is incomplete, just as the EU is not really supranational. And Russia has also travelled back to a very traditional view of defending its national sovereignty with hard power.

If Russia is now in renewed conflict with the West, it is not some simple replay of the Cold War. Thinking and capabilities have shifted on both sides. Nor is it just old-fashioned imperialist Russia reprising nineteenth-century great-power politics and out of tune with the post-modern West. Russia believes in the old-fashioned hard power of armies and missiles, but it is also a kind of 'post-modern dictatorship',[6] with a cynical understanding of the ways in which the West's technologies and foibles can be turned against itself.

Economic Europe Stagnates

This is not the place to rehearse all of the EU's economic problems, or the process whereby a private sector liquidity crisis in 2008 became a 'sovereign debt crisis' for so many EU states in 2010. The July 2012 promise by Mario Draghi, the new head of the European Central Bank (ECB), to do 'whatever it takes' at least provided a temporary end to the euro crisis. The ECB's promise to purchase government bonds in the secondary markets did enough to bring down borrowing rates. A new architecture was created for the euro: strict budget rules were made supposedly inviolable, banking oversight centralised, and the ECB printing presses let loose (though it was still not a proper lender of last resort). The euro had survived its first crisis, but it remained to be seen whether it would survive a second. And the EU still had a growth crisis. At the end of 2013, the eurozone's collective GDP was still 3 per cent less than its pre-crisis level in the first quarter of 2008. Some countries sputtered into growth, but not at the approximate rate of 3 per cent required to prevent their debt-to-GDP ratios getting ever bigger. Italy's GDP was still 8 per cent off its peak, and Greece's was a full 27 per cent. The ECB was unable to offer the kind of quantitative easing that in the USA and UK fuelled recovery (and possible future inflation). Recovery was also plagued by many types of moral hazard, as gamblers were bailed out and savers punished, undermining incentives to solve underlying problems. The renationalisation of banks and bank lending kept credit scarce.

After 2010, the new cliché was the virtuous north versus the indebted south, though it was the south that actually had more incentive to reform. But the southern EU states were certainly too preoccupied with crisis, reform or both to care much about Eastern Europe. They talked of the EU's 'absorption capacities' and such like, but what they really meant was that the east was not part of their world. Migration emerged as the new number one concern for almost every EU state, north and south; the rest of Europe was only deemed important as its potential source.

But the biggest difference in Europe was generational: twentieth-century enmities meant little if you had lived most of your life in the twenty-first. The threat of war meant nothing if you were under twenty-one. The EU was slow and bureaucratic, but it was also boring. The 2010s saw the rise of a new politics of protest, which was rooted in the personal politics of social media. What you felt about the system was what mattered,[7] and it was hard to feel anything about the EU rule book, the acquis communautaire. But youth was a poor predictor of attitudes towards events in Eastern Europe. Some were disaffected with their own political systems and susceptible to clever Russian critiques that mirrored their own; some were inspired by a good old-fashioned revolution in Kiev.

Energy Dependency

The EU was also divided by the politics of Russian gas – doubly so, in fact. It was not just that some states (like Slovakia) were entirely dependent on Russian gas, while others (like Spain) did not use it at all. The EU was also divided by what people thought about that dependency. The Baltic States imported all their gas from Russia, thanks to Soviet-era networks, but were extremely uncomfortable with the fact, as they thought it undermined their national security. Italy imported 30 per cent of its gas from Russia, but wanted more and the national energy company ENI was particularly keen to expand its Russia contracts.

The EU was further divided by what it thought about Russia's persistent habit of turning off the gas supply, 80 per cent of which traditionally came through Ukraine, first in January 2006 and then in January 2009, when there was a much longer mid-winter cut-off. Many parts of Europe lacked power. The one silver lining was that the crisis acted as a great experiment, demonstrating which countries could survive without Russian gas and which could not; which could be helped and which had to help themselves. The result was a programme of diversification and construction of interconnectors, and something called the Third Energy Package (see Chapter 10). But the impetus behind this new energy policy had faded by 2010. Much remained to be done and much of Europe remained dependent on Russian gas. Germany hooked up to the North Stream pipeline under the Baltic Sea in 2011, which made it less dependent on Ukraine, but more dependent on Russia. The political differences also remained: some were reluctant to antagonise Russia because it was an energy supplier; others thought it was precisely because of Russia's position as a major supplier (not a monopoly by any means) that it had to be challenged in other areas.

America Retrenches

The US was traditionally a much bigger part of the picture in Russia–Europe relations. But Obama's foreign policy has been the policy of priorities. It has also been an attempt to find a third way between the aggressive interventionism of the Bush era and the isolationism felt by many on the American left, as well as by the Tea Party on the Republican right. And any new US administration would have to have retrenched after the Bush wars in Afghanistan and Iraq, albeit perhaps not so far or so fast.

In this new utilitarian world, if you were part of the solution you would have America's friendship, and if you were part of the problem you would have its attention; otherwise you were out of the picture. The type of universal democracy promotion favoured by neo-conservatives was out of fashion, replaced by new metaphors like 'leading from behind' or America as an 'offshore balancer'.

The 'reset' of Russia policy announced by Washington in 2009 was more controversial. To its supporters, it was a means of securing more from the bilateral US–Russia relationship and solving other priorities, like cooperation in Afghanistan and Iran. To its critics it was a way of downgrading that relationship, and downgrading relationships with Eastern Europe even further. The post-war generation of East-Coast East-European intellectuals like Zbigniew Brzezinski was a declining force, less able to convince Washington of the region's intrinsic historical importance and of Russia's historical problems with its neighbours.

Competitive Reset

However, the Russian 'reset' was a perceived success in Washington at least. America's other resets or pivots or openings under Obama were less successful, and the US has few direct business interests in Russia (compared to, say, China). The EU was therefore encouraged to find its own reset consensus for Russia, pushing Eastern Europe even further down the priority list. Before the Ukraine crisis, most European states were cosying up to Russia, not the other way around. Russia was not encircled or threatened. Even NATO had a reset of its Russia policy under new Secretary General Anders Fogh Rasmussen after 2009 (see Chapter 2).

Germany, the EU's de facto leader since 2008, was already 'set'. Germany's Russophiles like to be known hubristically as the *Russlandversteher* – 'those who understand Russia'. To their critics they are the *Russlandknutscher* – 'Russia huggers'. They still use the rhetoric of *Ostpolitik* from the 1970s to justify a policy of business as usual under almost any circumstances.[8] But the original *Ostpolitik* had much bigger aims: post-war normalisation, opening relations with East Germany and Poland, and (for some) keeping alive the hope of a reunified Germany (or for others, putting the issue to one side). But for modern Germany, its Russia policy has been progressively downgraded to the mercantilist slogan of *Wandel durch Handel* – 'change through trade'.

Germany is the EU's foreign policy leader only by default: because it is the strongest economic power, not because its foreign policy makes sense. It could even be argued that Germany does not have a foreign policy in either of the obvious senses: hard power is ruled out by Germany's post-war history, and soft power always means protecting the gains from trade, not the use of trade as a policy weapon.

The UK, on the other hand, seems beholden to banks and big money: its protests over the Litvinenko affair (the assassination of a former Russian Federal Security Service (FSB) agent-turned-whistleblower in London in 2006) were muted until 2014. Corrupt Eastern European money has been able to run complicated schemes through the UK and its dependencies, as well as in states like Austria, Liechtenstein, Luxembourg and Switzerland. Until 2014, East Europeans were also able to place money and assets in plain sight, without bothering to hide it much. Italy is similarly beholden to big companies like ENI, not just to *Berlusconismo* and the frankly bizarre romance between Putin and Berlusconi. The Swedes dropped their objections to North Stream in late 2009. Even Poland was attempting a rapprochement which began before, but was temporarily accelerated by the Smolensk tragedy of 2010 – the death of President Lech Kaczyński and ninety-five others on a flight to, of all places, the site of the 1940 massacre of the Polish elite officer class by the NKVD. The government of Donald Tusk hoped for a business-friendly local 'reset', though ultimate results were limited.

Russia was, in other words, surrounded as much by friends as by enemies. And relations circa 2013 were, on the whole, somewhat better than they had been only a few years earlier. They were not completely harmonious, but nor were they completely disastrous. The war in Georgia in 2008 symbolised the duality: it led only to a short-term rupture in relations, even though it had, after all, been a war.

Europe and Russia

The enlargement of the EU and NATO to post-communist Europe, on the other hand, brought new 'divisions', but also new blood and fresh ways of thinking. The new arrivals had been kept waiting for so long that they wanted to throw some crockery once they were finally in, particularly with regards to attitudes to Russia. (They also hated being called 'new'.) The original purpose of the EU in Western Europe was the transcendence of historical enmities. Communist societies, on the other hand, were built on lies; post-communist leaders rightly thought they could only build new democracies if they began in truth. The original EU was an exercise in forgetting; post-communist Europe was about the recovery of memory – which meant dealing with Russia. It really mattered what happened in Lithuania in 1940 (or Ukraine in 1941), and not just because Stalin killed your father or your grandfather. The basis of local statehood was often contested: either it was justified by history or it was not. Too often, arguments about the past continue in and undermine the present. In the words of former Lithuanian Prime Minister Andrius Kubilius, there is no equivalent of Franco-German reconciliation in Eastern Europe, no burying of the hatchet between Russia and the rest, its collective neighbours. To the West, it often seems as though Lithuanians or Ukrainians are obsessed with what look like nineteenth-century historical debates and ethnic blood-and-soil arguments; in reality their statehood would be rootless without them.

Russia's 'Humiliation'

Russia had its own myths and memories, and not just about the communist era. The Russian elite, particularly under Putin after 2012, strongly believed that Russia had been constantly humiliated since 1991. This elite, under Boris Yeltsin, had a mild form of that belief in the late 1990s, but there was little trace of it in the early 1990s.

That is because it didn't happen. Deep-seated structural problems caused the USSR's decline, but not its collapse. The Soviet Union reached a negotiated end, and the only negotiators were Russians, Ukrainians and the leaders of the other then-Soviet republics. Whether the Soviet Union survived as a union depended on the members of that union. As the excellent recent book by Serhii Plokhy makes clear,[9] the West – and George Bush Senior's US in particular – did everything it could to slow the pace of collapse (since it was mainly worried about violent dissolution and the fate of Soviet nuclear weapons). Even in late 1991, independence for the Baltic States was seen as necessary but exceptional.

Russia was then humiliated domestically in the early 1990s by other Russians, the new oligarchic class that made itself so conspicuously rich. Only in foreign policy terms does Russia's argument – that the West (or just the US) has often acted in Iraq and elsewhere without constraint and with inconsistency – resonate with many other powers. But groupthink is a powerful force. It is a matter of fact that Russia's humiliation myth has become the conventional wisdom in Moscow, and is powerful enough both to coexist with and to outlast any 'reset' policy. *Despite* retrenchment under Obama, the Russian foreign policy establishment sees the US as an increasingly destabilising force. The bombing campaign against Libya by France, Britain and the USA in 2011, and Medvedev's failure to order a UN Security Council veto, was a first final straw. Then Putin was doubly emboldened by the Syria fiasco: first, because the West looked weak, and second, because Russia had got away with massive arms shipments, many through the Ukrainian port of Odesa.[10] So why not use the same tactics against Ukraine itself?

The Effect on Eastern Europe

After 2008, Obama's overstretched new US administration assumed that the EU would take on more responsibility for its 'backyard' in Eastern Europe, just as the EU itself was entering a profound internal crisis. Seen from the east, that crisis was multi-dimensional. It was above all economic, as the euro lurched from one crisis to the next. But the EU's travails were also perceived as a crisis of diplomatic effectiveness. The recoil of NATO from the region after the 2008 war in Georgia also shone a harsh spotlight on the EU's inability to play an effective security role in the region, or indeed anywhere. The EU's preoccupations with post-modern value politics and environmental issues were also perceived in Eastern Europe as luxury goods, while most in the east were forced to concentrate on necessities like statehood, security and the standard of living.

Europe was idealised in Eastern Europe in the early 1990s as a lost birthright. By the 2000s, Europe had settled into a symbol of quality, and of whatever a 'normal' life meant, from a rule of law to high welfare and living standards. But the global economic crisis hit Eastern Europe especially hard, and undermined the assumption that Eastern Europe would grow in prosperity in tandem. It was also not good at creating reform incentives. Post-communist states did more to reform in the immediate post-communist period and after the local mini-crisis in 1998. In some cases, like Russia, the recession was arguably too short to generate real pressure for reform, lasting only from the final quarter of 2008 until the second quarter of 2010. Russia was also able to run down its reserve funds to cushion the blow and keep the local recession shallow. The Swedish economist Anders Åslund argued that political regimes in the former Soviet states were too entrenched to reform this time, compared to 1998. The Baltic States were a notable exception, opting for a controversial 'internal devaluation', i.e. severe austerity and deflation, which led to quicker recovery, but also to 'population devaluation', i.e. out-migration. Between 1989 and 2011, the three Baltic States lost 1.5 million of their 8 million population, even according to official figures.

According to European Bank for Reconstruction and Development (EBRD) experts, Ukraine was the most vulnerable country of all. It had no reserves either of hard cash or of public support to cushion difficult reform programmes: 'Its economy is quite susceptible to external shocks in general [and] relatively small changes in its external environment can swing the entire economy in one direction or another, irrespective of whether those changes originate in the east or the west.[11] Ukraine was vulnerable to trade and output loss as a knock-on from recession in the EU area, had an exchange rate fixed to the dollar, was always in and out of external financing and International Monetary Fund (IMF) programmes, was highly dependent on world asset prices for its steel, minerals and chemical sales, and had 40 per cent of its banking assets owned by foreign banks at the start of the recession.

Ukraine did not have the buffer provided for commodity economies like Russia, Kazakhstan and Azerbaijan. On the contrary, it was highly sensitive to changes in the price of Russian energy. Ukraine also had many migrant workers in Russia, and so far as it got any foreign direct investment (the overall level was pathetically small), much of it came from Russia or from Russia offshore (i.e. Cyprus). Remittances were $9.3 billion in 2013, although as Ukraine is a large country that only made up 4.8 per cent of GDP.[12] Unlike most of its neighbours, Ukraine had not reoriented its trade towards Europe: 25 per cent of its exports went to the EU in 2012 and 26 per cent to Russia, with the rest going to other Commonwealth of Independent States (CIS) countries and emerging markets further afield like Turkey and Egypt (9 per cent between them).

European Neighbourhood Policy, Russian Neighbourhood Policy

In the 2000s, Russia paid more attention to NATO than to the EU. It thought the EU was ineffective and did not need to be opposed. As Gleb Pavlovsky complacently argued in 2007, 'the task of minimising the influence of the EU would be better left to Brussels'.[13]

In 2004, the EU launched something called the European Neighbourhood Policy (ENP). Critics argued that it was too broad, as it covered both Eastern Europe and the Mediterranean, and was badly timed, as it offered relatively little support to Ukraine, whose prospects briefly seemed transformed by the Orange Revolution, also of 2004. Zbigniew Brzezinski once said that it was based on a category mistake: its real goal was not to change countries like Ukraine, but to change Russia, by civilising the whole region from a distance – and transforming the periphery would not be possible without changing Russia.

The EU's 'Eastern Partnership' policy, launched in 2008–09 just as Eastern Europe was being swamped by the economic crisis, repeated the bad timing of the scheme it succeeded. The new policy decoupled the eastern and southern 'neighbourhoods', but it was torn between a policy of 'enlargement-lite' and a more geopolitical approach to Eastern Europe. Contrary to some expectations, the Eastern Partnership at least survived the Spanish and Belgian EU presidencies in 2010, and was then 're-launched' under the Hungarian and Polish presidencies in 2011; but it still threatened to be another technical talking shop like the Mediterranean Union – another EU initiative that still exists in an office somewhere, but has had relatively little impact on the ground.

The EU's policies may have struggled to transform Eastern Europe, but they did transform Russia, if not in the way that Brzezinski expected. Moscow adapted its policy to compete with the EU in Ukraine and the other Eastern Partnership states through what it thought were EU-style means, though Russia has a very warped view of 'soft power'. It concentrated on covert methods, such as bribing local politicians, setting up pro-Russian front parties and sending shadowy funding to new pro-Russian non-governmental organisations (NGOs).

Russia lost 8 per cent of its GDP in 2009, but most of its neighbours lost more. Unlike the West, whose natural instinct was to revert to utilitarian cost-cutting in recession, Russia was prepared to invest in making long-term strategic gains. Its worldview depends on great-power status derived from a central position as a pole in a multi-polar world. Russia also thought the economic crisis would replace flat 'globalisation' with lumpy 'regionalisation', and wanted to consolidate its region.

Russian state and corporate investments in the region grew steadily after 2008 (apart from in energy, steel and chemicals, most Russian companies were not really competitive further abroad). Russia's growing critique of the West also gained some traction in the region, often via Russia-funded organisations like Ukrainian Choice or the Eurasian Institute in Georgia. For example, the scaremongering reports in Ukraine on the costs of the EU Agreements, much quoted before the Vilnius Summit of 2013, came straight from a Russian-sponsored think tank, the Eurasian Development Bank.

Other Options for Eastern Europe

With little prospect of joining the EU, and with every prospect of being dominated by Russia, Eastern European states began to look for other options. One possibility was to try harder in the joining game. After 2009, Moldova tried a policy of 'pre-emptive implementation' by delivering change (biometric passports, tighter border controls) with no promise of anything in return. But this was like a sportsman taking strenuous exercise in the warm-up area, risking injury before the start of the actual game.

Georgia, on the other hand, after its Rose Revolution of 2003, often claimed to be better than the EU. The Republican US and certain anti-EU Europeans were big fans of Tbilisi's free-market or even 'libertarian revolution' (Chapter 9). President Mikheil Saakashvili claimed to be a big fan not of Brussels but of Singapore.

But there also developed a strong strain of what people in Moscow derided as 'collective Titoism',[14] which meant that states like Ukraine were not as subservient as they should be, and were constantly slipping out of the Kremlin's grasp, just as Tito eluded Stalin. For once, the Russians had hit on an important truth. Local states were weak, corrupt elites were entrenched, and their 'European choice' was often more virtual than real. Accordingly, local leaders used the game of balance both to extract resources from Russia and the West alike, and to excuse their lack of reform. The number of different names for this policy tells the story: in Ukraine it was called 'multi-vectored' foreign policy; in Belarus it was 'two-winged' policy; in Armenia it was 'complementarism' or 'sitting on two chairs at the same time'. De facto, such policies meant that such countries preferred their room for manoeuvre and did not really want to join up with either Russia or the EU.

But there were many different ways, good and bad, of running a 'balanced' foreign policy. In Ukraine, President Kuchma managed to keep everybody happy in his first term (1994–99), forging agreements with the EU, USA, NATO and Russia. But he dropped some of the balls in his second term. Foreign policy under Viktor Yushchenko (2005–10) was 'balanced', but only because other people disagreed with the president's broadly pro-Western course, resulting in inconsistency or gridlock. Viktor Yanukovych (2010–14) preferred blackmail, constantly using one side to leverage the other, which ultimately only annoyed everyone.

The Rise of Other Powers

The situation in Eastern Europe was also transformed by the rise of other powers. Eastern European states could then broaden their balancing game by seeking links to the 'WWW' (the World Without the West).[15] Turkey was closest, and several East European states actually wanted to be like Turkey – maybe not a potential member of the EU, but powerful enough to act according to their own terms. Turkey's hyperactive foreign minister, Ahmet Davutoğlu, liked to talk about Turkey as a pivotal country (*merkez ülke*),[16] the centre-point of concentric power circles from the Ottoman, Turkic-speaking and Islamic worlds. This included the Caucasus, where Turkey competed with Russia and the US, though it was least active to its north, towards Ukraine, Moldova and Belarus, where it tended to defer to Russia, given the considerable bilateral interest in business, tourism, energy supply and nuclear power. And no single East European state was as important a 'pivot' – not even Ukraine.

The big new power in the region, however, was China. Eastern Europe, to be honest, was not China's first port of call. In 2011, Beijing's trade with Moscow was worth approximately $80 billion, and its total trade with Ukraine, Belarus and Moldova was only around $12 billion. But Eastern Europe was a back door into the EU. And local leaders hoped that China would provide them with three things: money, even more balance or wiggle room, and a different model of governance. Moldova went through a phase of taking large (by its standards) Chinese loans for infrastructure projects, but since 2013 the EU has taken over as the leading infrastructure investor. Belarusian dictator Alyaksandr Lukashenka, on the other hand, had a much warmer relationship: China helped him to balance Russia. Whenever he faked a shift to the EU to cool Russian pressure, Brussels always mentioned human rights; but Beijing didn't care. China provided Belarus with total trade and other credits of $16 billion.[17] Its most intriguing plan was to build a $5 billion 'beachhead' city in the forests outside Minsk, near the airport and the M1 highway into Poland.

Ukrainian President Yanukovych was also a frequent flyer to Beijing. China wanted land and Yanukovych was happy to sell anything. A deal in 2012 led to a $3 billion loan, in exchange for corn. In January 2014, a deal was announced at the height of the crisis to lease China 7.5 million acres for fifty years – one-twentieth of Ukraine, or one-tenth of its arable land (an area roughly the size of Belgium). A month earlier, in December 2013, China proposed a $10 billion deep-water port project in, of all places, Crimea.[18] Once the Silk Road project took off (new transport routes to Europe), China would have direct land access to the European market via Ukraine.

As it had already shown in Africa, China imposed fewer conditions on its financial support in Eastern Europe, making the kind of conditionality engagement that is the EU's traditional modus operandi much more difficult to apply, as well as diminishing Russia's argument for maintaining historically predominant economic ties. China's powerhouse economy has also decoupled the ideas of democracy and prosperity, which were assumed to be different sides of the same coin in the 1990s. In a world that was increasingly multi-polar in ideas, as well as poles of influence, it was easier for East European elites to pick and choose.

The Vilnius Summit

All these forces came to a head in the run-up to the third summit of the Eastern Partnership in Vilnius in November 2013. Maybe this was not a big deal to most outsiders, but the Partnership had been twice upgraded since its launch and there were high hopes that not just Ukraine, but Georgia and Moldova, too, would shift decisively into the EU camp. That was not how things turned out.

The process was, of course, too technocratic. There is a common joke in Eastern Europe that 'Russia makes you an offer you can't refuse; the EU makes you an offer you can't understand.' The deal focused too much on trade, when the benefits of increased trade were all long term. Ukraine's share of trade with the EU was less than a third; its overall level of trade was also small – Germany's trade with Russia was €80 billion in 2012, more than ten times its €7 billion trade with Ukraine. Trade was also in decline, because of rampant corruption. One German retail chain, Real (part of Metro), pulled out of Ukraine just before the Vilnius Summit. Ukraine even failed the IKEA test: opinion polls showed that Ukrainians shared the middle-class dream of self-assembly furniture, but despite a decade of trying to enter the Ukrainian market, the Swedish retailer was put off by corruption.[19]

More generally, the 'Schuman method' that originally created the EU – start with economic integration (the Coal and Steel Community in the 1950s, the Single Market in the 1990s) and political integration will follow – did not work in Eastern Europe. The EU needed to pay more attention to the disfunctionalities of local societies, whose biggest problems were political – the lack of democracy and human rights, and the presence of rent-seeking elites.

That said, there was too much focus on one particular political problem and cause célèbre, the imprisonment of former Ukrainian Prime Minister Yuliya Tymoshenko in 2011 (see Chapter 3), even as a symbol of everything that was then wrong with Ukraine. After Tymoshenko went to prison, the Agreements were put on hold. There was then too much focus on what Ukraine had to do to restart the process, and not enough on its potential effects. Moreover, the EU was asking for Ukraine to change a lot, but was committing little. Russia, on the other hand, was prepared to prop up the regime without asking it to change at all. The short-term economic impact of implementing the Agreements in such poor countries was also underestimated, as was Russia's likely reaction. The EU made a bad job of explaining what it was up to, symbolised by Russian Deputy Prime Minister Igor Shuvalov's disastrous trip to Brussels in February 2013, when he was basically told that the process had nothing to do with Russia.

But the biggest problem was that Russia had decided to sabotage the policy, which it had decided was a threat to its vital interests. Maybe it was wrong: years of form-filling were all that lay ahead. But the Eastern Partnership was deemed incompatible with Putin's new grand alternative project, the Eurasian Union, scheduled to launch in 2015 (see Chapter 2). So Russia played hardball, without, of course, knowing what would follow. No one did.

Armenia was actually the first to abandon the process, in September 2013. But it was a much bigger shock when Ukraine walked away only a week before

the summit. Still, those who were in Vilnius, myself included, accepted a negotiating failure with Ukraine, but were mostly unaware of failure in broader
terms. But the summit started a chain of events to the east that led to repression
and an Uprising in Ukraine, followed by Russian invasion. And like many good
explosions, there was also an implosion, which would send shock waves back
westwards.

Conclusion

Post-modern Europe has to learn how to cope with old-fashioned hard power.
It also has to devise forms of soft power that work, including in competition
with hard power, and especially with states like Russia that normally have a
higher pain threshold. The award of the Nobel Peace Prize to the EU in 2012
was ironic, to say the least. The EU's expansion seemed to have come to a halt,
yet others, including many Ukrainians, still wanted to join it. On that view, the
new frontier of Europe in 2014 was somewhere in east Ukraine.

The EU also needed renewed vigour and sense of purpose; countries like
Ukraine could save Europe both from itself and from Putin's 'conservative
values' assault. After the patronising West–East lecturing of the 1990s, it was
time to recognise that Ukraine knew more about Europe than vice versa. The
'Ukraine crisis' was also a mirror of the crisis that has engulfed Europe since
2008. Oligarchs and bad bankers exist in both East and West. EU states do not
always uphold the values that they seek to impose on new members at home.

CHAPTER 2

Russia Putinesca

The key to understanding modern Russia is to realise that it is run by some very weird people. In the 1990s they were known as 'political technologists', ultra-cynical political manipulators who created a fake democracy because Boris Yeltsin couldn't build a real one, and who distracted the population with carefully scripted drama because the energy wealth had temporarily stopped flowing. The difference under Putin was that the Kremlin established a monopoly of manipulation, not just that the money from oil and gas started piling up again. Instead of politics being a competition of rival puppet-masters, there was only one. Vladislav Surkov, sitting in his office in the Kremlin, controlled every aspect of the political process. The power of grey cardinals is often exaggerated in history, but not this time. He stepped aside when he thought his job was done in 2011 – too early, as it happens, because the Kremlin was caught unawares by an unexpected wave of public protests. But Surkov was redeployed. He was in Crimea for a Valentine's Day visit in February 2014, a month before the annexation in March.

Putin's propagandists, on the other hand, love to contrast the 'good' 2000s under their guy with the 'bad' 1990s under Boris Yeltsin. The dark years of disorder and weaknesses were supposedly transcended by Putin re-establishing 'order', and, less plausibly, reining in the bad 'oligarchs'. This is a huge over-simplification: for one thing, Putin first rose to prominence as the defender of Yeltsin's interests, initially as the secret service chief destroying his enemies, and then as the signer of a decree protecting him from prosecution. The oppo-site black-and-white contrast – the democratic 1990s usurped by the autocratic 2000s – is also of limited value. Russia at least had pluralism in the 1990s, but it was also born in sin. Yeltsin's critics would include his destruction of a country (the USSR) by manoeuvring to displace Gorbachev through becoming Russian leader, rather than by replacing him at the Soviet level. Then there was armed conflict in Moscow in October 1993 and the unilateral and fraudulent imposition of a non-consensual constitution. Yeltsin was re-elected in 1996, but a change of power was never contemplated. Yeltsin was all set to cancel the vote while such a change was still a possibility.

Putin's era was also born in sin, both inherited from the Yeltsin era and of its own invention, by providing protection for the Yeltsin regime and launching Putin's popularity via the second war in Chechnya. A few of the 'oligarchs' of the Yeltsin era were eclipsed, but the Yukos Affair saw the rise of a new kind of kleptocracy, based around the so-called *siloviki* ('men of force', mainly former KGB) and 'Putin's friends'.

So the contrast between the decades is overdone. An alternative history would sketch how the culture of manipulation was developed in the early 1990s, and how problems of over-control became apparent by 2011. It would also describe how the current crisis in Ukraine is part of the attempt to export the same methods of manipulation and control.

Russia's Virtual Politics

Soviet totalitarianism didn't work, but it was not Soviet totalitarianism that collapsed in 1991. The Soviet state was not brought down by its crimes, or in the crucial hard-power contests with Nazi Germany and post-war USA. The post-totalitarian USSR of the Brezhnev era just petered out. Its failings were prosaic: it couldn't feed its population; the elite had more cabbage or apartment space than anyone else, but kept a jealous eye on real elite privilege in the capitalist West. The USSR was low on resources when it ended more with a whimper than a bang.

Russia and all the post-Soviet states were therefore also short of resources. Only Turkmenistan and Uzbekistan switched into hard-shell autocracies overnight, largely because of the strength of local clans and KGB networks. Other states that are authoritarian today, like Belarus, Azerbaijan and even Kazakhstan – and obviously Russia – were all fairly chaotic in the early 1990s. The energy-rich states built up resources to consolidate their rule over time. To stay in power, most of their rulers relied on manipulative techniques inherited from the Soviet era – techniques that never had sufficient time to become 'normal' (i.e. public) contested politics, even in Gorbachev's last few years. Their power was based on informal networks and 'corridor politics' (politics away both from the public eye and from a paper trail produced in offices). Their methods were contracted-out KGB services: agents everywhere, alongside agents provocateurs, divide and rule, *kompromat* ('compromising materials'), bribery and control. But its means were married to modern capacities. The political technologists were particularly skilled at manipulating information technologies, creating dramas that were literally virtual because they mainly existed on TV; or, later, at nudging, deflecting or reshaping the narratives of social media. Their natural language was Orwellian doublespeak. And as Orwell shrewdly pointed out, the control of language is the first step to the control of meaning, and the manipulation of meaning the first step to the manipulation of politics.

But the individual parts of the system did not work in isolation. They only functioned if they were held together by a big lie or meta-narrative – what Russians call, more lyrically, an artificial drama or *dramaturgiya*. The meta-narrative provided the script that everybody had to follow, kept elites and masses aligned, and ensured 'organised [i.e. inevitable] victory' (a favourite Bolshevik phrase) at election time. In 1996, the narrative was Yeltsin versus the Communists. Then it was Putin versus the Chechens for his first elections in 1999–2000. Putin versus the oligarchs worked supremely well in 2003–04. Then in 2007–08 it was 'Russia restored' versus all comers, and Putin passing on the torch of Russia's restored power to Medvedev.

It was easy to see that post-Soviet politics was sleazy, but it was less obvious that this was actually an alternative to more expensive repressive techniques. Russia in the 1990s did not have the money for a massive army, or even the old-style KGB; nor did it have the money to bribe people to keep them from protesting. But things then got more complicated in the 2000s, when energy wealth returned to Russia. Real GDP grew by 70 per cent between 2000 and 2008, and wages by much more. Russia could now afford its well-known social contract of growing prosperity in exchange for declining liberty. Except that this was never openly spelt out; acquiescence was easier if it didn't look like capitulation; social manipulation and psychological compliance were still important. The essential part of the system of control was still to direct the message or narrative; and the most important instrument of power in post-Soviet Russia has always been the media. Putin's response to the unprecedented opposition movement against him in 2011–12 included arrests and media clampdowns, but more important was to shift the narrative. Hence his 'conservative values campaign' to define the 'real Russia' and his new-found fondness for protecting Russians in the 'near abroad'.

But blanket propaganda does not work as well in the twenty-first century. It makes more sense to allow a contested media space, so that the local population feels it owns the narrative, even though that narrative has been manipulated for it. So media bans and internet filters are not universal. Russia does not yet have any equivalent of Beijing's 'Chinese Wall', censoring the internet. What it has instead is an army of interferers, whose techniques are much more post-modern: party managers and financiers, official scriptwriters, Kremlin bloggers, trolls and so-called *web-brigady*. Abroad, organisations like the Russia Today TV channel are successful because the Kremlin line is buried in a post-modern melange of 'alternative' views.

But precisely because there are gaps in the narrative, or because if you look closely enough you can see how it is done, life can still be very dangerous for those who seek to expose the truth behind the façade. The regime's most awkward critics can still end up dead, like Anna Politkovskaya. According to the Committee to Protect Journalists, as of 2014 of the 1,055 journalists killed in the world since 1992, 80 have been in Russia, with 56 'motive confirmed' and 24 'motive unconfirmed'.[1] Significantly, journalists are always targeted during times of protest or when the Kremlin is launching a new narrative. Russia toughens up when it thinks it needs to.

So the one thing that Russia had in both the 1990s and 2000s was this manipulative culture of 'political technology'. It was with good reason that I wrote a book called *Virtual Politics: Faking democracy in the post-Soviet world*, which came out in 2005. Political technology was born in the early 1990s and matured with the 1996 election. Its greatest success was to preserve Yeltsin's tottering regime in 1999. The 2003–04 elections then succeeded in squeezing all political life out of the mainstream and in pushing opposition to the margins. The campaign against Yukos brought one cycle to an end.

So there were some key differences between the 1990s and the 2000s – or more exactly between the period 1993–2003 and the years 2003–12. The earlier years were anarchic: the political technologists were guns for hire, all plotting against one another. For the political technologists themselves, they were almost fun.[2] The Yukos Affair in 2003 was about many things, but one key aspect was the final decisive showdown between the manipulators. The Kremlin wanted a monopoly. Yukos boss Mikhail Khodorkovsky was funding almost every political party, including the liberals and the communists, and even the ruling United Russia party, because, as a leading oligarch, that was what he was supposed to do; and he had one eye on the next elections in 2008. The Kremlin won and succeeded in squeezing the oligarchs – not out of politics, but out of political manipulation, which then became solely a Kremlin responsibility. Surkov was the only political technologist who mattered. Some of the old technologists retired, as they did not want a life as Kremlin drones. Others settled for a life as a sub-contractor. Surkov was then everywhere – he was even his own opposition. People became so inured to the system that they would offer their services without being asked. Anyway, being manipulated was profitable.

In one sense, however, once the dust duly settled there was less need for political technology. The population was quiescent, but the Kremlin feared that it wasn't, especially after Surkov and some of his old colleagues created the mostly phantom fear of rebellion spreading to Russia after Ukraine's 'Orange Revolution' in 2004. So political technology was in fact extended to new areas: to manipulating NGOs as well as political parties; to what was openly called 'counter-revolutionary technology' (building up the system's defences against protests – the Nashi youth group was the most notorious example); and to exercising Russian influence abroad. The Kremlin also proved adept at developing new ways of dealing with the new technologies that largely appeared after 2005 – the maturation of the internet and the arrival of social media. More subtly, the costs of regime maintenance were kept down by rendering the mass of the population complicit in the narrative. Apathy worked, too, and for a time the system even fed off the very disillusion it helped create.

The political technologists were cynical. But they also had to get out of bed in the morning. So they told themselves that what they did was perfectly normal. All politics is realpolitik, everyone manipulates the system, and political technology exists everywhere in the world – it's just that we supposedly disguise it a little more elegantly in the West. I interviewed one of the leading political technologists, Sergey Markov, in 2007. He wore slippers, as he likes to pose as a man of the people. 'All political technologies abolish the difference between the true and the not-true', he argued. 'These conditions are also in America, because of so-called post-modern society. New Times are coming for all countries.'[3] Markov's colleague Gleb Pavlovsky preferred to say, 'we live in a mythological era. We have gone back to the Ancient World where the distinction between myth and reality didn't exist.'[4] This is also suitably post-modern, as post-modern time is not linear. In the modern Age of Myth there was more freedom for propagandists; the two sides were tied to their relative ideologies during the Cold War.

According to Markov again,

normal institutions which [once] worked for democratic societies have declined, political parties [have] declined. Public opinion is changing, it's not disappearing, but it is becoming more artificially created. The legitimacy of key decisions still has a democratic background – but public opinion is much more organised. People believe they buy certain goods because they make the decision, but it's not true. Public opinion is made more and more by computers, which have no opinion of their own. They totally depend on what disk is inserted. All interest groups are fighting with each other for the right to insert their own disk.

Politics was just a type of competitive programming – a 'competition for the rights to programme public opinion'. 'In Russia, in most cases, we use normal things. There is no need to create something unique. But maybe it's something that's a little bit handmade' compared to the West, he concluded, with false modesty.[5] Again, the West supposedly only looked different because it had a grander façade.

This may have been what they said, but it wasn't true. Their methods were both deeply corrosive and often self-defeating. Western political systems have huge problems at the margins: declining institutions and falling voter participation, manipulation by our own 'oligarchs', politics as media and spin. But in Russia, the problems spread from the core. And far from everything being relative and all narratives having equal value, the system's ultimate weakness was that it rested on one big lie. Political technology was needed to disguise the reality of a kleptocratic regime whose fundamental underlying narrative – that Putin was the good tsar reining in the bad boyars to restore Russian might – was essentially false.

Russia's Virtual State

Putin claimed to have rebuilt a strong Russian state in the 2000s, but in reality it was held together with masking tape and 'political technology'. I also interviewed the leading Russian political technologist, Gleb Pavlovsky, in December 2007. His office sits across the Moscow river from the Christ the Saviour Cathedral, framed in a big window. Pavlovsky sits in front of it like a Bond villain – Donald Pleasence as Blofeld in *You Only Live Twice*, say. His line was, 'in the 1990s you couldn't use administrative structures [to rule]; we had to work through the reality we created instead'. 'Politics in Russia is not just a form of theatre. You have to build the theatre as well.'[6] Putin's presidency in the 2000s was indeed an age of construction, but it was as much about building myths as it was about building institutions. Political technology was, again, a low-cost way of simulating many things: democracy, public support, national unity and recovery. It was an alternative to control via repression, as the state was actually still quite weak. It meant that the West cottoned on late to the fact that Russia was not a democracy.

Markov put it slightly differently. He did not agree with my label of 'virtual politics', but for technical reasons:

> In Russia I think it was more like virtual politics in Yeltsin's time. Putin's time is the time of real politics. Political technologies now help to make real actions. They became part of real actions. We don't try to create an artificial

virtual world; we try to use different techniques to make a change in the real world. That's the basic difference. We don't want elections to look like people support Putin; we really want people to support Putin. This is the key difference. But in a situation where institutions are very weak, all these techniques are becoming very influential. They just occupy the vacuum where institutions should be. Once there are stronger institutions, there is less of a vacuum, and less need for such political technologies. From this point of view, in Russia we had a tremendous peak of political technologies in the '90s, but because institutions, step by step are becoming more influential, we have a diminishing of their role.[7]

But Russia's institutions were not recovering in strength as quickly as Markov would have liked. Politics was still highly personalised. The illusion of Putin's strong state rested on three myths: that the 'real action' that mattered most was conquest of the Caucasus; the idea that Russia was a BRIC economy (i.e. in the group Brazil, Russia, India and China, deemed to be at a similar stage of advanced development); and the creation of a 'vertical of power', Putin's favourite cliché.

But all three claims have been undermined. Ten years after the beginning of the second war in Chechnya in 1999, a new type of Russian nationalism emerged which inverted Putin's rhetoric of success with the slogan 'stop feeding the Caucasus' (meaning that Russia should cut its ties rather than fight to keep them). Economically, Russia managed a soft landing during the great global recession of 2008–09, but psychologically it was hit hard. The country now found it more difficult to depict itself as a rising power.[8] Finally, according to Pavlovsky, 'the vertical of power never existed; it was only ever a vertical of loyalty'.[9] The 'vertical of power' may have been a Russian tradition, but so was avoiding orders and responsibility. The impeccable authority in this case is the Russian writer Nikolay Gogol (who was half-Ukrainian), whose play The Government Inspector satirised the lengths to which Russians would go to ingratiate themselves with authority, in order to subvert that authority. Under Putin there was no 'vertical of administration'. The bureaucracy was treated like an army, and was given too many orders.[10] 'Governors demonstrate their loyalty, but are masters in their own fief, controlling all business, police and local media on their territory.'[11] The result was a crisis of implementation as bureaucrats subverted orders and avoided initiative and responsibility. Orders went down the vertical, but there was no communication upwards, or communication with the outside world. Even Putin himself said at the Valday Club in November 2011 that '80 per cent' of presidential decrees were not implemented by the regions.[12]

Medvedev

The choice of Dmitriy Medvedev as Russian president in 2008 was not a step away from this system, but a phase in its development. It was also a prosperity project. The economic boom that began in 2000 was still in evidence in early 2008. In Putin's first term, according to his own propaganda, he had restored the Russian state after the chaos of the 1990s. He had defeated the Chechen rebels and restored the writ of the Russian state in its other far-flung regions. In 2004, he then supposedly defeated the oligarchy – he did not abolish the class of rich men, but he claimed that the oligarchs no longer ruled as a class. So the choice of Medvedev in 2008 was designed to complete the job of restoring Russian power, by legitimising it abroad. Less well advertised was the need to legitimise the property grab by 'Putin's friends' after the arrest of Yukos boss Mikhail Khodorkovsky in 2003.

So the central problem of Medvedev's presidency was that the global economy crashed within months of his taking office. Even before the protests in 2011–12 there was a widening gap between two narratives. One saw the Russian middle class as the main winners in the recent economic growth. They were liberated to talk about 'modernisation', which Medvedev did on their behalf, without being able to deliver much. But most Russians were still on the up escalator, or wanted to be. Putin was now prime minister and concentrated on retrenchment, maintaining the social support he had built in 2000–08. His adviser Simeon Kordonsky argued that Putin had a better understanding of the aspirations of Russia's second society, the 'society of estates', the vast army of those dependent on the state.[13] And to be fair, the general population was not sacrificed as it was in the last Russian recession in 1998. Putin sought to interpret the great financial crash as a crisis of globalisation, and Russians would be sheltered in their own corner of the world. The reserve funds built up during the seven fat years were run down to cushion the lean years.

The war in Georgia in August 2008 was also a prosperity project, preceding as it did the collapse of Lehman Brothers by an entire month. Russia was at the peak of its relative power and wanted to use that power to restrain both President Saakashvili's Georgian state (which represented a very different type of post-Soviet regime – reformist and pro-Western, if imperfectly democratic: see Chapter 9) and the West's role in what it claimed was its 'sphere of privileged interests'. In the shortest of short-term senses, the calculation to go to war proved correct. Russian armed forces did not perform particularly effectively; they simply overwhelmed the Georgians by force of numbers. But the hoped-for demonstration effect in cowing Russia's neighbours was once again soon drowned out by the reorientation of priorities caused by the global economic crisis. And Russia itself turned briefly pragmatic and briefly inward.

In domestic policy, Medvedev was Robin to Putin's Batman. In foreign policy, Medvedev was Putin's 'scout'.[14] But despite the assumption after the initial change of power that Putin still called the shots, having Medvedev as president did make a foreign policy difference. Putin didn't want to undermine the credibility of his scout. Relations with the US improved during the initial phases of the 'reset' declared by Obama. NATO was removed as a burning issue soon after 2008; Georgian hopes of a Membership Action Plan were placed on the back burner, and Ukraine reined in its own ambitions after Viktor Yanukovych was elected president in 2010. New NATO Secretary General Anders Fogh Rasmussen steered the organisation to its own 'reset' with Russia after he took office in 2009. NATO no longer bet the business on expansion in Eastern Europe, but diversified the portfolio by cooperating on drug trafficking and international piracy. Russian cooperation then allowed the massive expansion of the 'Northern Corridor' to the Manas airbase in Kyrgyzstan and on to Afghanistan.

Putin Stumbles and Recovers, 2011–12

All three of the key Putin myths were slowly devalued under the Medvedev presidency, and the ever-loyal Medvedev contributed to their devaluation. So Putin's Russia needed a new narrative when he decided to return to the Kremlin in September 2011. Putin's initial failure to explain why he wanted to return, or to manufacture a drama in 2011, was not just hubris or oversight. The system then clearly struggled to find an internal logic without the element of strategic artifice. It was significant that the Russian word for the Medvedev–Putin job swap was 'castling' (*rokirovka*), a technical move at the back of the chessboard, rather than a bold attack.

The Kremlin was also getting lazy and over-reliant on 'administrative resources' to win elections – that is, simple fraud rather than 'sophisticated' manipulation. Voters in Moscow were outraged that they were 'outvoted' by voters in the North Caucasus – almost literally, given the inflated electorates and turnouts in the region. The 'carousel' that became notorious in the 2011–12 Russian election cycle was already regarded back in 2004 as a crude method in Ukraine. As it involved driving people around in a bus for repeat voting, it hardly merited the label of an election 'technology'. Virtual politics also fed the cycle of elite cynicism that generated it in the first place. Political technology not only masked the commodification of political power, but actually encouraged it. Elections cost a lot of money, and many officials over-concentrated on siphoning it off. Russian elections had also been emptied of real politics. Virtual dramas don't have real consequences. Russian politicians had gained a radical meta-freedom, but had not used it for anything other than self-enrichment.

Elite cynicism bred popular apathy. Electoral turnout was declining and becoming harder to manufacture – 60.1 per cent was claimed for the Duma vote in 2011. Russian turnout had been declining for years, compared to similar states where elections still mattered (e.g. 77.3 per cent for the third round in Ukraine in 2004). In Russia this time people were protesting as much against the fake turnout as against the fake victory for the ruling party, United Russia. They were protesting against the regime's theft of their authenticity by claiming that they had voted when they had not.

A hint of the deeper problem for the Kremlin was also provided by Pavlovsky: 'We have to prepare tranquilisation, not mobilisation.'[15] Mobilisation potentially meant lots of troublesome people – 'office plankton' was one of Pavlovsky's favourite phrases – making wearisome demands on the government. Pavlovsky claimed to prefer government 'for' the people rather than government 'by' the people. Putin's Kremlin made constant use of opinion polls in order to fine-tune manipulation policies, but to do it accurately. According to Pavlovsky, 'the first thing we did was kick out the sociologists who were fixing the figures'.[16] There was a feedback loop, but the manipulation came first, public endorsement came after.

It has often been remarked that Putinism rested on a 'social contract' of order and relative prosperity in return for less democracy. Less obvious was the psychological contract that asked people to look the other way while they were being manipulated. Virtual Russia was therefore always vulnerable to psychological revolution. The protests in 2011–12 were caused not by pocket-book issues, but rather by a psychological liberation from pocket-book politics, at least for the Moscow minority. The system was vulnerable to 'channel switching' – if the system depended on the message, it was vulnerable if Russians simply stopped listening. Particularly because the Kremlin had so overused Putin's charisma as a propaganda tool and exhausted much of his original impact. According to Konstantin Sonin, Putin used to be a strategic asset, but 'his PR has over-reached in the last three years. He was on TV too much, talking about culture and sport.'[17] Putin was famously booed at a kick-boxing event, but why was he there in the first place?

Nevertheless, Putin's omnipresence was more of a problem for the minority who were already disillusioned with him. Liberal Moscow loved to laugh at Putin 'discovering' Greek amphorae during a Black Sea dive, singing 'Blueberry Hill' or shooting a grey whale with a crossbow. And why not? It was all pretty funny. But Muscovites often seem to be laughing at the target audience as well. State TV still presented Putin's stunts with a straight face.

As Stephen Holmes and Ivan Krastev have argued:

Bombing is probably the best way to destroy a village; but to destroy a Potemkin village all that is required is to change the camera angle to reveal the improvised props holding up the flimsy façade. The post-election demonstrations were an expression of this revolutionary shift in perspective. In addition, the regime has succumbed to an aesthetic failure. Managed democracy was at heart a theatrical performance and it has failed in the way that mediocre performances can fail . . . the swap of roles between Putin and Medvedev spoiled the storyline of an open future.[18]

Without artificial drama, moreover, there was no distraction, and the election became a referendum on United Russia. Instead of the system creating lightning rods to channel and nullify dissent, the main regime party itself became the lightning rod.

An estimated 100,000 turned out to demonstrations in December 2011. Inexplicably, the organisers then took January off; but the February demonstrations attracted similar numbers, at least initially. For this minority, and only a minority, the emperor stood exposed – if not naked, then only partially clothed: Putin's ridiculous bare-chested hunting trips providing a suitable metaphor in the end.

The Grand Illusion was gone. The demonstrators had three favourite slogans: *Putin – vor!* ('Putin is a thief!') and *Rossiya bez Putina* ('Russia without Putin') were psychologically liberating – just chanting them in public displayed a lack of fear; the third was a play on the second slogan, *Rossiya bez puti* ('Russia without a path'), mocking Russia's new-found lack of direction. Though the one thing the demonstrators didn't have was a programme.

The opposition was dismissive of the Kremlin's rival methods. They mocked 'the administrative mobilisation of state workers'[19] and the use at pro-Putin rallies of migrants from Central Asia whose spoken Russian was often poor. Indeed, 'Tajiks for Putin' was a dangerous strategy in the longer term, given the rise of the new Russian nationalism.[20] The opposition also rightly saw Putin as simply trying to outnumber their own rallies with implausibly staged and strangely disengaged events, because the Kremlin was stuck in old paradigms of manipulation. In the words of Konstantin Sonin, 'the Kremlin thinks it's the TV message that matters . . . they think they can carry on with fraud and keep a lid on protests with media messages, and "anti-orange" politics . . . There is still too much emphasis on saying things rather than changing things.'[21]

But the TV message did still matter, and the opposition also neglected the extent to which its own liberated space was likewise an alternate reality. They were also trapped in the paradox of criticising elections in which they weren't actually taking part. Putin's rallies and campaign may have seemed implausible and artificial to them, but they created a form of reality for the majority of Russians who still got their news from state TV.[22] And it was the clash between these two completely different realities that made it difficult for the opposition to expand its appeal. Konstantin von Eggert even described the situation as the 'party of the internet' versus 'the party of TV'.[23] But the bad news for the opposition was that the TV party was much bigger. According to one Levada Center survey,[24] a massive 94 per cent of Russians still got their news mainly from the TV, and only 11 per cent from the internet, even though Russia has some 50 million regular internet users. An overall majority of 63 per cent trusted the news they heard on state TV,[25] which exactly matched Putin's vote.

On the other hand, there was no 'opposition' as such, just disparate groups that had 'switched channels'. The Moscow marches in December 2011 and early 2012 were, if anything, a little too catholic: everybody marched under a separate banner – liberals, nationalists, liberal-nationalists and all. No one really listened to the bad speeches from the public stage attempting to define an agenda. I was at the key rally on 4 February, when the temperature was at least –24°C, which did not help matters. The demonstrators thought they were consummating two separate convergences. The old liberal ghetto opposition from the 1990s was given space on the platform – a mistake, because its real political space was now smaller than ever. They stood alongside people like Aleksey Navalny who were both tech-savvy and newly nationalist, but not in the mould of Putin's original statist nationalism. Ethnic Russia mattered more than the state, and if necessary that Russia would be smaller: their key slogan was 'Stop feeding the Caucasus', as opposed to Putin's original 'There is no Russia without the Caucasus'. Arguably for the first time in Russian history, this was an introverted nationalism, committed to a practical Russia, without the bad bits, but also without so many migrants.

At the same time, older nationalist circles began to flirt with liberalism – or at least democracy, because democracy was necessary to oppose the regime. Such people had actually been demonstrating for years, in the much uglier annual 'Russian March' every November. There had also been anti-migrant riots on Manezh Square back in 2010. Significantly, it was these people that Putin wanted to co-opt, temporarily at least.

Putin's Conservative Values Project

Putin originally had no project for 2012, but he found one soon enough. His popularity had slumped – not disastrously by Western standards, but to below the magic 70 per cent threshold that had unlocked problems in the past. The answer was the 'conservative values project'. This ticked all the boxes. The first aim was to win the election by mobilising a 'Putin plurality' – not the super-majorities that had voted for Putin at the height of his popularity, but, minus the urban middle classes, the 'society of estates' would be enough for a simple majority. The second purpose was long-term divide and rule, splitting the new opposition by outflanking Navalny and the 'new nationalists'. Putin was clearly offended by the loss of what he thought was *his* middle class, the product of his economic boom. So the third purpose of the campaign was to redefine the protestors as somehow 'other'. Plus, more generally, an 'us versus them' campaign would put the opposition back in the box.

The fourth aim was to renew the elite. To Putin's paranoid mind, everyone around him had been disloyal during the crisis. Surkov had long talked of an 'offshore aristocracy'; now Putin decided that that group was vulnerable to pressure from the West and he launched a campaign to repatriate capital held abroad. Not that there was an immediate flood of cash back to Russia. Was there a property price crash in London or the south of France? Unfortunately not. Putin was right, though: the moneyed elite would be the weak link in the later parts of the story. But so-called 'internal sanctions' – restrictions on foreign accounts and travel bans on hundreds of thousands of key state officials – were applied gradually after 2012, before Western sanctions were considered in 2014.

There was also a shift within the elite balance of power, towards the so-called 'Orthodox oligarchs' like Konstantin Malofeev and Railways Minister Vladimir Yakunin (the former USSR manages to have both dowdy railways and super-rich railway bosses; revenue is limited, but huge amounts are siphoned off into satellite service companies, like SK Most and Transyuzhstroy). One long-term problem for Putin was that the elite were the least patriotic part of the population. But they were now well trained, and could spot a change in narrative when they saw one.

The conservative values project also helped Putin clamp down. To him and his more conservative coterie, the Medvedev interlude had seen a dangerous loss of control. The manipulation system had to be restored. It always worked best with fear in the background, so the demonstrators who had lost that fear needed to feel it again. Some people went to prison, some laws were tightened. The members of Pussy Riot were the most famous detainees: but 400 were arrested and twenty-seven were sentenced in total in an attempt to kill off the protests around Putin's inauguration day in May 2012. Navalny was convicted of embezzlement but released after only a day, with his sentence suspended. The opposition channel Rain TV lost its cable providers. Grani.ru and ej.ru were put on a blacklist of internet providers and Putin said the internet was a CIA plot. A new 'bloggers' law' in 2014 applied the same rules that currently govern the press to any site that received more than 3,000 hits in a day. The social network service Vkontakte was given new, Kremlin-friendly owners.

One political leader, Aleksandr Dugin, managed to talk of both a 'fifth column' (the remnants of the 2011–12 protests) and a 'sixth column' (regime insiders who failed to buy into the new project).[26]

But, again, to save on resources, it was actually more effective to use the us-and-them narrative to remind the demonstrators that they were 'them', no longer officially trusted and newly vulnerable to punishment. As with the Stalin era's campaign against 'cosmopolitanism', the campaign against post-modern Europe, against gay marriage and *pederasty* was really a coded battle against the system's opponents. Hence the neologism *tolerasty* – suggesting that misguided liberal values of toleration were simply creating a haven for the pederasts.

Economically, there was no more talk of 'modernisation', the buzzword under Medvedev's presidency. Kirill Rogov described the new programme as 'counter-modernisation'.[27] This meant amassing as many resources as possible to survive the metaphorical winter. 'Putin's friends' would get everything they wanted to maintain elite support, while the state distributed resources away from the 'creative classes' to the conservative masses and to inefficient parts of the economy – defence industries and remote regions in the eastern part of the country. Putin would accept the 'efficiency loss' in the short term.

One more advantage of the conservative values project was that it seemed to reinforce the other big project of Putin's return: the consolidation of a new political bloc in the post-Soviet space. This was a longstanding ambition that had gone under many names, but Putin now dubbed it the 'Eurasian Union'.[28] Russia claimed that the project would offer economic benefits, but the primary rationale was obviously political – to create a Russian-led bloc united in its opposition both to Western hegemony and to the West's post-modern rejection of 'traditional values'. Putin tried to turn the clock back a hundred years to 1914 – not to some high Soviet date like 1945, but to a time when Russia was both a major power in a concert of powers and a guardian of conservative values. And there was no Ukraine on the map in 1914.

Finally, it was belatedly discovered that some people in the West might take the conservative values project at face value. Useful idiots, on the right as well as the left, were prepared to buy the message, producing unlikely pieces like Patrick Buchanan's 'Is Putin one of us?'[29]

Geopolitics

Russia's other characteristic mode of thinking is 'geopolitics', which is in many ways the foreign policy equivalent of 'political technology'. Hundreds of books in Russian exist on the subject. There are even many books in Ukrainian on the Russians' obsession with the subject. Russia's version of geopolitics is conceived in lavish, even loving, old-fashioned great-power terms. Geopolitics, according to its advocates, is exclusively for the powerful. According to Aleksandr Dugin's definition, it is a 'worldview of power, the science of power and for power . . . a discipline of political elites'.[30] Russian geopolitics also views the whole world, and not just domestic politics, as a chessboard of neutral ciphers to be manoeuvred. Small states are subjects that do not deserve sovereignty. Sovereignty comes from strength, for which Vladislav Surkov liked to use the extremely long word *konkurentnosposobnost'* – which roughly translates as the 'ability to compete'. This view was not too far hidden in Putin's Crimea victory speech in March 2014: 'Crimea is our common historical legacy and a very important factor in regional stability. And this strategic territory should be part of a strong and stable sovereignty, which today can only be Russian.'[31]

The key to Russian geopolitics was the idea of a 'multi-polar world'. At the last count, there are more than 190 countries in the world, and by definition not all can be 'poles'. Poles need to attract (in this case) other states. What Russia has long advocated is better described by the Russian geopolitical thinker Vadim Tsymbursky in his book, significantly called *Island Russia*, as a 'multi-unipolar world'.[32] In this world, he argues,

> the basic parameters are set by the US, but in each region there are local powers that emerge to limit the actions of the superpower. They do not unite or offer an alternative world order, but they substantially restrict the ability of the superpower to advance its agenda . . . The US in the 1990s, on the other hand [and this is an important difference], ran a 'uni-multipolar' world. It imposed hegemony on regional leaders and gradually reduced their real influence.

Or rather the US thought it did: the unipolar world was always an illusion. The global reality was always more like 'one Great Centre and many sub-centres – or, as the Chinese say, one Super Power and Many Great Powers'.[33]

Tsymbursky claimed that his world was more stable than a world dominated by unrestrained American adventurism or unilateral 'democracy promotion'. The poles were supposed to balance each other. Russia would support other regional centres in standing up to Washington. The poles were also supposed to police the small states in their own unruly neighbourhoods.

Russian Neighbourhood Policy

So, over to Russia's 'pole'. In his victory speech following the annexation of Crimea in March 2014, Putin complained that after the collapse of the USSR 'the Russian nation became one of the biggest, if not the biggest ethnic group in the world to be divided by borders'. And Putin compared 'the aspiration of the Russians, of historical Russia, to restore unity' to the reunification of Germany in 1990.[34]

Similar statements were made by Russian politicians (of varying degrees of importance) throughout the 1990s and 2000s. But that certainly does not mean that the issue has dominated Russian politics ever since 1991, with Russia constantly bullying its neighbours to get its territory back. Most of the time Moscow simply didn't care, being preoccupied with internal tasks. Russia's initial policy towards its ethnic and linguistic kin was, to be honest, one of neglect. Yeltsin's wild capitalist bacchanalia wasn't too interested in highly sovietised factory workers living in crumbling estates in the suburbs of Donetsk or Riga. There was even a political party devoted to the issue of neglect, the Congress of Russian Communities, which won almost 3 million votes in the 1995 elections (like the League of Expellees in West Germany in the 1950s).

Russia has always tried to interfere in the internal politics and business life of other post-Soviet states. But in the 1990s it was relatively weak. In 2003–05, the 'coloured revolutions' – the apparently democratic uprisings in Georgia, Ukraine and Kyrgyzstan – created a heightened sense of threat. According to the reliably hyperbolic Pavlovsky, 'we had to fight for the streets'.[35] The Kremlin's version of what happened during those revolutions created an air of paranoia about foreign interference and domestic fifth columns. The booming Russian economy meant that Russia had resources to spend on counteracting that perceived threat. And the Yukos Affair had reshaped Russian politics to create state mechanisms capable of delivering those resources.

Russia saw itself as competing with the EU's 'neighbourhood policy' and its soft-power instruments. But Russia did not really 'do' soft power. It simply used the same political technology methods as it applied at home. According to the blunt and bull-headed Modest Kolerov, one of the key crafters of the neighbourhood policy in the late 2000s, 'soft power is dead. Soft power means creating points of pressure . . . points of infiltration, networks of influence . . . They [the other post-Soviet states] can struggle for their sovereignty, but it will cost them dear'.[36] This sounded more like 'covert power'. 'Soft power' for Russia seemed to be any means of coercion not involving tanks. But there was no neat alternative adjective; except perhaps for Tolstoy's phrase in *Anna Karenina*, the 'coarse power' of Russian society over the individual.

Russian neighbourhood policy also relied on the favourite political technology method of 'cloning'. I also talked to Sergey Markov about the use of political technology outside Russia. He said:

We should use political technology internationally in Georgia and Ukraine. I don't think of these countries as independent. First of all we should repeat what the United States is doing there. If we do ten times less than what the US is doing now, the result will be that a pro-Russian government will be in power in Ukraine. Now we are doing one hundred times less. The majority of the nation is in favour of Russia in Ukraine, so we just should help.[37]

I asked him what sort of things Russia should do exactly:

Think tanks, round tables, conferences, supporting media, exchanges, all these normal things. To help new leaders to appear, and to have roots for them in society, just normal things. You know that the Nashi movement was created to oppose the Orange Revolution, and that I am a teacher for this Nashi movement. I tell them: 'I am a big supporter of the Orange Revolution. But the Orange Revolution is not what Americans should make in Ukraine, but what we should make!' And it's a storm of applause every time!

So Russian 'neighbourhood policy' meant bribing local politicians and setting up pro-Russian front parties and sending shadowy funding to new pro-Russian NGOs. It meant spending at least $8 billion a year on PR.[38] It meant working through shadowy front companies like RosUkrEnergo in Ukraine, Prometheus in Greece, Overgas in Bulgaria, Emfesz in Hungary and Vemex in the Czech Republic. It also meant using the less shadowy Gazprom and its offshoots like North Stream and South Stream, polluting all the countries on its route. According to Andris Sprūds of the Latvian Institute of International Affairs, 'it's good that North Stream is where it is [its route from Russia to Germany being all under the sea]. If it passed through the Baltic States, it wouldn't be the states that controlled the pipeline, it would be the pipeline that controlled the states.'[39]

Modest Kolerov liked to think that this meant that Russia had a better, or more realistic, understanding of the region: 'We're better off because we're at home.' Whereas 'the EU is like Baron Münchhausen in countries like Moldova and Ukraine, pulling itself out by its own hair'.[40] But that really only meant a better understanding of venal post-Soviet elites. Putin's Russia was still far from interested in all the Russians outside Russia; just the ones who shared its values and technologies. In which case, non-Russians in the neighbourhood would do just as well, if they fitted Russia's modus operandi. Putin called his new policy and the NGO that promoted it *Russkii Mir* or 'Russian World'; but it was really 'Kremlin World'.

Information War

The final element in Russia's unholy trinity, alongside political technology and the love of geopolitics, is 'information war'.[41] Once again, literature is the clue. There are almost as many books in Russia with titles like *Information War* or *Information Geopolitics* as there are about political technology or geopolitics.[42] These are mostly written by one man – the 'political scientist' Igor Panarin, who is most famous for his prediction in 2008 that the US would break up into six parts within two years. Panarin is clearly no expert, then. (For anyone who is interested, he predicted that China would control the US west coast; the EU would take care of the east; Mexico would have the south-west; Russia would control Alaska; Japan would have Hawaii; and Canada would take the prairie states.)

What Russians mean by information war is a long way from 'soft power'. It involves not just the competition of ideas and information, but also the 'latent information management of the opponent's internal, economic and cultural processes' and 'information-psychological aggression based on economic, political and diplomatic pressure'.[43] The stress is therefore more on 'war' than it is on 'information'.

This is what the world would soon see during the crises in Ukraine, Crimea and the Donbas – blatant Russian manipulation of reality. 'Political technology', 'geopolitics' and 'information war' are not normal ways of thinking, or normal tool kits for domestic or foreign politics. They are pathologies. Put them together with the 'humiliation myth' and you have a sociopathic state. But the techniques that were first applied to domestic politics and then to small state neighbours would have completely different effects when they meant lying to and manipulating big powers that can fight back.

Conclusion

Returning to the law of variable consequences mentioned in Chapter 1, Russia's neighbourhood policy spun off in multiple directions after 2008. Both the EU and Russia were hit hard by the global economic crisis. Initially Russia talked more about things like 'selective empire' and 'control without responsibility' in its neighbourhood. But it soon realised that Europe had been hit harder and the US was preoccupied elsewhere. Russia was no longer so resource-poor and thought it could leverage that relative strength.

But the foreign policy turn also had domestic roots. After returning as president in 2012, Putin the pragmatist seemed to have become Putin the nationalist, albeit for pragmatic reasons. The moderate economic recovery in 2010–13 petered out by 2014. It would be easier to enter an age of austerity if national identity was on the up (unlike the EU, which had entered its age of austerity with the European idea in decline); and the new nationalism would replace the earlier pillars of the Putin myth. But this was a dangerous gamble: ideologies like nationalism can easily take over in weakly institutionalised authoritarian states. And it could also be rash: if the economic gains of the 2000s faded away too quickly and the new nationalist project ran aground, the system risked being exposed for what it was – a curtain of lies for the rich to hide behind.

Whatever was the more likely outcome, mobilisation was back. As Pavlovsvky complained, it had its problems. A state in permanent mobilisation risked over-heating. But permanent revolution suited the system better. The Kremlin's stumble into domestic problems in 2011–12 had not cured it of its addiction to political technology, but rather the opposite. But however good the Kremlin was at manipulating the virtual world of ideas and narratives, it would always clash with events on the ground, particularly if the Kremlin's rulers got trapped in a feedback loop; not only believing their own propaganda, but setting policy within the world of myths they had themselves created. This, then, was the background to the crisis of 2014.

CHAPTER 3

Yanukovych's Ukraine

Revolutions always disappoint; but few have disappointed more comprehensively than Ukraine's once-famous 'Orange Revolution' of 2004. That November, as the snow fell on photogenic crowds, gathered (as always) in Kiev's main square, the Maidan, Ukraine seemed to have it all. The attempt by a venal elite to rig the election was thwarted by massive, cheerful demonstrations mocking the old guard and singing in the new. The world's cameras lapped it up, focusing on the glamorous young Ukrainians deliberately placed at the front of the crowds and the glamorous Yuliya Tymoshenko on stage.

The whole post-Soviet world was at a turning point in 2004. In Russia, Putin had just arrested the country's richest man, Mikhail Khodorkovsky, in order to rewrite his succession deal with the Yeltsin elite. 'Putin's friends' were establishing their future mega-wealth through the seizure of Khodorkovsky's company Yukos. Ukraine had just been through a series of local corruption scandals (see below). The original Maidan protests in 2004 were therefore motivated by a sense that the hopes of the 1990s had given way to something worse in the 2000s. There was genuine optimism for change, and not just in Ukraine. The crowds in Kiev were an inspiration throughout the former Soviet Union. Adjectival revolutions sprang up everywhere – from the 'Tulip Revolution' in Kyrgyzstan in 2005 to the 'Umbrella Revolution' in Latvia in 2007.

Fast-forward to 2010, and Ukraine again looked a failure. After five years of infighting, egotism and missed opportunities, 'Ukraine fatigue' plagued Ukraine's friends and neighbours. Russia, which had not only tried to fix another election, but an election in someone else's country in 2004, was gifted the trope of 'Ukrainianisation', which Putin used constantly as a synonym for feckless talking-shop democracy. Viktor Yushchenko, the hero of the original Maidan, was replaced by none other than Viktor Yanukovych – whose attempts to rig the election in 2004 had sparked the original protests. He now had the chutzpah to stand with the ridiculous slogan 'The election was stolen from me five years ago, and I won't let it happen again'. Having won a fair election – the Orange Revolution did improve some things – he set about dismantling its every achievement and erasing it from history. But there was at least the hope that a country that has one revolution often has another, especially if the first wasn't so successful. That said, France had a long time to wait after 1789 until another change of monarchs in 1830 and a change of regime in 1848.

The Background

The main reason for all these ups and downs is that Ukraine has a predatory elite presiding over a deeply divided society. Ukraine is not the 'failed state' of Russian propaganda, but it has been incredibly badly governed more or less continuously since 1991. It won independence in 1991 only partly through its own efforts, but mainly because of the implosion of the Soviet order. The new Ukrainian state has always been weak and vulnerable to capture by regional clans and oligarchic and even mafia interests. It has always been difficult to form cohesive governments with coherent reform programmes, or even to form coalitions capable of challenging the power of the country's predatory elites. As a result, the economy has underperformed and corruption is rife. After the lost decade of the 1990s, economic recovery only began in 2000, but the small and medium-sized enterprise (SME) sector remained small and foreign direct investment (FDI) was minimal. Arguably, therefore, Ukraine had its first (Orange) revolution too early in 2004, before it really had a developed middle class.

In many ways the interesting question is therefore how come the Orange Revolution happened at all? One answer is that Ukraine did have some experience with democracy before independence in 1991 – less than most states in Central Europe and the Baltic Region, but more than many in the former USSR. The main trope in national historiography is the idea of 'Cossack liberty': unlike Russia, Ukraine's national history is not centred around the idea of statehood, as for most of its history it was ruled by other people – Poles, Russians and Communists – and Ukrainian Cossacks were refugees from, not servants of, the state, unlike the Russian Cossacks who pushed the frontier forward and, in the nineteenth century, were notorious for their treatment of Jews and other minorities. Ukrainian political culture is therefore different from Russia's. The state is not revered as an idea in itself; there is no cult of power or great-power status.

Moreover, Ukraine needs at least the discourse of democracy. Whoever rules in Kiev needs the argument that 'Ukraine is not Russia', the title of a (probably ghost-written) book by former President Kuchma (1994–2005), to justify their hold on power. And as Ukraine cannot be defined by touchstone issues of region, ethnicity, language, history and religion which divide more than they unite, this myth devolves by default to the political culture argument – the Ukrainians are 'more European' because they prefer compromise to confrontation and are less statist than the Russians. Or at least they used to be.

The Cossack tradition is overlaid with some historical experiences of pluralism, but mainly in the western territories that were part of the Habsburg Empire and then the inter-war states of Poland, Czechoslovakia and Romania. Most Ukrainians, who were subjects of the Russian Empire and then the USSR, experienced only the briefest flowerings of democracy after 1905 and in 1917.

On no occasion did Ukrainians experience democracy in their own state, however. They had competing visions of the borders of their putative community and disagreed about whether it should be part of some broader whole and, if so, whether that should be Imperial Russia, the USSR, the Habsburg Empire or Poland, or whether different parts should join up with different states. There were several attempts to set up an independent Ukraine in 1917–21, but no vote could be held that might have helped define, even retrospectively, the boundaries of the political community.

The west Ukrainian territories were not incorporated into the USSR until the 1940s, and a nationalist army, the Ukrainian People's Army (UPA), fought against that option until the 1950s. West Ukraine made the running in campaigning for independence in the Gorbachev era, but the west Ukrainian tradition is in fact many traditions, from which locals can pick and choose. The Habsburg idea of multi-ethnic *Galicia Felix* (Galicia being the name of the core west Ukrainian region centred on the city of Lviv) was succeeded in the 1920s by a fascistic 'nationalism of the deed', the purpose of which was precisely to cleanse the region of its historical multi-ethnicity. The violent tradition represented by the Organisation of Ukrainian Nationalists (OUN) and the UPA was superseded in turn in the 1960s by Soviet Ukrainian dissidents working within the system. 'Dissent' was, by definition, peaceful and civic, but violence was also abandoned because it didn't work. Ironically, the cult of the main OUN leader Stepan Bandera was readopted by many Galicians in the 2000s, especially the young, but this time as a symbol of local distinctiveness.[1]

The Galician Ukrainians like to think of themselves as the 'Piedmont of Ukraine' – the agent of national unity, like north-west Italy in the 1860s. But Galicia is largely rural, so this idea is usually rejected by the more urban, Russian-speaking east and south, where the vast majority of Ukrainians were under Soviet rule from 1921. Many Ukrainian critics complain that this majority population is 'post-colonial', denationalised, materialistic, subservient, clientelistic or even lacking in political culture.[2] Others bemoan the fact that political culture in Galicia is degraded. In the Gorbachev era, it was represented by the civic nationalism of the dissident-led movement Rukh; the years since 2010 have seen the rise of the ugly ethno-nationalist and anti-immigrant Freedom Party. Whatever the case, Ukrainians in different regions are still deeply divided by the lack of an agreed historical narrative. Most Ukrainian elections since 1991 have refought issues of identity, language and foreign policy orientation. Ukrainian politicians manipulate these issues to gain power, but revert to predatory behaviour in office; so underlying issues are never resolved and resurface at the next election.

The Soviet Union collapsed precipitously, and Ukraine's final decision to opt out was a key reason for that collapse. Ukrainians swung from 70 per cent voting to preserve the USSR in Gorbachev's referendum of March 1991, to 90 per cent backing independence in another referendum in December 1991. Ironically, this change was largely brought about by the promise that Ukraine would be better off economically outside the USSR. When the reverse proved true, support for independence fell back to about two-thirds.

Ukraine was independent, but there was no social revolution. The old communist elite remained in charge. The counter-elite – mainly former dissidents based in the Rukh movement – had been strong enough to win a quarter of the vote at elections in 1990–91 (in west Ukraine and among the Ukrainian-speaking intelligentsia), but not to win power on its own. Most Ukrainian nationalists were prepared to support the old elite, so long as they backed independence. But Ukraine was not well served by its first two presidents, as they sought to build a Ukrainian state more or less from scratch. First President Leonid Kravchuk (1991–94) had the uninspiring slogan 'We have what we have'. He thought it was so good he used it again as the title for his memoirs. His successor Leonid Kuchma (1994–2005) famously said, on becoming Kravchuk's prime minister in 1992, 'Tell me what kind of society we are going to build, and I will build it.' Ukraine, in other words, was not run by committed democrats or free-market enthusiasts.

Kravchuk was a typical former apparatchik.[3] With the partial exception of the west, society was atomised by seventy years of Soviet rule. The Soviet 'middle class' (technicians and intelligentsia) was hit hard when savings were wiped out by the inflation of the early 1990s; and the bureaucracy was the only real available instrument of power. Kravchuk therefore concentrated on 'state-building', which meant a centralisation of power, rather than building real grassroots democracy. His economic policy did not aim to build a true market economy, but rather to recreate a smaller version of the USSR, as its branch ministries and price, trade and production controls would also cement the new elite's new power. Kravchuk's response to growing economic difficulties in the spring of 1994 was not to undertake belated reform, but to contemplate stifling Ukraine's nascent pluralism.[4]

Kravchuk's economic policy was also dangerously incompetent, and he was increasingly out-manoeuvred by the 'red director' elite who had taken advantage of the chaotic conditions of the early 1990s to enrich themselves, trading in subsidised exports and exploiting price controls – and they wanted more. Ukraine was actually in a worse position than Russia: the fragile new national project made Kravchuk (and Rukh) reluctant to embrace 'big bang' economic reform, so Ukraine's semi-reformed economy had more opportunities for arbitrage. The 'red directors' backed one of their own, Leonid Kuchma, former director of the giant missile factory at Dnipropetrovsk, for president, after forcing early elections in 1994 by encouraging a series of strikes in eastern Ukrainian cities in 1993.

For these crucial elections, Ukraine was not quite pluralistic, but it was divided into two camps: Kravchuk fought on the achievement of statehood; Kuchma criticised the prioritisation of statehood over his own vague promises of 'reform'. Kravchuk won 45 per cent in the west and centre; Kuchma won with 52 per cent in the east and south. Kravchuk at least left office peacefully.

Kuchma was made of sterner stuff, and forced through a 'constitutional agreement' in 1995 as a prelude to a new constitution in 1996. Both greatly expanded presidential power, at the expense of transparency and accountability. The nationalist right was again complicit, because Kuchma shrewdly promised them what they wanted in terms of state symbols and formally entrenching the Ukrainian language. Kuchma also had to buy off the parties on the left with a long list of socio-economic rights that the state could not afford. Economically, Kuchma played a game of balance, as the 'red directors' were succeeded by an emergent class of 'oligarchs'. He parcelled out control of Ukraine's heavy industry to the rival regional 'clans' in a series of insider deals in the late 1990s and early 2000s: coal and steel in the Donbas, piping and petrochemicals in Dnipropetrovsk, engineering in Kharkiv, the trading entrepôt of Odesa, and the Soviet holiday industry in Crimea. Real economic reform was again delayed until this great property grab was over. Politically, with left and right parties increasingly passive anyway, Kuchma and the oligarchs were able to blunt any challenge to power by exploiting the local arts of 'political technology' – playing divide and rule and funding front parties to win parliamentary elections in 1998 and Kuchma's re-election in 1999.

Kuchma over-reached in his second term, however. In spring 2000, he claimed massive majorities in a referendum to further expand his presidential powers; but before he could ratify the changes in parliament with the necessary two-thirds majority, Ukraine was hit by the 'Gongadze scandal', named after the journalist Heorhiy Gongadze who founded Ukraine's first website devoted to political exposé and critiques of oligarchic corruption, and who disappeared in September 2000. In October, his headless corpse was found in woods outside Kiev. In November, sensational secret tapes emerged, supposedly made in Kuchma's office, in which the president angrily demanded that his subordinates deal with Gongadze in various colourful ways.

But the pressure for economic change was also building at this time. Ukraine was almost bankrupt, and in December 1999 Kuchma was forced to appoint a reformist prime minister, former head of the Central Bank Viktor Yushchenko, to negotiate with international lenders. His deputy, a former gas trader called Yuliya Tymoshenko, was appointed as poacher-turned-gamekeeper to clean up the energy sector. She made some progress in the gas sector, but coal and steel interests dug in deep. Ironically, the duo's reforms kick-started the economy, but that made it even harder to dislodge the oligarchs as they began to enjoy the fruits of belated growth. Once the Gongadze protest movement (dubbed 'Ukraine without Kuchma') fizzled out by spring 2001, the oligarchs brought down first Tymoshenko, who was briefly imprisoned, and then Yushchenko. Both founded new parties, which won a plurality but not a majority at the next parliamentary elections in 2002. Both of these were personal vehicles, however – Yushchenko's Our Ukraine party and the aptly named Tymoshenko Bloc. Ukraine has never had a reform party per se, nor a strong liberal party – nor strong political parties in general.

Kuchma survived, but was too weak to pursue his original intention of changing the constitution so that he could run for a third term in 2004. He was also less able to balance the clans, the strongest of which, based in the Donbas, imposed one of their own, Viktor Yanukovych, first as prime minister in November 2002 and then as presidential candidate in 2004. The strength of the Donbas came about through the rise of the local steel industry (see below) and because of its muscular, even thuggish, political culture. The opposition united behind Yushchenko. Ironically, a stronger Kuchma might have co-opted Yushchenko or backed a more centrist candidate, who might still have won. The economy had grown strongly in 2000–04 after the disastrous 1990s, and many oligarchs were starting to think about diversifying their options. Most stayed together as a cabal so long as Yanukovych looked the likely victor; but an outer ring of smaller 'minigarchs' thought they would be swallowed up by the Donbas clan if he triumphed. Others were worried that a controversial election would only deepen Ukraine's international isolation after the Gongadze affair.

The First Revolution

Divisions at the top made Ukraine 'semi-authoritarian', rather than truly dictatorial. Yanukovych's team fought dirty, assisted by Russian money and a Russian team of 'political technologists' – but arguably not dirty enough. The authorities were not strong enough to arrange a more decisive imposition of their planned result, but hubristic enough after 'managing' previous elections to think they would get away with rigging the vote. The most obvious 'half-measure' was that someone poisoned Yushchenko, but didn't kill him. The 'technologists' also tried to divert attention from issues of good governance and corruption by polarising Ukrainian east against Ukrainian west. Nationalist extremists were organised to demonstrate in unwanted support for Yushchenko, with a particularly notorious march through Kiev in June 2004 behind neo-Nazi flags and banners paid for by the 'technologists' (some of the same cast of characters would reappear in 2014). Finally, the technologists added almost a million votes for Yanukovych by hacking into the official count.

The opposition, meanwhile, expected fraud and was significant enough to pre-plan protest – but not the hundreds of thousands who suddenly flocked to the Maidan for mass demonstrations that would be known as the 'Orange Revolution' (orange being Yushchenko's campaign colour).

The huge crowds prevented Yanukovych's planned inauguration. Kuchma, to his credit, did not want bloodshed, and so he invited Polish President Aleksander Kwaśniewski to mediate – and to help him resist the pressure from Yanukovych and from Russia. Kwaśniewski was joined by Javier Solana for the EU. Once the international mission was in Kiev, a crackdown was unlikely, though it was briefly contemplated a week into the protests. But the crowd, although large enough to prevent the authorities declaring Yanukovych the victor, was not an actual actor. Different forces were divided as to what to do next. Radicals thought the regime was on its knees and could be dismantled: government institutions should be taken over, and Yushchenko should implement his campaign slogan of revolutionary justice: 'Bandits to Jail!' But in order to protect their interests, the richer oligarchs began building bridges with Yushchenko, who was naturally more cautious. There was, in any case, broad agreement on a non-violent, civil resistance approach.

Negotiations were therefore always likely, but the eventual agreements reached were highly controversial. Yushchenko's critics, including Tymoshenko, argued that he gave away too much from a position of strength, in particular the agreement to change the constitution and reduce the incoming president's power after the next parliamentary elections in the spring of 2006. Yushchenko was only inaugurated in January 2005, so he would have barely a year of full power. Then there was a behind-the-scenes amnesty not only for Kuchma, but also for the perpetrators of the election fraud (this was made public in October 2005), and seemingly a blanket immunity for all the former elite, symbolised by the return of the chief prosecutor from the Kuchma era, Svyatoslav Piskun, in December 2004. All as the price for a re-run election, which Yushchenko finally won in December 2004.

The Orange Soap Opera

The new 'Orange' period therefore failed to begin in truth, guaranteeing that controversies would continue to fester: there was no real investigation of Gongadze's death or Yushchenko's own poisoning; and as mentioned, in 2010, Yanukovych would be able to claim that the election was 'stolen' from him in 2004 – so his presidency would also be founded on a lie. Perhaps worst of all, the oligarchs had both an institutional framework to protect their power (the stronger parliament, the prosecutor's office, a corruptible judiciary) and were soon moving in to corrupt the new Orange team.

Their personal failings were important. Personalities clashed on a Shakespearian level – mainly Viktor and Yuliya, but there was a strong supporting cast, including Mrs Yushchenko as a cross between Eva Peron, Imelda Marcos and Lady Macbeth, and various players rushing in from the wings, like Petro Poroshenko. Even the courtiers were at each other's throats.

Nobody hit the ground running, despite the advice from Poland, in partic ular, to act quickly while the new leadership was still popular. Yushchenko declared victory in his inauguration speech and then went on holiday. According to his chief of staff: 'Yushchenko's first six months were spent travelling and collecting awards. No wonder it went to his head. I immediately cut down on his travel [from September 2005].'[5] Yushchenko was also much iller than he let on after the poisoning in 2004. If he spent half of his time travelling, he spent the other half receiving medical treatment.

Yushchenko was hopelessly prolix. One story relates how his advisers secured him a precious thirty minutes with Condoleezza Rice in 2006. After Yushchenko opened with a twenty-seven-minute monologue, Rice got up and thanked him for their 'interesting exchange of views'.

Yushchenko's key personal turning point was the affair of his wantonly wayward son Andriy in the summer of 2005. In particular, the ridiculous youth claimed to 'own' the Orange Revolution, as in having a monopoly on the sale of tourist merchandise (orange mugs, etc.), thus reducing it to a brand. President Yushchenko blamed the people and the media, not his son. According to his political adviser Rostyslav Pavlenko, 'The affair broke the moral contract with the people. Then all his political mistakes became evident. Moral capital was his key asset. Once he lost it, people looked only at political moves, and Tymoshenko was simply much better at this game. Yushchenko was not as charismatic as Yuliya, or even as clever as [Arseniy] Yatsenyuk [prime minister in 2014]. As an ordinary politician, he was bound to lose out.'[6]

In the end, 'Yushchenko wasn't a bad guy. He just got swallowed up by the system.'[7] Tymoshenko, on the other hand, still behaved like a businesswoman in government – and a post-Soviet one at that. She wanted to win, and making disposable deals with fellow politicians and their parties, companies or TV stations was simply how things were done. Politics was never about permanent beliefs or partners, just pieces to be moved to secure that ultimate victory.

Russia's Role

During the Orange Revolution there was a lot of nonsense talked about Russia's 'legitimate interests' in Ukraine, as if 'legitimate interests' included such unprecedented interventions. Russia seconded the political technologists who fixed the election, and it paid $500 billion for Yanukovych's campaign (albeit via a scheme whereby Yanukovych, as prime minister, overpaid Gazprom by a similar sum in the summer of 2004).[8] But Russia's role after the election, and its determination to poison the adventure from the start, has received much less attention.

In 2005, the new Orange leadership visited Moscow. Oleh Rybachuk, Yushchenko's chief of staff, tells the story thus:

Eventually Dmitriy Medvedev set me up with Putin. I was walking in Red Square when I got the call. Vladimir Vladimirovich [Putin] is waiting. He will see you in two hours. I hadn't asked for the meeting. Putin's opening words were 'You are selling the motherland' [the steelworks Kryvorizhstal]. I replied, 'Yes, but very expensively.' Medvedev then made me an offer. When I asked him about RosUkrEnergo, he said 'Our side is clear, transparent. I am supervising it. On your side, it's up to you. It's a good scheme. We made it with the [old] president. You're in power now, so it's up to you. It's yours. Go home. Talk to Yushchenko. Get back to me.'[9]

Rybachuk says the implication was clear. It was a massive bribe: $500 million a quarter, or $2 billion a year, was the Ukrainian share: 'This was an FSB-inspired scheme to corrupt Ukrainian politicians at the highest level.'[10] Russia has a long history of interfering in Ukraine. Rybachuk claims he refused, and 'my resignation was on Yushchenko's desk by February 2006. We limped on till September, but practically we stopped cooperating.'

But it made little difference. There was a demand for corruption from the Ukrainian side, as well as a supply from the Russian side. Rybachuk also says 'there was huge competition amongst the representatives of the Ukrainian business environment for this role of intermediary . . . Too many of our guys wanted to cut a deal with the Russians. All sorts of middlemen approached me – real Mafia guys . . . They thought I was a PR front, and real policy would be made by them . . . Another channel was found to Yushchenko.'[11] 'Yushchenko's gravediggers' were his brother Petro, the oligarch Dmytro Firtash and Mykhailo Doroshenko, editor of *Ukraïna Moloda*.[12] Jointly they killed the presidency: 'Doroshenko was totally corrupt. Knock on his door, he will sort everything. Everybody knew this.'[13]

A key meeting in the Carpathians in January 2006 took the scheme into the heart of government.[14] Cash was delivered straight from the National Bank of Ukraine. Petro was the cashier. Yushchenko retired with the contents of several national museums housed in his still-presidential palace – he was especially fond of Trypillian artefacts and Scythian gold; these often priceless pieces enabled him to bore visitors with his historical obsessions (according to Ukrainian nationalists, the Trypillians were an early Ukrainian civilisation that flourished from 5000 to 3000 BC). In 2013, Yushchenko claimed tactlessly that he was down to his last million.[15]

Little was therefore done to change the economic order, save for one symbolic 'reprivatisation' of the steel plant Kryvorizhstal in October 2005. Although Rinat Akhmetov, the richest oligarch of all, briefly sojourned abroad, there was no systemic challenge to oligarchic power – unlike Georgia after 2003. In fact, the constant rivalry between Yushchenko and Tymoshenko allowed the oligarchs to play divide and rule, rather than the other way around.

Economic policy concentrated on superficial populist measures, such as fuel and meat price freezes, rather than on tackling systemic problems, as had been briefly attempted in 2000–01. Historically, periodic economic pain has actually been good for Ukraine. The country never reformed its economy wholesale, like the Baltic States, but did just enough to survive when it was forced to – most notably when the recession of the early 1990s pushed it to the brink of collapse in 1994–95, and again after the local financial crisis in 1998–99 threatened it with bankruptcy in 2000. On the other hand, when the economy was doing well enough, politics was not conducive to reform. Hence the great missed opportunity of the years immediately after the Orange Revolution (also, arguably, in 2010, when the new authorities' business-friendly reform plans were quietly abandoned as the economy temporarily recovered).

Orange Government, 2005–10

The first 'Orange' government was led by Tymoshenko, but it collapsed amid infighting as early as September 2005. She was succeeded by the more 'business-friendly' Yuriy Yekhanurov, who had overseen the privatisation process under Kuchma, as a caretaker prime minister. Nevertheless, the voters gave the three Orange parties – the Tymoshenko Bloc, Yushchenko's Our Ukraine and the small Socialist Party – a second chance, with a narrow majority in the parliamentary elections of March 2006. But because the Tymoshenko Bloc was now the strongest of the three, Yushchenko refused to do a deal with it. As negotiations dragged into the summer, the Socialists sensationally defected to Yanukovych's Party of Regions to create an alternative majority, allegedly after another massive bribe. In desperation, Yushchenko cobbled together a final alternative coalition between Our Ukraine and the Party of Regions, along with the Socialists and the small Communist Party, to prevent the Party of Regions from governing alone.

It was a disastrous decision. Yanukovych returned as prime minister and set about aggrandising his power. The Our Ukraine ministers were soon forced out. Yanukovych's finance minister, Mykola Azarov, blatantly used every power at his disposal to bribe or force all the oligarchs back into the Party of Regions' camp. Then Yanukovych targeted the president's powers and a constitutional (two-thirds) majority in parliament, which he could only obtain by bribery and by breaking the new constitutional provision introduced for this very reason in 2006 – the so-called 'imperative mandate', which stipulated that deputies had to remain in the parties under which they were elected.

The result was a constitutional crisis in the summer of 2007, when Yushchenko attempted to dissolve the new parliament. Both sides bribed the constitutional court to rule in their favour, so it procrastinated. Various judges and the chief prosecutor were fired, the Tymoshenko Bloc withdrew from parliament to render it inquorate, and troops moved on government buildings. New elections were finally scheduled for September 2007, but only because Yushchenko privately agreed to another coalition between the Party of Regions and Our Ukraine.

But the voters unexpectedly gave the Orange politicians a third chance. The Socialists were hammered and the Tymoshenko Bloc once again took most votes. Yushchenko had to swallow his pride and reappoint Tymoshenko as prime minister in December 2007. This time she stayed in office for more than two years, when opposition might ironically have been a better option. She was prime minister when Ukraine was hit hard by the economic crisis in 2008–09, with GDP falling by 15 per cent in 2009. But it was not incumbency itself that killed Tymoshenko's chances at the next election. The Estonian and Latvian governments both won re-election in 2011 after austerity measures, because they explained what needed to be done and had a clear exit strategy. Tymoshenko, on the other hand, failed to present voters with a clear programme of 'pain but then gain'. She was all tunnel and no light. Economic reform was ditched while she tried to keep the economy afloat. Several oligarchs received large bailouts. Yushchenko again constantly undermined her, and disillusioned voters were not inclined to give the divided Orange camp a fourth chance.

The 2010 Election

By the 2010 election, Yanukovych had already been denied office once (in 2004) and been thrown out (in 2007). If the election had been closer – if Tymoshenko had won or come close enough to seriously test the outcome in the courts – Yanukovych was planning an 'anti-Maidan'. Regular party rallies in St Michael's Square were used as an excuse to keep the streets of Kiev full of his supporters: some elderly, some paid, some suspiciously youthful. The message was clear, though lost on most foreign observers – Yanukovych would not accept defeat with anything resembling good grace.

Tymoshenko's tragedy was that she could not convince enough voters that Yanukovych would be as bad as he turned out to be; too few voters were prepared to overlook her own faults; and Yushchenko stabbed her in the back once again. He won 5.5 per cent. His dwindling band of supporters pointed out that at least he had not fixed the result and was prepared to face his humiliation. Maybe so, but he did connive with Yanukovych: his last significant act, a decree to make Stepan Bandera a Hero of Ukraine, was so provocative to voters in eastern Ukraine, and so provocatively timed in between the two rounds of voting, that it seemed deliberately designed to mobilise votes against Tymoshenko. And Yushchenko also urged his supporters to stay at home. In the second round, Tymoshenko lost narrowly to Yanukovych by 45.5 per cent to 48.9 per cent. No less than 4.4 per cent of voters voted 'against all' (8 per cent in Kiev), and their number alone would have given Tymoshenko victory. A further 1.2 per cent of votes were declared invalid. But Tymsohenko's legal complaints soon fizzled out. She was the victim of her own failure to change the rules.

Breaking the Formal Rules

Yanukovych won a reasonably free and fair election, though he would have cheated if he had had to. But he was not elected with the powers he then seized. The opposite, in fact: ironically, one reason why many people voted for

Yanukovych was to balance the system. Tymoshenko was still prime minister, and the constitutional changes introduced in 2006 meant that she would stay prime minister until 2012. One reason why some were wary of voting for Tymoshenko was that she talked of 'clarifying' the constitution to give herself extra powers. Yanukovych said nothing, because what he did next was unconstitutional.

Defeated presidential candidates lose momentum pretty quickly, but the ouster of Tymoshenko broke all sorts of rules. The Orange parties had a majority from the last elections. That 'majority' was set in stone at the start of the parliament and could not be changed: MPs could not change sides – the 'imperative mandate' (see above) ensured that they had to stay in the parties under which they were elected (by proportional representation). The rules existed for a reason – to discourage volatility and the use of bribery and intimidation to promote 'political tourism', i.e. MPs changing sides. But that is precisely what Yanukovych did. At first seven, then twenty-eight of Tymoshenko's MPs were persuaded to abandon her. Seventeen members of Yushchenko's Our Ukraine also voted against her, as did three independents (plus the Communist Party and the Lytvyn Bloc).[16] The whole operation cost tens of millions of dollars. The renegades called themselves 'For Competitiveness and Reforms' and later 'Reforms for the Future' – part of an unconsummated plan to set up a second governing party to run alongside the Party of Regions (in imitation of the Russian system that partnered the ruling party United Russia with the pseudo-opposition party Just Russia). In February 2012, the project's 'manager' Ihor Rybakov was recorded offering another MP $450,000 to join, plus a $25,000 monthly 'allowance' – which gives some idea of the going rate.[17]

Tymoshenko's ousting was a key general turning point. This collective act of spinelessness, with all economic interests suddenly clustering around the new court, left Yanukovych free to push even further. A highly regressive legal reform in the summer of 2010 gave the executive complete control over the judiciary. The decision of the constitutional court to restore the old constitution in October 2010 was therefore only the icing on the cake. Except that there was a strong argument for saying that Yanukovych was now an illegitimate president, having seized so much power in what amounted to a constitutional coup d'état. The guardian of the constitution could have adjudicated – but unfortunately that was the very same constitutional court. (The Ukrainian constitution also contains a dangerous phrase about the president being the guarantor of the constitution.)

Hanna Herman, the then deputy head of the presidential administration, thought Yanukovych's first hundred days were reasonably successful: 'But there were parallel structures, which developed certain projects and solutions. Although we also worked in the administration, it seemed our proposals were rejected en masse. [People from Moscow, Kremlin technologists] were there from the beginning of his reign, but actively began to appear only in [later] years.'[18] The Kremlin's fingerprints were all over the Austrian bank accounts that Yanukovych and his cronies used to hide their assets.[19] The same local fixer, Reinhard Proksch, was also linked to Russian Deputy Prime Minister Igor Shuvalov.

Political Prosecutions

In 2010, the courts were nobbled. In 2011, the regime started putting its opponents in jail. In May 2011, charges were laid against Tymoshenko. She was accused of 'abuse of office', a crime from the 1962 Soviet Criminal Code. But there was no convincing smoking gun: the 'abuse' in question related to the January 2009 gas agreement with Russia. The Tymoshenko trial itself was held in one of Kiev's tiniest courtrooms to limit attendance, but that only made it noisy and chaotic. A young and inexperienced judge looked out of his depth and made no attempt to stop a string of prejudicial comments from government officials while matters were still sub judice. Tymoshenko, on the other hand, was imprisoned in August 2011, before the trial ended, on ill-defined charges of 'contempt'. In October she was sentenced to seven years and ordered to pay a fine of $188 million.

But she was not the only politician in jail. In May 2012, US Ambassador to the Organization for Security and Co-operation in Europe Ian Kelly counted 'thirteen former senior officials from the Tymoshenko-led government, including four cabinet ministers, five deputy ministers, two agency heads, one governor and the head of the state gas monopoly'.[20] More cases were laid after Kelly made his calculation.

Breaking the Informal Rules

Yanukovych may have won a free and fair election, but then he unconstitutionally aggrandised his power. What he did next with all his extra power was even worse. But Yanukovych also broke the rules of post-Soviet non-democracy – number one being that he didn't share the loot. Corruption was much more direct than it had been under Kuchma: whereas Kuchma controlled access to corruption opportunities, Yanukovych and his 'Family' ran the schemes themselves. Under Kuchma, there were rules about permissible theft: on the secret tapes made in Kuchma's office that emerged during the Gongadze scandal he says of one miscreant: 'You have put at least a hundred million in your pocket [but] you did it foolishly and stupidly . . . Any stupid inspector could see [through such] false schemes. Even a stupid one.'[21] Under Yanukovych, corruption was draining the bucket. Plus there were too many outright criminals involved. And there was license to the extreme; under the divided leadership of the Orange period there was no effective anti-corruption policy, but corruption was riskier, because there was no agreement on what was permitted.

Power was increasingly vested in a literal and metaphorical 'Family'. Commentators are used to the meta-reality of *The Godfather*. But it is far from coincidental that East European mafias behave according to the rules laid down by Marlon Brando at his daughter's wedding in the film – after all, they watched the movie too. 'Respect' means agreeing to the rules of the game. Once you are in, you are in for good, and you buy in to rule number one. 'Family' is both literal and metaphorical. Rules are as important as blood. In the film, Tom is not blood, but is part of the 'Family'. Michael is blood but is initially outside the rules and Don Corleone is at first upset when he opts in. And the less said about Fredo the better. Exchange of favours and mutual obligation ('One day, I will ask you to perform a service for me . . .') is another key rule, as is never going outside the 'Family'.

So it was perfectly natural that the Yanukovych 'Family' should consist of key actual family members who could be trusted – the president's elder son Oleksandr (born in 1973) but not the younger (and the president's wife was rarely seen), and confidants of a similar or even younger age who fronted the various schemes and scams, like Vitaliy Khomutynnik (born 1976) and Serhiy Kurchenko (born 1985). But the Corleones weren't running a country. If the main thing about the Yanukovych 'Family' was that it was too greedy, it was also too small, with fewer than ten leading figures (a key difference from Assad in Syria, who had an extended family of more than a hundred members and the Alawite sect as the regime's core support). Yanukovych's elder son personally vetted every regional police chief – power was concentrated at the very, very top.

According to Yuliya Mostova, the editor of Ukraine's main opposition paper *Dzerkalo Tyzhnya*, understanding Yanukovych was always easy: 'He wanted to be the richest man in Eastern Europe.'[22] The problem was well identified by leading economic and energy analyst Mykhailo Honchar: 'Yanukovych wanted to be both president and number one oligarch. Like all those other guys – Putin, Nazarbayev and Aliyev. Except they had energy and rents to distribute. Ukraine does not.'[23] That was why Yanukovych and his cronies jumped at the opportunity of developing local shale gas in 2013: suddenly they saw themselves sitting on top of a pile of money, with the world owing them a living – their ideal scenario all along.

So Yanukovych's regime was not simply a reprise of the Kuchma era after the Orange interlude. Kuchma ran the presidency as he used to run his rocket factory. The system of checks and balances was part of his managerial background. He preferred to deal with oligarchs horizontally. He believed that this made him more of a patriot than Yushchenko: 'The true Ukrainian nationalist is me, the former "Red director" Kuchma! . . . [You] can't have a national revival without national capital.'[24] According to one Ukrainian expert, 'Kuchma was more like a medieval European monarch in the way he dealt with his "barons"'. Yanukovych, on the other hand, acted more like an Asiatic despot: everything was organised vertically. Immediately below him was family and his inner mafia circle; then below them, various sycophants. So maybe that meant 'Kuchma was a little bit more European' than Yanukovych.[25] Except that his model of government was several hundred years out of date.

The election of Yanukovych did indeed raise corruption to another level. Initially, like Kuchma, he had to balance the oligarchs. But Yanukovych was a leading member of the group that emerged victorious from the Donbas gang wars of the 1990s, and they were not used to sharing anything. One by one, the circle of favoured oligarchs narrowed and power became increasingly concentrated in the hands of Yanukovych's literal and metaphorical 'Family', most notably his elder son Oleksandr and his associates like the baby-faced Serhiy Kurchenko. Political power was ruthlessly centralised, and so was corruption. And once it came to be increasingly monopolised by the 'Family', it exploded in scale. When the Maidan protests against Yanukovych were just beginning in November 2013 (actually sparked by the decision to abandon a key trade deal with the EU, but against the venality and brutality of the regime in general), Anders Åslund estimated the level of corruption at $8–10 billion a year to the Yanukovych 'Family'.[26] But once the protestors were victorious and Yanukovych had fled, more information became available. When Arseniy Yatsenyuk took over as prime minister, he initially claimed: '$37 billion of credit received have disappeared in an unknown direction . . . [and] the sum of $70 billion was paid out of Ukraine's financial system into off-shore accounts'.[27] To put this into perspective, $70 billion was equivalent to almost half of Ukraine's gross domestic product in 2013. Only 4.3 billion UAH (Ukrainian Hryvnia, or $430 million) were left in government accounts, Yatsenyuk said, and only $15 billion in the Central Bank's foreign currency reserves. Within two months, the estimate of total corruption by Yanukovych and his literal and metaphorical 'Family' had risen to $100 billion in just under four years.[28]

How Corruption Worked

Prosecutors and civil society were also able to give a better account of how corruption worked under Yanukovych. Gas was still the biggest area of 'traditional' corruption. The notorious RosUkrEnergo had lost its position in 2009, but a gas price discount agreed by Russia in 2010 actually made the situation worse, increasing the scope for arbitrage. A massive 7.5 per cent of GDP went on energy subsidies, including 2 per cent of GDP to the state oil and gas company Naftohaz Ukraïny. Åslund describes how Naftohaz bought 18 billion cubic metres of domestically produced gas per year at the extremely low price of $53 per 1,000 cubic metres, because it was supposed to supply hard-pressed domestic consumers. However, at least half of that gas found its way to industrial customers or straight to the companies of favoured oligarchs, or else went abroad for a price nearer the then Russian supply price of $410 per 1,000 cubic metres. As Åslund notes, 'the potential for privileged arbitrage here is enormous: $350 per 1,000m³ times 9 billion equals $3.15 billion. This is probably the main reason why Yanukovych so adamantly opposes increased gas prices.'[29] An investigation by slidstvo.info shows how 'Yanukovych's gas kings' divided up the domestic market.[30]

Insider privatisations were the key means of initially keeping non-'Family' oligarchs happy in 2010–11. Rinat Akhmetov, in particular, was able to add regional power companies to his empire. Dmytro Firtash won control of the local fertiliser industry. Nobody knows who bought the majority stake in Ukrtelekom in 2010.[31] But by 2012, the regime was running out of further assets to disburse.

State procurement was the biggest area of new corruption. Once physical assets threatened to run out, corruption was increasingly concentrated on the state budget. 'Over-payment was everywhere, in every ministry.'[32] Kurchenko was responsible for organising the pyramid and collecting the money up, along with Artem Pshonka, the general prosecutor's son. The chain led back to Yanukovych: 'He was the father, he could do anything . . . The cut was maybe 10 per cent under Kuchma, but 50 per cent under [former Prime Minister Pavlo] Lazarenko. Under Yanukovych it could be even higher.'[33]

In July 2012, all state-owned companies were exempted from open tender.[34] The amount of unmonitored, basically secret, procurement then simply exploded: it was 250 billion UAH ($21.1 billion) in the next twelve months.

Serhiy Kurchenko was key to the procurement scams. His chain of influence was made up of hundreds of fake Ukrainian companies and dozens of offshore firms, which worked on the principle of terrorist cells, divided into small groups that were not allowed to talk to each other.[35] Kurchenko also specialised in theft from state banks via questionable loans, like using the Odesa oil refinery to get two loans from the VTB Group worth $300 million and $370 million.

The same firms kept taking part in tenders conducted by one of the subsidi-aries of the Ministry of Energy and Coal. Billions were taken from the budget by these firms, even though they had nothing to do with these works and equipment. They exaggerated purchase prices by sixty times or more. Then they appropriated these funds through fictitious companies.

The same situation existed in the Ministry of Taxes: 'The former head of the department organised a number of front companies to minimise tax liabilities, leading to tax evasion amounting to over 6 billion UAH [$508 million].'[36]

Vitaliy Khomutynnik was the 'Family's' scam manager in the tax directorate – one of the so-called *smotryashchiye*, those who oversee and report back.

Another reason why procurement corruption took off in 2012 was that Ukraine had won the right to co-host, with Poland, the finals of the UEFA European Championship. Corruption in the Euro 2012 building process meant rake-offs of more than a third on most projects, especially after the incoming Yanukovych administration abolished competitive tendering for most contracts in 2010.[37] The Olympic Games in London in 2012 overran their original budget of £9.3 billion. But the Ukrainians spent even more, and they were only co-hosts. One investigation claimed a total cost of $14 billion;[38] *The Economist* estimated $13 billion.[39] But nobody really knows.

Ukraine concentrated on mega-projects. Four shining new stadiums went up in the host cities of Kiev, Lviv, Kharkiv and Donetsk. Kiev's new Olympic National Sports Complex cost an estimated $600 million, half as much again as the Allianz Arena in Munich built for the World Cup finals in Germany in 2006. Infrastructure upgrades have concentrated on airports, which is sensible enough for Ukraine's long-term business future, but ordinary Ukrainians do not see the benefit.

Scam procurement payments were often channelled through another favourite swindle using phantom companies that disappeared immediately after payments were made or simply never existed at all. These 'phantom firms [were] suspected of squeezing a total of 130 billion hryvnias ($11 billion) from Kiev's coffers over the past three years', at a time when 'the country's total tax revenue amounted to 210 billion hryvnias ($17.8 billion) in 2013'.[40] The way that the scam often worked was that state agencies pretended to buy goods or services from the phantom firm but, instead of delivering on the deal, the fake company secretly returned the money in cash, reducing the real company's tax liability in return for a cut of the money. The tax boss Oleksandr Klymenko ran one of the schemes himself. Klymenko had a vault 'equipped with a white-noise generator to beat eavesdroppers and furnished with clear plastic tables and chairs so those haggling over their spoils could see there were no listening devices attached to the furniture'.[41]

Fake bankruptcies were another popular scheme. State-owned companies would overspend, or fail to deliver product. They would then say they couldn't cover their bills and take a loan from a 'Family' bank. Then they would file for bankruptcy and the loan would disappear. The bank would then take over the company at penny cost – a form of privatisation without payment.

Another similar dodge involved forcing firms to pay into such schemes or overpay into oligarchs' own firms. For example, the oligarch who dominated Luhansk oblast in the east, Oleksandr Yefremov, forced the local Stakhanov ferroalloy plant to purchase gas at two or three times the normal price, which also allowed him to take it over.

VAT refunds have long been a problem in Ukraine. Companies had to pay bribes to move up the queue, or simply to get the refund at all. In the 2000s, this developed into a form of collusive corruption: companies would put in inflated claims and pay a commission on the refund, increasingly through shadowy intermediary companies, dubbed *firmy-prokladky*, meaning 'padding firms'. Once again, under Yanukovych this process was monopolised, and all organised under only one permissible channel. The payment to these types of companies was given the local euphemism of 'information services'.

Serhiy Kurchenko also specialised in evading customs. His VETEK company and subsidiaries imported 25 billion UAH ($2.1 billion) worth of oil in 2012–13 for refining, but pretended to re-export it, which allowed the company to avoid massive tax payments. The products were then sold in Ukraine though a chain of fictitious firms. Everyone had to buy from him.

Illegal coal mines, or *kopanky*, have existed in Ukraine for more than two decades, mainly in the Donbas region, the heart of the local coal-mining industry. Originally, they were a means for the local poor to try and scrape a dangerous living, but as soon as they showed signs of making reasonable money they came under the influence of organised crime and then 'businessmen' backed by state officials. Private companies were buying coal from up to 2,500 *kopanky*, processing it and selling it as if they had mined it themselves.

But once again, starting from 2010 the process was monopolised, in this case by the president's elder son Oleksandr Yanukovych. In 2012, 6.5 million tonnes of coal were mined illegally. Coincidentally, Yanukovych's MAKO company sold 6.65 million tonnes,[42] mainly to the two local state-owned electricity providers in the Donbas. In the six months over the winter of 2012–13 these bought 12 billion UAH ($1 billion) worth of coal from companies close to Oleksandr Yanukovych's circle.[43] Coal miners' trade unions estimated that if the annual amount was around 6–7 million tonnes, and with an average price for coal of about $100 per tonne, the annual output of illegally mined coal could be worth $700 million. The Yanukovych regime, in other words, robbed its home region as enthusiastically as it robbed the government in Kiev.

Ukraine under Yanukovych also saw an explosion of simple extortion. According to the Federation of Employers of Ukraine, the amount of bribes Ukrainian business had to pay officials reached 160 billion UAH ($13.5 billion) per year, mainly direct bribes and kickbacks paid during the procurement procedure, the return of VAT and customs.

So-called *raiderstvo* was another favourite tactic, but it was a world away from commercial raiding in the West. It meant the takeover of companies through violence or the threat of violence, or the use of *kompromat* and legal cases to undermine them. *Raiderstvo* was not challenged, but rather promoted by the law. One of the many functions of the destruction of courts' independence by the 2010 'legal reform' (in fact, an imposition of executive control over the judiciary) was to *monopolise* corruption and to use the courts for the legalisation, if not the legitimation, of *raiderstvo*.

The general prosecutor's office 'had a special office to monitor the most profitable businesses'. Any sign of financial health would trigger proceedings, inspections, and so on. In the 'light' version, bribes had to be paid to survive; in the 'heavy' version, owners would actually be imprisoned.[44] It would be hard to think of any action more inimical to economic growth.

The sheer scope and scale of all these schemes meant that the 'Family's' list of enemies grew rapidly. Not only was the Yanukovych system too narrowly-based, he also made too many enemies outside of it. (In George Orwell's *Nineteen Eighty-Four*, a precisely defined 85 per cent of the population are proles, who are, if not completely left alone, at least left to their entertainments.) The regime began by dispossessing oligarchs who had supported the Orange politicians. Then it turned on small and medium-sized enterprises. A tax reform designed to help SMEs turned into its complete opposite in late 2010, sparking protests known as the 'Tax Maidan' in November 2010. The tax-and-destroy policies were partly designed to feed the rich. They also had a lot to do with the regime's extremely poor grasp of basic economics. But, according to Oleksandr Danylyuk, the leader of Common Cause, they were also inspired by an existential mistrust of the emergent middle class: 'The middle class is always the most assertive class. The regime doesn't like people with freedom.'[45] The SME sector made up only 7–15 per cent of GDP.[46]

Meanwhile, 'Family' members and the broader elite exercised their full right to stand above the law in all areas. In 2012 and 2013 there were already several mini popular revolts against particularly egregious affronts. An eighteen-year-old girl, Oksana Makar, was raped, set on fire and left to die in Mykolaiv in March 2012, but her attackers were initially protected by their connections. The so-called *mazhory* – the sons and daughters of the elite, like China's 'princelings' – were notoriously legally untouchable. In July 2013, local residents in Vradiyivka, also in Mykolaiv, protested against the rape and beating of a local girl, this time by police.

By November 2013, the then thirty-year-old Oleksandr Yanukovych had estimated assets of $510 million.[47] Some of the richest men in Ukraine worked in the legal system, where, as the local saying has it, 'the law is for enemies; for friends everything is possible'. Chief Prosecutor Viktor Pshonka, the number one defender of the law in Ukraine, was neither Eliot Ness nor Girolamo Savonarola. But he was not just corrupt or lazy or guilty of turning a blind eye: he was himself the driving force behind many of the 'Family's' schemes, and was actively involved in their administration.[48] Pshonka's barnstorming departure from Ukraine was also emblematic. On 22 February 2014, two days after the worst violence in Kiev, he was filmed at Donetsk airport. The upholder of the law and his bodyguards simply knock down the metal detector and charge the gate to flee the country. The video does not show the later gunfight before they got on their plane.[49]

In February 2014, former Georgian President Mikheil Saakashvili recounted how, in private meetings, Yanukovych would boast about corrupting the judiciary:

> He would talk very loudly about how he had corrupted senior officials, in the supreme court and the constitutional court . . . He didn't care who he was talking to; the guy did not have any idea about morality . . . He would tell me at length about criminal cases. He would elaborate on every small detail, and was obsessed and fascinated with the fact that he could really play around with the courts. It's a sign of people who have had problems with the law in the past. It's also a very Soviet mentality; Stalin used to sign the verdict on every serious case.[50]

Mezhyhirya-Stan

Yanukovych lived in a vast estate at Mezhyhirya, north of Kiev, on the right bank of the river Dnieper, on the site of an ancient monastery (the name means 'between the hills'). He moved into the old Soviet-era complex in 2002, and started doing it up when he was first prime minister in 2002–04. But his delusions really took off during his second stint as prime minister in 2006–07. In fact, according to the (admittedly biased) source of Tymoshenko's deputy, Hryhoriy Nemyriya, Yanukovych's main concern at the time was not running the country, but running his estate. Yanukovych would not only hunt all weekend, but clear his Fridays for planning the hunt.[51]

But, in a foretaste of his downfall in 2014, Yanukovych was already too greedy. He constantly encroached on the powers of President Yushchenko, and his finance minister, Mykola Azarov, used his tax powers to harass Ukrainian business. The result was the political crisis of summer 2007 (see above).

Yanukovych reportedly agreed to the compromise of early elections in October, in exchange for two things: the promise that he would return as part of a grand coalition government with Yushchenko's party, and a secret Yushchenko decree that gave him control of Mezhyhirya.[52] No money was paid. However, Yanukovych pretended to own only 1.76 out of an area of 137 hectares (almost the size of Monaco); the rest belonged to an obscure offshore company Tantalit,[53] and then to various Austrian and British front companies, before the trail finally ended with an offshore based in Lichtenstein. In August 2013, the estate was transferred to key Yanukovych ally Serhey Klyuyev.

From 2008, Yanukovych started spending lavishly; although he was in opposition, he was obviously not cut off from serious money. He was also able to swat away an attempt by Tymoshenko to take the estate off him in 2009. Thanks to the hurry in which he left in February 2014, a special website, yanukovychleaks.org, was set up to show the details of the corruption involved. It reveals that Yanukovych managed to spend almost $30 million on renovations from 2006 to 2009.[54] Mezhyhirya eventually had a five-storey main residence, a three-storey guest house, a golf course, a yacht club with boating house, a helipad, a racecourse and stables, a zoo with kangaroos that failed to survive the Ukrainian winter, seventy cars in the 'garage', and greenhouses to supply food for Yanukovych directly (given his notorious fear of poisoning).

Then there were the fixtures and fittings. According to one Ukrainian journalist, Sergii Leshchenko, 'each of the mansion's Lebanese cedar doors cost $64,000. Three sets of wooden panelling for staircases came in at $200,000, wall panelling for the winter garden at $328,000, and cladding for a neoclassical column and parapet for a flight of steps at $430,000'.[55] Receipts left at the scene after his departure were for huge sums, up to $12 million. There was a golden loaf of bread and a priceless old book, *The Apostle*, printed by Ivan Fedorov in 1574. And there was a private chapel for the faithful to confess their sins. Among the documents uncovered after his flight were a '$12 million hand-written cheque to an undisclosed beneficiary [and] a €39 million chandelier supply contract'.[56] In 2012, as part of the preparations for the co-hosted UEFA European Championship, a motorway was built to link Mezhyhirya to Kiev. The airport is in the opposite direction.

The whole estate was surrounded by a five-metre fence, which proved invaluable when protestors first converged on Mezhyhirya in December 2013. The hunting estate next door at Sukholuchchya was circled by an anti-tank trench. The way the hunting grounds were run tells us a lot about Yanukovych's style of government. Only the president and a close circle of twenty-eight political friends were members of the hunting group known as 'Cedar'.[57] Each paid about $40,000 for the privilege in 2011; the price for such privileged access went up to $75,000 in 2012. But you also got your money's worth in booze: 'one hunting party in August 2011 saw . . . $22,000 spent on wine, champagne, and tequila alone'.[58] The documents also show Yanukovych funding other projects in return for favours, such as $1.25 million for the home of Vyacheslav Ovcharenko, head of the constitutional court.[59] Nearly $250,000 of taxpayers' money was spent on a large-animal enclosure.[60]

A series of front companies like Tantalit were linked to 'Family' pocket banks to ensure the flow of money: first UkrBusinessBank, then Radikal Bank.[61] A pocket charity foundation was part of the fake privatisation scheme. Other documents found at Mezhyhirya included accounting books detailing over-payment, fictitious contracts and double book-keeping, marked 'F1' and 'F2'.

After the Uprising in February 2014, the estate was overrun by curious but peaceful protestors. One tweet from an architect was addressed to the world's dictators, offering to do their palaces in a more minimalist style, to spare them embarrassment when the mob stormed their particular homes.

But Mezhyhirya was the key to understanding the elite's self-destructive greed. Their schemes drove the Ukrainian economy into the ground. But 'they lived in another reality. They didn't know when to stop.'[62]

No Cover Story

The ruling 'elite' were easy to mock. Their tastes were kitsch, their language and behaviour crude. But the regime also had no ideological underpinning. It was briefly fashionable in Kiev to talk of emulating the 'Turkish model' – Ukraine would also like to see itself as a powerful state on the edge of Europe increasingly able to act on its own terms. But Ukraine was not Turkey. Its economy is much weaker. Turkey's ruling Justice and Development Party keeps winning elections by delivering economic growth, even in 2014, after the 2013 protests in Taksim Square. Turkey stands at the centre of concentric circles of interest – neo-Ottoman, Turkophone and the business world. Ukraine doesn't really get on even with its tiny neighbour Moldova.

But such a brazenly kleptocratic regime needed a cover story. Being 'Russia-lite' wouldn't work. Instead, they relied on a highly divisive internal identity narrative, constantly inflaming domestic divisions to win elections. The crazy language about Ukrainian Nazis and fascists used in 2014 didn't come from nowhere. It was first used by Yanukovych's people about Viktor Yushchenko in 2004, when both Russian and pro-Russian media branded the seemingly pro-Western Yushchenko a virtual Nazi.[63]

Nor was the 2004 campaign a one-off. The Party of Regions ran a hysterical anti-NATO campaign in 2006, both before and after the elections. It based its

2010 and 2012 campaigns on mythical threats to the Russian language. So the rhetoric about west Ukrainian 'fascists' came easily in 2014. It was the default position. The threat that Putin seized on in 2014 had been largely inflamed by Russian and Ukrainian 'political technologists' over almost twenty years of playing with fire. And it was east Ukrainian, not west Ukrainian, politicians that were responsible for polarising the country.

The 2012 Elections

Parliamentary elections were due in October 2012. Once again, they were bitterly divisive. There was no longer any economic mini-recovery to celebrate. But the authorities were confident of victory, because they had changed the rules to revert to a system whereby half of MPs were elected in territorial constituencies, where corruption was rife. This also made the election very expensive, so 'opposition' parties were forced to buy into the system for support. The oligarchs were also spreading their bets, as they felt threatened by the rise of Yanukovych's 'Family'; but money from Rinat Akhmetov (Forward Ukraine, the part of Fatherland led by Arseniy Yatsenyuk), Dmytro Firtash and Russian circles (Ukrainian Democratic Alliance for Reform – UDAR) also reduced the real independence of the 'opposition'. The authorities also used 'political technology' to promote fake parties like Forward Ukraine, though its $80 million budget proved a colossal waste of money, and seeded the opposition parties with so-called *tushki*[64] – individuals who were known to be easily bribable, and who were pre-programmed to defect after the election.

So the ruling Party of Regions could ignore its growing unpopularity. Even with voter bribery and intimidation, it barely came first in the main proportional representation vote, but won 114 territorial constituencies out of 225, giving it 187 seats out of 450 overall. Most of the forty-four 'independents' duly joined its ranks, plus seven MPs from smaller parties.

The three main opposition parties all did well, although this reduced their incentive to cooperate with each other. A coalition based on Yuliya Tymoshenko's old Fatherland Party won 103 seats, and a new party UDAR (the acronym translates as 'Punch', the party being led by the boxer Vitaliy Klitschko) won forty. Tymoshenko was, of course, not allowed to stand, and it was impossible to judge the size of her sympathy vote, but it seems to have been a factor.

The 10.4 per cent and thirty-seven seats won by the Freedom Party were the biggest surprise. The party likes to depict itself as a 'moderate' new right party, like France's Front National, but its ugly face is barely hidden: the party even objected to Gaitana, Ukraine's 2012 Eurovision singer, because she was black. But the Freedom Party also harvested a classic protest vote, as it claimed to be the most radical opposition to Yanukovych. It was also boosted by the with-drawal of the traditional 'against all' option from the ballot paper; and the backlash against the Languages Law passed in July to raise the status of Russian, which prompted big protests in western and central Ukraine – whether or not this was cynically intended by the authorities. This being Ukraine, conspiracy theories abounded. The rise of the Freedom Party divided and discredited the opposition, which perfectly suited the authorities, who had covertly funded the party in the past. Party leaders were suspiciously prominent on TV channels owned by leading oligarchs.

This was the parliament that was still sitting when the Maidan protests began.

The 2012 elections were less democratic than previous elections under 'Orange' rules (parliamentary elections were held in 2006 and 2007), but not fully fixed – which is why the government and opposition both did well. But the trend was clear: it looked entirely possible that Yanukovych could run and win at the next presidential election due in 2015 – most probably by fixing the rules once again. Various scenarios were discussed, including a one-round election or simply selecting the president in parliament. Or – through a combination of fraud and 'political technology' – selecting an easy opponent for Yanukovych to face in a second-round run-off vote, such as the Freedom Party leader and nationalist

The 2012 Parliamentary Elections

	Headline percentage vote	Seats	Total
Party of Regions	30.1 per cent	73+114	187
Fatherland	25.5 per cent	61+42	103
UDAR	13.9 per cent	34+6	40
Communists	13.2 per cent	32+0	32
Freedom Party	10.4 per cent	25+12	37
Forward Ukraine!	1.6 per cent	–	–
Smaller parties	–	7	7
Independents	–	44	44

bogeyman Oleh Tyahnybok or the veteran leader of the Communist Party Petro Symonenko (whom Kuchma made sure he faced in 1999). In the meantime, the 'Family' was given even more power. Corruption escalated to new heights, although the economy moved into recession. The atmosphere grew increasingly fetid.

The Run-up to Vilnius

Ironically, Yanukovych could also have campaigned for the 2015 election with two key EU Agreements as his main achievement, to disarm his opponents. Negotiations with the EU on an Association Agreement, with, in EU jargon, a 'Deep and Comprehensive Free Trade Agreement' (in effect, swallowing about two-thirds of the bureaucracy of membership) had been going on since 2008. Ironically, the work was done by 2011, but Tymoshenko's imprisonment in October 2011 led the EU to put the deal on ice two months later. A year on, in December 2012, the EU defined three extremely vague sets of conditions involving 'electoral, judiciary and constitutional reforms' to unfreeze the process, adding ambiguously that they should 'possibly' be undertaken by the time of the Vilnius Summit for the EU's Eastern Partnership programme in November 2013.[65] Unwisely, the list was expanded (but not officially) to eleven points by Commissioner Štefan Füle in February 2013.[66]

Both the short and the long list contained a well-intentioned critique of everything that was wrong with Ukraine's judicial process, but no official mention of Tymoshenko's imprisonment. Nevertheless, her case turned out to be the key demand in practice; although exactly what was expected – Tymoshenko's freedom, an amnesty, or her escape to medical treatment in Germany – was also ill-defined. A special Ukraine mission led by former Irish politician Brian Cox and former Polish President Aleksander Kwaśniewski visited Ukraine twenty-seven times, but its mission had too narrow a focus and the Ukrainian authorities constantly exploited it by offering a few minor concessions to Tymoshenko's prison regime. Not that the demand for Tymoshenko's release should not have been made, but it should have been embedded in some broader process.

Moreover, by front-loading the challenge to the legal system, the EU was basically asking Yanukovych to dismantle his system of power. Ukraine therefore worked on the requested reforms as slowly as it could, to string the EU along. A new criminal code was introduced, which was a slight improvement. Draft reforms on 'improving judicial independence' and reforming the Procuracy were deliberately left in their very early stages.

But by the summer of 2013, there seemed no way of getting round the EU's fixation on the Tymoshenko case. Two things then forced the negotiations off track. First, Ukraine switched to bribery mode. Instead of the EU making demands of Ukraine, things were suddenly the other way around. EU negotiators grew increasingly frustrated as their Ukrainian counterparts came up with new claims at every meeting for the potential costs of the agreements, mainly cobbled together on the basis of Russia's threats to wreck the Ukrainian economy – though it was actually politically convenient for Yanukovych to claim he was being bullied by Russia. As Brussels officials sardonically put it in private, these were mainly 'oral presentations', without too many figures to hand. When figures were used, they came from a Russian-backed Ukrainian think tank.

Second, Ukraine *was* actually being bullied by Russia. In mid-August, Russia closed its borders to virtually all physical exports. Heavy industry in east Ukraine was deliberately targeted. So were particular Ukrainian oligarchs who favoured the EU agreements, such as Petro Poroshenko, who ironically sold chocolates to Russia. The initial forecast of the actual, rather than merely predicted, damage of Russia's measures was between $2 billion and $2.5 billion in the second half of 2013, which was about 1.5 per cent of GDP;[67] the figure was later refined to $500 million.[68]

On the other hand, Russia also had some carrots to dangle. It understood the Ukrainian leaders' greed and lack of 'European values' perfectly well. The most notable part of the supposed Russian strategy document for dealing with Ukraine, leaked in August, was the stated desire to 'influence the President's family business . . . with the aim of creating and enhancing the dependence of this business on Russian structures'.[69] Serhiy Kurchenko was often present at Putin–Yanukovych meetings, leading to speculation that the 'Family' was trying to create some new version of RosUkrEnergo.

At the same time, the leading Russian nationalist Aleksandr Dugin laid out three options for Ukraine.[70] First, given what he called 'the incoherence of the Ukrainian national idea, and the fickleness of Ukrainian politics, its grotesque and almost farcical character', was the division of the state in two. Second was 'a complicated game with the pragmatic [*sic*] leadership of Ukraine' to pressure it into joining the Eurasian Union, given economic crisis and the declining pulling power of the EU. Third was converting west Ukrainian nationalism from foe to friend – which was never likely. Dugin did live in a bit of a dream world. Russia plumped for option two, but it is significant that option one was already being discussed.

The Final Breakdown

With the EU, meanwhile, Ukraine demanded more and more money in compensation for putative losses. In private, EU officials said Ukraine was claiming that it would need €13 billion to implement EU standards and €12 billion to compensate for lost trade with Russia – per year. Prime Minister Azarov eventually got as far as translating that into an overall figure, over several undefined years, of between '150 and 165 billion euros' to help Ukraine with modernisation.[71] Azarov tastefully mocked the idea of a billion euros in aid: 'What is a billion euro? It's nothing. It helps a beggar on the porch.'[72] As a footnote, by 3 December, Azarov's demands had come down to €10 billion.[73]

This was pretty much back to front. Broadly speaking, the Central European and Baltic States that joined the EU in 2004 were keen to do so. They did the hard work of transforming their economies and societies before accession, because of the greater long-term benefits of membership. In Ukraine, the Yanukovych elite expected the West to pay them, rather than the other way around, and to disburse benefits before, during and after signing any agreements. They also had no understanding of the broader consequences of using bribery as a substitute for foreign policy. The Ukrainian elite was running out of friends in the West, and its only friend in the East was as cynical and predatory as it was.

On 21 November 2013, only a week before the Vilnius Summit, Ukraine dramatically pulled out of the deal. Protests began in Kiev, one again on the Maidan, but they were initially quite small. Arguably, the EU was saved from a bad deal – even if it had agreed to just some of Ukraine's outrageous list of demands. Stefan Füle, the EU's enlargement commissioner, was ready to fly to Kiev with, according to the *Financial Times*, 'a package including expedited trade support, promises of new gas supplies and backing for resumed aid from the International Monetary Fund'.[74] Many of these were good ideas in themselves, but cumulatively they only created a bidding war that allowed Ukraine to wriggle free of its commitments rather than stick to them. Yanukovych even tried to bargain at the summit itself. There was a last-minute drama at the Kempinski Hotel in Vilnius.[75] But the hosts were tired of his behaviour. The Lithuanians released a video showing him being snubbed or criticised by other leaders. Angela Merkel's comment that 'we see you here, but we expected more' was something of an understatement.[76]

Conclusion

Yanukovych went home to the protests. There was open speculation in Vilnius and Kiev about whether he was cynical enough to order the violent repression of the demonstrators as soon as he left the summit. According to his warped Mafia logic, to do so while he was meeting foreign leaders would show disrespect; as if they wouldn't be equally outraged by a few hours' difference.

CHAPTER 4

Maidan 2.0

The protests originally known as #Euromaidan started on 21 November 2013, when the government suddenly dropped its plans to sign the Association Agreement with the EU. The original 'Maidan' – the protests on Kiev's central square of that name – was in 2004, though some would go back to when the square was first occupied by student protestors in October 1990. Even before the volte-face, there were already plans in the making to hold some kind of demonstration on 22 November, as this would be the ninth anniversary of the outbreak of the Orange Revolution protests in 2004.[1] The organisers planned to gather in frustration and lament the general state of Yanukovych's Ukraine, but they had no real plan for a 'Maidan 2.0'. There was no model for how to organise new protests that would be successful in a way that the original protests had not been. Rather, the point was to mark the failure of the original project.

If anything, things were worse than in 2004. As ordinary Ukrainians grew disillusioned with politics, a whole local industry of pay-demonstrations grew up. Students and the poor would sell their services to any bidder. I came across one well-drilled column in Kiev in April 2013 near the Maidan. When I asked them what the demonstration was about, people cheerily replied 'money'. When I asked for specifics, they said they didn't know, but 'the bosses will tell us, before the rally'.

Demonstration, But Low Expectation

Paid demonstrations were the new norm. So the first thing that demonstrators did this time was carry signs saying 'We are not paid'. At least this meant the authorities were caught off guard: both at the start of the protests and as they

1 Ukraine

continued, they assumed that the protestors would soon go home. When the authorities organised their own fake counter-demonstrations, they posted guards – not to keep the two sides apart, but to stop their commitment-challenged crowd from wandering off. Copious amounts of alcohol were also supplied to the government crowds. The idea that thousands of ordinary Ukrainians might simply stand up for what they thought was right was not how they thought the world worked. To the regime's way of thinking, they could only be financially out-gunned; so the Maidan must have been paid for by their opponents – either the West (which they had been pretending to be eager to join) or the domestic oligarchs outside the 'Family' (whom they had been trying to expropriate and destroy).

They were wrong. 'Know your enemy' is a good rule. Although initially small, the demonstrations had the same initial spark as in 2004. What matters with such things is not a few percentage points stolen in an election, or the fine print of some EU documents, or even several billions stolen from the state budget. What matters is a sense of opportunity closing, of hope for change being lost, of individual life-chances disappearing. The Association Agreement process with the EU at least forced Yanukovych to compromise and to pretend. Without it, he could do what he wanted. The 2015 election would be fixed and

Ukraine would become like Russia or Belarus. This was true for both individuals and the country in general. As with other social media protests, the Maidan was initially about themes of authenticity and self-validation.[2] Hence the chosen name of the 'Revolution of Dignity'.

Much has been made of how the Maidan demonstrations began with a tweet by the journalist Mustafa Naim, who worked for *Ukraïnska Pravda*, the website set up by Heorhiy Gongadze before he was murdered in 2000. But Naim had something like the same original Maidan model of peaceful and carnival-like demonstration in mind. The original attendees were only a few hundred strong, mainly his followers and friends. The next few days of protest were manned by the intelligentsia and students. But they remained small-scale in the first week, before the final collapse of relations with the EU at the Vilnius Summit. Parliamentary leaders like Arseniy Yatsenyuk joined in with belated tweets,[3] but were far from setting the pace. There were also early differences between one group on the Maidan and another 'more political' demonstration two hundred metres away on European Square. But the first Sunday demonstration, on 24 November, under the label 'For a European Ukraine!' attracted some 100,000 people.

New media technology was more important than in 2004. The 'Euro-Maydan' Facebook page garnered 75,000 'likes' in its first week and had 300,000 by the spring. Twitter's@EuroMaydan had nearly 100,000 followers. Hromadske TV ('Civic TV', online interviews via hand-held cameras) debuted at the same time as the protests and helped feed the Maidan's spirit of self-organisation and start-up activism. The well-known paradoxes were nevertheless present: Facebook and Twitter can assemble a crowd, but you can't negotiate via SMS. Protestors got their news from websites (51 per cent), Facebook (49 per cent) or the local equivalent VKontakte ('In Contact', 35 per cent), but that left them in an 'alternative reality' to the audience of state TV.[4]

At the Vilnius Summit a week later, on Thursday and Friday, 28–29 November, the demonstrators were the main crumb of comfort for the minority of EU politicians who were aware of their existence. Some NGO activists staged a mock signing ceremony on behalf of their unwilling government; but EU sympathy was equally symbolic. A rearguard action was expected at best, and a crackdown was widely feared. This was exactly what happened in the small hours of the very next morning, 30 November. True to form, Yanukovych had gone hunting, having allegedly ordered Andriy Klyuyev, head of the National Security Council, and his deputy, Volodymyr Sivkovych, to do the dirty work.[5]

Protestors (seventy-nine, according to official figures) were savagely beaten on the square and in adjoining streets, and as they were pursued. But, brutal as this was, it was the wrong amount of violence: enough to provoke, but not enough to cow. Time and again, the authorities applied a similar formula – of zero concern for human dignity, but, among some members of the elite, concern for foreign reaction. Within this limit, the key miscalculation was that the Maidan protestors were like their own paid protestors and would simply run away; but by the evening, some 10,000 were back in the square. More protestors (70 per cent) were now motivated by their desire to protest against the violence used by the authorities, than against Yanukovych's failure to sign the EU Agreements (54 per cent).[6]

A second route to dispersal was attempted the next day, 1 December. The city authorities banned further demonstrations, but hundreds of thousands were now on the streets. The trade union building on the north side of the square was occupied, and so was the Kiev city council building down the main street on the other side. But a group of several hundred that went up the hill from the Maidan towards the presidential administration building was infiltrated by provocateurs, who duly staged fierce fights with the police.[7] Most were fake nationalists – some from the recently organised Right Sector, but mainly from the Social-National Assembly and Brotherhood, which was linked to Putin's favourite Ukrainian, Viktor Medvedchuk. Implausibly, they had somehow got hold of a bulldozer in the middle of the city. Even more implausibly, the leading 'Ukrainian nationalist' leader Dmytro Korchynsky had a long tradition of working for Kremlin organisations and speaking at pro-Putin summer camps in Russia. The riots marked the first decisive intervention of the moderate oligarch and former foreign minister, Petro Poroshenko, who worked hard to contain the situation on the ground.

Spot the Fascist

This plan failed to achieve its immediate aim, however: it did nothing to discredit the demonstrations domestically, at least in Kiev, although it was the start of a deluge of propaganda aimed at eastern Ukraine. Over time, though, a sufficient number in the West bought the idea of right-wingers as the primary organisers of the protests, particularly with the growing noise made by the Right Sector movement.[8] A torch-lit march through Kiev in honour of the World War Two Ukrainian nationalist hero Stepan Bandera on 1 January was such a stupid idea, it had to be a provocation.[9]

There was a desire to make this a national revolution, of the type that the Central European states or Baltic States had in 1989 or 1991 and that Ukraine had missed out on. A certain amount of nineteenth-century nationalism was also to be expected when Ukraine was being treated in nineteenth-century terms, with 'great powers' negotiating over its head. Plus, with the country under growing Russian pressure, it was hardly surprising that patriotism was on the rise.

But this was the twenty-first century. Despite using flags and slogans from an earlier era (actually the 1940s), most Maidan activists had a pretty accurate sense of what was wrong with their country: namely, obscene levels of corruption rooted in post-Soviet political and business culture. The rhetoric about Russia's overbearing and malign influence on Ukraine was reasonably accurate, as was the idea that Ukraine's Russian-speaking comprador bandit elite (normally called 'the regime of internal occupation') was not restrained in its plunder by any sense of responsibility for national patrimony. Even the idea that the 'creole' elite artificially maintained a post-Soviet neo-Russian culture in Ukraine as a cover for its theft was not a million miles from the truth.

That said, the whole point of the Maidan was that there was no overarching Big Idea. Spontaneity and authenticity were its leitmotifs. Even Right Sector was defined more by the desire for direct action than by nationalism: its most sophisticated slogan was 'Against the regime and integration' (the latter with Russia, presumably, but it was ambiguous). Its main leader Dmytro Yarosh was from east Ukraine, near Dnipropetrovsk. He claimed that 40 per cent of members spoke Russian.[10] Timothy Snyder has argued that 'the revolution in Ukraine came from the Left. Its enemy was an authoritarian kleptocrat, and its central program was social justice and the rule of law'.[11]

The armed struggle of the 1940s was not a relevant precedent, other than demonstrating a previous generation's commitment. The Cossack era was further in the past, but a more direct source of inspiration. First was a general willingness to stand and fight. Second was the use of Cossack principles to organise in 'hundreds', later echoed in the 'Heavenly Hundred' dead. There was also a delegate system in nearby towns and villages to send protestors to Kiev on *vakhta* (guard duty in 'shifts') – a pot of money would be raised, and individuals would draw on it for successive trips to the Maidan. On the fateful Thursday, 20 February, the fighting was accompanied by two bare-chested Cossacks with topknots beating a call to arms on kettle drums. Powerful stuff.

But the actual Western 'analysis' of the Ukrainian right wing was full of holes. The Freedom Party was indeed full of racists and demagogues, but won 10 per cent of the vote in very specific circumstances in 2012. Their vote in west Ukraine increased because of economic problems; and their vote spread to Kiev because they promised to provide the most resolute opposition to Yanukovych, while claiming the other opposition parties were part of the 'system'. But in the very different circumstances of the Maidan, the party was already in sharp decline: its raison d'être was usurped as the protestors were clearly more radical than they were – this was all the more obvious when the party tried to bask in their glory. Polls clearly showed declining support, so it was then a mistake to include the party in the new government formed in the spring (see below). Its support crumbled even further once Yanukovych was gone: party leader Oleh Tyahnybok would get only 1.2 per cent of the vote in the May 2014 election. The later phases of the protests vindicated direct action, not nationalism per se.

Then there was the new group Right Sector; but they were not the only actors on the Maidan and they were latecomers anyway. They were first heard of in November, but only came to prominence after 16 January. They were also small: in January, Right Sector claimed around 300 'fighters', but only one of the 'hundreds' on the Maidan. After the February events, numbers grew, but it is hard to say to what extent. One source claims 800 to 1,500 nationally with 200 to 250 fighting on Hrushevsky Street in late January.[12] Another source claims 2,500 at most after the Uprising.[13] Right Sector was 'entryist', like an old-fashioned Trotskyist sect, but there is no evidence of successful radicalisation of any larger groups. Much of the negative publicity around Right Sector came from crude black PR from Russian media.[14]

As is often the case with small radical groups, Right Sector was anyway a fissiparous coalition. There was a 'neo-Nazi fringe', consisting of the White Hammer group, Patriot of Ukraine and the Social-National Assembly, but 'the main group behind the Right Sector is "Tryzub" (Trident) which is far from neo-Nazism, racism and anti-Semitism. Its ideology can be interpreted as national conservative.'[15] White Hammer – obviously a dubious name – was expelled in March 2014.

Then there was a failure to look at who later went into government – which was the Freedom Party, not Right Sector, plus some Maidan activists. Only Andriy Parubiy at the National Security Council could be considered close to the far right. Serhiy Kvit at the Ministry of Education, and Tetyana Chornovol were radical, but independent. Kvit was, in any case, a former university rector.

There were also already serious questions about Right Sector and its origins, its covert links to the regime and the part played by political technology in creating it as the latest *pugal* ('scarecrow') to replace the declining threat of the Freedom Party. Many of its constituent parties and members had been nationalists since the 1990s, but that gave them a long record of collaboration with the security services. One sub-group, the Ukrainian National Assembly–Ukrainian Self-Defence (UNA–UNSO) acted as provocateurs to discredit the 2001 'Ukraine Without Kuchma' campaign and then ran fake demos in support of Yushchenko during the 2004 campaign, funded by Kuchma's presidential administration. No fewer than four fake nationalists, including Dmytro Korchynsky, stood as 'technical candidates' in 2004 to try and discredit or take votes off Yushchenko. Tryzub was linked to the Ukrainian Security Service. Another group provided muscle to defend election fraud by the ruling party in 2012.[16] Patriot of Ukraine worked for Hennadiy Kernes, mayor of Kharkiv. UNA–UNSO tried to hijack the Vradiyivka protests in July 2013 (see Chapter 3), and sell their attempt to 'control events' to the government.

Right Sector was also allegedly financed by government figures like Firtash and Lovochkin. In late January, Andriy Klyuyev offered Right Sector millions to withdraw.[17] Its members were regularly mysteriously absent during the main violence. One Right Sector leader, Dmytro Yarosh, met Yanukovych in secret on the final fateful Thursday, 20 February.[18] *After* the uprising, Right Sector played an even more controversial role (see Chapter 8).

Parts of the Western left, in particular, are addicted to an outdated 'anti-fascist' narrative. Even in the 1930s and 1940s this narrative was abused by the USSR – when 'fascists' were those who opposed Soviet policies. This is also one reason for the assumption that fascists are all in Central and Eastern Europe, because that is where so many Nazi collaborators were, while further to the east lay Russian victims of fascism. Numerically, non-Russian Soviet citizens suffered more because they were occupied for longer, and all occupied countries collaborate to some degree. Ukraine has right-wingers like anywhere else, but the idea of a rebirth of war-time fascism was absurd. The real scandal was the role that such propaganda would play during the Russian annexation of Crimea and the fighting in the Donbas. There are more fascists in Russia than in Ukraine; and they are in, or close to, power. The real problem would be the legacy of violent uprising and the general relationship between the Maidan and the interim government once the uprising was over.

The Maidan Becomes a Camp

The first week of December also saw the beginnings of serious organisation for the protests, particularly because there seemed little hope of political progress. On 1 December, a 'Headquarters of National Resistance' was set up in the trade union building on the north side of the Maidan. The first 'self-defence' units were created and the first proper barricades went up.

Unlike in the early days of the 2004 protests, however, the regime's ranks stayed reasonably solid. A trickle of early defections did not become a flood. The ruling Party of Regions easily defeated a first attempt to unseat the government on 3 December – the motion won only 186 out of 450 votes. Talk of the inner circle of oligarchs splitting up (especially Firtash and Akhmetov) came to naught. However, the outer circle's business interests were threatened by the 'Family'; Petro Poroshenko's Roshen chocolates were under sanction, and Ihor Kolomoisky's airline AeroSvit was bankrupted in 2013. They therefore spread their bets, with their media coverage at least. Poroshenko's Channel 5,

Kolomoisky's 1+1 and another channel TVi linked to another oligarch, Davyd Zhvaniya, provided increasingly open coverage of events.

A 'Last Chance' march (at the time it seemed a perfectly reasonable title) on 8 December, with a target of a million participants, was the biggest demonstration yet (though nobody could, of course, accurately count the numbers). Its success led to demonstrators trying to expand their base by seizing parts of the government district. The Lenin statue at the other end of the main street from the Maidan was photogenically toppled (the one on the Maidan was removed after it was covered in graffiti in 1991). But this proved premature: the protestors had to surrender their new positions on 9 December. 'When we blocked the government district, we expected huge numbers of people there . . . But too few came', said Andriy Parubiy, the future head of the National Security Council of Ukraine.[19] Then, on 10 December, the tide flowed the other way. The authorities had missed their chance to nip the protests in the bud; but Yanukovych and his coterie again showed their contempt for EU leaders with another attempted clampdown while EU foreign policy supremo Catherine Ashton was in Kiev, trying to negotiate compromise. They also showed their nervousness about closing off all their options, however, by adopting totally different tactics this time. Police joined shields and pushed protestors slowly back (though they also whacked heads). The early hours of 11 December marked the first successful defence of the Maidan, with up to 25,000 reinforcements flooding in. The bells of St Michael's Monastery of the Golden Domes sounded the alarm, as during medieval defences of the city (the monastery had been destroyed in Stalin's time and rebuilt in 1999).

Who Were the Demonstrators?

It was premature to talk of a middle-class revolution back in 2004. The old Ukrainian middle class was destroyed under Soviet rule. The old Soviet middle class – the 'humanitarian and technical intelligentsia' – was wrecked by the inflation of the early 1990s. In 2004, the Ukrainian economy had only just begun to recover, and GDP had only been growing since 2000. By 2013, the middle class was bigger, but its motives were defensive: many protestors were entrepreneurs or small-business owners fed up with the predatory state. The SME sector had been subject to the greed of the Yanukovych 'Family', to rampant *raidertsvo*, and to the authorities' tax-and-destroy policies since 2010. So in many ways, this was a classic revolutionary J-curve effect – a middle class that was on the rise and then saw its position threatened.

But not everyone on the Maidan was middle class. Over time, research showed that the protestors became more male, less based in Kiev, and more likely to be from smaller towns and regions. The average level of education also went down, hence the often populist message at the sharp end. The organisers of the research, who carried out three surveys during the protests (on 7–8 December, 20 December and 3 February), labelled their changing character as a transition from 'Maidan-the-meeting' to 'Maidan-the-camp' to 'Maidan-the-fortress' (using the Cossack word *sich*).[20]

The number who came from Kiev fell from 50 per cent to 19 per cent to 12 per cent. The number who came from the regions rose from 50 per cent to 81 per cent to 88 per cent. By the time of the third survey, 42 per cent were from small towns (less than 100,000 inhabitants) and 20 per cent from villages. In the last survey, some 27 per cent were classed as 'specialists' and 17 per cent entrepreneurs. But there was no simple overall picture. What stood out was that most were outsiders: either regionally or occupationally they were on the edge of, but suffering from, the Yanukovych system.

Tactics

In December 2013, just after the Russian offer of financial aid to Ukraine (see below), one of Russia's most notorious former 'political technologists', Marat Gelman, mocked the whole idea of successive Maidans in the tweet: 'Maidan installation sold for 15 billion – most expensive art object ever.' An object, moreover, that had been bought by a discerning Russian collector (Putin) – a reference to Russia's attempt to offer an alternative deal to the EU. Gelman had largely left his career as a post-modernist arch-manipulator for a similar career as owner of a chic Moscow art gallery. Some Western commentators like Anne Applebaum also argued that the coloured revolution 'model is dead', mainly because of the power of those it seeks to oppose:

> corrupt oligarchs, backed by Russian money and Russian political technology, are a lot stronger than anyone ever expected them to be. They have the cash to bribe a parliament's worth of elected officials. They have the cynicism to revive the old Soviet technique of selective violence . . . learned to manipulate media . . . [and] crafted a well-argued, well-funded, alternate narrative about Western economic decline and cultural decadence.[21]

Many Ukrainians secretly agreed. But there was no uniform strategy towards state institutions and the organs of power. In the early phases of the protests, demonstrators took the classic 'coloured revolution' approach and tried to win over or disarm the aggressive intent of the Berkut special forces police. Then they started throwing rocks at them. The Berkut increasingly lived in their own world. Russian *politruki* ('political instructors') were reportedly infiltrating their ranks, giving them lectures on how to demonise the enemy. Their Facebook fan page[22] duly filled up with anti-Semitic, racist and homophobic content, and with bragging about violence used against protestors.[23] Many of the messages were identical. The regime also made sure that the Berkut were well paid. Where necessary, their salaries were topped up by the most loyal oligarchs, like Vadym Novynsky. Berkut were getting $500 per day, and $1,000 if they saw 'action'.[24] They were also from the 'right' part of Ukraine: in the final week of the crisis, the majority of the Berkut on the streets were from Sevastopol and Crimea (206 out of 1,241), the Donbas (180) and other regions of the east and south (490).[25]

The idea of a charm offensive against the Berkut quickly disappeared. According to pollsters, support for the idea of creating 'armed formations independent of the state' among Maidan protestors went up from 15 per cent in early December to 50 per cent in February. Support for negotiating with the authorities went down from 51 per cent to 27 per cent.[26]

But what next? Activists made good use of information strategies to publicise the regime's crimes and violence. The wealth of the 'Family' was detailed at www.yanukovich.info; the culpability of key officials at personalaccountability.info. The project 'Don't be a brute!' at skoty.info/ aimed to expose and limit militia violence. Maidan activists made good use of other technologies to publicise their cause and deter the regime from too much violence in front of the world's TV cameras and smartphones. Someone had the great idea of using drones to fly over the houses of government officials, showing their opulence.

In late December, a new group emerged called 'AutoMaidan'. Its members consisted of several hundred car owners, which by definition made them a little bit more middle class. Partly, they helped supply the Maidan, ferrying volunteers, food and firewood. They also patrolled the streets, especially as the authorities resorted to informal groups of thugs (see below). But the group also emerged out of frustration with just occupying the Maidan. Members drove in mass pickets to government buildings, most notoriously out towards Mezhyhirya on 29 December. This privately infuriated Yanukovych, and AutoMaidan activists were suddenly at the forefront of repression.[27] More than 1,500 of the drivers were stripped of their driving licences in court, while dozens of cars were torched. The busiest single night was 30 January, when twenty vehicles went up in flames, including at least thirteen from a list later found at Mezhyhirya. According to the Emergencies Ministry, 129 cars were torched in the first two weeks of January. The future minister of youth and sports, Dmytro Bulatov, was one of the leaders of AutoMaidan protests and was kidnapped on 22 January. More than a week later he was found in a village outside Kiev; he had been badly beaten and a part of his ear had been cut off.

Through December, several other groups coalesced. Common Cause dated back to 2010, when it had played a leading role in the 'tax Maidan' protests by small and medium-sized business owners. It was therefore largely based in the Kiev middle class, and favoured direct but non-violent action. Right Sector was formed on 20 November, and was little interested in such nuances. The key overarching non-structural structure was called 'Self-Defence' (nothing to do with the right-wing UNSO with a similar generic name), which was as much an idea as it was an organisation. Sub-groups organised as 'hundreds', which facilitated the affiliation of other groups, including AutoMaidan and Afghan veterans.

Civil Sector of Maidan was an umbrella for various NGO support networks. Euromaidan-SOS publicised human rights violations. An All-Ukrainian Maidan Association was established on 22 December, with various NGOs sitting on its Public Council (though the majority of protestors were increasingly reluctant to be organised by anyone other than themselves). Its official 'Manifesto', issued on 29 December, had little impact.[28] Only 6 per cent of protestors had been organised by civic groups (rising to 13 per cent in February), though this was more than those who came because of the appeals of political parties (2 per cent, rising to 3 per cent in February). A massive 92 per cent (84 per cent in February) came on their own.[29]

Staccato Repression

There is no doubt that Yanukovych would have unleashed more violence if he could have got away with it: he was brutal enough with his own colleagues. But state violence on the scale of Tiananmen Square in 1989 in the post-modern interconnected world is hard to imagine. Everyone remembers the picture of the Chinese flag-waver in front of the tank, but that was afterwards. There are no pictures of the clearing of the square itself – but now there would be. Ukraine is also a medium-sized state with no nuclear weapons, energy monopoly or any other obvious get-out-of-jail card to pre-empt international condemnation. This was one of the things that Yanukovych hated most, and a key reason why Ukraine wanted to develop its shale gas. But a resource-rich future was still many years off.

The authorities' first moves were clumsy. Journalists and cameramen were targeted during the violence on 30 November.[30] The attempt to clear the Maidan on 11 December was more cautious. In late December and January, the regime developed more cynical tactics of what might be called 'off-screen repression'. The authorities understood that the new media aren't that new: they still follow the law of the photogenic. There were more news stories in the

West about nationalist stone-throwers than there were about government snatch squads. Good reporters picked up and reported on those who were beaten or disappeared away from the Maidan, but there weren't many pictures. The risk of global reaction was therefore lower.

Plus, things were getting more personal in late December and early January. Activists were publishing the crimes and corruption of individual ministers. AutoMaidan members were driving to their houses. Protestors were lying down outside the Procuracy building.

Growing numbers were beaten away from the world's cameras and smartphones. Kidnappings of activists became increasingly common. Medical treatment became a real problem, as injured protestors were snatched from their hospital beds. Huge numbers were processed by Ukraine's far-from-independent judiciary.[31] After Yanukovych fled Mezhyhirya, Ukrainian journalists discovered all sorts of documents abandoned in haste. One was the diary of his security chief, Konstantin Kobzar. It contained a chilling series of entries regarding the journalist Tetiana Chornovol, who was chased by thugs in cars and brutally beaten in the early hours of 25 December, Christmas Day in the West (the Orthodox Church still uses the Julian Calendar, which lags by eleven days). Chornovol blamed Yanukovych personally, as she had been investigating the financing of Mezhyhirya and other lavish regime residences. The diary entries read:

Chornovol went to Maidan.
  2310 Turned off phone
 2350 Turned phone on. On Khreshchatyk
  2350: Operation (*zachistka*) started
 1 am: They have finished (Clean).[32]

This exactly matches the time at which Chornovol was driven off the road, beaten and left for dead, with horrendous facial injuries.

But the regime held ranks. Initial stories of scores of defections proved false, though a handful of MPs quit the ruling party. Yanukovych's chief of staff tried (but apparently failed) to resign. The system was still intact, at least its security part. But it was all stick and no carrot. Russia's bailout in December was carefully calibrated to keep Yanukovych's head just above water. There was no extra money to spread around. But Yanukovych's natural instinct was still to bully. According to one UDAR MP, it was 'physical threats for smaller guys, threats to destroy the businesses of bigger guys'.[33] At one session of parliament, Yanukovych threatened *Ya Vas posazhu* ('I will put you in jail'). At one private meeting he shouted: 'So, we have a mutiny, right? You'll all get fifteen years.'

Yanukovych descended on parliament to make all sorts of physical threats to pass the 'dictatorship laws' on 16 January (see below). According to a source close to the oligarchs still in the government camp: 'In some ways that was the start of his downfall. We were primed to vote for something else. He used up a lot of political capital. There was an understanding we wouldn't be ambushed again.' But the threats worked: the laws went through; and all the soft-liners secured was a promise that next time there would be no voting on unseen proposals. Voting would solely be with official cards.[34] MPs only had themselves to blame for being sheepish enough to vote through the measures in the first place.

The *Titushki*

According to one opposition MP, 'The regime had been building up its security forces for three years [since 2010]. It was 40 per cent ready in November 2013, as it was expecting the main confrontation to be in 2015.'[35] The militia were effective, or (more exactly) prepared to be brutal, but they were only 6,000 strong. The extra factor in the equation was increasingly the notorious gangs of hired thugs, who even had a special name: *titushki*. The Ukrainian authorities have always employed agents provocateurs, and thugs were kept in the background in case Yanukovych lost the 2010 election. But organised bands of militant hooligans were a new phenomenon. The name first became commonplace in 2013, when, in May, a 'Rise Ukraine!' rally in Kiev was attacked by thugs and 'anti-fascists'.[36] One of their number, Vadym Titushko, a 'sports guy' from Bila Tserkva, a small town outside Kiev, managed to beat up two journalists and gifted his name to the phenomenon. *Titushki* were all similar young men – either the burly type from sports clubs, or else from the ranks of the poor or underemployed. Their ranks included 'people from a number of backgrounds, like off-duty police officers and state security workers, members of more or less legal combat sports clubs, workers at industrial plants owned by pro-government forces, members of criminal gangs, and common convicts, and most likely also groups of football fans'.[37] Many had criminal records, so they were recruited by local police, who told them they had to 'do service' or else dormant punishments would be activated. Others were poor and desperate for money – which was also a serious indictment of Yanukovych's Ukraine, as the initial going rate for their services was only 200 to 500 UAH (from $17 to $42) a day, plus equipment.[38] By January, however, the figure was $100 a day.[39]

Like the Berkut, the *titushki* needed financing. The key figure in channelling money to the shadowy gangs was the 'Family' front man Serhiy Kurchenko, who headed a group directing ministries and local administrations to provide quotas.[40] In Kiev, the *titushki* were coordinated by the former interior minister, Viktor Zubrytsky, the director of Kontakt media holding, which gave the then interior minister, Vitaliy Zakharchenko, some deniability and distance, although he directly coordinated the anti-Maidan media campaign himself. Many *titushki* came from the provinces, where they were also used to stop copycat Maidan demonstrations spreading. 'Russian *titushki*' in Donetsk and Luhansk were financed by the president's son, Oleksandr Yanukovych,[41] and the oligarch Yuriy Ivanyushchenko. In Kharkiv, money came from the Mercury Bank.[42] *Titushki* were supported on the ground by the authorities. Discreet yellow ribbons were worn, so that they could identify each other.[43] Some even had police IDs.[44]

By definition, the *titushki* had no real ideology, despite the slogans of 'anti-fascism'. But as events moved into 2014, there were attempts to create a real 'movement' – which was basically a contradiction in terms. The fight club Oplot ('Stronghold') from Kharkiv were '*titushki* plus'. They had more of a crude credo: cult of force, common Slavic values against fascist west Ukraine, and Putin's conservative values project. Kharkiv was also home to the Ukrainian Front organisation's founding rally on 1 February – a bizarre collection of fight-club members, former policemen and the Night Wolves, the favourite bikers' gang of Russian President Vladimir Putin. This 'project' had direct Russian support and was far from welcomed by Ukrainian President Yanukovych, who thought he could crack down on his own.

But the *titushki* were, by definition, undisciplined. They were therefore responsible for some of the worst violence against protestors, particularly on 21 January (the 'night of the *titushki*') and in the final week of protests. They were responsible for almost a dozen documented deaths, though many of their victims were among the 'disappeared'.

The Russia Agreement

The Maidan activists had even more to worry about after Russia and Ukraine signed a grand 'Action Plan' on 17 December 2013. For the Maidan activists, this was a double blow: it confirmed the closure of the European option and seemed to give the Yanukovych regime the resources it needed to survive and even prosper: trade restrictions were to be reviewed, and Russia promised to fund $15 billion of Ukrainian debt – but would eke it out quarterly. The price of gas would fall to the level in Germany (plus transit): $268.50 per 1,000 cubic metres, rather than $410. But the bailout wasn't really for the economy as a whole. The first tranche was $3 billion, and half of that immediately disappeared into the collective pocket of the Yanukovych 'Family'. As with previous deals in 2004 and 2006 (see Chapter 3), Ukrainian and Russian elites were supposed to share the loot; so much of the $15 billion would eventually come back to Russia. The other Ukrainian oligarchs were given a bone: beleaguered steel and pipe exporters were offered some relief, and deals were cut for aircraft and shipbuilding.

Russia cleverly made the deal medium term: there was more than just immediate debt relief. The long-term question of whether Ukraine was to join the Russia-led Customs Union was parked. But Russia assumed that, by parcelling out its assistance, Ukraine would grow even more dependent. The bailout was aptly summarised by opposition leader Arseniy Yatsenyuk: 'The only place with free cheese is a mousetrap.' The Ukrainians would end up selling more to the Russians than even Belarus ever had. Yanukovych would pass the tipping point where, instead of using his country as collateral in a positive-sum bargaining game between Russia and the West, he had to sell more and more at the margin simply in order to survive, especially as he was more dependent on Russia first to get to, and then try to win, the 2015 election.

Could the Maidan Have Fizzled Out?

In early January 2014, there was a sense of drift. Numbers were down, with a hard core of 1,000 to 2,000 on rotation duties. Sunday rallies were now institutionalised, acting as the equivalent of Friday prayers in the Egyptian Revolution; around 50,000 came out on Sunday, 5 January, even though there was no official call. But the original momentum seemed lost. Some of the factors that helped make for an original broad coalition now worked in the other direction. The coalition was too catholic, its various parties unwilling to criticise one another. The 'Maidan Republic' was a symbolic independent space in the centre of Kiev; but it could look isolated at the same time.

The regime continued to hold its ranks, and there was a sense that the protestors needed new tactics. Achievements were few, though many of those originally arrested had been freed and the idea of Ukraine joining the Customs Union was on the back burner. The Maidan could not engage in 'normal' politics. Five repeat elections were held on 15 December in seats where the authorities had simply stopped the count when their candidates were clearly losing, back in 2012. The authorities used the same old 'administrative methods' of vote-buying and ballot stuffing to win in four of the five. The opposition was therefore maybe not as strong as it looked – at least in the sense that it could not derail the government machine. The official parliamentary opposition failed to put up much of a fight. Even though the protestors were dominating the streets of central Kiev, the authorities still won. One of the rerun elections was in Kiev and three were near the capital. But the authorities' 'victory' also radicalised the opposition, as it could only expect more of the same at the presidential elections due in 2015.

But if Yanukovych had sat out the protests, he may well have survived. That said, his use of violence away from the Maidan was double-edged: on the one hand, it worked – the costs of protest were high; on the other hand, because it worked, many activists felt it was time for one last push while they still had the chance.

Many opposition leaders and activists also feared a repeat of the Yugoslav scenario of 1996–97, when demonstrators first tried to topple Slobodan Milošević. The West encouraged a legalistic compromise, which Milošević then used as a cover to repress the opposition. He was not removed until the 'bulldozer revolution' three years later, in October 2000.

The Dictatorship Laws

But life was also becoming more difficult for the authorities, and they made the mistake of moving first. Their arms may have been twisted. When Yanukovych fled Mezhyhirya he left some of his diaries behind. One records a secret meeting with Putin on 8 January near Valdai, during which the decision was allegedly reached that the Ukrainian authorities would fully suppress the protests and approve new repressive laws.[45]

The protests had now been going on for almost two months. The authorities chose to try and bring them to an end – not (yet) with the physical force that had failed in the past, but with a new law banning more or less everything. In farcical scenes in parliament on 16 January, the bill was rammed through with 235 votes in favour – except there was no real voting. Normal voting procedures were disrupted, and on several votes the tellers counted 235 votes, in a show of hands, in just five seconds.[46] With no logic or attempt at credibility, the authorities sought to criminalise everything the opposition had been doing over the past two months. Ukraine copied the Russian law that requires NGOs receiving money from abroad to register as 'foreign agents'. It would be illegal to take part in peaceful protests while wearing a hard hat or any uniform, or carrying any type of flame; and – striking at the modus operandi of the Maidan – it would be unlawful to set up tents, a stage or even a sound system without the permission of the police. Driving in an organised group of more than five cars was illegal (because of the AutoMaidan), as was blocking access to someone's residence. Collecting information about judges – i.e. exposing corruption – was made illegal. The 'government' (the exact agency was not defined) could decide to 'prohibit access' to the internet. MPs could be stripped of their immunity immediately, without due process. Denying the crimes of fascism, or of fascist accomplices, was criminalised – this would presumably render unlawful the right-wing Freedom Party's celebration of war-time Ukrainian nationalists.

I could go on; the list was long. But the measures did not cow. They were both comical and threatening, but also a sign of weakness – the authorities clearly could not arrest everyone in Kiev. But above all, they were counter-productive. Many protestors asked, 'Why wait?' According to one journalist: 'If you can be arrested for wearing a hard hat or writing a Facebook post, why shouldn't you throw a Molotov cocktail or a cobblestone? As the risk of large-scale repressions became real, Maidan erupted.'[47]

Calls for dialogue were not going anywhere; the government was moving in a sharply authoritarian direction, and the mood of many on the street was radicalising. The authorities' longer-term plans were not clear – they had sticks, but few real carrots. The official opposition never had much of a plan. The more radical protestors and the social networks had yet to develop one. The sense of vacuum was also fuelling the frustration.

The Battles on Hrushevsky Street

The key events began on 19 January on Hrushevsky Street, round the corner from the Maidan and the start of a climb up the hill to parliament. In Soviet times, it was Revolution Street (i.e. the 1917 Revolution) and Kirov Street, but after Ukrainian independence in 1991 it was renamed after Ukraine's national historian. In fact, the very worst fighting took place right outside the Institute of History building, usually a soporific site of quiet contemplation.

After yet another Sunday rally, this time of more than 200,000, at which many protestors wore comedy headgear, there was a march on parliament, which was disrupted by a police blockade of cars and buses at the foot of the Hrushevsky hill. The stage was set for another stand-off in a different part of town. There were many sightings of alleged agents provocateurs, given that a turn to violence was what some in the regime had always wanted. But there also seems to have been a desire, at least among younger protestors, for more direct action. The scenes of violence were therefore not staged, but real. The 'official' opposition (the parties in parliament) was increasingly discredited – particularly after Vitaliy Klitschko, leader of UDAR and a former boxer, was sprayed with a fire extinguisher.[48] The Freedom Party had been trying to hijack the protests to prove its toughness, but was now outflanked by ordinary members of the Maidan 'hundreds'.

The stand-off continued for four days, with protestors now throwing rocks and Molotov cocktails. According to one Ukrainian journalist, 'the Ukrainian protest belonged to all classes and were a mix of multiple realities; a combination of nineteenth-century national revolution and an Occupy protest, a rebellion of repressed businessmen, an anarchist commune and a warrior camp'. The Maidan was 'a place for medieval weapons such as a catapult and a ram, and almost non-stop online broadcasting and streaming. The first catapult on Hrushevsky Street, the location of the January clashes, was constructed from drawings found on the Internet and uploaded to a smart-phone right next to the front line'.[49] Protestors also built crude rocket launchers for firing Molotov cocktails like fireworks. On 22 January, two protestors were shot dead, leading to temporary retreat; but the space was soon reoccupied. For those with a historical frame of mind, this was a bitter irony: 22 January is Unity Day – the day when rival independent governments in Kiev and in west Ukraine briefly united in January 1919.

Despite not seeming to have been a provocation, the violence had the effect many had feared. The militia polarised against the protestors, and the protestors polarised against the militia. The next step was the occupation of government buildings from 24 to 29 January, largely by activists from the group Common Cause. According to the group's leader, Oleksandr Danylyuk, 'we organised the occupation of government buildings as an alternative. We wanted to focus attention back on the government, not on the militia', to prevent the polarisation of all against all. 'We wanted to be radical, but non-violent.'[50] The authorities were taken off guard and three ministry buildings were temporarily seized. The activists did not stay long in the Ministry of Energy, because they reluctantly accepted that, given Russian pressures, energy was a national security issue. But, according to Danylyuk, 'We only left the Ministry of Justice because the official opposition parties told us Yanukovych was about to make real concessions.' The leaders of Fatherland and UDAR were 'not only brakes on the opposition, but played the role of internal riot police on the Maidan. They stopped us from doing anything other than stand in the square.' Activists were forced out of the third building, the Ministry of Agriculture, by rival activists from the Freedom Party. Six were hospitalised. The Freedom Party, Danylyuk complained bitterly, 'only used violence against other protestors.'[51] But his group still believed in non-violent *action directe*. Common Cause's next idea was to occupy government buildings on 9 March, which is the birthday of the national hero, the poet Taras Shevchenko (1814–61).

The Regions

There were many other 'Maidans' – similar demonstrations in other towns and cities across Ukraine. Some tried to become permanent, with varying degrees of success: the camp in Dnipropetrovsk was attacked as early as 26 November. As in Kiev, the mood was radicalised in late January. It was also emboldened. There were still only 6,000 militia nationally; so if the Berkut was reinforced in Kiev, it would be short of numbers elsewhere. This led to eight state buildings being overrun in western and central Ukraine on 24 January, plus two more the next day. According to one UDAR MP, this was the one time that Yanukovych lost his cool in private. During yet another round of fruitless negotiations with the official opposition, his tone changed each time an aide brought him news of oblast administration buildings being seized in west Ukraine, one by one. 'After the fourth note appeared, he was prepared to talk about compromise.'[52]

The wave of occupations spread throughout central Ukraine, leaving Kiev isolated; but was stopped in the 'soft east', where other demonstrations in Dnipropetrovsk, Zaporizhzhya, Poltava and Sumy were repressed by militia and *titushki* on 26/27 January. Without such tactics, the regime may have been overwhelmed even earlier; there were plenty of actual and potential Maidan supporters in the east. But once such tactics were used, there was a mobilised 'anti-Maidan' minority available even after Yanukovych's flight.

Zig-Zag

The regime's incoherent responses to the demonstrations were due to internal splits, and to being caught between competing external pressures. Russia was pressing for a hard line, so it also supported domestic hardliners, particularly Interior Minister Zakharchenko, who was fond of saying (in the traditional way of authoritarian policemen) that all would be well if he was given a free hand.[53] Russia re-imposed export restrictions on 29 January. Serhiy Lovochkin finally resigned as head of the presidential administration and was replaced by Andriy Klyuyev on 24 January. Klyuyev was also a hardliner, but in a different way: he favoured grinding the opposition down with 'non-Maidan repression', endless fruitless talks and divide and rule tactics. He was also responsible for what amounted to the 'political technology' strategy of building up the 'nationalist threat'. The administration's links to Russia grew stronger, if anything.

Events did not reach the dénouement predicted by some when parliament sat again on 28 January. In fact, the possibility of compromise hinted at over the preceding weekend disappeared once more. Russia was already going slow on its promised aid package, presumably to stiffen the authorities' resolve. Nine out of twelve of the repressive laws 'passed' on 16 January were repealed – but not all. The law on 'the public denial or justification of the crimes of fascism' was maintained to target the right-wing Freedom Party, at a time when many in the West were buying the story that the protests were no longer worth supporting because of the over-prominence of that party.[54] Mykola Azarov stood down as prime minister, but the new acting prime minister was none other than Serhiy Arbuzov, one of the 'curators' of the Yanukovych 'Family'. This was the exact opposite of Yanukovych's apparent offer the previous weekend to set up a coalition government. In Mezhyhirya, Yanukovych was increasingly reliant on a 'Family HQ', but as much to maintain financial schemes as for security.

A new 'amnesty law' was controversially passed in the government version and boycotted by the opposition – once again with credible reports of fraudulent 'voting' – after Yanukovych himself had again descended on parliament to issue all kinds of threats. The 'amnesty' would only apply if protestors left buildings first; which they were now supposed to do within fifteen days. So the law was actually a threat rather than a concession. Chief Prosecutor Viktor Pshonka and others were pressing for a full state of emergency.[55] With almost no publicity, the government adopted plans on 27 January to increase the size of the main militia forces six-fold, raising the complement of the two main units, the Berkut and the smaller Grifon, from 5,000 to 30,000 men. 'Civil defence' forces would also be introduced. The Special Fund (i.e. state reserves) would be raided to find the money to pay.

Conclusion

On 31 January, it was announced that Yanukovych was ill and indisposed, adding even more uncertainty to the situation. He returned on 3 February. The EU continued to dither over calls for sanctions. The mood on the Maidan grew more radical. The stalemate could have continued longer than it did, but the stress was increasing.

CHAPTER 5

The Uprising

The revolution I saw in Kiev in February 2014 was an old-fashioned popular uprising – the kind you read about in textbooks on the nineteenth century. I saw a few nationalists with flags and slogans, but I also saw old women helping cut up the pavements, and every variety of citizen forming human chains to pass the stones for the young men to throw on the front line. The neatest signs of evidence of civic support were the cardboard boxes at the entrances to the encampment on the Maidan with 'cigarettes for the defenders' written on them in Ukrainian or Russian. Local teenagers, showing off in front of their mates, were enthusiastic donors.

But this was a radicalised citizenry. Three things had changed the mood since late January. One was the 16 January repression laws. The second was the regime's increasingly savage off-screen violence: protestors were snatched from their hospital beds; activists were seized at night, beaten and dumped in local forests. The third was the ineffectiveness of negotiation. Yanukovych was duplicitous, and the parliamentary opposition did not speak for the Maidan. Every time an agreement was signed between the parliamentary parties and the president, the protestors ignored it or put on a show of force to demonstrate that they were not consulted.

So the protestors got more and more militant, and the regime got more and more brutal.

Tuesday, 18 February

A march on parliament, dubbed the 'peace offensive' (the contradiction was deliberate), began at 8.30 a.m., with an estimated 20,000 people. First were the hundreds, then Self-Defence, then ordinary Kievites. Someone played Beethoven's 'Ode to Joy'. But things turned violent around 10 a.m., after the speaker of parliament refused even to table the discussion of changing the government and constitution. The regime was always closing or preventing discussion by dubious methods – the speaker abusing his powers or MPs blocking the rostrum if they couldn't get their way (also a favourite opposition tactic). But it was now closing down the hope of a negotiated way forward at the most volatile time. Soon there were running battles between protestors and militia, and the headquarters of the ruling Party of Regions was set on fire. According to a later official report, this was a provocation initiated by Ukrainian Security Service (SBU) agents, who had infiltrated protestors' ranks.[1] Two people died.

By the early afternoon, police had regained control on Institutska Street, the street leading up towards the government district from the Maidan, using guns. But there was mayhem where protestors were more isolated and the *titushki* were concentrated, half a mile away on the other side of parliament, near Mariinsky Park. Perhaps twenty people were dead.[2] Running battles were fought all afternoon as most protestors moved back to the Maidan. The metro was closed. An ultimatum was issued to clear the streets by 4 p.m.

The regime's response was 'Operation Boomerang' (the SBU operation) and 'Operation Surge' (mounted by the Interior Ministry). The long-feared attack on the Maidan began on Tuesday night, at 8 p.m., but it did not take the expected form. Two opposing armies faced off, throwing missiles at each other. This was not a full-on assault, though two armoured personnel carriers were stopped and burned. The fact of the matter is that the Maidan's defences were necessarily pretty amateurish: the protestors had piled up lots of snow and seen out the winter, but now it was almost all melted and they had tried replacing it with sand. Trees, advertising hoardings and rubbish bins were all dumped on the barricades. This would have not have held back a tank assault, but there are reports that the army twice refused to be dragged in.

Alpha Group stormed the House of Trade Unions. Protestors fled the buildings because it was set on fire, and Alpha Group, which had taken over the top three floors of the building, had to make off the same way it came – through the roof.

The *titushki* were now on the other side of the Maidan from Institutska Street, around St Michael's Square. With weapons handed out by the Interior Ministry, they killed six people.[3] The best estimate was that twenty-six were left dead on the day.[4] The official opposition once again sat down with Yanukovych at 11 p.m. The assault on the Maidan was clearly faltering, so they could at least buy relative peace for the next day, but at growing cost to their reputation for too much compromise.

Wednesday, 19 February

According to one Maidan leader, 'the regime thought if they killed a dozen people, then that would be enough'.[5] But it wasn't. The protestors lost territory, but stood firm. The next day, Wednesday, Yanukovych did not leave Mezhyhirya until just after midday, presumably because he was first overseeing the attack on the Maidan and then digesting the consequences of its failure. He may already have decided to flee. Or at least flight was the double-or-quits option he decided on at the same time as raising the stakes with an even more bloody attack on the protestors. Video footage at Mezhyhirya show Yanukovych packing (not doing it himself, obviously) over the course of the three days before he fled Kiev, starting on 19 February after the failure of 'Operation Boomerang'. The scenes can be watched on YouTube: art, cash and guns are piled into vans with unseemly speed.[6]

Wednesday was largely an interlude, as both sides plotted the next phase. However, the *titushki* were by now increasingly out of control, mixing brutal beatings with simple robbery. At least one more victim was killed in the morning.[7] The centre of Kiev shut down to a greater degree – though some restaurants at least remained open. The authorities announced an 'anti-terrorist operation', a state of emergency in all but name. Yanukovych appointed a new and apparently more biddable chief of the general staff. In the evening Akhmetov phoned Yanukovych in the 'bunker' and urged restraint. That evening was relatively calm after yet another meeting with the official opposition troika at 9.50 p.m. However, the call for a truce was rejected by AutoMaidan and Right Sector.[8]

European Commission President José Manuel Barroso also placed a call. The combination of internal and external pressure did have an effect.[9] Hence the staccato pattern of repression. Hence also the shock at the next day's events, which were not part of the previous pattern.

Thursday, 20 February

Ludicrously, Yanukovych declared 20 February to be a day of national mourning. In a chillingly inept TV broadcast late on Wednesday, he claimed to believe in dialogue, even though 'speaking frankly, I have advisers who are trying to turn me towards harsh options, to the use of force'.[10] Chief Prosecutor Pshonka was again demanding a full state of emergency.[11]

The protestors counter-attacked at 7.30 a.m. to try and reverse the losses of Tuesday. The government forces seem to have been caught unawares, as they were preparing to change tactics. Many Berkut were captured or retreated. The first sniper shot was fired at about 9 a.m.[12] Those behind the barricades or in no-man's land were shot professionally through the head or heart. With 75 per cent of victims the bullets went straight through.[13] Photographs later showed that the snipers were based in nearby government buildings and in the presidential administration.[14] Their firing positions were about two hundred yards uphill from the Maidan, at positions across and by Institutska Street, from the Ukraine Hotel on the left and the National Bank and Cabinet of Ministers on the left. One sniper was allegedly round the back of the Maidan, at the Kozatsky Hotel.

Ukrainian sources have hinted that a team under Yanukovych's personal control had been in place for weeks. The snipers were led by a Colonel Sergey Asavelyuk from the Interior Ministry, Sergey Kusyuk of Berkut special forces, and a group of Alpha led by Oleh Prysyazhny and 'Myron' Bychkivsky.[15]

It would later be alleged that the Russian Defence Ministry and FSB had supplied 'two separate Russian groups – involving 30 special agents in all' who 'conspired to plan and carry out an "anti-terrorist" operation' and 'also supplied Ukraine's law enforcement with more than five tonnes of various grenades and explosives that were used against peaceful activists.'[16] Two groups of twenty-four and six FSB agents had been based at an elite Kiev suburb, Koncha Zaspa, at various times since December. Valentyn Nalyvaichenko, who took over the Ukrainian Security Service (SBU) after the Uprising, says his organisation paid for their stay, provided them with security, and made joint plans for the Euromaidan crackdown of 18–20 February. Moreover, twenty-six FSB agents were present at an SBU shooting range on 26 December, he alleges.

Nalyvaichenko also claimed that 'Somewhere around January 20th, two military cargo aircraft from Chkalovsk, Russia, landed in Hostomel and Zhulyany airports near Kiev . . . They delivered 5,100kg of explosives, impact munitions and additional weapons.'[17] He also said twenty-six FSB were involved in planning the crackdown.[18] Another source lists a delegation of twenty-seven 'Kremlin and FSB officials' who arrived in Kiev on 20 February.[19] And Ukrainians would point out that Russia had done this kind of thing before: putting snipers on the roofs in the South Ossetian city of Tskhinvali when their candidate was losing the 2011 election, and targeting President Sergey Bagapsh of Abkhazia in 2004 (fortunately he had his own guys to protect him).

But new Interior Minister Avakov did nothing to stop the snipers destroying the chain of evidence: they were able to take all their firearms, the journal for issuing and returning weapons, and other documentation. Kusyuk and sixty-two others were able to flee to Russia, and many took part in the fighting in the Donbas.[20] Oleksandr Yanukovych allegedly took some of the weapons himself.[21]

When the sniper slaughter began, Maidan activists were prepared to fight back. Common Cause had two groups with military experience, and they were authorised to use arms if the government attacked first, having got their weapons 'from various sources'.[22] Some groups could listen in on the snipers' conversations. As a result, two snipers were killed – one on Institutska Street, near the National Bank, and one in the Hotel Ukraine, at about 11 a.m. The others then panicked.[23] The key buildings uphill from the Maidan were now occupied as both the snipers and Berkut fled – in part to comb for evidence.

Some Right Sector showed arms on the stage at the Maidan the next day.[24] But this was not an armed revolution: the Maidan hundreds were barely armed, or even protected. I saw an advertising hoarding being ripped down for use as a shield. Protestors hid behind trees. This time, for obvious reasons, I stayed further away; but I was still close enough to the edge of the Maidan to have to stumble aside at the regular shouts of *korridor!* – 'make way' – for the wounded or already-dead to get through.

According to the investigative MP Hennadiy Moskal, 196 police and militia were also injured between 18 and 20 February, and seventeen died.[25] Sixty-seven militia were captured on 20 February, but released the next day.[26] Police stations in Lviv were overrun on 18–19 February. More than a thousand fire-arms disappeared – some could have made their way to the Maidan. Other weapons were allegedly handed out by the security services to discredit the protestors.[27] Either way, the regime's defenders sensed a turning tide – the opposition might soon out-gun them, as well as out-fight them.

But at heart, this was a low-tech conflict. The protestors won with rocks and Molotov cocktails against snipers. They swarmed rather than attacked with precision. When one of their number was shot, they were prepared to keep going. Their bravery may even have increased the death toll. Seventy more dead was the initial estimate for Thursday alone.[28] Another 166 were unaccounted for.[29] According to the Health Ministry, 622 were injured and 405 hospitalised, but most sought to avoid hospital.[30] Militarised funerals as early as Friday created a new national myth of blood sacrifice.

Friday, 21 February

In retrospect this was the end, though it did not look like it at the time. At 3 p.m., Interior Minister Zakharchenko reportedly issued orders to 3,500 militia to carry arms. Armed special forces reportedly returned near the Maidan towards midnight.[31] There was plenty of flight from the government's ranks, but still no real rebellion. The claim that the oligarchs now moved decisively to bring Yanukovych down does not hold water.[32] They defected late as part of the general panic, but they did not induce that panic: defeat on the streets of Kiev did so.

Parliament's motion to end the police action on Thursday evening, 20 February, was undoubtedly a watershed, but only thirty-five Party of Regions

MPs were present.[33] A bare majority of 236 MPs supported the motion, but only 238 out of 450 were present. Seventeen MPs formally left the Party of Regions, followed by another five late in the evening. The rest had other things to do, with documents to destroy and businesses to protect.

Three EU foreign ministers, Sikorski of Poland, Steinmeier of Germany and Fabius of France, who later left for China, arrived for emergency negotiations on the Thursday morning. Putin sent the Russian human rights ombudsman Vladimir Lukin to join them. Andriy Klyuyev and Andrey Portnov, Yanukovych's legal 'expert' (who used to work for Tymoshenko), played a part as intermediaries and swapped the roles of good and bad cop, making it extremely difficult to get concessions out of Yanukovych. Klyuyev would set political booby-traps; Portnov acted as the 'legal' refusenik blocking any constructive compromise (he would soon end up in Russia, openly working for Russian interests). Overnight talks broke up at 7.20 a.m. on Friday. At a meeting with the Maidan Civic Council there was strong criticism of any deal that left Yanukovych in power and failed to flesh out transition mechanisms.[34] Sikorski said it was the best deal he could get: 'If you do not support this, you will have martial law, the army, you will all die.'[35] The Maidan Council reluctantly agreed.

Later the plans for an even bloodier assault on the Maidan were released. 'At least one helicopter would be deployed, as well as armoured personnel carriers, supporting thousands of army soldiers to back up 22,000 law enforcement personnel comprised mainly of riot police and the national guard ... It was planned to involve up to 10,000 fighters and internal forces and about 12,000 police officers, including 2,000 Berkut.'[36] The operation would have used as a pretext an alleged plot by Right Sector to set off bombs at government buildings. Traffic, electricity, water and telecommunications would be shut off in the city centre during the operation, while four television channels said to be independent or opposition-leaning would have been shut down before and during the operation.[37]

But Yanukovych had to make some kind of deal. An agreement was finally signed on Friday at 6.45 p.m. The 'Orange' constitution would be restored, leading to a national unity government. A new constitution would be written by September. Yanukovych would remain as president, but new elections would be held in December. They were actually due in March 2015, so three months early was no big deal. New election laws and a new Central Election Commission (CEC) would oversee the vote (the then CEC being totally corrupt). There would be an investigation into the violence conducted, under joint monitoring by the authorities, the opposition and the Council of Europe, and there would be an amnesty for protestors arrested since 17 February. The agreement also stated that:

The authorities will not impose a state of emergency. The authorities and the opposition will refrain from the use of violence . . . Both parties will undertake serious efforts for the normalisation of life in the cities and villages by withdrawing from administrative and public buildings and unblocking streets, city parks and squares . . . Illegal weapons should be handed over to the Ministry of Interior bodies.[38]

Parliament voted unanimously, 386–0, to return to the 2004 constitution, and then 332–0 in a vote to suspend Interior Minister Zakharchenko, who had direct authority for the slaughter. The 'anti-terrorist operation' was suspended. Another bill introduced changes to the criminal code, allowing for the release of Tymoshenko.

Russia claims that this was a binding agreement, though bizarrely the Russia envoy Vladimir Lukin did not sign it. But Yanukovych was negotiating in bad faith and ultimately just fled. He was not forced out by the West. Far from levering him out, the USA and EU did everything they could to get Yanukovych's people and the parliamentary opposition to agree to the compromise. In fact, they were in danger of propping him up. Nor was Yanukovych forced out by the crowds, who were still concentrated in the centre of Kiev, at a safe distance. Even if he was afraid of ending up like Romanian communist leader Nicolae Ceaușescu, chased away by his own people and subject to arbitrary 'trial' by his own entourage, Yanukovych was still several steps ahead. He was not in any immediate danger, and protestors had not crashed into his office, though they had occupied the vacated presidential headquarters just up the hill from the Maidan.

About a hundred militia had surrendered to Maidan activists by late Friday morning.[39] Their colleagues hastily left their positions around parliament just after lunch.[40] But at the same time, there were reports of heavily armed Berkut reinforcements on the way into town from the airport.[41] According to Ukraine's leading paper, Interior Ministry troops and most Berkut had already abandoned Yanukovych, but his own 200-strong security detail and the elite Alpha unit remained loyal. He also had plenty of armed *titushki* to defend him. Twelve buses with heavily armed personnel were seen in Kiev.[42] The SBU only stopped the anti-terrorist operation a day later, on the Saturday. So the situation was still confused.

The everyday forces of public order, on the other hand, knew what some of their number had just done. They stood aside as protestors walked into the presidential building on Bankivska Street. But there was no general looting or vengeance. Captured militia were treated well and released. In fact, this softly-softly approach allowed most of the sniper force to escape. Some politicians were already fleeing, followed by the police – in almost all cases in that order.

The belated announcement of Western sanctions on 20 February added to, but did not cause, their panic. What Yanukovych probably feared most was that those around him would not protect him, given that he had issued so many threats to them to stay in line. Like many bullies, he was also a coward.

At a public meeting on the Maidan that evening, one leader of the 'hundreds', Volodymyr Parasyuk from Lviv, raised the prospect of renewed action if Yanukovych did not resign by 10 a.m. the following day. He finished his emotional speech by threatening action 'with arms'.[43] This was more a personal commitment to his fallen comrades than an appeal to all to join him; still less was it the united threat of all those then present.

The moderate leader of one of the parliamentary opposition parties Vitaily Klitschko was booed when he announced the EU-brokered deal.[44] Russians constantly claim that 'no sooner than it had been signed, the deal was rejected by the Maidan',[45] and so there was a coup d'état. But this is false. The deal was being criticised – and for good reason – not rejected. There was no voting process on the public square. The Maidan Public Council reluctantly backed the deal by thirty-four votes to two.[46] If Yanukovych ran away simply because one rabble-rousing speech got a big cheer, then that was his own personal choice.

Yanukovych actually fled because he had finished packing. Preserving what he could of his wealth seems to have mattered more to him. Ukrainian prosecutors estimated that he took $32 billion (out of his supposed $100 billion total graft) to Russia with him, much of it literally crossing the border in trucks.[47] That kind of round-but-precise figure was suspicious. How did they count it? It would amount to several trainloads. But Yanukovych certainly sent a lot of money ahead. He got back to Mezhyhirya quite early, given the circumstances, at 8.55 p.m.; and he left when the packing finished at 4 a.m. He was undoubtedly planning his next move, but does not seem to have issued any significant orders other than to complete the packing. Yanukovych departed with twenty-one bodyguards in two helicopters for the secret government residence Obukhiv, near Kharkiv.[48]

Yanukovych was removed from office by parliament later that day, Saturday, 22 February. Here, corners were cut. According to the constitution, impeachment was a long process with several hurdles, and the final hurdle was high: a vote of three-quarters of MPs, or 338 out of 450. The vote to oust him was supported by 328. According to one MP:

> This was not an impeachment as such, but a 'change of power by consensus', a form of 'political-legal' solution by a unanimity vote (supported by ALL factions). If such a consensus had not been reached, there would have been more bloodshed. Parliament had to take responsibility and consolidate power,

which was falling apart after Yanukovych withdrew himself (*samousunuvsya*). The Berkut . . . wanted to surrender to some legitimate power, and not to Right Sector.[49]

Oleksandr Turchynov from Yuliya Tymoshenko's Fatherland Party was voted in as acting president. Russia considered this a wholly illegitimate, rather than imperfect, process. One reason for insisting that Yanukovych was still the real president was that he was persuaded to ask for Russian military intervention on 4 March, once he was in Russia – which was the closest thing that Russia had to legal cover for the annexation of Crimea. But it was poor cover: Yanukovych in exile failed the 'effective political control' test now established in international law and designed to prevent minority or exile factions in civil wars constantly calling for outside help.[50]

Yanukovych was not the only one to flee. Energy Minister Eduard Stavytsky left behind $5 million and fifty kilograms of gold in bars, plus gold, platinum and diamond jewellery.[51] Kiev's city airport at Zhulyany on Thursday evening was like a scene from a Martin Scorsese movie, with fleeing oligarchs taking money in hand luggage and fur-clad women tripping over their heels. Former Interior Minister Zakharchenko and 'Family' cashier Kurchenko bolted to Belarus on 21 February. Interestingly, Belarus President Lukashenka didn't want them around, and the local KGB (still called the KGB) told them to leave for Russia by 6 p.m. the next day.[52]

Saturday, 22 February – Yanukovych's Flight to Kharkiv

Whatever the purpose of Yanukovych's flight to Kharkiv, it failed.[53] In 2004, during the Orange Revolution, an assembly in the Luhansk city of Severodonetsk had made separatist noises and persuaded Viktor Yushchenko to compromise with the outgoing Kuchma administration in Kiev and give up many of the powers of the presidency he was then certain to win. Yanukovych's purpose this time was unclear. He may already have been fleeing. He may have been stopping off before catching up with his money. But there was an assumed political aim parallel to the events in 2004: either to declare a new capital in the east or to use Kharkiv as some kind of powerbase to return to power in Kiev.

Whatever the case, he made the wrong choice of city, and his Kremlin contacts soon agreed. Kharkiv had been the capital of Soviet Ukraine until 1934. But, unlike Severodonetsk, which is a chemical industry town close to the Russian border, Kharkiv is a centre of science and relatively high-tech industry, with a local intelligentsia and 300,000 students, many of whom were at the big pro-Maidan rally the preceding day. Its universities also have about 20,000 foreign students, who are essential to keep the establishments going. Kharkiv likewise has a more diversified economy and some of Ukraine's surviving SMEs. That said, in the 1990s it was also known as the *stolitsa musorov* – the 'cops' capital' – due to the dominance of its notoriously corrupt police and former KGB.

Politically, the previous Ukrainian Front rally organised in Kharkiv on 1 February had not been a resounding success.[54] Most of those present had been *titushki* or Oplot, with not enough 'respectable' politicians from the east and south. The meeting was shifted to a hall in a working-class district of the city and besieged by pro-Kiev demonstrators outside. This put off others when a similar rally of 'delegates from southern and eastern Ukraine' was held in Kharkiv on 22 February, two days after the massacre in Kiev. 'Akhmetov instructed everyone close to him not to attend', which led to too many empty seats in the venue.[55] The rally was held while events were still unfolding in Kiev, and local elites looked as though they would largely be left in power. And indeed they were: so they were fairly quiescent until Russia intervened in Crimea. Kharkiv, although it was the former capital, was not like the Donbas and had never run the country in recent years. Kharkiv elites were used to coalition-building, not going out on a limb, and their leaders knew that they would face retribution if they failed.

There was not the infrastructure in Kharkiv to support a new capital. Most importantly, there was no concentration of armed forces. Despite some separatist speeches, Kharkiv's unsavoury leadership duo, the foul-mouthed Mykhailo Dobkin and Hennadiy Kernes,[56] announced that they would lead a rally outside – then drove away as fast as they could, heading straight for Russia. Pshonka's flight convinced the would-be separatists that they had no force behind them (see Chapter 3). And Yanukovych never appeared publicly.

Russia claims it feels 'betrayed' by the events of 21–22 February. In the first place, this is plain wrong: Yanukovych ran away from the deal; no one broke it. Second, it is rank hypocrisy: Yanukovych can safely be assumed to have been in full communication with the Russians when he fled to Kharkiv. Getting cold feet seems to have been a joint decision. But had Yanukovych still claimed to be president in the east and/or had he set up a rival seat of government in Kharkiv (or anywhere else), there can be little doubt that Russia would have supported him, and that would have been a much more radical breach of the principles of the 21 February agreement.

To Crimea, via Donetsk

That same Saturday, Yanukovych went to Donetsk, arriving at about 4 p.m. He tried to fly to Russia in his Falcon jet, but some brave official apparently refused permission because of the lack of documentation, though it seems unlikely he would have acted alone. Then Yanukovych went to see Ukraine's richest man, Rinat Akhmetov, and asked for his support. Akhmetov told him his time was up and he should resign.[57] Yanukovych was then driven to Crimea, having once again failed in an attempt to flee by helicopter near Mariupol, half-way to Crimea. First he went to Yalta, from where 'the route was led by security chief [Konstantin] Kobzar, coordinating the plan of action with Russia'. They were waiting for some money.[58] Yanukovych then reached Sevastopol, and left three days later.

Three weeks on, two AgustaWestland AW139 helicopters ($10 million each) and Yanukovych's Falcon 900 executive jet ($33 million) made their way independently to Moscow's Vnukovo airport: the Falcon via Switzerland, the helicopters via Moldova.[59]

The Aftermath in Kiev

Activists made a good job of substituting for the disappearing police, but only in the very centre of Kiev. Given the potential vacuum of authority there was minimal disorder. The Russian media soon gave up on its claims that Kiev was engulfed in anarchy; its bogeymen were fascists rather than looters. The protestors gave the newly released Yuliya Tymoshenko a pretty lukewarm reception when she addressed them from a wheelchair on Saturday. She already looked like yesterday's politician. Officials in the new government were stopped and lectured about their motorcades sweeping around Kiev as if nothing had changed. Precisely because the protestors stayed committed and stayed on the Maidan there was no mass vengeance or vigilantism elsewhere. There were a few exceptions involving Right Sector (see Chapter 8), but Kiev was back to normal within weeks.

The political purism of the Maidan leaders was reinforced by the murder of over a hundred of their number in Kiev, already entered into martyrology as the *Nebesna Sotnya* ('Heavenly Hundred'), beginning with the highly charged funeral services held on the Maidan. Within weeks, Lenin statues had been pulled down and streets renamed in central Ukraine. Most had already been changed in the west, but the fashion was now not for the nationalists of the 1940s but for names like 'Maidan' or 'Heroes of Nebesna Sotnya'.

Paradigms of Resistance

Ukraine had something resembling a revolution in February 2014. But it was not the same as any of the old paradigms of revolution: the sweeping social change after the French Revolution of 1789 or the Russian Revolution of 1917, the professional revolutionary seizure of power by the same Bolsheviks in

1917, the Central European 'non-revolutionary revolutions' in 1989, or the 'revolution-as-carnival' model of the coloured revolutions of the 2000s. Despite being once again endorsed by the fans of the veteran American activist Gene Sharp and his model of non-violent resistance,[60] this was clearly a more complicated affair. There were therefore interesting but complex lessons to be drawn for both protestors and autocrats across the globe.

The Ukrainian protestors mixed up the old and the new. The Maidan demonstrations lasted three months, and it was not long before many argued that passive resistance was not enough. Many thought the largely unsuccessful 'coloured revolutions' a decade earlier had been too peaceful to enact real change. Nor was leaderless revolution or network revolution using social media for mobilisation sufficient. Cobblestones used to be a symbol of revolution à la française – the Russian band Pussy Riot had a song 'Release the Cobblestones' – and sure enough, they became a key symbol of the Ukrainian Uprising, as protestors went back to old-fashioned methods of throwing Molotov cocktails and bits of their own city at the Berkut. But the protestors were also innovative. They developed other methods of communication to hold their lines together, including text messaging to define where it was safe to move and later where the snipers were located. They also devised novel modes of organisation, drawing on local Cossack traditions to band together in 'hundreds', with sergeants rather than an overall leadership structure. There was also an old-fashioned willingness to fight and even die for the cause. There wasn't exactly professionalisation, however. The victory on the final Thursday came about by swarming at the enemy. Statistics may prove that non-violent revolution is still more likely to be successful, but future protestors will likely mix up their tactics in the same way.

For autocrats, the new conventional wisdom is that large-scale repression is too costly in the modern media age. The key tipping point is the exposure and condemnation effect if public violence is seen on global TV or transmitted online by smartphones. The lessons from Ukraine were complex. The authorities might have nipped the protests in the bud with maximum violence as quickly as possible. They could have succeeded when they escalated repression, but took it 'off screen'. They failed when they used too much conventional violence, gunning people down in the streets; that could not have looked worse on the world's TV and computer screens. They did not have the capacity to impose the 'sniper-plus' plan.

Conclusion

And then it was quiet. Ukraine was not about to collapse. There were pockets of discontent and a few die-hard Yanukovych supporters, but the cynical elite at least knew which way the wind was blowing. The best evidence for that was provided by the early super-majorities in parliament: 328 out of 450 MPs voted for Yanukovych's ouster; 386 for the return of the old constitution. There was little trouble before Russia decided to make trouble.

To some, this was 'Gettysburg on the Maidan',[61] already the birth of a new nation. To others, it was a threat to the whole post-Soviet order. And Putin had been here before. One reason why he decided not to back the Kharkiv scenario at the last minute was that he did not want to be back in the same losing situation as in 2004. Something more radical was needed this time.

CHAPTER 6

Crimea

It is often said in Russia – and repeated in the West – that Khrushchev 'gave away' Crimea as a 'present' to Ukraine in 1954, when he was probably drunk. However, he followed what counted as legal procedure in the Soviet Union at the time – although he was perhaps guilty on the second count, as drunken decision-making was the norm in the USSR. Petro Poroshenko describes life as a minister under Ukrainian President Kuchma, when four litres of alcohol were often consumed at a sitting (i.e. five bottles of vodka, presumably between them, though he wasn't clear on that point): 'this was a normal Soviet thing, a test of bureaucratic competence'.[1] It didn't make for a very efficient bureaucracy, of course. The word 'present' is only a metaphor anyway. Far from being a boon, the transfer of Crimea was designed to make Ukraine less Ukrainian by adding so many Russians.

The idea of an 'eternal Russian' Crimea is also nonsense. Here is Putin's victory speech in March 2014:

In people's hearts and minds, Crimea has always been an inseparable part of Russia. This is the location of ancient Chersonesus, where Prince Vladimir was baptised. His spiritual feat of adopting Orthodoxy predetermined the overall basis of the culture, civilisation and human values that unite the peoples of Russia, Ukraine and Belarus. The graves of Russian soldiers whose bravery brought Crimea into the Russian empire are also in Crimea. This is also Sevastopol – a legendary city with an outstanding history, a fortress that serves as the birthplace of Russia's Black Sea Fleet. Crimea is Balaklava and Kerch, Malakhov Kurgan and Sapun Ridge. Each one of these places is dear to our hearts, symbolising Russian military glory and outstanding valour.[2]

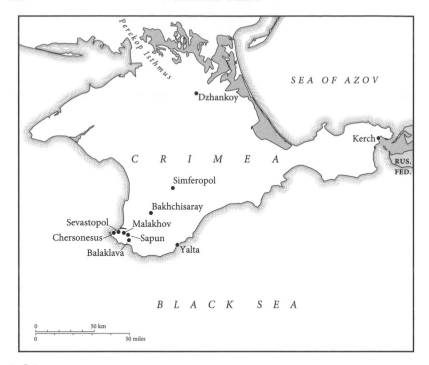

2 Crimea

In fact, the Crimean Tatars have the strongest claim to the history of the peninsula. The Russian Empire annexed Crimea in 1783, but it was only ever truly
Russian from the Crimean War of 1853–56 until 1917, and then from 1945–54
(it was a separate Soviet Republic from 1921 to 1945). The idea that the transfer
of Crimea from Russia to Ukraine under Khrushchev in 1954 was an arbitrary
act that flew in the face of history is therefore false (according to Putin, it was
Khrushchev's atonement for his crimes as party boss in Ukraine in the 1940s).
By my calculation, Crimea was Russian for seventy-three years after 1853; then
it was Ukrainian for sixty years from 1954 to 2014, which isn't so different.
Before that, it belonged to the Crimean Tatars for at least 400 years.

As a date, 1944 is in any case arguably more important than 1954. The
Crimean Tatars were deported en masse just after the USSR reoccupied the
peninsula in May 1944, as, at various moments in the war, were the Bulgarian,
Greek, German and Armenian communities. War and devastation meant that
the population of Crimea was only 351,000 in the summer of 1944.[3] It was
2 million in 2014, and so the vast majority were new settlers. Modern Crimea
is therefore not so much Russian as Soviet. Crimea is full of giveaway place
names, introduced when the Crimean Tatar presence was artificially erased

overnight: Lenin region, First of May district, and so on. Crimea had a special Soviet niche as a local version of Florida, full of dachas and holiday complexes for factories and trade unions from all over the USSR, plus the Black Sea Fleet, leading to a large number of retirees and former military. Though one thing that was undoubtedly significant about the transfer in 1954 was that Crimea missed out on the Soviet-backed Ukrainianisation programme elsewhere in Soviet Ukraine in the 1920s; this only made Crimea even more Soviet.

Island Crimea: Always a Melting Pot

Crimea has long had links to the Slavic world. Christianity spread north from Byzantium and through Crimea in the tenth century, though legend goes back to the supposed exile of Pope Clement in Crimea until his death in the year 99. But the Christian influence went first to Kiev before Moscow was even founded – or, if we don't bother about who was first, Christianity came to what is now Ukraine, Belarus and Russia (and partially to Lithuania) collectively after 988, not to Russia alone. The local Orthodox community in Crimea was based in the old Greek city of Chersonesus, but as an island of settlement in a multi-ethnic patchwork. The Mongols arrived in the thirteenth century and their descendants established the Crimean Tatar Khanate, which flourished from the 1440s to 1783 and outlasted all other remnants of the Golden Horde; Kazan and Astrakhan were conquered by Ivan the Terrible in 1552 and 1556. Historians on various sides dispute the extent to which the Crimean Khanate remained an independent state or became a protectorate of the Ottoman Empire after 1475. But this was also the period when the intermixing of the native peoples of the peninsula (Scythians, Sarmatians, Tauri, Goths) with Turkic tribes (Kipchaks, Kumans, Khazars, Pechenegs) and the Mongols created a Turkicised and largely Islamicised Crimean Tatar ethos, initially known as the 'Tats'. There is also a more marginal theory that modern Crimean Tatars are more narrowly the descendants of the Slavs' and Mongols' opponents – the Kipchaks or Polovtsians, who dominated southern Eurasia from the ninth century until their defeat by the Mongols in 1241. It is sometimes argued, therefore, that the Crimean Tatars should be more simply known as 'Crimeans' (*Qirimlar*), that is, *the* Crimeans.

The Crimean Tatars remained the majority population until Russian annexation in 1783 (83 per cent, or 171,000 measured ten years later). When the Russians invaded, they had no decent maps of Crimea and had to borrow them from the British Museum. There was little formal Russification until the Crimean War, during and after which an aggressive programme of Christianisation sought to turn the peninsula into the 'Russian Athos'.[4] (The twenty monasteries of Mount Athos, the first of which date from the ninth century, are in north-eastern Greece, but are under the direct authority of the Orthodox Patriarch in Istanbul.) The 'historical' Crimean Christian population of about 50,000 at the time of the annexation in 1783 was largely made up of Greeks and Armenians,[5] not Russians. The Greeks pre-dated the Crimean Tatars by more than a thousand years. Armenians fleeing the Seljuk invasions in the eleventh century formed *Armenia Maritima*, one of the largest parts of the medieval diaspora until 1475. Then there were the local Germans, who were invited to settle in Crimea and the southern steppe by Catherine the Great; and the Bulgarians, refugees from the Ottoman wars either side of 1800. Crimea was also home to the Krymchaks, who spoke a Turkic language and were culturally akin to the Crimean Tatars, but who wrote in Hebrew characters, and the Karaim, who were also Turkic speaking but more thoroughly Jewish (though messianic and anti-rabbinical). Both groups claim to pre-date the Crimean Tatars on the peninsula. At the time of the first census in the Tsarist Empire in 1897, Russians made up only 33.1 per cent of the population; they were still outnumbered by the Crimean Tatars (35.6 per cent).

The half-century after the Crimean War was indeed a golden age of Russian Crimea. Christianity was aggressively promoted, precisely because its position was not dominant. The Orthodox Church even put forward the idea that the Crimean Tatars were not Mongol latecomers but part of the local Crimean ethnic mix who were 'Islamicised' and therefore could be 're-Christianised'. In the future, this would ironically be one of the foundations for the idea of the Crimean Tatars' 'indigenous' history. The great Aleksandr Nevsky Church was completed in Yalta in 1892; and St Vladimir Cathedral at Chersonesus in 1876 (destroyed in World War Two, it reopened in 2004). Pushkin and Chekhov set stories in Crimea, although usually as a place of exotic adventure. The highly emotional Russian nationalist writer Aleksandr Prokhanov celebrated the return of Crimea in 2014 as 'the sacred Russian firmament, the altar of the sacred religion, a bastion of great power, the great naval harbour . . . Livadia, with its palace where the Tsars rested . . . [and] Yalta, where Stalin, Churchill and Roosevelt met for their conference, and the Generalissimo drew in the sand the contours of the post-war world'.[6] Well, yes to some of that; but Crimea is also home to the Palace of the Khans at Bakhchisaray and the great Juma-Jami Mosque, founded in 1552. It is estimated that there were 1,600 mosques and religious schools in Crimea in 1783.

The Ukrainians have just as much claim as the Russians to the era of Crimean and Kievan Christianity between the tenth and the thirteenth centuries. Ukrainian historians also stress the importance of cooperation between the Cossacks and Crimean Tatars for control of the steppe from the sixteenth to the eighteenth centuries – though they fought each other just as often. But one

CRIMEA

recent book on the 'History of the Statehood of Ukraine' essentially celebrates parallel projects – governments in Kiev and the west alongside the Crimean Tatars in the south. There is even a myth that the flags are basically the same colour and the Crimean Tatars' national symbol is the same as the Ukrainian, just upside down. More generally, the longer view of Ukrainian history sees Crimea as the key to access to the sea and a role in the wider world. Ukrainian settlement has waxed and waned. In hard times, the population has concentrated in the forests further north; in good times it has moved down the mighty rivers (the Dnieper and the Dniester) that flow due south to reach the Black Sea.

The Crimean Tatars

The Crimean Tatars were in a comfortable majority at the time of Russian annexation in 1783, but their numbers fell sharply with successive waves of out-migration, mainly to the Ottoman Empire – the first even before annexation, during the Russo-Turkish War of 1768–74; the second immediately after annexation; and a third after the Crimean War of 1853–56.

But at the time of the 1917 Revolution, the Crimean Tatars still made up about a quarter of the local population. They benefited from a certain amount of power-sharing after the Bolsheviks established a Crimean 'Autonomous Soviet Socialist Republic' in 1921 (i.e. Crimea was a separate republic, *not* part of Russia); but they suffered from two terrible famines in the early 1920s and 1930s, and the purges of the 1930s (which in Crimea began after 1926). According to the historian Alan Fisher, 'between 1917 and 1933, approximately 150,000 or 50 per cent of the Crimean Tatars had either been killed or forced to leave the Crimea,'[7] even before the deportation of the rest in 1944.

The deportation of the remainder (in Crimean Tatar, *Sürgünlik*) is the central point of reference in Crimean Tatar and Crimean history. In May 1944, the Crimean Tatars were accused of collaboration with the German occupiers and of desertion, and were deported from Crimea en masse. Since most adult Crimean Tatar men were either at the front fighting at the time, 86.1 per cent of the original deportees consisted of the elderly, war invalids, women and children.[8] The main deportation, on 18 May, was then followed by another wave, consisting of the Crimean Tatar soldiers serving in the Soviet armed forces. Some Crimean Tatars had indeed defected to the German side – one estimate is just over 9,000 – but 20,000 had been mobilised into the Soviet armed forces since 1941.[9] Moreover, Crimean Tatars made up about a fifth of local partisans.[10] The Soviet authorities were clearly also motivated by longstanding stereotypes concerning the 'treacherous' Crimean Tatars, by a desire to make Crimea more firmly Russian (and less Ukrainian), and by aggressive geopolitical rivalry with Turkey at the time. In 1897 there were actually more Muslims in Russia than in the Ottoman Empire – 20 million, as opposed to 14 million. The north and east of the Black Sea was also Muslim, not just the south. Some 3 million Muslims had left Russia by the time of the 1917 Revolution. Stalin was determined not to reverse the process, and wanted to 'destroy Turkey's "frontline security zone" in the Caucasus'.[11] Hundreds of thousands of other deportees included the Meskhetian Turks (Georgian converts), Kurds and Khemshils (Armenian converts), Chechens, Ingush, Balkars and Karachays.

At least 180,000 Crimean Tatars in total were deported to Siberia, Central Asia and the Ural Mountains.[12] The loss of life during the deportation (in guarded and sealed cattle-trains, without food or water, and in appallingly unsanitary conditions) was substantial. According to NKVD estimates, 27 per cent of the population perished in the first three years alone.[13] Crimean Tatar analysts in the 1960s put the figure as high as 46 per cent, almost half of the population, perishing in the first years following the operation.[14]

After Khrushchev's 'secret speech' in 1956, in which he denounced Stalin, many other deported peoples were allowed to return home – even the Chechens. But not the Crimean Tatars. A decree in 1967 withdrew the charges of collaboration, but this was given little publicity outside Central Asia and stopped well short of full rehabilitation.

The Crimean Tatars were only able to return to Crimea in the very late Soviet period, after 1989. Ironically, an assistance programme was drawn up in Moscow in 1989, but remained largely unimplemented at the time of Soviet collapse. By 2014, just under 270,000 had returned to Crimea, with perhaps another 100,000 left in Central Asia, plus several million of Crimean Tatar descent in the diaspora, mainly Turkey.

Crimea After 1991

After 1991, all three main groups in Crimea felt they were minorities. Ethnic Russians were a local majority (58 per cent, or 1.2 million according to the 2001 census), but were nationally a minority in the new Ukrainian state. For Ukrainians, on the other hand, this was the only region in the new state where they were in a minority (24 per cent). Moreover, the local Ukrainians were highly Russified – the Ukrainianisation campaign of the 1920s had passed Crimea by, and so there were almost no schools, newspapers or other Ukrainian cultural institutions in Crimea. The Crimean Tatars had increased their numbers to about 13 per cent, but of course claimed to be an artificial minority.

As the Soviet Union fell apart, several contradictory votes were held in Crimea. It became a republic once again, after a referendum in January

1991 that won 93 per cent support. The manoeuvre was accepted in Kiev, in order to prevent the Russian majority threatening to secede. The local elite ensured that the referendum referred to their desire to be 'a subject of the Soviet Union and a party to the [proposed new] Union Treaty', but the latter demand was soon irrelevant – the USSR would be gone within months (although in Crimea, 87.6 per cent backed the preservation of the USSR in the March 1991 referendum). The new Autonomous Republic of Crimea remained part of Ukraine, and so joined it when the Ukrainian parliament declared independence in August 1991, a decision confirmed by over 90 per cent in an all-Ukrainian referendum of December 1991. The vote in favour in Crimea was 54 per cent.

This majority – albeit a narrow one – came about for two reasons. First, as elsewhere in Ukraine, the local communist elite, led by Mykola Bahrov, fell in line with Ukrainian independence. Second, sufficient numbers of Crimean Tatars had already returned to vote and convert a plurality into a majority. But there was also an irreconcilable pro-Soviet and new Russian nationalist alternative. The first attempt to convert autonomy into independence came as early as 1992, but ended in another constitutional compromise. The second came when Kiev miscalculated by assuming that Bahrov would win an election for Crimean 'president' in 1994; in the event he lost heavily to Yuriy Meshkov, who led the self-explanatory Russia Bloc. But Meshkov's visit to Moscow to plead for help from Boris Yeltsin was badly timed: Yeltsin had just used tanks against his communist and nationalist opponents in Moscow in October 1993, including plenty of hard-line volunteers from Crimea. Meshkov came from the same milieu, and so Yeltsin wouldn't talk to him, and by December 1994 Russia was embroiled in the Chechen war (the 'wrong war', according to Aleksandr Solzhenitsyn, no less).

In 1995, Ukrainian President Leonid Kuchma made good use of the new Ukrainian security services to disband the rebels. The only real enthusiasts for rule from Kiev, however, were the Crimean Tatars. Kuchma had to make a deal with the locals – stay out of separatist conflicts and you can steal all you want. Crimea in the 1990s was notorious for its bloody local mafia wars. According to Wikileaks,[15] the Seilem organised crime gang (named after the popular cigarette brand 'Salem'), with a base among local Armenians, was responsible for fifty-two contract murders in two gang wars in 1991–92 and 1995, as it fought with the more Slavic Bashmaki gang, named after Viktor Bashmakov, with links to Transnistria, the separatist region in Moldova. Connections with both Nagorno-Karabakh and Transnistria were logical, as Crimea threatened to become another de facto state. But after 1995 the mafia moved into politics, making money on the privatisation of local land and holiday businesses.

Crimea's lucrative corruption opportunities were also fought over in Kiev. The key oligarchs all had operations there, but had to cooperate or compete with Russians to a much greater extent than in the rest of Ukraine. Dmytro Firtash's interests started in the north (the chemical industry), then spread along the shore to both east and west via the local gas utility Krymgaz. The central steppe of Crimea was the space for solar and wind energy businesses owned by the Klyuyev brothers. There was more to share in the south and around Sevastopol, including for Oleksandr Yanukovych and the Cedar hunting club from Mezhyhirya.[16] Rinat Akhmetov owned the local electricity supplier, agribusiness and the Avlita cargo port in Sevastopol. There were high hopes of big money from energy, especially in potentially lucrative offshore deposits, hence a bitter skirmish over the oil company Vanco during Tymoshenko's second stint as prime minister in 2007–10.[17]

The Crimean Tatars meanwhile had a well-organised protest movement dating back to the 1960s – in part because they had so little to lose. In June 1991, an elected assembly, dubbed the Second Qurultay was organised in Simferopol (the first having been in 1917), which passed a Declaration of National Sovereignty of the Crimean Tatar People. It claimed that 'Crimea is the national territory of the Crimean Tatar people, on which they alone have the right to self-determination ... The political, economic, spiritual and cultural revival of the Crimean Tatar people is possible only in their own sovereign national state.' The Qurultay and its plenipotentiary body, the Mejlis, also claimed to be the sole legitimate representative voice for the Crimean Tatar people; that is, a parliament rather than a political party or NGO. The Qurultay was re-elected every five or six years (in 1996, 2001 and 2007), with 50.5 per cent turnout claimed for the most recent round of voting in 2013.[18]

In practice, self-government has been difficult to organise when the Crimean Tatars make up just over 13 per cent of the local population. There have been some experiments, such as a quota of fourteen seats for them in the local elections of 1994. A 'Council of Representatives of the Crimean Tatar People Attached to the President of Ukraine' was set up in 1999, which oversaw several practical improvements to Crimean Tatar life in the early 2000s.

The assertion of parallel representative authority is, however, an awkward claim for any sovereignty-minded state. Among Ukrainian President Yushchenko's many failings was his neglect of the Crimean Tatar issue. According to the leaders of the Mejlis, 'we were surprised by his indifference,'[19] the most plausible explanation for which was Yushchenko's relative Ukrainian nationalism and his concern that Crimean Tatar demands for sovereignty were a threat to the Ukrainian state-building project on the peninsula.[20]

Crimea under Yanukovych

Originally, when Yanukovych became president in Kiev, Crimea was run by local bigwig Vasyl Dzharty, but he died of lung cancer in August 2011. His successor, Anatoliy Mohylyov, was much less of a player. His role was simply to open the door to a wholesale takeover by Yanukovych's cronies. As many of them came from Makiyivka, near Donetsk in east Ukraine, in Crimea these guys had the magnificent (if sinister) nickname of the *Makedontsy* – the 'Macedonians', as in ancient Greece, the outsider rulers from the north.

Mohylyov publicly referred to the Crimean Tatars as 'Hitler's henchmen'[21] and revived the local gangsters. Yanukovych told the veteran Mejlis leader Mustafa Dzhemilev in private that the Mejlis was being punished for voting against him. Conversely, he said: 'Join my team and all your problems will be over.'[22] According to Dzhemilev, all this divide and rule 'was done in parallel with the Russian FSB'. He also claimed that a rival like Rustam Temirgalyev was an 'agent of the GRU [military intelligence]'.[23]

So Yanukovych's government set about fostering a loyalist Crimean Tatar movement instead, though many also detected the hand of Russia. This was known as the Kazan Party, as it claimed life was better for the Volga Tatars under the Russians in Kazan. A new generation of Crimean Tatar businessmen was also manipulated, as 'business' on the peninsula was always riddled with mafia and political connections. In August 2010 Yanukovych neutered the Council of Representatives by deposing Dzhemilev as chair and replacing many Mejlis members with the radical Milli Firka National Party instead (the 'National Party' named after the first Crimean Tatar party, originally established in 1917).[24] Other Uncle Tom parties included the Crimean Tatar Popular Front, the NGO Sebat ('Fortitude') and New Generation, all peddling either a collaborationist or faux-radical line.[25] The main Crimean Tatar Muslim body, the DUMK, was also challenged by a new 'Spiritual Centre for the Muslims of Crimea'. Veteran leader Mustafa Dzhemilev, born in 1943, whose youngest son was caught up in a murder case in May 2013, retired in October 2013. In the ensuing leadership contest, his long-term deputy, Refat Chubarov, just held off Remzi Ilyasov, representative of the proxy forces, who was allegedly close to another pro-Russian businessman, Aziz Abdulayev.

With its corruption and ethnic divisions, Crimea was always one of the worst-governed parts of Ukraine (which is saying something). For once, analysts consistently predicted trouble in the right place. But few expected that Russia would attempt such an audacious land grab. That said, anybody who wanted to make trouble had plenty of material to hand.

Surkov's Footprints?

Fast-forward to 2014, and there was a coup in Ukraine, involving masked men with guns. But, as pointed out in the introduction to this book, it was in Crimea, not Kiev. The first element in the unfolding saga was the flight of the Berkut from Kiev. After the Maidan, the notorious militia, with so much blood on its hands, dispersed back to its home territories. At a rally in Lviv attended by priests, its members asked for forgiveness. Others were basically on the run. If they stayed in Ukraine, they faced murder charges. If they defected to Russia, they could be heroes. The local Crimean Berkut members were already back in Sevastopol by Saturday, 22 February, only two days after the massacre in Kiev. Their bus stopped in the middle of town, where they were treated as heroes and given flowers, to cries of 'Well done lads!', 'Glory to the Berkut!', 'Heroes!' and 'There should have been more!' – meaning, more dead in Kiev. The Berkut 'heroes', though, still kept their masks on.[26]

In a crude parody of events in Kiev, the next day a local businessman, Aleksey Chaly, a Russian citizen whose grandfather had been commander of the Black Sea Fleet, was elected 'people's mayor' at a public meeting thronged with militia. This was the first coup, and served as a dry run for the subsequent takeover of the whole of Crimea.[27] It was also a classic, but tawdry, 'political technology' technique, called 'cloning' – copying other methods, in this case the popular involvement on the Maidan, to claim moral equivalence. If people in Kiev could do it, why not in Crimea, too? Even though the events were entirely different.

Two days later, on 25 February, the authorities in Kiev took the inevitable decision to abolish the national Berkut. According to the investigative MP Hennadiy Moskal, 'the first to rise in revolt were the Sevastopol Berkut; they were then joined by fighters from special units from other regions of the country'.[28] Moskal says the operation was led by the leader of the Sevastopol Berkut, Sergey Kolbin.[29]

We do not know how much of the rest of the Crimean operation was pre-planned, or whether it simply took advantage of the Berkut. Many Russian sources say plans were first drawn up after the war in Georgia in 2008: one theory is that it was an option for after the 2015 Ukrainian election, if a pro-Western candidate won, or to derail any Ukrainian attempt to join NATO.[30] After the Uprising in Kiev, the Russians may have feared the abrogation of the 2010 Kharkiv Agreement that prolonged the lease of the Russian Black Sea Fleet in Sevastopol until at least 2042. If the original timetable was restored, the lease would run out in 2017. But we do know that Putin's key aide Vladislav Surkov made a Valentine's Day visit to Crimea, just *before* the events in Kiev spiralled out of control. The speaker of the Crimean Soviet, Vladimir Konstantinov, also went to Moscow on 20 February.

The operation was also allegedly a 'public-private partnership', involving finance from the Russian oligarch Konstantin Malofeev, one of the sponsors of the Orthodox Church and its crazier prelates. His company, Marshall Capital, was presumably named after the money-laundering islands of the same name. Malofeev funded Chaly, the 'people's mayor' of Sevastopol, to the tune of $1 million.[31] A trip to Simferopol was supported by the Russian Orthodox Church on 30 January.[32] In the ultra-cynical world of Russian politics, Malofeev allegedly sponsored Right Sector as well.

Surkov may also have sensed the brewing revolt against the Yanukovych clique. He seems to have ignored the ruling Party of Regions during his visit, probably because he wanted a more pliable and ultimately more easily disposable instrument. So Surkov and his Orthodox oligarchs looked instead to the remnants of the Russian nationalist movement from the early 1990s. There wasn't much of it left: whereas Yanukovych's Party of Regions won eighty of the hundred seats in the 2010 Crimean elections, the two small pro-Russian parties, Union (i.e. the Soviet Union) and Russian Unity, won only five and three respectively. The Party of Regions won 48.9 per cent of the vote, Union won 5.3 per cent and Russian Unity only 4 per cent. It was widely mentioned when Russian Unity's leader Sergey Aksyonov suddenly became the new 'prime minister' of Crimea that he was hardly electorally popular. Rather less noticed was the fact that Surkov had a pretty narrow choice of openly pro-Russian politicians to anoint.

The local Russian nationalists had also merged with the local mafia after 1995 (see above). For Surkov, this was probably a net advantage, as it made them biddable. Konstantinov ran a property company Consol, which owed a fortune to Ukrainian banks of more than 1 billion UAH, or $130 million,[33] and money to Russian banks, too. With numerous building projects unfinished, he was being pursued by his creditors through the Ukrainian courts in 2013–14. Aksyonov, known as the 'Goblin' in mafia circles in the 1990s (he was allegedly in the Seilem gang), rode on Konstantinov's coattails and owned a small TV station and bank.[34] Both Aksyonov and Deputy Prime Minister Rustam Temirgalyev had links to Dmytro Firtash; Temirgalyev had ties with Russian businessman Dmitriy Sablin, who was born in Mariupol. Firtash helped finance Aksyonov's 2010 election campaign, which supposedly left the Goblin $5 million in debt.[35]

Surkov, a man with literary pretensions, may also have recalled the cult novel written in 1979, *The Island of Crimea*, which was also penned by an Aksyonov – Vasiliy Aksyonov – who imagined that the Whites had hung onto Crimea at the end of the Civil War in 1920 (like the anti-communist Kuomintang in Taiwan after 1949). But Aksyonov's Crimea was both flashier and seedier: both the capitalist West and the anti-West – more like Hong Kong.[36] The novel's anti-hero, Andrey Luchnikov, invites the USSR to annex Crimea because he is nostalgic for an imaginary Russia that has long since disappeared. The most famous line in the book is his lament when his scheme backfires: 'Things get out of control, you know what I mean?' Possibly the coincidence played on Surkov's mind.

But needs must. After the Uprising in Kiev, it initially looked likely that a new coalition would run Crimea, made up of Crimean Tatars, local Ukrainians and pro-Maidan activists, supported by ultras from the local Tavria soccer club and locals opposed to the old ruling clique. At a rally in Simferopol on 26 February, 'Crimean politicians discussed the independence of the peninsula, not from Ukraine, but from the ... "Macedonians"'. One Crimean MP, Volodymyr Klychnykov, declared: 'The branch of "Macedonia" in Crimea is closed.'[37] Rather marvellously, at the rally the Crimean Tatars were chanting both 'Allahu Akbar!' and 'Glory to Ukraine!', the latter in Ukrainian. Twenty were injured in clashes and two were killed (one trampled, one a heart attack). The assembly therefore delayed a decision on holding a referendum to loosen ties with Kiev. The next day the local pro-Russian parties, backed by the Berkut and local anti-Maidan 'Self-Defence' militia, took over instead.

The Crimean Coup

It took only sixty men with Kalashnikovs to seize power in Crimea the next morning, at 4.20 a.m. on 27 February. The government was changed at gunpoint, a motion on secession was passed at gunpoint, and a motion organising a referendum to confirm the decision was passed at gunpoint. Militia accompanied MPs during toilet breaks. Communications were cut and mobile phones confiscated. Only a select few were allowed into the Crimean 'parliament' building anyway. Most Russian sources say sixty-four local MPs out of the hundred were present, and fifty-five voted for Aksyonov, a bare majority. Other sources including one local MP Nikolay Sumulidi say thirty-five or thirty-seven, below the quorum of forty.[38]

Most of the masked men seem to have been Berkut from Crimea and, reportedly, some other parts of Ukraine, plus some 'volunteers'. Soon they would form the core of a new expanded Crimean Berkut. Many were fast-tracked to receive Russian passports. Some got Russian medals. Russian political technology played a role in recruiting local civilian protestors in support, including 10,000 in Sevastopol alone. Elite mobile units from Russia, including GRU and probably FSB, may have helped organise the Berkut. According to one source, the operation was assisted by special forces from the Russian 45th Airborne Regiment.[39] Other sources maintain that Russian ships, recently returned from the Sochi Winter Olympics to Sevastopol, 'landed more than one thousand men on the peninsula' the day before, on 26 February.[40] Some forces had seemingly left the Black Sea Fleet base in Sevastopol, as the main Sevastopol–Simferopol road was blocked. Some Russian Cossacks from the Kuban allegedly arrived in Crimea in mid-February.[41]

The Military Operation

The Berkut-plus forces also seized an Interior Ministry arms store in Sevastopol, and blockaded the isthmus that connects Crimea with the rest of Ukraine. During the following night of 27/28 February, the full-scale Russian military invasion of Crimea began, starting with the seizure of Sevastopol and Simferopol airports.[42] Oleksandr Yanukovych owned Simferopol airport and simply let the Russians in. The soldiers – without insignia, personal documents or mobile phones – were dubbed the 'little green men' by local journalists; but they were actually from the 'military units of the Black Sea Fleet; from the "East" Chechen battalion, the 31st Guards brigade, the 22nd brigade of special GRU [Main Intelligence Directorate] troops, and other military units'. They were approximately 30,000 to 35,000 in number.[43] There were no conscripts, though possibly some private contractors. Best not to dwell on the pretence that local forces could assemble so many ships and guns so quickly. In April Putin admitted, 'of course, Russian servicemen did back up the Crimean self-defence forces'.[44]

State institutions simply swapped sides.[45] The 'Macedonians' had hollowed out the local elite. Moskal chronicled how the structures he used to command slid out of Kiev's grasp (he had a long career in the Interior Ministry and SBU, including two stints in Crimea): 'The directorates of the [Interior Ministry] and SBU in Crimea have distanced themselves from performing regular duties and are just watching how events unfold', Moskal wrote despairingly on Facebook on 28 February. 'I am particularly surprised at how the SBU in Crimea and Sevastopol and the military intelligence directorate in Sevastopol could simply sleepwalk through all this.' The new Crimean interior minister, Igor Arvutsky, simply handed over control. Crimea's border guards were equally passive, allowing coastguard vessels to be trapped in harbour.

But the initial military situation on the Ukrainian side was far from hopeless. Ukraine had 20,000 troops in Crimea, almost two-thirds of the Russian number. It was not until 11 March that Russian forces were properly stationed in defensive positions, including the deployment of twenty-two artillery units at the isthmus near Perekop and Grad missiles at Dzhankoy,[46] after reinforcements apparently crossed the Strait of Kerch the previous day.

But the Ukrainian forces did not get any orders. They should have concentrated in one place or evacuated in good order, as the interior troops managed to do. An Alpha unit was stationed within twenty kilometres of Simferopol, but was not ordered into action. As the veteran Crimean Tatar leader Mustafa Dzhemilev pointed out, 'they have mostly been trained to fight Crimean Tatars', not local Russians. He even speculated that if they had recruited any Crimean Tatars, those would have proved more loyal servants of the Ukrainian state.[47]

Ironically, it was Belarus's supposedly pro-Russian dictator Alyaksandr Lukashenka who spoke for many in a bizarre interview for Ukrainian TV:

By acting like that Ukraine's current government has virtually acknowledged that Crimea is not their territory. Why did they leave? Why did they pull out the military units? Why did they not stand up and fight if the land was theirs? In my darkest nightmares I cannot imagine the same thing happening to Belarus, God forbid . . . I would take up arms and fight on my own . . . I am the president of the country. People have elected me for this purpose . . . They were supposed to protect their land . . . Did your leaders do it? They did not. Did your military do it? They did not. You packed up your toys and left.[48]

The Ukrainian military had also suffered from decades of neglect and corruption. Yanukovych wasn't even the kind of tin-pot dictator who likes to review troops in uniform. He spent heavily on the interior troops and militia, and, for different reasons, on the customs service. But not on the armed forces, which took 1 per cent of GDP, compared to 5 per cent in Russia. Even going by official figures, internal defence spending was actually higher than national defence spending – $2.1 billion, over $1.9 billion – and the militia budget was topped up by oligarchs as the protests in Kiev got more serious. The Interior Ministry employed 358,000, of whom 33,000 were militia forces; the armed forces had only 139,000.[49] Russia had six years of military reform and expanding budgets after the war in Georgia in 2008; Ukraine had six years of military decline.

Yanukovych saw the Sevastopol base housing the Russian Black Sea Fleet as a business asset with only one buyer, and so he sold it in 2010 (agreeing to the longer lease until 2042, which even in 2010 was deemed treasonous by many). He also signed agreements with Russia to beef up his capacities for domestic control; these led to the Ukrainian security services filling up with actual Russians, at a pace that was accelerating in 2013. Oleksandr Yakymenko, Yanukovych's last head of the SBU, was born in Russian-speaking Estonia and worked in the Russian armed forces and Black Sea Fleet until 1998.[50] Yanukovych's last two defence ministers were Dmitriy Salamatin, a Russian-speaker from

Kazakhstan, and Pavlo Lebedyev, born in Russia, who had business interests in Crimea and with the local gas lobby. Vyacheslav Zanevsky, who was head of Yanukovych's presidential guard and an informal 'gatekeeper' to the president, was a Russian citizen.

Yanukovych's abandoning of NATO aspirations and declaration of non-bloc status in 2010 led to totally misguided threat perception and contingency planning. Most Ukrainian forces were left in the west of Ukraine, where Soviet planners had placed them, under the Western (Carpathian) and Southern (Odesa) Operational Commands.

None of this was preordained. In 2003, when Leonid Kuchma was president of Ukraine, the Russians had attempted to seize Tuzla Island in the Strait of Kerch between Russia and Crimea. Kuchma stood firm, there was no real response from Russian nationalists in Crimea, and Russia backed off.

The 'Referendum'

The Crimean Soviet initially scheduled a referendum for 25 May, but brought it forward to 16 March. It then claimed that 96.7 per cent voted for union with Russia on a turnout of 83.1 per cent. Russia was used to such dictator-majorities, but this one wasn't even ethnically plausible – 24 per cent of the population were Ukrainian and 13 per cent Crimean Tatar. A more important figure was the 25,000-plus Russian troops stationed in Crimea. Even one Russian report found that while the overwhelming majority of residents of Sevastopol voted to join Russia (turnout of 50–80 per cent), the turnout for all of Crimea was from 30 to 50 per cent, and only 50–60 per cent of those voted to join Russia.[51] A poll taken in the second week of February before the coup and the annexation showed 41 per cent in Crimea supporting union with Russia, which may have been just about right, given a certain radicalisation of opinion and the drastic change in the political climate before the 'referendum' a month later.[52] Although there were reports of a '15 per cent turnout' in some Crimean Tatar regions,[53] Mustafa Dzhemilev claimed that the Crimean Tatars' participation was minimal and that only 34 per cent voted in Crimea overall.[54]

Putin then surprised many by annexing Crimea within days. A treaty was signed on 18 March and ratified by the upper house of the Russian parliament on 21 March. After the war in Georgia, Russia had doubled the controversy by recognising Abkhazia and South Ossetia within days – but as independent states, not as new parts of the Russian Federation. And this was perhaps not a good precedent anyway, as so few had followed suit (none of the other post-Soviet states recognised Abkhazia and South Ossetia; only Nicaragua and Venezuela did so, plus a handful of money-seeking Pacific island states).

Transnistria has remained unrecognised for years, even by Russia. But this time Russia wanted to go the whole hog and avoid Crimea remaining in similar limbo. Putin had no desire to wait around for the rest of the world to recognise Crimean independence, and may also have calculated that key states would be more likely to adjust de facto, if not de jure, to annexation. For the time being at least, though, he ignored Transnistria's request to be annexed, too.

The Pirate Republic

In March, Prime Minister Medvedev unwisely said 'all of this is our headache now'.[55] Crimea could cost Russia $20 billion, even in the short term. In the breakaway Transnistrian region of Moldova, people had talked for years of the *Putinskaya nadbavka* – the 'Putin extra' for the budget and local salaries and pensions. Once the euphoria of annexation was over, the Russian press speculated that Crimea would cost $2.6 billion annually to top up the budget, and $2.9 billion for development, for at least four years.[56]

Given the popularity of its southern coast at least, 25 per cent of the population were pensioners. The local tourist industry relied on unofficial income – people let their flats out to visitors – but tourism collapsed in the summer of 2014, apart from some Russians keen to make a point. Some 70 per cent of tourists used to come from the rest of Ukraine.

Crimea would be the next mega-project after the Sochi Olympics. Without further invasion of southern Ukraine, Russia had no land link to Crimea. Estimates for the cost of the proposed new bridge over the Strait of Kerch rose from $1.5 billion to $6 billion or $7 billion within just four months.[57] Money would flow in, to make Crimea a showcase and to buy local loyalties. But criminals were already in charge; according to informal accounts, Aksyonov and his colleagues were given two years to enrich themselves, then they would be out. But with Ukrainian oligarchs trying to protect their fragile empires and new Russian oligarchs moving in,[58] the mixture was toxic. Sevastopol was predicted to become a new smuggling hub and Black Sea Fleet supply ships were exempt from customs inspection.

And Chechen oligarchs were first in the queue. The Chechenisation of Crimea was hardly the aim of the March referendum. Tolstoy and Chekhov would certainly not have approved. But Ruslan Baisarov, a billionaire close to Ramzan Kadyrov, the thuggish ruler of Chechnya, was Putin's unofficial envoy to control (the takeover of) business in Crimea, especially in tourism, with plans for a new resort for 40,000 tourists and the 'redevelopment' of the ancient Crimean Tatar capital at Bakhchisaray. In 2014 Baisarov took over the Stroygazkonsulting construction company, close to many of 'Putin's friends' (see Chapter 10). Russia immediately legalised gambling in Crimea, and the Chechens were supposed to be in charge. A radicalised Crimean Tatar move- ment next to a Las Vegas-style fleshpot run by the Chechens did not seem like a good idea.

The fear of sanctions had an effect on mainstream Russian business: major Russian banks were reluctant to set up, and Aeroflot was reluctant to fly. Unfortunately, that opened the door to Grozny Avia from Chechnya instead. There was also a Grozny battalion placed at Dzhankoy. All of this was both the ironic opposite and the fulfilment of Aksyonov's novel *Island of Crimea*.

The Crimean Tatars as Ukraine's Last Hope

There was no immediate descent into disorder, as there was in the Donbas. But Crimea was not safe if you were on the wrong side. In March, seven local Maidan and AutoMaidan activists were kidnapped, as documented in an early UNHCR Report.[59] But most vulnerable were the Crimean Tatars, the main organised political force on the peninsula. Conversely, too many voices in the West wrote off Crimea as 'lost' to Ukraine, because it was now 'controlled' by Russia. Russia did not yet control the 270,000 Crimean Tatars.

Ironically, the Crimean Tatars would have had expanded influence over a possible new Crimean government whose formation was prevented by the coup on 27 February. Their leaders then initially appealed for calm, and instructed supporters to stay at home, but called for a boycott of the referendum on 15 March. On 29 March the Qurultay voted for 'national self-determination'. According to the UNHCR, as of mid-April, 5,000 had fled Crimea, mainly Crimean Tatars.[60]

Putin's victory speech boasted of the benefits of multi-ethnic Russia:

> Crimea is a unique blend of different peoples' cultures and traditions. This
> makes it similar to Russia as a whole, where not a single ethnic group has
> been lost over the centuries. Russians and Ukrainians, Crimean Tatars and
> people of other ethnic groups have lived side by side in Crimea, retaining
> their own identity, traditions, languages and faith.
>
>   Crimean Tatars returned to their homeland. I believe we should make all
> the necessary political and legislative decisions to finalise the rehabilitation of
> Crimean Tatars, restore them in their rights and clear their good name.[61]

Putin issued a decree on 21 April to make Crimean Tatar an official language and create a 'national-cultural autonomy', while backtracking on initial talk of giving the Crimean Tatars a 20 per cent quota in local administration. On the same day, the Mejlis building was attacked. Aksyonov was, after all, a Russian nationalist.[62] ATR, the Crimean Tatar news channel, was threatened, and a law on land seizure was mooted (the Crimean Tatars have been at the centre of controversy over supposedly 'irregular' settlements – i.e. self-builds).[63] First the veteran Mejlis leader Mustafa Dzhemilev and then his successor, Refat Chubarov, were banned from entering Crimea. Ukrainian and Crimean Tatar language schools began converting to Russian. In June the Mejlis decided on a boycott of the local assembly elections called for 14 September.

Russia was building up a loyal faction to eventually displace the Mejlis, made up of the 'business group' around Remzi Ilyasov, those already co-opted under Yanukovych (the Popular Front, Milli Firka), a handful of ideological Eurasianists and *Kazany* led by Rustam Temirgalyev, the deputy prime minister, who is actually a Volga Tatar. In the debate after annexation, one faction within the Mejlis wanted to be more radical. But Temirgalyev argued that he could protect the Crimean Tatars from within government. This was maybe a bad call, as he resigned from that government in June. But at another Mejlis session in April delegates took a more moderate line, and Deputy Chair Lenur Islyamov, a businessman who ran ATR TV, was delegated to be deputy prime minister, and another Russophile, Zaur Smirnov, to chair the Crimean Nationalities Commission.

This could be justified in the longer term by resurrecting the pan-Turkic and 'Eurasian' ideology of the founder of the modern Crimean Tatar national movement, Ismail Gasprinsky (1851–1914), even arguing that the Crimean Tatars were natural Eurasians – the marriage of Slavs and Turks, the northern forests and the southern steppes.[64] Only the gerontocratic Mejlis leadership, according to Russian propaganda, supposedly held back the dialogue with Russia because it was addicted to Western grants.

But there was a real risk of the Crimean Tatars ending up stateless, if they refused to take up Russian citizenship (like the ethnic Georgians left behind in Abkhazia). Or else the peninsula could end up like Abkhazia, only nominally Muslim; or like Palestine, with a radical intifada.

Strategic Implications

Ukraine no longer has a navy. Its ships were based in one of Sevastopol's smaller bays before the annexation. Its one big ship, the frigate *Hetman Sahaidachny*, was involved in anti-piracy operations off the coast of Somalia at the time of the annexation, and managed to return to Odesa, its future role uncertain. Back in Crimea, the bays allocated to the old Ukrainian navy have been taken over. On 2 April Putin signed a law abandoning the 1997 Black Sea Fleet

Agreement (and the 2010 Kharkiv Agreement), according to which the size of its navy was regulated and any upgrade had to be approved by the Ukrainian authorities. The old complement is likely to be expanded by six new frigates, six submarines and several smaller ships. Most controversial, however, has been France's planned sale of two Mistral helicopter carriers to Russia for €1.2 billion, one of which is actually called the *Sevastopol*.

As Crimea is a peninsula, it has projection. For Russia, Crimea is the eastern outpost of Eurasia. It can dominate southern Ukraine as far as Odesa and even Moldova, which can be reached by Iskander missiles. Russia and Turkey will be the only major naval powers in the Black Sea, much as in the nineteenth century; though the US may try and build up Romania as a counter-balance (with implications for Moldova).[65] Romania and smaller states like Georgia have traditionally encouraged in 'extra-regional powers' to balance the big two. Ukraine once hoped to make that the big three, but will now have to settle for being one of the alliance of smaller states. That said, on the positive side the Black Sea Fleet and its black ops are no longer a factor in Ukrainian politics.

Conclusion

In June 2014, the Moscow newspaper *Novaya Gazeta* published a list of those who later privately received 'service awards' for their role in the annexation of Crimea, including 'prominent members of United Russia, bikers [the Night Wolves], soccer fans, nationalists and people with a rugged criminal past' – plus numerous high-level Kremlin officials.[66] In August, Putin's favourite biker gang, the Night Wolves, starred in a grotesque propaganda show in Simferopol, broadcast on primetime Russian TV, which featured Ukrainians goose-stepping in swastika formation. If that reminds you of Mel Brooks' 'Springtime for Hitler', it wasn't remotely funny.[67]

In many ways, Crimea was therefore unique. Only Putin knows if he had always planned to move on to east Ukraine after annexing Crimea. But the Crimean operation, in the format now dubbed 'hybrid war',[68] seemed in his terms to have been a success.

CHAPTER 7

The Eastern Imbroglio

The next act of the drama took place in eastern Ukraine – most acutely in the Donbas, in the far east of Ukraine next to Russia, but not adjoining Crimea (there is no land link between the two). It has the second-highest proportion of ethnic Russians (38.5 per cent in 2001) and Russian-speakers (72 per cent by 'native language') in Ukraine. But you wouldn't expect anybody to fight over the Donbas. It is full of the kind of smokestack industry – coal, steel and chemicals – that has largely disappeared in Western Europe, thanks to recession, the euro crisis and Chinese competition. Eastern Ukraine also has some of the worst pollution in Europe. Local industrial dinosaurs include steel mills built before 1917 and mines at depths of up to 1,200 metres with such old seams that the journey to work can be half an hour – that's half an hour *after* you have reached the mine and the bottom of the mine shaft. Illegal and highly dangerous open mines, little more than holes in the ground, are also big business. The number of deaths per year in mining has averaged 300 since 1991.

It was therefore hard to imagine Putin giving a second speech which eulogised the history of the Donbas in the same way as he eulogised 'eternal Russian' Crimea. Even in World War Two, the local defeats as the German armies swept east towards Stalingrad in 1942 were more notable than the region's reconquest in September 1943 (the great tank battles at Kursk were further north, over what is still, for the moment at least, the Russian border). Putin could maybe name-check the most famous resident of the Donbas, the champion miner Aleksey Stakhanov, whose coal-hewing exploits launched the original Stakhanovite movement in the 1930s (he allegedly cheated, with teams of helpers hidden underground). Donetsk also has a decent football team called Shakhtar Donetsk (*shakhtar* means 'miner'), but most of its star players were

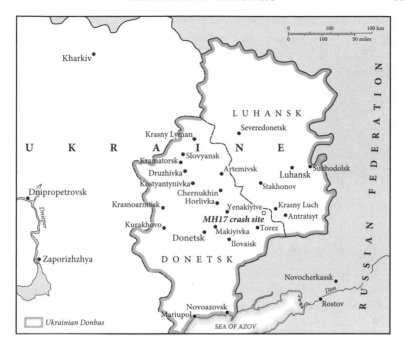

3 The Donbas region

second-string Brazilian imports. Bankrolled by Ukraine's richest man, local oligarch Rinat Akhmetov, the team won the UEFA Cup in 2009. Whether it would survive in a Russian league is another question. It certainly wouldn't have much competition in an independent league of the Donbas.

The big grimy towns of the Donbas have a multi-ethnic history, and are proud of their melting-pot labour culture. In Russian historiography, the land was largely terra incognita, apart from some early frontier settlement at its northern fringes, before its conquest under Catherine the Great in the late eighteenth century and its subsequent settlement and industrialisation. That said, this view is somewhat incompatible with the idea of 'eternal Russian' Crimea, which was conquered at the same time.

The Ukrainian view is that the region was part of the *dike pole* – the 'wild field' of the western end of the giant Eurasian steppe. It was not an addition to empire, but the margin of the Ukrainian heartland, regularly occupied by the Ukrainians and their ancestors over millennia in peaceful times, including the 'Ukrainian' Zaporizhzhian Cossacks after 1576. It was also, on and off, loosely controlled by the Crimean Tatar Khanate, which dominated the northern Black Sea coast east of the river Dnieper and as far as the river Don from the 1440s to 1783.

Putin increasingly referred to the region as part of 'New Russia', a tsarist term for the whole of eastern and southern Ukraine. Or sometimes just 'South Russia': Putin's big set-piece speech after the annexation of Crimea on 18 March 2014 repeated the point about Khrushchev's 'gift' in 1954, but said similar things about the whole of south-east Ukraine:

> After the revolution, the Bolsheviks, for a number of reasons – may God judge them – added large sections of the historical South of Russia to the Republic of Ukraine. This was done with no consideration for the ethnic make-up of the population, and today these areas form the southeast of Ukraine.[1]

Most explicitly, during his annual phone-in in April 2014, Putin said:

> what was called Novorossiya (New Russia) back in the tsarist days – Kharkov, Lugansk, Donetsk, Kherson, Nikolayev and Odessa – were not part of Ukraine back then. These territories were given to Ukraine in the 1920s by the Soviet government. Why? Who knows. They were won by Potyomkin and Catherine the Great in a series of well-known wars. The centre of that territory was Novorossiysk [actually almost 400 miles south-east of Donetsk], so the region is called Novorossiya. Russia lost these territories for various reasons, but the people remained.[2]

This was bad history. 'Novorossiya' (New Russia) was an invented label for a new set of Imperial Russian territories in the nineteenth century, not a twenty-first century reality. Crimea had some minority Russian nationalism – maybe close to 40 per cent – but certainly not the 97 per cent claimed in the 'referendum'; but east and south Ukraine was much more of a mixture, defined in fact by its multiple identities and creolic mixture (which were good for blurring lines of confrontation, but bad for organising civil society). Ironically, the region's Kremlin backers learned the same lesson when they started trying to set up their own movement in the Donbas. Kharkiv and Dnipropetrovsk have histories very different from the Donbas. Much of the rural edges of the south and east were historically linked to the fluid borders of central Ukraine. The industrial towns of the Donbas are still surrounded by Ukrainian countryside. The port of Odesa at the other end of 'New Russia' was certainly new, but had a highly specific local identity, having been founded only in 1794.

The Geopolitics of the Donbas

The Donbas was not Crimea. It traditionally stood alone. The region had little in the way of overseeing state authority until the very late tsarist era. There was both a strong local anarchist streak (ironically the Ukrainian Cossack myth turned in on itself) and a readiness to acquiesce to power exercised from outside if sufficiently strong – but little tradition of public politics in between. Civil society was almost non-existent, and so was a culture of compromise; instead there was an intense informal culture of 'looking after one's own' and of 'winner takes all'. The population was often transient, and life was tough; criminal gangs with exotic names like the Malakhovs and Sibryakovs were a feature of Donbas life from the very beginning.[3]

The Donbas was proudly alone. But the people's pride also had a flip side: a phobia that everyone else was out to get them. According to one poll taken in 2013, only 13.2 per cent in the east had ever been to the West (EU, USA or Canada), compared to 32.8 per cent in west Ukraine and a national average of 20.6 per cent. Mind you, only 45.3 per cent in east Ukraine had ever been elsewhere in the former USSR.[4]

But the Donbas also has its internal differences, which was one reason why the separatist networks that were set up in 2014 were so complicated. It is formally divided into two oblasts anyway: Donetsk and Luhansk. Viktor Yanukovych was from the central coal-mining belt, where he grew up a teenage tearaway in the 1960s. Further north were the big industrial towns, like Slovyansk and Kramatorsk in Donetsk, or Stakhanov and Severodonetsk in Luhansk. They had more of a technical intelligentsia than the big coal towns, though for all the locals' residual fondness for Soviet culture the Donbas as a whole never had a classic proletariat: settlements grew up piecemeal and were often semi-rural, and the humanist intelligentsia were few and far between.[5] Slovyansk is no longer the heart of the Donbas, but it was the heart of the separatist movement in 2014. It is actually the oldest town in the region, having been founded in 1645 by Imperial Russian interests to extract local rock salt. The coastal area in the south is surprisingly empty, the town of Mariupol being the only major settlement. The north of Luhansk and the far north of Donetsk, above the town of Krasny Lyman, are agricultural and relatively Ukrainian (even Ukrainian-speaking), part of the historical Cossack lands of 'Slobidska Ukraine', centred on neighbouring Kharkiv. In a similar fashion, the western parts of Donetsk are also rural and similar to neighbouring Dnipropetrovsk.

The Donbas, like Crimea, was also divided in the 1990s by bitter gang wars, often ethnically based. The winners were the most violent, including some of Ukraine's most powerful men under President Yanukovych, and including Yanukovych himself. The gangsters of Tatar origin, led by Alik the Greek, were the original victors. Rinat Akhmetov was his protégé: he grew up controlling local markets, but inherited Alik's empire after the latter was spectacularly murdered, along with six of his bodyguards, by a bomb at Shakhtar Donetsk football stadium in 1995. Yanukovych grew up a petty criminal, but then seems to have fallen in with more serious criminals in jail and with the KGB outside. This allowed him to move up in local administration through Communist Party ranks, where he is credited with organising the key scheme to supply local business with cheap coal and coke at the expense of the state. By the late 1990s, Akhmetov and Yanukovych had forged a natural partnership of business and political muscle. Local mafia groups still existed, but now worked for them.

Burden or Jewel?

The Donbas liked to depict itself as the engine-room of first the Soviet and then the Ukrainian economy; others see it as an outdated industrial behemoth to be dropped as soon as possible. As of the last (albeit way out-of-date) official census in 2001, Donetsk and Luhansk had a population of 7.4 million, which was 15.2 per cent of the Ukrainian total.[6] But the locals were not that loyal to their region: the population had fallen by 1.3 million by 2010 – a much faster rate than for Ukraine as a whole, indicating out-migration more than simple poor public health; thus its share of the overall population had dropped to 13.4 per cent.[7] As of 2011, the Donbas produced $30 billion of Ukraine's then $181 billion GDP, or 16.6 per cent – punching slightly above its declining demographic weight, but not enough to make the region the economic powerhouse that locals claim. And it needed 20 per cent of Ukraine's gas consumption to get that far. A 22 per cent share of Ukrainian exports hardly suggested that it was over-performing either. Moreover, the entire economic model of the Donbas depends on subsidies to local oligarchs that are carried by the Ukrainian state – at least $1.5 billion a year.[8] Most tellingly of all, the Donbas only contributed 7.1 per cent of the national Ukrainian budget before the unrest. Kiev quite clearly subsidised the east, not the other way around.[9]

The other aspect was dependence on Russia. The Donbas – or to be more exact, the local steel, mining and chemical industries – needed Russian gas. On the other hand, the Russian boycotts that began in the summer of 2013, and the crisis itself, changed trade patterns: in the first quarter of 2014, the percentage of Ukraine's trade with the EU and Turkey was up from 28 per cent to 41 per cent, compared to the first quarter of 2012. The share going to the Customs Union three of Russia, Belarus and Kazakhstan was down from 34 per cent to 23 per cent. The decline of Russia was also true in the Donbas: 43 per cent of Donetsk exports went to the EU and Turkey, 17 per cent to the Customs Union three; for Luhansk it was 51 per cent versus 39 per cent (Donetsk sold more to other markets).[10] That was not a typical quarter-year, of course. Local heavy industry at least was still highly dependent on Russian orders. Local railway freight car manufacturers, for example, almost shut down in late 2013.

When the crisis began and turned the Donbas into what one Ukrainian writer called a 'criminal Mordor',[11] there were some intellectual voices who openly expressed the heretical thought that maybe Ukraine would be better off without the region; possibly economically, but definitely politically, without its political culture corrupting government in Kiev. The idea that the Donbas should be allowed to vote on whether to stay or go and leave the rest of Ukraine in peace was actually first expressed by the writer Yuriy Andrukhovych back in 2010.[12] Now he was joined by other intellectuals,[13] whose ideas began filtering through social media in Kiev where there was also some criticism of the apathy and criminality of the east. But, as Ukraine was fighting for the Donbas at the time, such sentiments remained subdued. They were certainly taboo for politicians.

'New Russia'

In Crimea, Sergey Aksyonov represented a marginal political party. His brand of Russian nationalism had been more of a force in the 1990s, but in the 2010 elections won only 4 per cent of the vote. Yet, low as that was, it was actually more than his counterparts in the Donbas. A motley crew of activists belonged to tiny groups that were technically registered as Ukrainian parties, such as For a United Rus (later the Russian Bloc), or branches of parties from Russia, like Russian National Unity or the National Bolshevik Party; but none had anything resembling electoral success. The best result any had ever managed was in the 1998 Ukrainian elections, when something called the Social-Liberal Union (SLOn, which means 'elephant') won a massive 0.9 per cent in Ukraine as a whole, but 0.5 per cent in Donetsk. In 2012, the Russian Bloc won only 0.4 per cent in Donetsk, or the impressive total of 7,937 votes.

Even this tiny number were divided: some wanted to join Greater Russia, some were federalists, and others were localists. Few were, in reality, inspired by their most prominent supporter in Russia, Aleksandr Dugin and his mystical Eurasianism.[14] In 2014, Dugin became obsessed with the idea that a new and 'more pure' Russia would be reborn in 'New Russia'. One of his websites (rossia3.ru) was full of claims such as, 'New Russia creates new personalities', 'New Russia – the new name of Russia's Resurrection', 'New Russia as a challenge to all levels of the oligarchy'. Unfortunately, this was absurd. Locals may not have liked the purist version of Ukrainian nationalism that they claimed to see coming out of west Ukraine, but they weren't 'new' or 'pure' Russians either. Most were happy with their fuzzy identities: many locals spoke both languages; they had mixed marriages – many would therefore even reject the concept of 'mixed'. The Ukrainian critic Mykola Ryabchuk identified a local phenomenon he called 'it's-all-the-same-ism' – Russian and Ukrainian culture overlapped, or were compatible, or were just 'the same'. A local class-based identity as 'ordinary workers' made more sense to many, especially as that covered almost everybody, the local oligarchic class being rather small.

In Crimea, Aksyonov and his small band of colleagues could at least hope to revive some dormant pro-Russian sentiment. But there was no mass welcome for Russian activists in eastern or southern Ukraine. There was no handing out of flowers; no celebration, as in Sevastopol. One reason was that the Donbas didn't have much history before 1917. The idea of historical legitimacy for a separatist movement based in the short-lived Donetsk-Kryvy-Rih Republic of 1918 had little resonance, as it only lasted a month; though that did not stop local historian Vladimir Kornilov republishing his book on the subject,[15] and its black-blue-red flag occasionally appeared at demonstrations.

According to a massive opinion poll conducted throughout eastern and southern Ukraine in April 2014, a mere 15.4 per cent as a whole supported separatism and union with Russia (7.1 per cent definitely; 8.3 per cent more or less). The figure was higher but still only 27.5 per cent in Donetsk and 30.3 per cent in Luhansk (11.9 per cent and 13.2 per cent definitely). The same survey demolished the myth of *Novorossiya*, of a united arc of territory called the 'south-east'. The south and Dnipropetrovsk were much more loyal to Kiev. There was a certain amount of duality throughout the east and south; but only in the Donbas did the plague-on-all-their-houses spirit prevail. Overall only 31 per cent thought the new acting President Turchynov was fully or more-or-less legitimate, but the figure was a mere 14 per cent in Donetsk and 8 per cent in Luhansk. A larger number, 43 per cent, thought the national parliament was legitimate, as it still contained MPs that the south and east had voted for in 2012; but again that fell to 32 per cent in Donetsk. On the other hand, only 20 per cent thought Yanukovych was still the legitimate president (only 10 per cent 'fully'), and that figure was not much higher in Donetsk – 33 per cent in total, of whom 19 per cent said 'fully'.[16]

Neither set of figures was overwhelming. Most people were either agnostic or indifferent to all. A similar duality emerged from a question about what happened on the Maidan: 42 per cent in the south and east backed the statement that it was a 'citizens' protest against corruption and the arbitrary dictatorship of Yanukovych'; while 46 per cent saw the events as an 'armed coup d'état, organised by the opposition with the help of the West' (both pretty leading questions). In Donetsk, the figures for the two statements were 20 per cent and 70 per cent, respectively, which showed a worrying degree of alienation from the new authorities in Kiev.[17]

Anti-Fascism

Putin initially claimed implausibly that Russians and Russian-speakers were subject to constant discrimination in east Ukraine:

Time and time again attempts were made to deprive Russians of their historical memory, even of their language and to subject them to forced assimilation. Moreover, Russians, just as other citizens of Ukraine, are suffering from the constant political and state crisis that has been rocking the country for over 20 years.[18]

This was chimerical. So 'anti-fascist' propaganda suddenly went into overdrive instead. Right Sector moved part of its operations to Dnipropetrovsk at the end of April; but early reports of Right Sector activity in east Ukraine seem to have been bravado or Russian propaganda. According to the well-informed military blogger Dmitriy Tymchuk in early May, his network of analysts 'hasn't seen evidence of pro-Ukrainian partisan activity'.[19]

In reality, there was a different dynamic at work. The Soviet narrative of 'anti-fascism' was first revived during the 2004 presidential election and the subsequent Orange Revolution, when the seemingly pro-Western Viktor Yushchenko was depicted as somehow both 'Bushchenko' – a stooge of US President George Bush – and a little Hitler, seeking to revive the anti-Soviet Ukrainian nationalism of 1941.[20] The 'fascist threat' advancing eastwards was even more ubiquitous in 2014, via the classic elisions and sophistry of Soviet historiography.[21] The 'Great Patriotic War' started in 1941, not 1939: Nazism was an existential threat because of its threat to Russia/the USSR after 1941, not because of its previous crimes. Moreover, this threat was the primary, sometimes almost the *only* negative feature of fascism, not the Holocaust (Nazism and fascism are interchangeable terms). In the modern 'anti-fascist' narrative, 'fascism' has long escaped the geographical bonds of Germany and Italy; the label applies to anybody who embodies the same existential threat. So all Ukrainian nationalists are fascists by definition.

Even the EU and the US, or NATO, or the West in general, are 'fascistic'. As Sergey Glazyev, Vladimir Putin's adviser on Eurasian integration, put it, bizarrely conflating so many factors, 'the main engine of modern euro-fascism is euro-bureaucracy directed from Washington'.[22] This is all classic political technology, because at a distance it makes no sense whatsoever. But close up, propaganda like the notorious poster in Crimea showing the swastika superimposed on the peninsula was crudely effective so long as it was embedded in a bigger narrative, or bigger lie. The first thing that the Russians did after the annexation of Crimea was create a monopoly for Russian TV. As fortunes ebbed and flowed in the Donbas, control of TV switching back and forth was almost as important as the changes in territorial control.

In fact, it was the pro-Russian side that looked more like real fascists.[23] Russian National Unity, one of the Russian nationalist organisations active among the east Ukrainian separatists, managed to combine in its logo both Soviet and recently invented 'anti-fascist' imagery (mainly the orange and black ribbon of St George) *and* a modified swastika. This was either pitch-perfect post-modernism or plain crazy.

The 'Family'

There seem to have been four overlapping 'projects' that kicked off the trouble in the Donbas. First, the Yanukovych 'Family', particularly the deposed president's elder son Oleksandr, directed operations on its home turf. Then Russia sent in a new version of the 'little green men', who organised a motley band of local activists and criminals. Thirdly, some of the key players in the annexation of Crimea wanted to repeat their success in the Donbas. And finally local oligarchs like Rinat Akhmetov initially bet on their own puppet groups to increase their bargaining power with Kiev – which did not turn out well.

The Yanukovych network had been built up over many years. The entire local administrative and police system owed its primary loyalty to the 'Family'. It was strongest in the triangle north-east of Donetsk city: Yanukovych's home town of Yenakiyeve, plus Makiyivka and Horlivka. Other parts of the clan ran other cities: former Prime Minister Azarov's son was big in Slovyansk; former Prosecutor General Pshonka ran Kramatorsk. They intersected with criminal groups like the Sarkisian gang.[24] Russian money also allegedly came via Viktor Medvedchuk, President Kuchma's former chief of staff, now Russia's most reliable ally in Ukraine, to strengthen these networks in the immediate run-up to the Uprising in Kiev.[25]

The Yanukovyches, father and son, fled Kiev with massive amounts of money. No one knows how much. Loose talk in Ukraine of '$30 billion' or more defied credibility, as that would have meant several trainloads of cash, but they also had access to funds secreted abroad. And Russia rather thought they should spend their wealth in return for protection. Viktor Yanukovych's new bolthole in the chic village of Barvikha, on the edge of Moscow, reportedly cost $52 million, and is almost as kitsch as Mezhyhirya – more like a castle than a pied-à-terre. But at least Yanukovych can share the company of fellow refugees: his near neighbours include the former president of Kyrgyzstan, the deposed boss of Adjara (a former separatist region in Georgia) and part of Slobodan Milošević's family.

Yanukovych's son stayed down south, probably just over the Russian border in Rostov. There was also money coming from other Ukrainian oligarchs with bases in the Donbas: Yuriy Ivanyushchenko, Serhiy Yefremov and Oleh Tsaryov, who bizarrely at one point actually stood in Ukraine's presidential election.[26]

Oleksandr Yanukovych channelled in most of the initial money. He was also responsible for intimidating local networks to cooperate with the separatists. The 'Family' had *kompromat* on everybody and could threaten to hand it over to the security services if they did not cooperate. All of Oleksandr's enterprises – like MAKO (his main holding company: construction, trading, coal, energy) and the All-Ukrainian Development Bank (VBR) – carried on working in Donetsk. Money was handed out through the back door. According to local activists, 'in the local banks of VBR and Sberbank people collected money in huge plastic bags; some of MAKO's managers organised the first demonstrations and assaults on buildings; they were seen on Lenin Square [the site of the main demonstrations in Donetsk] in March/April'.[27]

The whole militia was appointed by Oleksandr Yanukovych. The Donetsk Berkut 'promised to fight to clear their reputation, but then defected to the enemy'.[28] Local police were inactive or else simply switched sides. They were appointed to guard the 'Family', not to uphold the law. The Donetsk militia had about a thousand men who stood by. Their head was Konstantin Pozhyvanov, who used to work for Akhmetov. One Ukrainian military analyst claimed 'the local Interior Ministry heads handed over their buildings and offices (allegedly "captured") to the separatists for a fair amount. Bargaining started at $100,000' per building.[29]

The police also had lists of criminals whom they had exploited and armed to attack pro-Maidan activists both locally and in Kiev.[30] Local mafia boss Armen Sarkisian from Horlivka organised the attacks by *titushki* on earlier Euromaidan rallies in Donetsk in January and February,[31] and later brought his militants to Kiev. Media reports suggest that they killed several protestors in the capital, including six near St Michael's Square on the night of 18/19 February – one of them the journalist Vyacheslav Veremiy.[32] Then they returned to the Donbas, where 'It is said that these guys received two cars of brand new weapons'.[33]

Now that the 'Family' was so exalted, however, even in exile, it mainly recruited mafia guys indirectly:

The Family is not as closely connected with mafia structures, as with the police in every region – from regional divisions and above. The police themselves lead the bandits. The Family has influence on the border police, customs and tax. There is a 'platform' for the transfer from cashless circulation into cash, protected by the SBU. Direct contact is with mayors, prosecutors, directors of enterprises. All these people are 'on the hook' of the Family. So [mobilisation] is not done through criminals but through officials and security forces.[34]

The Locals

But the 'Family' needed foot soldiers, even if it had to pay them. The first attempt to seize power – when Pavel Gubarev, a minor local loudmouth who allegedly worked as a costumed *Ded Moroz* ('Grandfather Frost', or basically the Slavic Santa Claus) was elected 'people's mayor' on 1 March by a crowd in the centre of Donetsk (a pale imitation of the Kiev Maidan) – did not have the desired effect of sparking some kind of popular uprising: 'By declaring himself governor, Gubarev doomed his pro-Russian rebellion to failure. Instead of the promised 50 thousand people the following day, there were only around 5 thousand.'[35] Gubarev was arrested five days later. He had links with Russian National Unity, but the far right was simply too marginal in the Donbas.[36] The first separatist leaders were an ugly mixture of criminals, far-right radicals and nobodies.[37] Denis Pushilin, who later claimed to be the head of state of the 'Donetsk People's Republic', worked for the notorious tawdry pyramid scheme MMM. One commentator characterised the whole movement unhelpfully as 'lumpens against Ukraine'.[38]

'Cloning' the Kiev protests cut both ways. Simply electing a 'people's mayor' from among a few hundred people at a public meeting was not what happened in Kiev and risked looking ridiculous. Leverage didn't work the same way as in Crimea. Thirty armed men could not swing the whole of southern and eastern Ukraine. The general population was harder to shift, and the elites had more options and were not about to be ordered around by the likes of Gubarev. The whole operation was also the wrong way round: a hollowed-out elite in Crimea was bounced by the coup, followed quickly by the 'referendum' and annexation; in the Donbas, the elite were supposed to do the groundwork to make an eventual vote possible. So-called 'Putin tourists', Russians bussed in from over the border, were used to bolster numbers at street rallies. This also didn't work, so Russia decided on special operations instead.

Nor was there any general uprising elsewhere in southern and eastern Ukraine. Without the influence of the 'Family', the reality was that in just a week after the Uprising in Kiev, local elites had made their peace with the new authorities. In Kharkiv the separatist movement dried up once local politicians, and local mafia, decided to cut off the money flow.[39] In Dnipropetrovsk the leading oligarch Ihor Kolomoisky imposed order and marginalised former

Party of Regions leaders like Dmytro Kolesnikov and Oleksandr Vilkul (linked to Akhmetov), who had suppressed local protests in support of the Maidan in January.[40] Kolomoisky, or his deputies, also seemed increasingly to act as a patron for Right Sector.[41]

In Odesa there was tragedy on 2 May, when a pro-Ukrainian demonstration was attacked by 'anti-Maidan' forces, including, once again, local thugs. But this time, the tables were somehow turned and the anti-Maidan group found itself in the minority. Six were killed in street fighting, with the police largely shielding the anti-Maidan forces until they fled into the local trade union building, where fire then killed most of the further forty-two who died. Anti-Maidan detainees were released after another demonstration two days later.[42] Rival local mafia groups were involved with some of the demonstrators, fighting to control the city's three ports, the 'seven mile market' (Ukraine's biggest market, but also a centre for money laundering) and the oil refinery, which used to belong to the 'Family's' youthful front-man Serhiy Kurchenko (it now belonged to the Russian bank VTB).

Russia's Role

On 26 February, Putin announced 'exercises' on the Ukrainian border. On 1 March, the Russian parliament voted to approve any use of military force in Ukraine. On 13 March, earlier reports of a military build-up were confirmed, though exact numbers never were, for obvious reasons. NATO and American sources estimated 40,000 to 50,000 by the end of March.

The troops served many purposes. In 'hybrid war', the potential use of conventional forces is as important as their actual use. The troops leveraged the power of the rebels in the Donbas, and Ukraine was restrained from using too much force against them for fear of triggering an actual invasion. The West was diverted into constantly speculating about what Putin might do next, rather than helping Ukraine deal with the situation on the ground. And too many people were prepared constantly to shift the 'red line' as Putin kept taking steps forward. Deterring an actual invasion was seen as an actual success, as if Russia had not already invaded de facto.

The second attempt to take power after the 'people's mayor' fiasco began with the seizure of administrative buildings in the Donbas on 6 April. As usual, a stronger reaction from Kiev might have slowed things down, but none came and police and SBU buildings were taken on 12 April. Russia had called up reinforcements. By mid-April, 'the situation on the ground [was now] mostly handled by people with ties to the Family, as well as instructors from Russia'.[43] The head of the self-proclaimed Donetsk People's Republic told a press conference that 'a "single command" had prepared the pro-Russian operations in Crimea and in other parts of Eastern Ukraine'[44] – at this stage at least.

The two key incomers from Crimea were the 'political technologist' Aleksandr Boroday,[45] and the paramilitary organiser Igor Strelkov (his real name was Girkin; the nickname Strelkov has its roots in the word *strelok*, meaning 'shooter').[46] 'Together with other members of the GRU, stationed in the Crimea, a total of thirty people on April 8 led by Strelkov took the Kerch crossing to Rostov-on-Don, where the intelligence centre was situated.'[47] GRU agents were providing coordination in command and control roles. There were also consultations in Moscow, before Strelkov crossed the border to Slovyansk on 12 April, where he seized the city council building with twenty men.[48]

So again only a hard core began the protests, but others got sucked in, including local radicals whom Russia had been cultivating for years, some genuine enthusiasts, and volunteers attracted by a going rate advertised on social media of $300 to $500 a day. 'The core group was trained by Russian military instructors, mostly in Krasnodar in the Kuban.'[49] The operation worked a bit like English football riots, with a hard core of professional hooli- gans, plus those prepared to join in. The pattern became so well established that wage rates were set: $500 for a 'storm'; 500 UAH for standing at a demon- stration; 200 UAH for women who blocked vehicles.[50]

But increasingly, the region filled up with Russian nationalist volunteers direct from Russia. It would be hard to imagine a bigger irony than the fact that many of these had been Putin's opponents during the demonstrations in 2011– 12, and during the earlier anti-migrant 'Russian Marches' and rioting on the Manezh Square in Moscow in 2010. Perhaps it was like the Saudis exporting their radical troublemakers, or the USSR its most militant internationalists during the Spanish Civil War. Many were recruited by Orthodox oligarchs like Malofeev or by the Russian security services.

Akhmetov's Dangerous Game

Ukraine's richest men were playing a duplicitous game both in Kiev and in the regions to try and preserve their influence. The richest of them all, Rinat Akhmetov, had always thrived with less oversight, bleeding subsidies from the state and not paying taxes. He wanted to keep that going, and put pressure on Kiev to back off from his empire; but he probably didn't really want an inde- pendent or Russian Donbas either, as nobody would then pay his bills.

Denis Pushilin and his 'Donetsk People's Republic' was allegedly Akhmetov's puppet project.[51] Gubarev claimed that 'two-thirds' of activists were initially paid by Akhmetov.[52] It was also claimed that Akhmetov made a secret visit to

Moscow in late March or early April to see Putin.[53] He was reportedly interested in Russian bank loans and in protecting his various businesses in Crimea. In 2013, Akhmetov's steel company Metinvest had taken on a new finance manager, previously linked to Gennadiy Timchenko, one of 'Putin's friends'.[54] Others sold themselves more clearly to Russia: Akhemtov's rival oligarch Oleksandr Yefremov, the former governor of Luhansk, was a more frequent visitor to Moscow, setting himself up as Russia's friend from the very beginning. Yefremov went back to Luhansk to stir up trouble as early as 20 February.[55]

One journalist characterised the leaders of the Donetsk People's Republic as 'sitting for a month in the building they had seized in downtown Donetsk; they do not shoot at anybody (they are either lightly armed or not armed at all), they put up banners, organise rallies, and in general do not threaten anyone with anything, but create a convincing picture of Donetsk separatism'.[56]

But others wanted more than a 'convincing picture'. By the time Akhmetov woke up to the danger, he had done untold damage to his long-term interests. By May, his home in Donetsk, mysteriously built in the middle of public botanical gardens, was under siege. For the 'King of the Donbas', this was an unprecedented loss of face, after trying so hard to protect his own empire from challenge from below and from other oligarchs, this is precisely what he now achieved.

Akhmetov's miscalculation was also due to the fact that playing with separatism had worked in 2004 – it had been enough to convince a timid Yushchenko to strike a feeble bargain to become president. Akhmetov presumably thought he could do the same thing again. But this time, the separatism was real, or at least grew increasingly so. Paradoxically, however, the originally stage-managed rebellion also empowered the previously powerless. The Donbas had been run by communists, mafiosi and oligarchs – with the difference being mainly one generation growing into the other. Now there was a strong element of a peasants' revolt – the revenge of the ordinary folk to whom the Donbas was supposed to belong.

The Passive-Aggressive Donbas

The Donbas leaders copied the Crimean scenario by announcing their own 'referendum' for 11 May. Initially the task seemed impossible: the Donbas was contested territory. The separatists controlled an archipelago of towns and roads, but not the region as a whole. The city of Slovyansk was the first centre of operations, for three reasons. First, 'Family' control was stronger there than in the regional capital of Donetsk, home to networks controlled by Akhmetov. Second, Slovyansk was actually a lake resort: it was one of the oldest settlements in the region, and it sat on the main road from Kharkiv to Rostov. Now Russia was trying to do the same as it did in Georgia in 2008, when it cut the main east–west highway. Third, it was easier than taking Donetsk, a city of almost a million people. The hope seemed to have been that once a small base was established, the rest of the region would follow, either voluntarily or once suitably 'encouraged'. While the hard power of guns and fighters was based in Slovyansk and Kramatorsk, the 'soft power' of political technology – agents provocateurs, Putin's tourists and paid demonstrators – would leverage the bigger cities. Donetsk, home to the rival 'Donetsk People's Republic', was initially almost quiet.

The referendum could only go ahead if the local authorities in other areas allowed general voting. This they did, once again under pressure from the 'Family', showing that a combination of intimidation, alienation and indifference might allow the radical minority to get what it wanted.

Another factor was the plasticity of local public opinion. According to the April 2014 opinion poll quoted above, only 27.5 per cent in Donetsk backed union with Russia (11.9 per cent definitely). But even this minority did not fully back the separatists: only 12 per cent in the east and south, with 18 per cent in Donetsk, supported the 'actions of those who seized local government buildings with arms in your region'. Only 33 per cent thought Russia was 'justly defending the rights of Russian-speaking citizens in the south-east', but that figure rose to 47 per cent in Donetsk. A majority of 54.1 per cent thought Russia was 'unlawfully interfering in the internal affairs of Ukraine' – 32.9 per cent in Donetsk.[57] Even by July, local support for separatism had only gone up to 37 per cent.[58]

On the other hand, certain events seem to have radicalised opinion in the middle ground to an undetermined extent, particularly the deaths in Odesa on 2 May, and on 16–17 April and 9 May in Mariupol, southern Donetsk. On the latter occasion, the celebration of Soviet Victory Day, at least twenty people were killed when security forces allegedly overreacted to an attack on a local police station. Many locals seem to have sided with the rebels. One of Russian propaganda's more effective lines was claiming the Ukrainian police and army were running a *karatelnaya operatsiya* ('punitive operation') – a phrase commonly used in Soviet times to describe the bloody acts of war-time Ukrainian partisans.

When the two local 'referendums' were held on 11 May, however, Donetsk separatist leaders asserted that 89 per cent had backed 'independence' (the ballot used the Russian word *samostoyatelnost*, which actually means 'standing on one's own') on a 75 per cent turnout. The vote in Luhansk was supposedly a 96 per cent 'yes' on an identical 75 per cent turnout. Most opponents stayed at home, so turnout was the more significant figure. Acting Ukrainian President Turchynov claimed that voting was only 30 per cent in Donetsk, and 24 per cent in Luhansk.[59]

One leaked phone conversation between Aleksandr Barkashov, the leader of the Russian National Unity party, with local activist Dmitry Boitsov says a lot about how democratic the referendums actually were:

> Boitsov: If we do not get support, if Russia does not bring its troops . . . we will be fucked up. I am cancelling the referendum set for the 11th, because it can't be held. We can't conduct it lawfully as long as those cocksuckers are here.
>
> Barkashov: Dima, there is no way that you cancel it, it will mean you got scared.
>
> Boitsov: No, we are not scared at all. We simply can't hold it. We're not ready.
>
> Barkashov: Dima, just flog whatever you want. Write something like 99% down. Are you going to walk around and collect papers? Are you fucking insane?! Forget it, fuck them all.
>
> Boitsov: Got it.
>
> Barkashov: Write that 99% . . . well not 99%. Let's say 89% voted for the Donetsk Republic. And that's it. Fucking shit![60]

The official declared result in the referendum was 89 per cent.

But, if it wasn't for the passive-aggressive Donbas, the vote wouldn't have taken place at all. Putin's strategy may have been to build up the separatists' authority to force Kiev to negotiate with them. But the local population was allowing the tail to wag the dog.

Boyars versus Otamans

The separatists did not have much of a longer-term plan of action, other than hoping that Russian troops would be brought in. Meanwhile, parts of eastern and southern Ukraine seemed to be heading back to the medieval era, increasingly dominated by local barons (in Russian, *boyars*). An initial plan promoted by oligarch Ihor Kolomoisky had been to make himself and three other oligarchs local governors: Viktor Pinchuk refused to run Odesa or Zaporizhzhya; Akhmetov declined the post in Donetsk, which went to another steel magnate, Serhiy Taruta, who struggled to make any impact; so Kolomoisky himself ended up the most powerful of all. His post in Dnipropetrovsk was the geographical key to preventing the revolt from spreading, and his early successes gave him ever greater license. The local militia were under his control, as were some of those fighting further east. He posed as general protector of the east, supposedly even offering a bounty for intelligence on pro-Russian separatists or for the surrender of weapons. Posters offering '$10,000s for a Moskal' (a pejorative term for a Russian), supposedly sponsored by his Privatbank, were reportedly faked.[61] Kolomoisky also installed his ally Ihor Palitsya as the new governor of Odesa, and Andriy Verevsky (a 'minigarch' – his Kernel company sells sunflower oil) in Poltava. Kolomoisky aggressively pursued his interests in Kiev (see Chapter 8) and seemed to be campaigning against Akhmetov, too – so some of the information against the latter may have been black propaganda.

This was a classic cycle in Russian history: the boyars were strong when the tsar was weak. An alternative metaphor comes from Ukrainian history after the Revolution in 1917. Around that time there were various governments in Kiev, but by 1919 they had little authority in the east and south, where a unique local mixture of warlordism, anarchism and Cossack traditions of self-government created scores of rival leaders – called *hetmany* or *otamany* – whose local forces often simply defended local towns or villages from outsiders. The area around Kherson, south of Dnipropetrovsk, even had a self-contradictory 'anarchist government' under Nestor Makhno.

By mid-May 2014, the Donbas was descending into similar chaos and threatening to become like Chechnya in the early 1990s, with different factions taking hostages and raiding neighbours. Different towns had different leaders; different factions even controlled different streets. In one building it was 'the fifth floor versus the fourth floor'.[62]

Most forces were initially in Slovyansk, where, according to Ukrainian sources, they were backed by a hundred Russian special forces, as of the middle of May.[63] Slovyansk was home to Strelkov's group, which also ran neighbouring Druzhkivka and Kostyantynivka. Nearby towns were run by other warlords; Zdrilyuk in Kramatorsk and Bezler, aka 'Bes' (the demon) in Horlivka – most had a *nom de guerre*. Bezler's group was one of the main suspects in the shooting down of the Malaysian airliner in July (see below). In Donetsk, there was the Donetsk People's Army, the Russian Orthodox Army and the Berezin group, but the two main forces were Oplot, under Aleksandr Zakharchenko (mainly made up of police auxiliaries), and the mysterious Vostok (see below), both thought to be closer to Akhmetov.

In Luhansk there were more Cossack groups, given its closer proximity to Russia and the Don region. One group under Nikolay Kozitsyn was based near Antratsyt; another was near Krasny Luch. Valeriy Bulatov headed something called the 'Russian United Army of the South-East', which did not have the power to unite anybody. The Prizrak ('Ghost') battalion under Oleksiy

Mozgovoy was active in the south, while the defence minister of the 'Luhansk People's Republic', Igor Plotnitsky, was busy in and around Luhansk.

The number of fighters kept changing, but it was never more than 10,000. One calculation estimated 4,500 Russian fighters in the Donbas by mid-May.[64] Strelkov, Berezin, Vostok, Oplot and the Cossacks had the biggest groups. Strelkov had maybe 2,000 men, while Vostok and Oplot had 2,500.[65]

Anarchy in East Ukraine

That was a lot of different groups. Some clearly had, to different degrees, agendas of their own. For Russia, there were disadvantages to playing a longer game: local proxies were harder to control at a distance. In Crimea, Aksyonov was at least a proper puppet. By late April, there was increasing anarchy in the Donbas: too many straightforward criminals had been recruited. And there was fighting over Russia's money.[66] Cash arrived on a Monday, and was spent by Wednesday. Everyone was drunk until then. Then they did some fighting with Kiev's forces before the whole cycle started again.[67] In July, drunken militants were filmed indiscreetly complaining about Russia's inadequate deliveries of tanks and infantry fighting vehicles (BMPs).[68]

Amnesty International recorded some cases of abuse by pro-government forces, but the vast majority of allegations of abduction and torture were levelled against separatist pro-Russian groups.[69] Ukrainian activists were dealt with early on. The Ukrainian SBU recorded Bezler's conversation with Vyacheslav Ponomaryov, the self-proclaimed mayor of Slovyansk, during which Bezler urged him to 'deal with the corpse; make sure he's dragged out of here as soon as possible; he's lying and stinking here'.[70] The body was presumed to be that of Volodymyr Rybak, who served on the Horlivka city council for the opposition Fatherland Party and who disappeared after tearing down the separatists' flag from the city hall. His body was later found dumped in a river, having been tortured.

Kidnapping became big business. Amnesty International referred to both the UN Human Rights Monitoring Mission's estimate of 222 cases of abduction between April and June, and the Ukrainian Interior Ministry's estimate of 500.[71] At least 250 were still being held hostage in mid-July: 150 in Luhansk and 100–120 in Donetsk and Horlivka.[72] Looting and theft were commonplace, particularly as the militias sought to supply themselves. Strelkov liked to dress up for historical military re-enactment societies, but he could also be ruthless. He apparently ordered the shooting of looters, on the basis, bizarrely, of Stalin's declaration of martial law for the Soviet Union in June 1941.[73]

There seems to have been a partial coup d'état (if the expression can be applied to a fake state) on 29 May, when Vostok battalion kicked out some of the militants from Donetsk. There had long been rumours of Chechens arriving – supposedly 2,500 in Luhansk by mid-May,[74] reportedly paid $300 a day[75] – and of a so-called *dikaya diviziya* ('wild division').[76] Vostok was the name of a Chechen battalion in the 1990s, but despite much speculation,[77] the one here (or its leadership at least) seems mainly to have been made up of defectors from the local Alpha unit of the SBU, previously close to Akhmetov. Either way, its purpose seems to have been to rein in some of the anarchy, when Ukraine's forces were starting to have some successes on the ground.

The Anti-Terrorist Operation

Kiev launched its official 'anti-terrorist operation' against the rebels on 13 April. The choice of words was unfortunate (to put it lightly), as they were the very same as had been used by Yanukovych and his henchmen during the February Uprising in Kiev. The new authorities' definition of a 'terrorist' was also far too broad, too often a synonym for 'separatist', covering anyone who might have waved a flag or thrown a stone.

Ukraine still had the right to establish order on its sovereign territory. Previous measures had, however, been laughable. The governor of Donetsk and leading oligarch Serhiy Taruta (he made his fortune in steel) offered to build a ditch to keep the Russians out, which was even less use than the Maginot Line. As in Crimea, Ukrainian forces initially proved inept: the leadership of the National Security and Defence Council was amateurish; the army was painfully underfunded and was humiliated in Crimea; and the security service, the SBU, was thoroughly infiltrated by the Russians. In desperation, the authorities even turned to the elite Alpha unit – the very force that had killed demonstrators in Kiev in February; but its members proved less willing to lay down their own lives. Attacks on the separatists in April simply led to the defection of more men and the loss of more equipment.

As in Crimea, there were underlying reasons for underperformance. The armed forces had been chronically underfunded under Yushchenko and then criminally underfunded under Yanukovych, who had built up the militia to protect himself, but was not interested in protecting the national interest. In fact, the situation was even worse: arms and equipment were simply sold off. The SBU now accused its own former boss, Oleksandr Yakymenko, of running an arms-smuggling racket. One irony of the situation after the protests in Kiev was that there was not much crowd-control hardware – shields, helmets, and so on – to use in the east.

In May 2010, a Russo-Ukrainian spy agreement had led to massively increased cooperation (penetration might be a better term). According to Dmytro Tymchuk, counterintelligence activities against Russia were shifted from top priority to priority number four in autumn 2010, during Yanukovych's first year as president. Tymchuk added that the counterintelligence budget was severely cut, and counterintelligence activities in eastern Ukraine scaled back to almost zero.

But the new government reformed after a slow start. After early defections, the remnants of the regular army were supposedly more reliable. Some US non-lethal aid began to trickle through. In April, the new Interior Minister Arsen Avakov announced plans to create new militia forces. These tended to be of two types. The first were the battalions that were formed by local oligarch governors as an alternative to *both* the corrupted militia in the Donbas *and* the harder-to-control Maidan activists, who would fight for ideological reasons. There was a suspicion that these were (or would become) private armies to defend oligarchs' business interests.

The second were volunteer forces, incorporated after accelerated training into a National Guard under the Ministry of the Interior and new battalions under the Ministry of Defence. About 20,000 were added after the annexation of Crimea. They were not self-organised, but incorporated as official units. The first battalion, 400-strong, that went straight to the outskirts of Slovyansk, was made up '100 per cent of those who stood on the barricades on the Maidan'.[78] This was a mixed blessing: the new recruits were well motivated, but could be represented as outside forces. They were also politicised, and depoliticising them was not part of their training. Allegations of their ill-discipline were somewhat one-sided, given the behaviour of separatist forces in the Donbas.[79] Some of them were too disciplined. Official sources claimed that they had 'moral strength, which was good for inspiring the regular army, too' – which was again double-edged.[80]

These new forces initially mainly manned the containment checkpoints. The regular army was used for more proactive tasks, but professional security forces (the SBU) were held back. Heavy weapons were not used.

This seemed to be only a short-term strategy until the election for a new Ukrainian president was over at the end of May (see Chapter 8). Thereafter the authorities were less vigilant in policing who actually turned up to fight or to make political points. If Right Sector's presence was initially a Russian propaganda myth, it was soon a reality.[81] Nationalist and populist politicians like Dmytro Yarosh and Oleh Lyashko were allowed to play stunts, turning up in uniform in the east. Lyashko was seen interrogating the former 'defence minister' of the Donetsk People's Republic, stripped and bruised, as early as

7 May.[82] Lyashko formed a 'Ukraine' battalion.[83] On 9 July he went to Slovyansk, just after the separatists fled, to be filmed berating the chair of the city council.[84] Yarosh's Right Sector seemed to be able to present itself as a semi-official part of the anti-terrorist operation, where a group under Semen Semenchenko (the *nom de guerre* of the leader of the Donbas battalion) fought in Kurakhovo, just west of Donetsk city.[85]

The Ministry of Defence also collected donations from ordinary citizens via SMS, which was nicely patriotic but no way to run a serious anti-insurgency campaign in the long run. The scope of crowd-funding efforts expanded significantly over time, via such sites as the People's Project (www.narodniy. org.ua), as well as www.armyhelp.com.ua and the Ukrainian Freedom Fund (ukrfreedomfund.org) for raising money from abroad. Such sites were impressively transparent. In June, the world's first 'people's drone' was assembled from donated parts for $35,000.[86] But the main government budget was feeling the strain by the summer (see Chapter 8).

The first serious Ukrainian counter-attack was on 1 May. The operation was now headed by a KGB veteran, Vasiliy Krutov. Ukraine first cleared the areas where the separatists had only ever had limited influence – the rural areas of western Donetsk and northern Luhansk. Outlying towns such as Mariupol and Krasny Lyman were freed by June. But fierce fighting continued over the border crossings. On 26–27 May, twenty-six people were killed in the 'Battle of Donetsk airport', which had been rebuilt for $900 million for the Euro 2012 football championship.

At the same time, national unity talks started on 14 May, and international talks in Geneva and Berlin. The round tables helped calm some of the separatists, but Russia had prepared a carefully laid trap by inserting Viktor Medvedchuk as a key participant. Medvedchuk is the former chief of staff to President Leonid Kuchma (1994–2005). Putin is godfather to his daughter, and Medvedchuk had spent the last few years serving Russian interests, as head of the anti-EU NGO Ukrainian Choice. The Russian plan was to install him as governor of Donetsk, alongside a similar figure in Luhansk, the political chameleon Nestor Shufrych. Putin would appear as peacemaker. The two Donbas regions would then remain semi-detached parts of the Ukrainian state, but the separatists would know that Medvedchuk answered to Putin. Akhmetov would presumably be a partner to Medvedchuk. So the Donbas would be under Russian control in all but name.

Ukraine agreed a ceasefire from 20 to 30 June. But it was unilateral: twenty-seven Ukrainians were killed in those ten days. Critics argued that Ukraine had been making gains, and it allowed the separatists to regroup and resupply. A tentative peace proposal reached in Berlin on 2 July was quickly superseded by events on the ground. Its key conditions – control of borders, release of all hostages, monitoring by an OSCE mission – were never met.[87] At least that meant that the 'Medvedchuk plan' also lost relevance.

The Paradoxes of Hybrid War

If this was a 'new kind of war',[88] then that war was more successful in Crimea than in the Donbas. As the conflict dragged on, Putin was clearly embarrassed both by the lack of a quick victory and by the disorder on the ground. In his victory speech after the annexation of Crimea, he had proudly boasted that 'there was not a single armed confrontation in Crimea and no casualties'.[89] The 'fascist threat' appeared out of nowhere in 2014, and then waxed and waned on Russian TV just as quickly. Aleksandr Dugin suddenly found himself dismissed from his Moscow university post. Moreover, Putin could not easily use conventional forces when he was in denial mode. Nor would it be easy to plausibly deny the origin of the kind of heavy weapons that the separatists now needed.

Petro Poroshenko's ceasefire also came at a time of increasing internal dissent among the separatists, whose leaders reportedly threatened to shoot anyone who was prepared to disarm.[90] Russian state border guards reportedly shot at a number who were trying to escape back to Russia.[91]

When operations restarted on 1 July, the Ukrainians were again successful. They were now more like a home army fighting against a set of militias. The new recruits fought well, while the separatists remained splintered and disorganised: Ukrainian blood was worth more than Russian treasure. There were even allegations that the new patriotic Ukrainian army was prepared to fight a little dirty, with Grad ('Hail') multiple-rocket launchers used in densely populated areas. The Azov, Shakhtar and Donbas battalions all had controversial reputations.

Slovyansk was retaken in a massive symbolic victory on 5–6 July, forcing Strelkov and his fighters to retreat to the less friendly territory of Donetsk. The separatists' area of control was reduced to a strip of territory that included the big cities of Donetsk and Luhansk; but if they dug in there, they would be hard to dislodge. Strelkov seemed to have money again, this time to rebuild a mercenary army. According to a leaked tape, he was prepared to 'stop public transport and blow up nine-story buildings on the outskirts of the city . . . what the fuck is up with that?' According to the unidentified speaker, Strelkov is 'Colonel Batshit Crazy, let's be honest'.[92] His men's double-edged justification for everything, from the chaos to taking goods without payment, was 'We came from Slovyansk', which won them few new friends.[93]

The death toll now far exceeded that on the Maidan (though the nature of the conflict meant there were no exact figures). By early June, separatists had supposedly killed 181 people, including fifty-nine from the Ukrainian armed forces;[94] in turn, they claimed to have killed over 500. The UN recorded 356 dead between mid-April and mid-June.[95] As of 15 July, the Ukrainian National Security and Defence Council's official figures for casualties since the beginning of the anti-terrorist operation were 258 Ukrainian army personnel killed and 922 injured, with forty-five remaining in captivity.[96] The assistant UN secretary-general for human rights, referring to official sources, stated that 423 people had been killed between 15 April and 20 June 2014 (from the beginning of the anti-terrorist operation up to the Ukrainian ceasefire). This figure also included civilians.[97] A calculation by the *Kyiv Post* from official sources, published on 18 July, listed 550 civilians dead (sixteen children) and 275 Ukrainian army, of whom fifty-two had died since 10 July. The newspaper counted 86,609 refugees, but gave no estimate of the number of separatists killed.[98] By the end of August, the UN recorded 2,593 deaths, at a rate of thirty-six per day.[99]

Flight MH17

The striking initial success of the Ukrainian July campaign led the separatists to call for more supplies from Russia. SBU transcripts show them complaining to their GRU handlers that 'we are having a very difficult time now'.[100] The separatists had to fight to keep the border open, or else be encircled. Also in the second week of July, several of the local puppets were replaced by people Moscow could trust more, like Transnistrian 'minister for state security' and veteran separatist Vladimir Antyufeyev as local 'deputy prime minister'. Antyufeyev had organised separatist movements in both Latvia and Moldova, and kept a tight lid on Transnistria until 2012 – while also organising its smuggling rackets. There was also evidence that Russia was refinancing the rebels.[101]

Further leadership changes, none with anything approaching a cover story of local decision-making, followed in July and August. Even Strelkov, perhaps the victim of his own personality cult, took 'a vacation'. Russia's proxies started building state structures for a 'freezing option'. On 24–25 June, the two 'parliaments' of Donetsk and Luhansk declared a united 'Federated Republic of Novorossiya'. They also announced plans for their own central bank. Various figures, such as the pro-Russian Ukrainian MP Oleh Tsaryov, were touted as the 'Republic's' figurehead leader.

But resupply was what mattered most. On 13 July, about a hundred armoured personnel carriers and other vehicles crossed the border from Russia.[102] Ukrainian sources estimated another 400 extra fighters.[103] More than ten Ukrainian aircraft were shot down in June and July, including a transporter carrying forty paratroopers and nine crew on 13 June, two helicopters, and either one or two SU-25 fighters on 16 July, the day before the Malaysia Airlines tragedy.[104] There were many reports of fire coming from the Russian side of the border. Three jets were shot down from Russian territory. Grad multiple-rocket launchers were used from Russia.[105] Supplies crossed the border from two staging points in Novocherkassk (ironically a famous site of anti-Soviet demonstrations in 1962) and Briansk, including 'T-64 tanks, Grad multiple-rocket launchers, various armoured personnel carriers equipped with cannons, BUK advanced radar-guided surface-to-air systems, shoulder-fired rocket launchers as well as sniper rifles, mines, grenades and automatic weapons.[106] The even more advanced Tornado multiple rocket launchers were also allegedly moved in.[107] As Prime Minister Yatsenyuk was fond of saying, 'there is no civil war in my country'[108] – the hybrid war looked more and more like a normal war with Russia.

According to the SBU, one particular item that crossed the border at Sukhodolsk around 1 a.m. on 17 July was the BUK anti-missile system, complete with crew. There were also three Gvozdika self-propelled artillery weapons. The separatists could be heard boasting 'we already have BUK. We'll be shooting them all to hell.' One calls the system 'a beauty'.[109] By the afternoon, it had been moved to Hornostoevka village. Two minutes before the tragedy, one fighter reports to the separatist leader Bezler ('Bes') that a plane is approaching: 'a birdie flew towards you . . . high and strong'. Bezler tells him to 'report to those above'.[110] Within minutes, 298 people were dead. By 4.40 p.m. Bezler reported to the GRU that 'we have just shot down a plane'.[111] Though he later blames a group of Cossacks stationed at Chernukhino, Strelkov initially boasted on his website that 'we just shot down an AN-26 plane near Torez; it's scattered somewhere around the Progress mine. We warned them not to fly in "our sky"'.[112]

When the awful truth sinks in, the first priority is to cover up. One of the handlers says 'our friends from high above are very much interested in the fate of the "black boxes". I mean people from Moscow . . . They must be under our control . . . All that you find must not come into someone else's hands.'[113] The BUK returned to Russia that night. The rest of the world watched in horror as the original tragedy was then compounded, as access to the crash site was obstructed, bodies and body parts rotted in the heat, and evidence was tampered with or allegedly carried off by looters.

The international outcry put Putin on the back foot. Intelligence suggested that the Russian crew may have actually fired the missile. But the background to the tragedy was that Russia was upping its support for its retreating proxies. It wasn't likely that Putin cared about them personally. But he did care about potential strategic defeat. That was far from certain, but it was now a distinct, rather than a distant, possibility. The US had already hardened its stance on sanctions the very day before the disaster. The EU now followed suit.

Convoys

But further setbacks for the separatists followed, so Russia did not stay quiet for long. In August it announced that it would send a 'humanitarian convoy' of over 200 trucks to the Donbas (OSCE observers eventually counted 227). Ukraine was rightly extremely distrustful, first because Russia was the aggressor, so had no moral right to offer to salve the gaping wound it had itself cut open. Moreover, the mission could have served as cover for any number of ploys. A full search of every truck was difficult. The drivers could have stayed behind and no one would know who they were. 'Provocations' could easily have been arranged, the mission could easily mutate into other forms of support. It was also obviously a means to buy time, and redefine Russia's mission to make trouble, providing another means towards long-term engagement and keeping Ukraine unstable. The Ukrainian government alleged that many of the trucks were empty and that factory equipment was stolen from two hi-tech factories making ammunition and radar systems before the vehicles headed home.[114]

The convoy was also cover for other convoys. In late August, Russia poured in enough men, tanks and armoured personnel carriers to support a counter-offensive, after President Poroshenko dodged Putin's harsh terms at a meeting in Minsk. Putin could reverse the military tide, but only with what were increasingly obviously military means, although the EU, as ever, remained reluctant to call them such. The German press was actually counselling Ukraine (rather than Russia) to back off, as too radical a defeat in the Donbas might 'provoke' Putin.[115] But at the end of August, NATO estimated that there were at least 1,000 regular Russian troops in Ukraine. The Committee of Soldiers' Mothers of Russia went much higher: 10,000 to 15,000 had served in total, 7,000 to 8,000 were then in Ukraine, and 200 had died.[116] These kinds of numbers were big enough to give many Ukrainians second thoughts. Russia may have already sent in sufficient forces to turn the tide, and the West had done nothing.

Massacre at Ilovaisk

It was typical of Putin that a major offensive was launched on 23–24 August, the latter being Independence Day in Ukraine. Ukraine's response was perhaps equally typical: they had been pointing to Russian involvement all along, but their short-term military strategy was based on the assumption that the Donbas rebels could be defeated as Russia would not dare escalate further.

Russian forces broke the sieges of Donetsk and Luhansk cities, opened up a much bigger border crossing and advanced along the Azov coast towards Mariupol, threatening to open up a land-link to Crimea. The biggest losses, at least 300 dead, were suffered by the volunteer battalions who were surrounded on three sides at Ilovaisk, a small railway town on a major supply route south-east of Donetsk. Many were ambushed as they retreated. The volunteer leaders accused the government and regular army of at best, neglect, and at worst, of wanting them out of the way.

But the regular army also took a pounding. The Russian forces no longer bothered hiding. In fact, they made sure to be deliberately in plain sight, to force the Ukrainians to give up on hopes of victory, and to show that the rest of the world would do nothing to stop the plainest possible forms of Russian intervention (thus the mocking claims that any Russian troops were either 'lost or on holiday'). Poroshenko duly accepted a ceasefire on Russian terms on 5 September, presumably calculating that the October elections at least could then be held. But the terms were so unfavourable it was difficult to see the ceasefire holding.

Conclusion

Unlike Crimea, the conflict in the Donbas dragged on for months, though poten-tial future options were becoming a little clearer by the summer. Both sides predicted a 'Transnistrian scenario' – the formation of a statelet strong enough to survive on its own. Ukraine's offensives were designed to stop that happening, to reduce the separatists' territory and resources to the point where a precipitous collapse was likely. Russia was using all available means to recalibrate the conflict to prevent that from happening, and keep the conflict going. By the end of August, it looked as if Russia might be able to tip the balance, because the West had not converted its outrage over the MH17 tragedy into a policy to reverse the military build-up that had caused it. This Transnistrian scenario might then rumble on for decades, which would be the point (the original ceasefire in the Transnistrian conflict was in 1992). It would most likely end up not a 'frozen conflict', but a variable-temperature conflict to control whoever was in power in Kiev: sometimes with a little bit more war, sometimes with a little bit more nego-tiation, but fundamentally on and on indefinitely.

The Ukrainians had scented victory in the early summer and then felt the pain of retreat at the end of August. The conflict would likely ebb and flow. Even if Kiev reconquers the region, the act of reconquest could cost it local support. Only a minority supported the original revolt, but war changes facts and emotions. Many are now alienated from both sides. Even Semen Semenchenko, the nationalist commander of the Donbas battalion, managed to combine both scenarios, predicting 'first we will have a long and very bloody war, followed by many years of an Ulster-like scenario'.[117]

CHAPTER 8

Ukraine's Unfinished Revolution, or a Revolution Barely Begun?

Ukraine had something resembling a revolution in February 2014. Petro Poroshenko was elected president in May because he seemed to combine the hope for reform with the promise of order and stability. He even said in his inauguration speech that order must come first: 'The time of inevitable positive changes has come. To implement them, we need first of all peace, security and unity. A real war, planned and unleashed in the Ukrainian Donbas, became an obstacle for enormous opportunities that opened for the European moderniza-tion of Ukraine after the fall of tyranny.'[1] This did not necessarily mean this was the quickest revolution in history, over before it really began. But it did mean that many already had doubts about what, realistically, the Ukrainian revolution could hope to achieve. Maidan activists talked of root-and-branch change (or, for the younger generation, of systemic 'reboot'). Ultimately, this would be the bench-mark: people wanted more than in 2004, when they didn't get much further than a change of leaders. But with the country at war in the east and such an entrenched *ancien régime*, it was an open question how much change was actually feasible.

The 'Maidan' after the Maidan

The Maidan physically remained in the centre of Kiev until August, with some hard-core activists still encamped. The Maidan was part museum, part memo-rial – both where people were killed and where the snipers were, on Institutska Street, leading up the hill to the government district. When I visited again in May, the whole area still smelt of burnt rubber. Cobblestones, which were emblematic of the February Uprising, were used to make art and to spell out statements like 'Stop Propaganda, No Fascism Here!' But one test of

4 Eastern Europe, Russia and the Baltic States

'normalisation' was the growing series of complaints about the traffic and local restaurateurs' loss of business. The overspill on Khreshchatyk Street was cleared up in June; all but a few remaining areas were cleared in August.

Some Maidan activists joined the new battalions and fought in the Donbas (see Chapter 7). Some set up bodies to press for reform. There were further demonstrations, such as the action against the Russian embassy on 15 June, when the then foreign minister raised eyebrows by calling Putin a 'dickhead' (*khuilo*); or the peaceful march on Akhmetov's luxury Kiev residence in July, with some taking a dip in his swimming pool. Many were gearing up to campaign for new parliamentary elections in the autumn as one last revolutionary act.

But the relationship between the various Maidan forces and the new government lacked clarity. Some more formal coordinating organisations emerged during the protests, like the Maidan Public Council, the All-Ukrainian Union 'Maidan', Civic Sector and Reanimation Reforms Package, which aimed to score all post-Maidan government policy initiatives.[2] Particular bodies monitored particular sectors, like the Centre for Military and Political Studies. But the Maidan forces had yet to launch an influential party or parties apart from the Democratic Alliance, which won two, but only two, seats on the Kiev city council in May. Most were at least authentic new voices, apart from the largely moribund 'Public Council' of the great and the good. But they would need a change in election rules if their voice was to be heard alongside well-financed traditional parties.

On the other hand, most Maidan activists were politically purist and talked about monitoring the government from outside. The minority of reformist government ministers spoke warmly about the value of the Maidan keeping them on their toes, but they would soon grow weary of constant carping. More Maidan activists could actually join, rather than just criticise, the government.

Disorder

As with the Uprising itself, there were many myths about the Ukraine that emerged thereafter, many deliberately sown as part of Russian 'propaganda war'. The first is that it was revolutionary, in the sense that normal power had collapsed and been taken over by men with guns from the Maidan.

Some of the police and some of the traffic cops melted away, but there was no mass looting. Some of those who got guns very late in the Uprising kept them, however. There was a swaggering element around Right Sector, which now took over the Dnipro Hotel, around the corner from the Maidan, as its headquarters. Whatever its origins, Right Sector was now split between genuine hard-line nationalists and opportunists who were prepared to sell themselves to political sponsors and criminal elements. Most of the fakes, some '30% to 50% of their guys', belonged to the extremist sub-groups which had a long history of collaboration with the security services.[3] The same groups collaborated with Oleh Lyashko, whose Radical Party was on both the right and the left, but had always been a populist 'political technology' project of leading oligarchs, making Lyashko a 'clone Robin Hood'.[4] The 'Social National Assembly' in particular linked up with Lyashko, who added its activists to a belated amnesty law for Maidan protestors. The Azov battalion that eventually went to the Donbas included many of its number.

There were allegations that 'Family' oligarchs were now supporting Right Sector to provide a 'scarecrow' image to cover their activities in east Ukraine.[5] Early reports of Right Sector activity in the Donbas seem to have been bravado or Russian propaganda; eventually it would be real enough (see Chapter 7). Right Sector was evicted from the Dnipro Hotel at the end of March, leading to parliament voting on a weapons hand-in the next day and an attempt to storm parliament after the death of one Right Sector activist, Oleksandr Muzychko, in a shoot-out in west Ukraine.

But Right Sector already looked like yesterday's men. After posting a picture of the Eurovision Song Contest winner, bearded drag queen Conchita Wurst, under the headline 'Do we need this kind of "Europe"?' Right Sector was condemned for being a mirror image of Putin's nationalists.[6]

The New Government

Another myth was that the new government was dominated by extreme right-wingers. Its biggest element was, in fact, Yuliya Tymoshenko's old party. There were originally five parties in parliament: before February, the Party of Regions governed with the Communists, while the parliamentary opposition troika was made up of Tymoshenko's Fatherland Party, Vitaliy Klitschko's UDAR and the right-wing Freedom Party. UDAR bowed out of coalition negotiations, which left two groupings, if the Party of Regions was to be excluded. Fatherland did not want to govern on its own, and thought, wrongly, that the Freedom Party was a proxy for the moral authority of the radical forces on the Maidan.

But the decision to include the Freedom Party in government was nevertheless disastrous: its ratings were in steep decline, and its presence fed the Russian narrative of a nationalist takeover. The new government could easily have included more non-party and NGO activists instead. The new leaders also made the wrong compromise with the old regime, including too many odious members of the old guard, rather than grassroots representatives from eastern and southern Ukraine. The symbolic presentation of the new government to the Maidan at a public meeting on 27 February, a week after the worst day of killings, at a so-called People's *Viche* ('Assembly') also turned out to be a less than brilliant idea. This was not a voting process, although names were booed and cheered; but Russia was later to use a bastardised version of the idea in the open-air 'people's elections' in Crimea and the Donbas.

The acting president and prime minister both belonged to Fatherland. The rest of the government was split roughly nine to five, the ratio of party strengths in parliament. The Freedom Party had several non-controversial portfolios, but also defence and the Procuracy. Andriy Parubiy ran the National Security Council. The same ratio applied to regional governors. Maidan and NGO activists ran the 'humanitarian' ministries (health, education, culture, youth and sport), plus two new para-agencies: the Anti-Corruption Bureau, led by the journalist Tetyana Chornovol, now recovered from her savage beating; and the Lustration Committee, headed by Yehor Sobolyev, founder of the Svidomo Investigative Journalism Bureau.

The new authorities made another crucial early mistake: on 24 February, parliament repealed the 2012 Language Law (passed by Yanukovych to bolster his party's support before the parliamentary elections that October). Acting President Turchynov soon vetoed the change, but the damage had been done. The change would not have meant that the Russian language was suddenly in danger of disappearing in south-east Ukraine; only its monopoly was in danger: in Crimea, the Donbas and most other cities of the east and south, Russian predominates.

In Ukraine as a whole, the Ukrainian language is underused. The population is 79 per cent Ukrainian, but many speak Russian. There are various ways of measuring the prevalence of the two languages, but one yardstick is that 43 per cent speak Ukrainian at home and 39 per cent Russian, with 17 per cent saying both (data for 2011). But even the Ukrainian-speaking population is underserved. As of 2011, the top eight TV channels only had 22 per cent of their primetime content in Ukrainian; only 30 per cent of total newspaper circulation was in Ukrainian.[7] So successive governments have believed in an element of positive discrimination for Ukrainian – not to make it hegemonic, but to reverse its long-term decline. Perception is what matters in such cases, though, and Russian propaganda went into overdrive on the threat to all Russian-speakers in Ukraine.

The Birth of a New Political Nation

Putin did much more to divide Ukraine. His view has always been clear enough: he has always said that it is not a real country. That view isn't all that unusual: many Russian politicians say the same. Even Boris Yeltsin spent half of his presidency refusing even to visit Kiev, though things did improve after the State Treaty signed in 1997.

In 2013, Putin visited Kiev for the 1,025th anniversary of the Baptism in 988, when the Prince of Kiev introduced Christianity to this part of the world. Putin called him 'Vladimir', which is his own name – Vladimir Vladimirovich ('Vladimir, son of Vladimir'). In Ukrainian, Vladimir is spelt Volodymyr – and calling him 'Volodymyr Putin' always raises a laugh in Kiev. This is what Putin said afterwards:

> You know, whatever happens, and wherever Ukraine may go, we still meet again sometime and somewhere. Why? Because we are one people. And [despite] angry nationalists on both sides, the nationalists we have in our country and in Ukraine, in fact it's true. Because we have one [common] Dnipro Kievan baptismal font, without doubt we have common historical roots and common destiny, we have a common religion, a common faith, we have a very similar culture, language, traditions and mentality ... As far as this part, Ukraine, is concerned, it is a land and we understand and remember that we were born, as I said, within a common Ukrainian Dnipro baptismal font, Rus' was born there, and we all come from there.[8]

The exact Russian words used by Putin were telling. For we are one 'people', Putin used the Russian word *narod*, which is the normal term for an ethnic, not a state, identity, and for the common folk who preserved their ties despite shifting borders and shiftless politicians' decisions. When Putin called Ukraine a 'land', he used the Russian word *krai*, meaning a territory, rather than a separate country. The reference to Ukraine as 'this part' came after a section where Putin talked about the Russian state, implying that Ukraine was a part of its history. Even more bluntly, and in ungrammatical English, Putin said in August 2014, 'it seems to me that the Russian and Ukrainian people [*narod*] is [*sic*] practically one people'.[9]

At the ill-fated NATO summit in Bucharest in 2008, Putin lectured George Bush on a similar subject, when the question of offering Ukraine and Georgia a 'Membership Action Plan' to join NATO one day was under discussion:

> Ukraine, in its current form, came to be in Soviet-era days . . . From Russia the country obtained vast territories in what is now eastern and southern Ukraine . . . Crimea was simply given to Ukraine by a CPSU Political Bureau's decision . . . one third of the population are ethnic Russians. According to official census statistics, there are 17 million ethnic Russians living there, out of a population of 45 million. Some regions, such as Crimea, for example, are entirely populated by ethnic Russians. There are 90 percent of them there . . . If the NATO issue is added there, along with other problems, this may bring Ukraine to the verge of its existence as a sovereign state.[10]

This is seriously confused. Leaving aside the spurious history for a moment to concentrate on Putin's demographic 'data', according to the last official census statistics (from 2001), the Russian population in Ukraine was 17 *per cent*, not 17 *million*. 'One third' refers to the roughly one-third of the population who said Russian was their 'native language', not those who were actually Russian. The '90 percent of them there' in Crimea is the number of Russian-speakers in Crimea – the ethnic Russian population was 58 per cent. Unfortunately, Bush was not well placed to provide Putin with a detailed historical rebuttal.

But in Ukraine it was increasingly common to claim that Ukraine was actually *more* unified after Putin's onslaught, and that the Maidan had led to the birth of a new 'political nation'. The idea of a 'Ukrainian political nation' has in fact been around since even before independence in 1991. Other criteria for defining the nation, such as ethnicity, language or religion, are too divisive. But a 'political nation', a civic identity, rather than a narrowly Ukrainian identity for all Ukrainian citizens, was initially only a slogan, an empty box. The political community, the *civis*, needs a myth of why it exists. The Orange Revolution could have helped define a new national identity, but it proved divisive. Once back in power after 2010, Yanukovych tried to have it removed from school textbooks.

Poroshenko's inauguration speech addressed one element of the problem: 'Until now, many people thought that we got independence without any difficulty'. But now 'the Heroes of Nebesna Sotnya died for it.'[11] The Uprising was the central new national symbol. So was fighting for the Donbas. There was some early sociological evidence that regional differences on key issues were shrinking rapidly. According to one survey in March, the same 91 per cent in western and central Ukraine 'completely condemned' the Russian Duma's decision to give Putin authority to use troops in Ukraine; the figure for southern Ukraine was 65 per cent, for eastern Ukraine 55 per cent.[12] Another poll showed little sense of a threat to Russian language rights, rising only from 4 per cent to 24 per cent, west to east. Support for Ukraine remaining a unitary state was 86 per cent in the west and still 45 per cent in the east.[13] Putin's rating in Ukraine fell from 47 per cent in October 2013 to 16 per cent in April 2014. In south Ukraine it fell from 57 per cent to 14 per cent, and in east Ukraine (minus the Donbas) from 62 per cent to 19 per cent – much the same as in Ukraine as a whole. Only in the Donbas itself did it stay high, barely down from 63 per cent to 60 per cent.[14]

Pro-European sentiment was also on the rise.[15] Support for European integration rose by 11 percentage points in just one month (February to March 2014), from 41 per cent to 52 per cent; while support for the Russia-led Customs Union fell from 36 per cent to 27 per cent. A July poll showed the number of EU supporters rising to 61 per cent; even supporters of NATO membership outnumbered opponents by 44 per cent to 35 per cent.[16]

Ukraine was certainly less polarised, having lost one of its poles – Crimea. The future of the Donbas was unclear. There were early signs of more cohesion in the centre. All of which provided grounds for hoping that Ukraine's famously 'weak', overlapping or hybrid national identity might consolidate in the longer run – assuming things went well.

Ukraine might also be cured of the idea of 'Grand Ukraine'. Ukraine's original nineteenth-century nationalists saw themselves in mirror-image competition with Russian nationalists. If the latter had the slogan of Russia stretching 'from the Carpathians to the Pacific', Ukrainian nationalists wanted a Ukraine stretching 'from the Carpathians to the Caucasus'. Twentieth-century Ukrainian nationalists like Yuriy Lypa even talked of an 'imperial Ukraine' dominating the Black Sea, Caucasus and beyond. Soviet propaganda played on similar themes in the 1940s, when Stalin's annexation of west Ukrainian territories was celebrated as creating 'Great Ukraine' (*Velyka Ukraïna*) and making Ukraine the 'second republic' in the USSR.

Mykhailo Hrushevsky, the father of Ukrainian history and briefly state president in 1918, also wanted as big a Ukraine as possible, in three parts. Galicia in the west would connect Ukraine to Europe; 'Greater Ukraine' would connect Ukraine to Russia; and Crimea was the key to Ukraine's natural orientation, via its river systems flowing to the south-east, to the Black Sea, to the Caucasus and to a wider world of 'Ukrainian Orientalism' (a strong tradition in Ukrainian intellectual life, centred on the appropriately named Ahatanhel Krymsky, 1871–1942). Without Crimea, Ukraine would lose its historical links to the south and to the Caucasus. It would also be virtually landlocked. To the north-east of Crimea, the Sea of Azov would be pretty much a Russian sea. To the west of Crimea, Odesa could be blockaded, and has anyway always historically been a law unto itself, an entrepôt beholden to no one.

A Ukraine without much access to the sea would not suffer in nineteenth-century terms, foreign naval support being not so crucial these days; but in twenty-first-century terms it would have a much weaker position in energy geopolitics and its attempts to find alternatives to Russian supplies. Its outreach to countries like Georgia would be curtailed.

The counter-argument is that a smaller Ukraine would be more manageable. Too many of its leaders have behaved as if Ukraine is more important than it actually is, and as if the world owes them a living. Ukraine's leaders have also liked to talk of their country as a 'bridge' or 'crossroads' between east and west, north and south. Well, it might also be a good thing if Ukraine was a bit *less* of a bridge, if a smaller country didn't overlap so much with so many neighbouring worlds.

Poroshenko Becomes President

With Yanukovych gone, new presidential elections were scheduled for 25 May. Given the low expectations at the start of the campaign, the election could be counted a success. The separatist threat in the Donbas remained contained, and there was no major 'provocation' elsewhere. That said, only a tiny number from Crimea were able to vote, and could only do so by voting elsewhere in Ukraine.

Turnout was a respectable 60.3 per cent, compared to 66.8 per cent in the first round and 69.1 per cent in the second round at the last election in 2010. Crimea was not included in the figures, but the Donbas was, so separatist forces cut the turnout by an estimated 7 per cent overall. But voting was still possible in many areas of the Donbas: according to the Central Election Commission (cvk.gov.ua), it was 15 per cent in Donetsk and 39 per cent in Luhansk. In neighbouring regions, such as Kharkiv with 48 per cent, voting was less than the average, but there was no sign of a mass boycott or mass inability to vote. In fact, nowhere was the vote level particularly high. Even in Kiev, it was only 62 per cent. And nowhere was it overwhelming: the highest level was in Lviv, in west Ukraine, at 78 per cent. At least that meant the election was less geographically lopsided.

The favourite was the 'chocolate billionaire' Petro Poroshenko, who had personally campaigned in support of the Maidan, backed by his TV company – and, some said, by his money, too. An oligarch as president was obviously deeply paradoxical. But the Party of Regions was discredited, the leaders of the parliamentary opposition parties had looked opportunistic and behind events during the protests, and the election was too soon for the new generation of Maidan and NGO leaders. Poroshenko won outright in round one. In fact, many voters may have voted for him instrumentally: as they saw his bandwagon rolling, they spotted a chance to avoid the three-week wait until the second round, with a tense security situation getting worse.

Poroshenko initially promised to put his business interests in trust, though that had not happened by the time he was elected. He also had assets that were vulnerable to Russian pressure, including a chocolate factory just over the Russian border in Lipetsk (which was subject to on-off Russian sanctions; Roshen has 12 per cent of the Russian market), and a ship-repair business in Sevastopol.

Yuliya Tymoshenko, newly released from prison but not a new face (even her old hairstyle was back), failed to reinvent herself, running an old-style campaign full of populist promises and deal-brokering with corrupt local elites, reportedly including Akhmetov.[17] Even her initial hyperactivity reflected badly, as she acted like the acting president. She also made several miscalls, calling for a state of emergency in the Donbas, which would have played into Russia's hands. Her attempt to set up her own militia led by a former Berkut officer came to naught. Tymoshenko won a respectable 12.8 per cent, which was enough to survive; and her many supporters in government, among local governors and in the judiciary were sure to dig in for the long haul.

The election also showed the minimal level of support for the far right, especially compared to many European countries voting in elections to the European Parliament on the same day. The 'nationalist threat' of Russian propaganda was always a wild exaggeration. Oleh Tyahnybok, leader of the Freedom Party, won only 1.2 per cent, and Dmytro Yarosh, leader of Right Sector, the Kremlin's favourite bogey, won even less – just 0.7 per cent. By comparison, Marine Le Pen in France won 24.9 per cent in the Euro elections, the even nastier Jobbik in Hungary won 14.7 per cent, and the neo-Nazi Golden Dawn achieved 9.4 per cent in Greece.

The one exception was Oleh Lyashko, who won third place overall – exactly the kind of publicity-seeking provocateur the election did not need. Lyashko exploited 'anti-politics' sentiment to win 8.3 per cent. In a sense, this was paradoxical in post-revolutionary Ukraine. Maybe it made Ukraine a little bit more European, as Lyashko was like the Five Star movement in Italy or (more exactly) the Self-Defence populists in Poland. But Lyashko stank of old-style political technology: his stunts were all over oligarch-controlled TV, as he confronted half-naked separatists and urged the reconquest of Crimea 'tomorrow'. So was his emblem: a stylised pitchfork to confront his enemies in the shape of the

Ukrainian letter 'sh' in his surname. On past form, this kind of political project had three purposes: to distract from real issues like 'lustration' (the purging of compromised officials from the old regime), to provide a 'scarecrow' for the east of Ukraine and the west of Europe, and to sneak oligarchs' supporters into power behind Lyashko. He also took votes off Tymoshenko, which was logical, as Lyashko's main sponsor was her long-time enemy.

Mykhailo Dobkin, the candidate of the Party of Regions, the old ruling party under President Yanukovych, limped in with a mere 3 per cent – but then he was campaigning to keep his sponsor Rinat Akhmetov's options open, not campaigning to win. Another oligarch with a moderate image, Serhiy Tihipko won 5.2 per cent, mainly in southern and eastern Ukraine, where he hoped to re-launch his party. Tihipko's slogan was 'Peace above all', a neat inversion of the traditional nationalist slogan 'Ukraine above all'.

On the one hand, the absence of a strong eastern candidate in the leading bunch meant that the vote for Poroshenko was not too polarised – he led in every region of Ukraine, including the east and south. In fact, this was the first election in more than a decade where Ukraine was not split down the middle. But on the other hand, the east and the south had no direct voice in either the government or the presidency.

Results of the May 2014 Presidential Election

Petro Poroshenko	54.7%
Yuliya Tymoshenko	12.8%
Oleh Lyashko	8.3%
Anatoliy Hrytsenko	5.5%
Serhiy Tihipko	5.2%
Mykhailo Dobkin	3.0%
Vadym Rabinovich	2.2%
Olha Bohomolets	1.9%
Petro Symonenko	1.5%
Oleh Tyahnybok	1.2%
Dmytro Yarosh	0.7%

Promised and Stalled Reform

Many reforms were promised, including by Poroshenko on the campaign trail. By August 2014, however, hardly any had been delivered. Some had been begun but faced challenges; others had seemingly completely stalled.

Ironically, Ukraine made most progress in what is often one of the most difficult areas: namely rewriting the rules of the game via constitutional reform. The basis of Yanukovych's authoritarianism was the strong-arming of the constitutional court in October 2010 to agree the restoration of the more presidential 1996 Constitution, rather than the more 'balanced' version adopted after the Orange Revolution in 2004. In February 2014, Ukraine went back to the old 'Orange' constitution; but it was readopted in haste and has never worked well in practice, leading to constant conflict between president, parliament and prime minister. After the annexation of Crimea and conflict in the Donbas, there was also an urgent need to give the regions more power.

As so often in Ukrainian history since 1991, parliament and the president wanted different things. Different proposals sought to tidy up the division of responsibilities in different ways. Parliament wanted to make impeachment of the president easier, after the mess of trying to remove Yanukovych in February; President Poroshenko wanted to leave the procedure pretty much the same. Poroshenko also wanted more power over key appointments, particularly in the Procuracy and the SBU, and over a new watchdog agency, the Orwellian-sounding State Bureau of Investigations. Parliament and the president struggled over who would be responsible for any declaration of a state of emergency.

Significant 'decentralisation' was also promised. Ukraine's four levels of government would become three – central, oblast-regional and local communities (*hromady*) – as an alternative to formal federalism, which the authorities in Kiev feared would lead to the 'Bosnianisation' of the state. The middle level would have much more power, including on the issue of whether to introduce Russian as a second local language. But one possible source of future trouble was that the *hromady* would have the right to petition for internal border changes – which could threaten a possible break-up of the Donbas, by giving western regions to neighbouring Dnipropetrovsk, for example. The president could also appoint special 'representatives' in the regions, who might undermine local democracy. The constitutional court in Kiev would also have the right to rule on the constitutionality of actions by lower-level units, which the president would then attempt to enforce through his representatives. In the short term, this was clearly a reserve mechanism in case there was further trouble in the regions; but it was a recipe for conflict in the longer term. The first Ukrainian President Leonid Kravchuk, for example, also experimented with presidential representatives in 1992, but they did not last long.

Limited 'Lustration'

One of the central Maidan demands was the 'lustration' of the system – that is, the removal of the people who misgoverned the country under Yanukovych. The Maidan movement established two organisations: the Lustration Committee headed by Maidan activist Yehor Sobolyev, and the Anti-Corruption Bureau led by the journalist Tetyana Chornovol. Both initially operated as non-governmental civic organisations. Consisting mainly of volunteers and operating through grassroots activism and social media, they had made commendable efforts in trying to push reforms forward, but were often patronised by the central government as amateur enthusiasts. The two bodies were underfunded, and openly clashed with the new government over initial attempts to carry out the lustration of judges.[18] The Interim Special Commission of the High Council of Justice was appointed to sit for one year: five members are from the Lustration and Anti-Corruption bodies, but they are outnumbered by five representatives of the parliamentary factions and five from the Supreme Court (the old judiciary). While the Lustration Committee pushed for a more radical approach to tackling corruption, parliament continued to turn a blind eye to the continuation of illicit practices.

The more general problem was that so much of the old regime remained intact. Almost the only casualties of the revolution were those who ran away – though even some of these continued to operate shadowy business interests within Ukraine.

Following the ousting of Yanukovych, parliament effectively became the key decision-maker, setting and enforcing the agenda. Its informal modus operandi remained effectively unchanged: internal webs of influence were still dominated by oligarchs who hid behind formal political parties. The Party of Regions had lost more than half of its members, but mainly to the new so-called centrist factions and to the ranks of the 'independents'. The coalition parties (Fatherland, Freedom Party, with UDAR's voting support) lacked a majority on their own, and, strikingly, had failed to gain members since February. So they resorted to the same old ways of making deals behind closed doors.

The 'super-majorities' that forced through changes in February and March could no longer be relied on. Voting in parliament was much tighter and the new 'centrist' oligarchic factions held the balance of power: first Economic Development with forty-one seats, linked to Ihor Kolomoisky, and Sovereign European Ukraine with thirty-five seats, linked to another oligarch Ihor Yeremeyev, joined in June by the often openly pro-Russian For Peace and Stability. The much-trumpeted new Procurement Law, for example, was a worthy attempt to crack down on the biggest source of corruption under Yanukovych, but it was only passed by one vote, and at the second attempt. Most of the rest of the government's reform agenda was stalled.

The collapse of the new government on 24 July was therefore, on balance, a good thing (Yatsenyuk remained formally as prime minister, but could do little). With the major exception of ongoing finance for operations in the Donbas, parliament was not doing much anyway: a caretaker government would do just as well. At the time of writing (August 2014), new elections are slated for 26 October. But the polls appear highly volatile. The Party of Regions barely registers in single figures and the Communists could be banned. Fatherland and UDAR will most likely return to parliament, but Poroshenko's Solidarity party has been up and down, partly because it is not yet a real party, and partly because Poroshenko's role in it is unclear. Oleh Lyashko's populist Radical Party has been rising fast in the polls. He is easy to dismiss as a marginal lunatic, but in fact his brand of oligarch-backed populism is entirely emblematic of the new Ukraine. Oligarchs dominate the old parties, and most of the 'new' ones too. Kolomoisky might turn his dormant Ukraine of the Future party into a serious project. No new party has had much support in east Ukraine, so the risk of low turnout there is high.[19]

Factions in Parliament, as of 2 September 2014 (there are 450 MPs), Compared to June 2013[20]

Current Coalition	*September 2014*	*June 2013*
Fatherland	86	92
UDAR	41	42
Freedom	35	36
New Centre		
Economic Development	41	–
Sovereign European Ukraine	35	–
For Peace and Stability	38	–
Independents	94	34
Old Guard		
Party of Regions	77	207
Communists (the Communists' faction was dissolved in late July)	–	32

What Future for the Oligarchy?

For many, 'reform' in Ukraine has been synonymous with dismantling the ruling oligarchy. One or two individual oligarchs are in trouble. Firtash and Akhmetov will struggle to hold onto their assets in Crimea. Ironically, the separatists in the Donbas have run a strong populist campaign against them. Ukraine's richest man, Rinat Akhmetov, has tried to balance both sides to protect his assets in the Donbas, but he is losing room for manoeuvre. Only one oligarch has even temporarily been in jail, however: Dmytro Firtash was placed under arrest in Austria in March on a US warrant. His bail was a record €125 million. So there has obviously been no general witch-hunt.

At the time of writing, collectively the old oligarchy was at least temporarily stronger. The 'Family' was down, if not yet out; not only were the other oligarchs freed from its constant threats against them, but the tide was turned as 'Family' assets were suddenly vulnerable to takeover. Kolomoisky had at least three 'Family' members in his sights. In one leaked phone call from Serhiy Kurchenko in Moscow, he asks Kolomoisky for 'protection', but Kolomoisky sounds like the aggressor.[21] (When Kurchenko was smuggling oil into Ukraine, it was distributed through Kolomoisky's network of petrol stations.) Kolomoisky also provided 'protection' for the interests of Vitaliy Khomutynnik, another youthful 'Family' member, and his interests in the financial system; and was warring with Ihor Yeremeyev over the state owned UkrTransNafta, Ukraine's oil transportation system.[22] Even Akhmetov might be a long-term target.

Oligarchs run the regions as a price for insulating them from the separatist movement in the Donbas. Most obviously, once again, this has been Ihor Kolomoisky in Dnipropetrovsk. In return for supposedly providing 'order' and preventing the separatist virus spreading from the Donbas, he has run his own militia, and his businesses have remained untouched. He has also exercised power in Kiev; while one of his allies has taken over as the new governor of Odesa. But Kiev has also allowed the old guard to stay on in cities like Kharkiv, after they cut off funding to local separatists.[23] Many of the new battalions fighting in the east were supported by the oligarchs, which will make it even harder to take the arms out of Ukrainian politics in the longer run.

In politics, the oligarchs have been playing the old game of musical chairs behind the scenes. Former Party of Regions members have been selling their support in parliament in exchange for being allowed to continue their illicit practices, as well as for being offered political appointments and preferential access to the coffers of the state. Increasingly, however, it has looked as though there is a big division between one camp, headed by Kolomoisky, and another, headed by Firtash and Serhiy Lovochkin, the former head of Yanukovych's presidential administration. There has been a bitter media war between the two camps. Kolomoisky has been happy to spend a few pennies from his own pocket on army supplies, because he has personally been doing much better behind the scenes: he dominated the new European Choice faction in parliament and Tihipko manoeuvred in his orbit. Firtash and Lovochkin have sponsored Poroshenko and Lyashko. Yeremeyev of UkrTransNafta, Kolomoisky's rival, has been in their orbit. Lovochkin has backed Oleh Lyashko's Radical Party, spreading the group's bets.

In Kiev it was often claimed that 'there was no alternative' to using the oligarchs to establish order in the east: the official institutions were simply too weak. This was false and fatalistic. Ukraine could not remain in the dangerous situation where it effectively had two presidents – Petro Poroshenko as the elected president in Kiev, and Ihor Kolomoisky in Dnipropetrovsk. Ukraine may have a new political nation, but it has yet to build an effective state. More traditional sinews of power clearly need to be strengthened and reformed: the armed forces suffered major neglect under Yanukovych; the security services were thoroughly infiltrated by Russians; and the tax and customs services were deeply corrupt. Reform of the Procuracy had barely begun by the time the government fell, resulting in a rowdy demonstration outside the Kiev offices on 18 June. Ironically, the new Procuracy was supposed to be investigating massive corruption in the construction of its own new office building.

Russian Pressure, Russian Influence

Institutional weaknesses are the main reason why there is still a powerful Russian lobby within Ukraine, despite the ongoing 'anti-terrorist operation'. Ukraine is still a weak state, open to too many forms of influence.

Many members of the old Russia lobby fled to Russia during or after the Uprising in February. But many remained, and Russian money can still buy new allies. Until new elections were held, there was still a Russia Group of maybe twenty in parliament.[24] Many official parties contained so-called 'grey cardinals' who represented oligarchs' interests, and often Russian interests, behind the scenes.[25] Needless to say, they cared little about lustration or reform. One example was the deputy party leader of UDAR, Vitaliy Kovalchuk;[26] another was the head of presidential administration, Serhiy Pashinsky, considered to be Tymoshenko's 'grey cardinal'. The most powerful figure still in the shadows was allegedly Andrey Portnov, the former 'legal adviser' to Yanukovych.[27] Portnov had actually fled to Russia,[28] but was allegedly charged with maintaining his influence in the legal system, and obtaining a new constitution and political system more to Russia's liking. Many figures linked with both Yanukovych and Portnov still held key positions in the judiciary: Yaroslav Romanyuk still headed the High Council of Justice, and the new head of the Arbitration Court (the key court for business disputes) was Bohdan L'vov, an old ally of Portnov's.

Piecemeal Reform

Clearly, the type of 'big bang' reforms that the Baltic States adopted in the early 1990s or that Georgia implemented after the 2003 Rose Revolution under President Saakashvili (see Chapter 9) would not be possible in post-Uprising Ukraine. A piecemeal reform was much more likely, though it could gather momentum if new parliamentary elections were held and swept the old guard out of power, or if the situation stabilised in the east. Political obstacles were the real problem. The idea that economic reform would lead to social explosion in east Ukraine was false, and was the same old hack thinking that had held Ukraine back since 1991. The swift introduction of market prices for energy, plus a targeted compensation programme, would strengthen the central government's position by showing that it was doing its best to help the poorest members of society. It would also undermine the main source of corruption in Ukraine.

At least the threat of bankruptcy was put off, although GDP was predicted to fall by between 3 per cent and 5 per cent in 2014. The generous loans provided to Ukraine were, in part, a leap of faith, offered before most major reforms were possible, though Ukraine did meet the key IMF technical demands (a floating currency, higher energy prices). The EU promised €11 billion over seven years. This figure would include €1.6 billion in macroeconomic financial assistance, with €610 million to be provided in the short term, as well as €1.4 billion in grants, including €140 million to be disbursed in 2014 to strengthen institutions and financial capacity. A further €8 billion would come from the European Investment Bank (EIB) and the European Bank for Reconstruction and Development (EBRD), plus a possible €3.5 billion from the Neighbourhood Investment Facility.

The IMF's programme was worth $17 billion, with $3.2 billion provided up front. The World Bank aimed to provide up to $3.5 billion by the end of 2014. The US offered a $1 billion loan guarantee, plus $184 million for crisis response, security assistance, reform assistance and building law enforcement capacity. By the summer, however, it was clear the money was not enough; most went simply to serve previous liabilities. The currency continued to fall and inflation rose towards 20 per cent. Kiev was without hot water in August. The government imposed an emergency 'war tax' of 1.5 per cent. Significantly, the newly patriotic general population would have to pay, not the oligarchs. Even more significantly, 'patriotic' energy oligarchs like Kolomoisky succeeded in shifting the burden towards unpopular metals oligarchs like Akhmetov.

The government had some initial successes. A good procurement law was passed, but so was a bad environment law drawn up under Yanukovych. A programme to help small and medium-sized businesses only covered certain sectors, and did not provide the general bonfire of controls that was needed. Its architect, Economy Minister Pavlo Sheremeta, resigned in frustration in August, as did Tetyana Chornovol, frustrated at the lack of progress in fighting corruption.

The biggest change was that the EU trade deal that had caused so much controversy was finally signed in June. The hope was that it would gradually transform Ukraine over ten years, like the EU Customs Union with Turkey which came into effect in 1996. Whether the new rules would apply in the Donbas remained to be seen.

Conclusion

Ukraine could not afford to wait to improve its ramshackle state and economy until the war in the east was over. In fact, the war taught the opposite lesson. Russia would always try and prevent Ukraine's progress, whether the war was on or not. Ukraine's armed forces made gains in the summer precisely because they had been reformed. Putin's appeal in the Donbas was only partly cultural; it was also based on persuading locals that they should walk away from a failing state. If Ukraine were ultimately to be seen as a success story, it could not win back the Donbas by force alone. And vice versa: if the post-Maidan Ukraine became a better country, it would have more pulling power in the east.

A true reformist government might take power after the elections due in October 2014, especially if the conflict in the Donbas is minimised by then. Many oligarchs are worried at the thought of thousands of radicalised fighters returning from the east, to press for true 'revolution'. Retrospective solidarity might help: having sacrificed so much, there would be strong pressure on any new government to deliver change. A new Maidan – a new round of popular protest – is always possible. Unfortunately, the more likely short-term scenario is mobilisation without reform. The October elections are likely to make parliament more patriotic, but not necessarily more reformist. A consolidated majority of patriotic parties would be a transformation, given the divisions that have plagued Ukraine ever since independence in 1991; but more than two decades of dysfunctional statehood look likely to be harder to change.

CHAPTER 9

Other Hotspots

The crisis wasn't just about what Russia might do next. The Uprising in Kiev might encourage other copycats, as the Orange Revolution had briefly done after 2004. More prosaically, whether or not it was part of a new wave of global or local democratisation, it could encourage politicians in Eastern Europe and elsewhere to do the nitty-gritty work of reform. The policies recommended by the EU were not the only type of reform, but one immediate effect of the Crimea annexation was to bring forward to June 2014 the signing of key EU agreements with Georgia, Moldova and Ukraine.

Then there was the question of how other autocrats might react. Azerbaijan used the crisis to crack down on the local opposition. So did Georgia, which had good claim to be an imperfect democracy. In Belarus, Lukashenka made the opposite calculation, and seemed to be tempted to broaden his political base by building bridges with Belarusian nationalism. The rest of the former USSR had more than its fair share of dictators, but there were plenty of others in the world who would be shoring up their defences in different ways.

Many parts of the world further afield didn't care too much. The UN vote on 27 March condemning the annexation of Crimea had a hundred votes in favour and eleven against, with fifty-eight abstentions and twenty-four absent. Belarus and Armenia voted against, as did a motley group of states like Syria and Cuba. China abstained, but so, too, did a large number of developing states, which saw this as a local quarrel between a US–European bloc and a Russian bloc.[1] Others were emboldened to take similar steps. China took a more aggressive line towards Vietnam, both because in this relationship China was Russia, while Vietnam was Ukraine, and because Russia was Vietnam's traditional patron and was busy elsewhere. China has also been accused of using fishing boats and merchant ships as conflict proxies, like Russia's 'little green men'.

Russia and Its Neighbours

But the most obvious consequences were indeed local. Why would Russia stop at Crimea, when it had incurred so few real costs for its action, and when it had defined such a broad agenda? Putin had started on a lot of unfinished business, attacking the entire post-Soviet settlement. He was already well known for saying in 2005 that the collapse of the USSR had been the 'greatest geopolitical catastrophe of the twentieth century'. Now he added:

> Back then [in 1954], it was impossible to imagine that Ukraine and Russia may split up and become two separate states. However, this has happened. Unfortunately, what seemed impossible became a reality. The USSR fell apart. Things developed so swiftly that few people realised how truly dramatic those events and their consequences would be. Many people both in Russia and in Ukraine, as well as in other republics hoped that the Commonwealth of Independent States that was created at the time would become the new common form of statehood. They were told that there would be a single currency, a single economic space, joint armed forces; however, all this remained empty promises, while the big country was gone . . .
>
> The Russian nation became one of the biggest, if not the biggest ethnic group in the world to be divided by borders.[2]

Putin went on to compare 'the aspiration of the Russians, of historical Russia, to restore unity' to the reunification of Germany in 1990.

This was a massive revisionist agenda. But after the annexation of Crimea, it was an open question whether Russia had the resources to destabilise everybody at once. And if Ukraine was successful in containing the separatist problem in the Donbas, that would hugely reduce the risk of overspill in other areas. If not, then all of Russia's neighbours, friend and foe, had reason to be worried.

Moldova

Most obviously next in the firing line were the two states closest to finalising agreements with the EU, namely Moldova and Georgia, whose agreements were fast-forwarded to signature in June 2014. Russia does not have the same tactical advantages everywhere that it had in Ukraine, and different pressure points for different states. It might be unable to push on all fronts while it was preoccupied in Ukraine, but it was rightly feared that it would when it could.

Moldova is Europe's poorest country, but it has some semblance of democracy, or at least of turnovers of power. Moldova had two one-term presidents in the 1990s; then the Communist Party, which hadn't bothered to change its name for 'marketing' reasons,[3] ran the country from 2000 to 2009; then a pro-European group of parties called the Alliance for European Integration (AEI). But Moldova is also small, and it is often claimed that 'five men rule the country'.[4] Under the Communists, the party leader, Vladimir Voronin, controlled the state. The number one local 'oligarch' was actually his son Oleg, who ran the local sugar business (among other things). Then there was Anatol Stati and his Ascom Group, which had business in Romania and in Central Asian energy and funded the opposition Liberals. The third oligarch, Vladimir Plahotniuc, originally existed in the shadows, running various schemes with Oleg Voronin and managing the Communist Partys' offshore accounts – in fact managing them so well that he was able to take much of the money when the Communists lost power in 2009. In 2012, Plahotniuc's fortune was estimated at $1.7 billion,[5] when Moldovan GDP was $7 billion.[6] A fourth oligarch was Vlad Filat, who made his original fortune in the 1990s, with RoMold Trading over the Romanian border in Iaşi. He may have skipped a customs payment or two, but now ran the business-friendly Liberal Democratic Party.

The Communists lost power in 2009, not to a 'coloured revolution', but after their botched repression of a botched attempt at revolution. Alleged fraud gave the Communist Party a majority in the April 2009 elections, but one short of the magic number of 61 seats out of 101 to elect a new president. Protests were hijacked by government provocateurs, leading to hundreds of arrests and four alleged deaths in police custody. Voronin blamed the Romanians and Stati, the oligarch, for funding the opposition Liberal Party, backed by his Pan-Romanian friends – the Romanian National Liberal Party and the clan surrounding former Romanian Prime Minister Adrian Năstase.

The crackdown polarised politics. Privately, the EU was urging compromise, which would have kept the Communists in power. But intransigence won the day. Two successive failures to elect a new president meant new elections. Voronin thought he had protected himself by attacking Stati, but he was looking at the wrong threat. Over the summer, several defectors from the Communists, including Marian Lupu, speaker of parliament since 2005, joined the small opposition Democratic Party, which tipped the balance in the next elections. In September, Voronin offered Lupu a bribe of first $5 million, and then

$10 million, to keep the Communists in power.[7] Lupu claimed he haughtily refused – because he was already backed by Plahotniuc.

The elections in July 2009 gave the new opposition coalition, dubbed the Alliance for European Integration, a tiny minority, and Filat became prime minister. The coalition governed for a year and a half, though allegedly unconstitutionally, as it was now its turn to be unable to elect a new president. It took a third round of elections in November 2010 to give the coalition a working majority, but even then not as big as it had hoped. Politics was much more polarised after 2009. There was no political earthquake to destroy the Communists' support base: elections were always on a knife edge.

But in 2009 the EU had just launched its Eastern Partnership project, and, with the Baltic States already members, Ukraine in the doldrums and the neo-liberal project in Georgia more popular in Washington (see below), the EU was in search of a success story. The AEI also benefited from its opponents still calling themselves 'Communists'. The coalition was able to depict 2009 as Year Zero, with nothing before having been worthwhile. Within two years, Moldova had gained a reputation as the top performer of the six Eastern Partnership states. It was awarded a big increase in aid – up from €57 million in 2009 to €122 million in 2012. By 2011, Moldova could claim to have one of the fastest-growing economies in Europe, with GDP growth of 15 per cent in three years, before a slowdown in 2012. Moldova negotiated its Deep and Comprehensive Free Trade Agreement with the EU in sixteen months, and visa-free travel to the EU was agreed in April 2014. Moldova joined the 'open skies' programme in 2012, leading to plans to send budget airlines to the country. The government pushed through many key sectoral reforms: economic courts were dissolved in 2011, an anti-discrimination law was passed in 2012, as was a law on police (2013) that abolished the Soviet-style traffic cops and introduced an independent General Police Inspectorate.

But the reforms were not as deep as in Georgia. According to one EU ambassador, the Moldovans were keen to adopt the 'European way' as their default option, but with little local ownership, so that reform ran out of steam after two years: 'They are too externally focused. Their default position is the import of the "European standard" best practice – without giving it roots. There's not a lot of local generation of ideas.'[8] There was no signature 'Moldovan' economic policy. There was no flat tax, and the country considered itself too poor for neo-liberalism. The closest equivalent to such a touchstone policy was the local programme of free economic zones, which provided spare parts for Mercedes and BMW.

But the AEI was badly designed at birth – or more exactly, at its rebirth. The 2010 elections were also close. Putin sent his right-hand man, Sergey Naryshkin, to the Moldovan capital Chişinău to try and persuade Lupu, Plahotniuc and other members of the Democratic Party to defect back to the Communists. He did not succeed, but encouraged the Democrats to secure a high price for not defecting, with the signing of a secret agreement in December 2010 (leaked in 2012)[9] to partition not just ministries, but also supposedly neutral state institutions and the economy itself. The Liberal Democrats ran the customs, and the Liberals the airways and railways, via the Ministry of Transportation. The Democratic Party was allowed to control the whole justice sector: the courts, the Procuracy and the National Anti-Corruption Centre (NAC) (which turned into its ironic opposite). Its legal powers were used to soften up and take over businesses targeted by Plahotniuc and to shift state bank accounts (the telecoms and postal service, Chişinău airport and the health and education ministries) to his Victoria bank. Plahotniuc took over Publika TV in the summer of 2012.

Prime Minister Filat meanwhile had a role in the customs (75 per cent of the budget) and controlled Tutun-CTC (a tobacco factory in Chişinău) and Aroma (alcohol).[10] Two notorious deals in 2013, to sell the Banca de Economii and Chişinău airport to shady Russians, were allegedly approved by Filat.

After nine hundred days without a head of state, the jurist Nicolae Timofti was finally elected president in March 2012. Ironically, the key extra votes came from Communist defectors. This should have given the AEI fresh wind. But Filat turned on his opponents, withdrawing the licence of the pro-Communist NIT TV, and backing a law banning the use of communist symbols, including the hammer and sickle. The opportunity to do something about the Democrats' state capture arose in early 2013, after a local businessman was shot on a hunting trip attended by Valeriu Zubco, the Democrats' prosecutor general. Zubco was accused of orchestrating a cover-up and forced out of office in January. The Democrats instantly fought back, using the NAC to launch investigations against leading Liberal Democrat ministers, including Filat. The accusations were amplified on Plahotniuc's TV channels.

The two sides traded blows, but there was no knockout punch. Plahotniuc was removed as deputy chair of parliament in February; Filat was defeated in a confidence vote in March. Foreign Minister Iurie Leancă was made acting prime minister instead. Filat secured vague promises to depoliticise the legal ministries, but could not remove Plahotniuc's team. In May, the AEI was re-formed as the 'Pro-European Coalition', with a smaller majority of fifty-three, and limped on.

Russian Pressure Points

A change of power back to the Communists in the elections due in November 2014 is Russia's big hope. Corruption is the second factor that makes Moldova most vulnerable to Russian pressure. It has fed popular disillusion with both the Communists and the governing coalition. However, no fewer than four attempts to bribe MPs to bring the government down failed over the winter of 2013–14. Russia even channelled the bribery through local crooks:[11] the Ukrainian raider Vyacheslav Platon and a Russian mafioso, Renato Usatii, who was allegedly involved in the notorious attempted assassination of Russian banker German Gorbuntsov in Canary Wharf in the heart of London's banking district in 2012. The bribery attempts were not entirely unsuccessful: seven or eight MPs were now a law unto themselves, making it almost impossible for the coalition to pass much-needed new laws.

The authorities also played dirty. Plahotniuc was behind a virtual 'Party of Communist-Reformers of Moldova', set up in spring 2014, which had the same Russian initials as the real Communist Party (PKRM). He was also placing his own agents in the Communists' ranks, hoping they would defect after the election.

Russian shadow capital controlled an estimated 70–80 per cent of the banking system: sucking liquidity out of the system would be one easy way to cause a quick crisis. Moldova still had a big agricultural economy, and Russian measures taken against fruit and vegetable exports, as well as the wine ban in place since September 2013, would add to the Communists' support, especially in the Russian-speaking north. Some 200,000 semi-permanent migrant workers in Russia, plus another 100,000 seasonal migrants, were also vulnerable.

Energy was the sector where the EU thought it could do most to reduce Moldova's vulnerability. But Gazprom has fought a tough rearguard action against a planned interconnector across the western border into Romania (from Ungheni to Iaşi), using its 51 per cent share in Moldova Gaz and the subsequent capture of the local Economy Ministry, run by the Democratic Party, to constantly slow the process down. Gazprom first disputed who should own the interconnector, then pushed for multiple tenders, and finally tried to keep the pipe diameter to an 'emergencies only' minimum. But the pipeline was finally opened in August 2014, though Moldova now needs a new compressor station and an onward pipeline to Chişinău to be truly self-sufficient.

Moldova also has no real intelligence service, and its armed forces are weak. So it would be unable to resist local 'little green men', particularly if they began operations in local ethnic-minority regions. Also, Russia has been growing frustrated with its attempts to buy local supporters. No one has proved reliable – at least no one has stayed bought for ever. Some Moldovans have even been resistant to bribes. So making trouble on the ground is an attractive option. One region, Gagauzia, which is home to just under 150,000 Turkic-speaking

Orthodox Christians, held a referendum in February 2014, in which 98 per cent backed closer relations with the Russia-led Customs Union and 99 per cent backed Gagauzia's right to declare independence 'should Moldova lose or surrender its own independence' (possibly referring to better relations with the EU). The referendum was financed by a Moldovan Russian oligarch, Yuriy Yakubov.

The other problem region is Transnistria, the region largely on the other side of the Nistru river that Chişinău lost in the 1992 civil war. Moldova is not like Georgia, however, where all politicians have to stress the importance of national unity. Ordinary Moldovans place the Transnistrian problem very low on their list of priorities. Many politicians in Chişinău are happy to ignore it, others to collude with its business elite.

But the contradictions of Transnistria's economy were an important lesson for the Donbas. Half the region's estimated $1 billion GDP comes from industrial goods, nearly all of which are exported, since there is a lack of a local market. Paradoxically, therefore, Transnistria has a very open economy. It also lives beyond its means, with a massive fiscal and trade deficit. External debt is 400 per cent of GDP, compared to only 80 per cent for the Right Bank. Transnistria is dependent on 'funds generated through sale of Russian gas, cash remittances from expatriate workers, and funds received from Moscow'.[12] Less than 10 per cent of GDP comes from small and medium-sized business. By the late 2000s, Transnistria was costing Russia several hundred million dollars a year. The region consumes two-thirds of Moldova's gas, and, as of 2012, got it for $75–$137 per 1,000 cubic metres, compared to Moldova's $391. Chişinău, meanwhile, was burdened with the ever-increasing debt ($3.7 billion at the end of 2012).

Then there is 'Putin's premium' (*Putinskaya nadbavka*). Russia pays to keep the budget afloat, even directly topping up local pensions, which are double those in Moldova (though still only about $100 a month). Prices are also lower. In return for its financial largesse, Russia (or more precisely, Russian oligarchs) have been allowed to run local heavy industry. Alisher Usmanov ran Rybnitsa (Rîbniţa) steel and cement plants; Anatoliy Chubais's Inter RAO runs the power plant at Kuchurgan (Cuciurgan). The rest of the economy is run by the bizarrely named 'Sheriff' group, controlled by local hood Viktor Gushan, including the giant Tirotex textile factory.

Chişinău and the EU are hopeful that Transnistria will want to share in the benefits of any future trade agreement. But Russia could just as easily lean on it to make trouble. Flashpoints along the demilitarised zone have been frequent. Tiraspol, effectively the capital of Transnistria, could also exploit the competition between the 'two Moldovas'. About 70 per cent of Transnistrians are thought to have kept their options open by keeping their Moldovan passports. In several villages in the demilitarised zone and in the Right Bank proper, locals take Transnistrian pensions because they are higher, raising the threat of westward border creep.[13]

Georgia

Georgia had its reform burst after 2004. Moldova took its reform ideas straight from the EU – 'local ownership' of poorly explained plans was often a problem. In Georgia, a new team swept into government after the 'Rose Revolution' of 2003 – young, Western-educated and highly ideological. They were therefore not typical of the country as a whole: 'Saakashvili's problem was always that his was a minority government.'[14] It was this sense of distance from ordinary Georgians that brought the government down in the end. Nevertheless, for almost ten years the country fizzed with the energy of reform; and Georgia was the most obvious example for post-Maidan Ukraine to follow.

Like the Baltic States in the early 1990s, Georgia benefited from taking a 'big bang' approach to reform – not worrying too much about fine-tuning sequencing, but throwing in all the change at once. Some things still came first: the arrest or expulsion of Georgia's notorious mafia bosses (*vory* in Russian, *k'urdebi* in Georgian) – 'which', one Georgian official joked, 'was good for us, but not so good for Austria or Spain.'[15] According to another, 'our first step had to be reforming the instrument of compliance', the legal and prosecution service, 'before we could then use it'.[16] Harsh sentences for corruption came early on, and prosecutions were facilitated by racketeering laws. A radical neo-liberal approach to the economy then sought to slash taxes, controls and red tape. Unlike the EU, the Georgian reformers realised that post-Soviet bureaucracy was normally a bad thing: the same institution might be a rule-applying bene-factor in Bavaria, but a source of nepotism and income from controls in Tbilisi. They therefore believed in minimal citizen contact with the state. The results of low-level police and traffic cop reforms were spectacular. Then, because 'computers don't take bribes', Georgia made great strides in e-government, becoming one of the most transparent countries in the world.

But not everything was rosy. The conflict with Russia was used as an excuse to cut corners, to build a strong security state, to harass the opposition and to excuse a tougher line on law and order at home – a bad precedent for Ukraine. If often left the government thinking it was above its own rules. The family mafia of the Shevardnadze era morphed into a party mafia, with oligarchs affiliated to Saakashvili's United National Movement (UNM) running energy busi-ness and TV, and being awarded lucrative government contracts.

On the other hand, the shiny new hotels in Tbilisi and Batumi were not typical of rural Georgia, which was poor, conservative and still addicted to clan politics. It was this 'other Georgia' that defeated the UNM at the parliamentary elections in October 2012, despite the strength of the 'security state' built up by Saakashvili. Money also helped. The opposition coalition Georgian Dream was a broad coalition with a liberal minority; but it was also an alliance of Church conservatives and old-style Soviet bureaucrats, held together by the largesse of billionaire Bidzina Ivanishvili. It was the first time in Georgian history since 1991 that a peaceful transfer of power had occurred.

Georgia is still a poor country. On World Bank figures, its GDP per capita in 2012 was still only $3,508, ranking it eleventh out of fifteen post-Soviet states. The fundamental contradiction for the Saakashvili team was that they were pursuing a modern, or even post-modern, project in a poor and patrimonial society. In a sense, they ran ahead of the game – in part because they concentrated on mechanisms and institutions, while informal culture carried on closer to the ground and in the regions. The anti-corruption reforms that also sought to minimise citizens' contact with the state likewise detached too many citizens from the state, throwing them back on informal networks and survival mechanisms and creating something of a vicious circle. Under Georgian Dream, there was a danger of creeping re-patrimonialisation, as the culture crept back through the institutions.

Ivanishvili's 2012 campaign played heavily on his wealth and the implicit changes that it could bring. He found himself topping up the funding for the 2013 agricultural season to the tune of over 200 million Georgian Lari ($115 million). Creeping re-bureaucratisation and the return of nepotism therefore threatened the path-breaking public sector reforms that were still an example for many others in the former USSR, not through frontal assault but by erosion from within.

Several ministries saw the return of nepotism, and the state bureaucracy began to grow again. Old employees returned to the police force, where some of the professionalisation reforms of the Saakashvili era were reversed. It was this creeping change of culture that was probably most insidious, rather than any full-frontal assault on the 'low-level' achievements of the Saakashvili years, which were still valued by the general public. It was more just a sense that 'the Ivanishvili government is bringing back a post-Soviet belief that bureaucracy can deliver'.[17]

Prime Minister Irakli Garibashvili has reportedly created an inner government, staffed with former law enforcement officials from the Shevardnadze era, the clan of his father-in-law. 'Political prosecutions' were numerous, but became a flood after the June 2014 local elections were safely out of the way, with almost the entire UNM leadership facing charges, including Saakashvili. The lessons for Ukraine were clearly mixed.

Challenges from Russia

Putin's Russia did not like Saakashvili's Georgia. According to a Georgian deputy foreign minister, 'We represent a challenge for our big neighbour, not just for geopolitical reasons, but because we are challenging the founding myth of Putin's ideology – that democracy Western-style cannot be implemented in this part of the world without leading to anarchy.'[18]

The extent to which Russia helped Ivanishvili topple Saakashvili is hotly disputed. To Saakashvili's team, the fact that Ivanishvili had made his fortune in Russia meant that he played by the Kremlin's rules; the fact that he was able to make good on his promise to sell his assets after entering politics for a reasonable price was even more suspicious. Certainly Ivanishvili's Georgia has been more open to certain types of Russian pressure, including in areas where some have thought Georgia was immune. One myth is that so much of the country is occupied anyway that Russia could not do any worse. The other is that Russia could not apply economic pressure, as trade had almost disappeared even before the war in 2008, since Russia first introduced sanctions in 2006.

In fact, significant changes in the occupied territories of Abkhazia and South Ossetia soon followed the annexation of Crimea. In late May 2014, a Moscow-backed 'people's coup', similar to the ones in Crimea and the Donbas, toppled Abkhaz President Aleksandr Ankvab and replaced him with the more pliable Raul Khajimba after early elections in August. In June, 'parliamentary' elections in tiny South Ossetia (21,000 votes were cast) were won by the United Ossetia Party, which favours unity with North Ossetia under Russian auspices. One or two Crimea-style 'referendums' on annexation by Russia could follow. Khajimba's followers have threatened to expel remaining Georgians from the Gali district. Tensions have also been raised by 'borderisation': the formal demarcation with fences and barbed wire through the middle of villages – a process that always seems to grab some extra Georgian land. Even bigger claims have been made to 'historic Ossetia', targeting neighbouring Georgian territory in the staggeringly beautiful highlands of Kazbegi. There is also the opposite possibility – of offering Tbilisi some kind of renewed confederation with the two regions if it gives up everything else, including NATO and EU membership aspirations. In other regions, Georgian control over Adjara is now secure, but Russia could stir up the Armenian minority in the southern region of Samtskhe-Javakheti.

Georgia is less vulnerable to Russian pressure on energy and trade than is Moldova or Ukraine, but it is not immune. Georgia under Saakashvili solved the chronic problems of energy supply that led to frequent power cuts. It expanded hydro-electric power and imported gas from Azerbaijan, though oil imports from Russia also rose. The restoration of trade under Ivanishvili saw exports to Russia quadruple from $45 million in 2012 to $190 million in 2013, including 50 per cent of wine exports – i.e. back up to a level where the loss of the market might matter again. Georgia's most sensitive economic pressure point is remittances: in 2013, the country received $1.48 billion, 54 per cent from Russia. The free trade deal with the EU would therefore not change fundamentals, or commit Georgia to the EU.[19]

Georgia is not so vulnerable to 'little green men' – its security and intelligence forces are much stronger than Moldova's. More subtly, however, it is vulnerable to the reappearance of Georgian Russophilia, especially if disillusion sets in with the EU and NATO and fuels a parallel revival of Georgian nativism. The Georgian Orthodox Church is extremely conservative. It used to be the main national institution – historically, when Georgia was occupied or divided, Georgia was deemed to be 'wherever Georgian was spoken at prayer'. However, the Stalin purges were ruthless and turned the Church into a more pro-Russian institution. In the modern era, the Church has therefore served as a base for pro-Russian and 'Eurasian' NGOs that have mushroomed in number since 2012.

The Baltic States

The other countries with large numbers of ethnic Russians or Russian-speakers are the three Baltic States and Kazakhstan. The latter is a Russian ally, though there are fears that a long-term succession crisis – President Nazarbaev, born in 1940, is now seventy-four – could become a secession crisis in the northern regions where the minorities are concentrated. The Baltic States have a more particular worry. While 'late reformers' like Moldova and Ukraine have found that Russian pressure has made it very hard for them to deliver that reform, the Baltic States had no such problem in the early 1990s. Their problem is, were those reforms enough? Have they rendered the countries safe, now that all three are members of NATO and have been in the EU since 2004?

Maybe the Baltic States were lucky in facing less pressure from a weak Russia in the 1990s. In fact, Russia actually pushed the Baltic States away in the most difficult years, 1992–94, with trade boycotts and energy cut-offs only increasing the case for rapid reform. On the other hand, the fabled lure of EU membership as an incentive to reform was weaker than it seemed at the time.

Often it was the other way around: the Baltic States were constantly being told the time wasn't right, and they had to push hard to get where they are now.

Immediately after 1991, the Baltic States made the difficult transition that Ukraine never managed. From a starting point not that different from the other post-Soviet states, in 2012 the Baltic States' GDP per capita, according to World Bank figures, was around $14,000 to $16,000 (Estonia was the highest), compared to under $4,000 for Ukraine.[20] They also had to cope with a severe recession in 2008–09, but made tough retrenchment choices: they refused to devalue their currencies as a short-term panacea for getting out of recession, opting instead for 'internal devaluation' (basically a euphemism for austerity and deflation), and by 2010 were recovering well. But they have also suffered population devaluation, with significant out-migration that began even before 2008.

The local Russian-speaking populations have fallen particularly fast since 1991. This has aided Russian PR which has used the figures both as a sign of general weakness and as an indication of discrimination (though Russia's own population had declined from 148.7 million in 1991 to just under 142 million in 2009). But large minorities remain. Many have taken the path to local citizenship: Estonia and Latvia largely restored the status quo ante of 1940 – historical minorities have full rights, post-war migrants do not. In Estonia, 100,000 hold Russian passports and another 100,000 are non-citizens, meaning about 150,000 have gained citizenship since 1991; in Latvia there are just under 300,000 non-citizens, down from 715,000 in 1991.

In Lithuania, the titular group is more dominant and the Poles are the traditional minority, but in language terms Lithuania actually has the most Russian-speakers of the three: 63 per cent of the population stated a knowledge of Russian in the 2011 census, compared to 42–43 per cent in Latvia and Estonia; and that figure has actually gone up, from 60 per cent in 2001 (as did knowledge of English, up from 17 per cent to 30 per cent).[21] The main reason is that Lithuania's media market is not so separated into Lithuanian and Russian spheres. It overlaps more – in both directions, so that Lithuanians are more fluent in Russian and Lithuanian Russians are more fluent in Lithuanian (Lithuanian Russians are also better versed in Lithuanian than are Poles).

Russian Influence

Moscow has had a 'diaspora policy' in the Baltic States longer than anywhere else, going back at least to the last years of the Gorbachev era. However, as argued in Chapter 2, the 1990s were largely years of neglect, when Russians throughout the former Soviet states complained that Moscow was doing

Population Change in the Baltic States, 1989–2011
('Eastern Slavs' means Russians, Ukrainians and Belarusians)

Estonia

Population in 1989:	1.566 million
Population in 2011:	1.294 million
Total loss:	272,000 (including 73,500 Estonians, 194,900 Eastern Slavs)
Population composition:	69.7% Estonians, 27.9% Eastern Slavs (16% non-citizens – 368,000 people)

Latvia

Population in 1989:	2.667 million
Population in 2011:	2.070 million
Total loss:	597,000 (including 102,600 Latvians, 446,200 Eastern Slavs)
Population composition:	62.1% Latvians, 32.4% Eastern Slavs (13% non-citizens 671,000 people)

Lithuania

Population in 1989:	3.675 million
Population in 2011:	3.043 million
Total loss:	632,000 (including 363,000 Lithuanians, 222,800 Eastern Slavs)
Population composition:	84.2% Lithuanian, 7.5% Eastern Slavs (less than 1% non-citizens – 280,000 people)

Overall Population Loss

1.501 million (539,000 titulars, 864,000 Eastern Slavs, 97,000 others)

nothing to help. The beginnings of a new approach were laid out in Russia's 1999 Compatriots Law, which began a process of outreach, not just to ethnic Russians, but to all 'non-titulars' living in former Soviet states – and even titulars who retained some Soviet traits.[22] But things really changed after Ukraine's Orange Revolution in 2004, which Kremlin officials regarded as a Western-inspired NGO-fronted 'special operation' in their own backyard. They determined to follow suit.

The second phase, then, saw Russia attempt to saturate 'its' population with the same methods of control that it used for its own domestic population. The Baltic States were, however, democracies. On the one hand, that gave gleeful Russian political technologists more freedom to exploit. On the other hand, it meant they could not set the rules. Russia quickly realised that the narrowly ethnic parties of the 1990s (such as For Human Rights in a United Latvia or the Russian Party in Estonia) were a dead end, as did local Russophone voters, as they were unlikely to take power. In their place there emerged two broad-church parties: Harmony Centre in Latvia and the Centre Party in Estonia. Both Tallinn and Riga are now controlled by 'roadblock' mayors from these parties: Edgar Savisaar, whose capacity for scandal has not diminished over the years, has been mayor of Tallinn since 2001, apart from a break in 2004–07; Nils Ušakovs, leader of Harmony Centre, has been mayor of Riga since 2009. In the 2013 Riga city elections, Harmony Centre won an absolute majority of 58.5 per cent, in alliance with a local party – Proud to Serve Riga! – and with many ethnic Latvian votes. Proud to Serve Riga! is headed by a local oligarch, Andris Ameriks; Latvian oligarchs have been squeezed out of local politics since the 2008 recession and may be using Russian-speaking parties as a way of returning to national politics.

These parties are mainstream, but they are still assisted by Russian money and dirty tricks.[23] Some money is channelled through NGOs like Russkii Mir and '9 May' (Victory Day) in Latvia, or through Baltic Media Alliance, the owners of the Russian-language First Baltic television channel. It was claimed that the Russian Foreign Intelligence Service secretly funded Nils Ušakovs' 2009 mayoral campaign.[24] During the 2011 elections the Estonian Security Services (KAPO) accused Edgar Savisaar of taking €1.5 million from Vladimir Yakunin, the head of Russian railways, for his Centre Party, which won 26 of the 101 seats. In 2013 Savisaar was also accused of laundering money through a Swiss bank account, after the party's entire €470,000 balance was withdrawn in cash.

Russian-style campaigning dirty tricks have also been exported to the Baltic States, with training programmes run by Kremlin political technologists like Modest Kolerov. In Latvia, local equivalents like Jurģis Liepnieks have done the dirty work, often through mudslinging websites like puaro.lv and pietick.lv (which means 'Enough!' and made money by publishing *kompromat*). 'Thirty rouble army' bloggers and trolls are very active, often in the local languages. On the Delfi portal and news comment network, three IP addresses provided 60 per cent of all comments.

Parties have been flanked by NGOs like Russkii Mir ('Russian World'), set up in 2007. Latvia also has For the Mother Tongue (known by the acronym 'Zarya') and, as of 2013, the Latvian Non-Citizens' Congress and the 'Parliament of the Non-Represented'. The NGO Freedom of Speech was used to fund the Freedom Party, backed by the oligarch Andris Šķēle in the 2006 elections.[25] Gazprom funds the Kontinental Hockey League (KHL), where announcements are in the local language and Russian. Dinamo Riga was sponsored by the Russian company Itera.

The mass media is the third, but in many ways the primary, element of Russian influence – especially TV. By the end of the 2000s, a bifurcated media market had effectively been created in both Latvia and Estonia, with Latvia remaining more Russophone because of business, trade and transport links. The Latvian media is therefore half Russian: 'Three out of the six most viewed channels in Latvia have content produced in Russia.'[26] The third most popular channel is PBK (First Baltic Channel), with an audience share of 11.3 per cent, which in any case 'devotes 80% of its airtime to re-broadcasts of productions from Russian Channel 1'. Fifth and sixth are NTV Mir Latvia (5.3 per cent) and RTR Planeta Baltija (5.2 per cent), which both 'broadcast directly from Russia'.[27] The popularity of First Baltic Channel actually grew in the recession, because it was better financed than its rivals.

On the internet, the Regnum site is popular, despite being propagandistic. The Russian presidential administration backs rubaltic.ru. The Delfi portal attracts 60,000 hits a day, and is more successful than the Estonian public broadcaster's attempts to set up a Russian-language website – rus.err.ee. But it is not just the viewing figures. According to Latvian analyst Andis Kudors, 'Russian mass media in the Baltic States is not just a business project, but a part of Russian foreign policy.'[28] The Russian mass media increasingly targets the existential foundations of the local 'national idea' and spreads the trope of Latvia (in particular) as a 'failed state'. The Baltic States are depicted as small and lacking influence. During a 'trade dispute' in 2013, Russian 'health and safety' chief Gennadiy Onishchenko called Lithuania a 'microscopic new political formation',[29] indicating all too clearly that Russia's real purpose has nothing to do with trade: Russia was beating up Lithuania because it held the presidency of the EU during the run-up to the crucial Eastern Partnership Summit in November 2013. Centre Party Russian MP Yana Toom predicted that the

Estonians would die out.[30] Baltic leaders are depicted as crazy extremists who do not fit into the European mainstream. Soviet myths about 'voluntary' annexation and war-time collaboration are resurrected, in particular via the three books published by the Moscow-based Evropa publishing house in 2006,[31] linked to the political technologists Gleb Pavlovsky and Sergey Markov. In 2012, a Russian-backed book on the history of the south-eastern Latgalian region tried to portray a history of the 'Latgalian ethnos' separate from that of the 'Latvian Balts'.[32] The Latvian media, meanwhile, does not plumb the depths of Latgalia. Locals are more likely to vote for United Russia than are actual Russians in Russia. 'Locals believe in the TV Russia, not the real one' – helped by the fact that they do not have to live there.[33] In 2013, however, First Baltic Channel over-reached itself: its news service was banned for three months in Lithuania after it aired a programme claiming that the events of January 1991, when Soviet forces killed thirteen in an attempt to suppress the Lithuanian independence drive, had been a provocation staged by the Lithuanians themselves.

The local energy network is the final element in Russia's influence grid. First is control of the three main 'national champions': Gazprom controls 37 per cent of Eesti Gaas, 34 per cent of Latvijas Gaze, and 37 per cent of Lietuvos Dujos. Another 10 per cent of Eesti Gaas and 16 per cent of Latvijas Gaze used to be held by the Russian company Itera, which was taken over by Rosneft in 2013, meaning the entry of another key Russian player controlled by 'Putin's friends' into the Baltic market. Second, Russia also controls the smaller gas distribution companies like Itera (Estonia and Latvia) and Dujotekana, Stella Vitae and Vikonda (Lithuania) – and it is worth noting that the local Baltic markets are actually important revenue sources for Russia, thanks to market pricing. Third come other companies linked to the energy grid, like Latvenergo. The owners are often key political players, such as Viktor Uspaskich, former owner of Vikonda; Rimantas Stonys of Dujotekana in Lithuania; and Itera's Juris Savickis in Latvia, who has backed Russophile parties like For a Good Latvia. These networks are more capable of penetrating titular political parties, especially in Latvia and Lithuania, where parties are usually small and ephemeral, making them more vulnerable to influence. Estonia is an exception, with its more stable and dominant centre-right.

In Latvia, Gazprom used to work through the leading oligarch Andris Šķēle, and the Ministry of Economics is still stuffed full of guys from Latvenergo and Latvian Gas (owned by Itera and Gazprom). As a consequence, Latvia's new independent energy policy is taking forever to develop. Some progress has been made on reducing energy dependence on Russia. In 2009, the EU introduced the Baltic Energy Market Interconnection Plan (BEMIP). Electricity connections are planned for Estonia to Finland (Estlink was operational from 2007, Estlink 2 will follow in 2014) and Lithuania to Sweden (NordBalt, due for completion by the end of 2015), with LitPol planned to link Lithuania and Poland. Initially, all three states pursued separate liquefied natural gas (LNG) projects, but Lithuania moved ahead, with the Klaipėda LNG terminal due to be completed by the end of 2014. Lithuania's gas market is twice the size of Latvia's, but the project risks becoming a white elephant in a world of shale.

Instead of being an 'energy island', the Baltic States are now an 'energy peninsula'. Estonia is a net energy exporter; Latvia has concentrated on keeping consumer prices down, and so has no grand projects, unlike Lithuania, which has five in total: three interconnectors, LNG and mothballed nuclear expansion, plus possible shale gas reserves – and a floating LNG terminal should be operational off the Lithuanian coast at Klaipėda by the end of 2014.

The next linkage task is transport. Modern Riga has a shiny new hub airport, and a theme park exhibit of rusty Soviet planes. Tallinn's airport is small and new; Vilnius's is just small. But 'the railway map hasn't changed. It's cheaper for some of our exporters to sell all the way in Central Asia. Our competitive advantage runs out at the German border.'[34]

The Post-modern Phase

A third phase of Russian influence began in the 2010s, providing a foretaste of how Russian propaganda would work in the West during the Ukraine crisis in 2014. Elections in Latvia and Estonia in 2011 showed that the Russian parties could not yet take national power: they were only partially 'post-ethnic', and the Russian-language electorate was only so big. But successive fly-by-night populist parties were easier to influence. Moreover, new media meant new possibilities. Putin's post-2012 conservative values project dictated a broader approach; according to the leading Lithuanian specialist Nerijus Maliukevičius, 'you need the reach to throw in the message',[35] and working only with Russophones limited potential reach. The ghetto limit was reached first in Lithuania, where the ethnic Russian population is only 5.8 per cent. Russian-backed TV in Lithuania began broadcasting news in Lithuanian and subtitling Russian programmes in 2012. More intriguingly, Russia began trying to work with a broader range of 'strategic resources'. As the Eurasian nationalist Aleksandr Dugin cynically predicted way back in 1997: 'In Poland and Lithuania the main geopolitical partners of Eurasia should become the forces insisting on a non-Catholic orientation in politics.' Dugin went on to list a motley crew of Russian targets, more or less the same as in the 2010s: 'supports of secular "social democracy" [i.e. former communists], "neo-pagans", "ethno-centrists", Protestants, Orthodox religious communities, ethnic minorities. In addition, ethnic tension in Polish–Lithuanian relations is an extremely valuable element, to be exploited and, if possible, exacerbated.'[36]

Russia's new policy was less about controlling the commanding heights of a media fifth column, based in TV, and more about exercising modal influence in an interconnected world. In Lithuania, Russia sought to connect with greens, parents' rights groups, anti-shale and anti-capitalist groups, plus campaigners against the CIA prisons scandal, the local nuclear power plant, local banks and paedophiles. Russia could not dictate the agenda of such groups, but it could insert messages. It could connect one with another via 'cross-branding', so that anti-fracking groups could link to, or post material from, 'parental rights' groups, and vice versa. Russia could provide resources to help activists translate opinion into action, paying to get them onto the street and into lobbying positions. Russia was sometimes an organiser, sometimes a multiplier, helping the rise of the 'expert' website ekspertai.eu or anti-fracking groups like skalunai. info, and anti-Chevron campaigns on Facebook. The information sources for such sites and networks were often Russian: the Lithuanian State Security Department (VSD) has also criticised their anonymous funding.[37] Significantly, these networks had 'a tendency to coalesce around topics which are of relevance to Russia: anti-NATO, anti-EU, anti-energy security, anti-VSD'.[38] The modus operandi of these often virtual 'radicalising networks' also suited Russia: their members tended to be gullible, conspiracy oriented and anti establishment. Traditional blue-collar conservatives are especially vulnerable, and losses to one particular populist party – Way of Courage – cost the ruling party five to seven seats and potential survival in government at the 2012 Lithuanian elections.[39] The ultimate message is that Lithuania is clannish and corrupt. Ultimately, the interests of Gazprom and Rosatom are defended, and long-term policy-making for the Lithuanians rendered more difficult. The campaign to build an LNG terminal has been slowed down, and Chevron pulled out of a tender for shale exploration after the government changed the law to make it less attractive.

Russia has also increasingly worked through proxies and new instruments in the Baltic States, knowing that it cannot win elections outright. One such tool is the referendum. In Latvia in 2012, Moscow pushed for a referendum (unsuccessful) on making Russian an official language, in order to re-radicalise the leadership of Harmony Centre. In Lithuania, the gas company Lietuvos Dujos covertly financed the (successful) 2012 referendum campaign against a new nuclear power station (to the tune of $8 million),[40] and infiltrated the Green movement and village action groups, mostly Russian, who live near the proposed site. Linas Balsys, a journalist who once worked for President Grybauskaitė, organised the anti-nuclear campaign from his 'Green Policy Institute'. Some money allegedly came out of the Russian embassy.[41] The use of proxies is particularly important in Lithuania, where the Russian minority is small: 'In Lithuania it's impossible to work through the local Russian organisations – they're too divided.'[42] Russia has funded the local Polish minority instead – in kind, help with demos, and the like.

The Baltic States are robust. Their restored independence since 1991 has already lasted longer than their original independence between the wars. But some fear the tide may turn back in favour of Russia. According to Lithuanian President Grybauskaitė, 'they are influencing our media, some politicians; they are buying people in our media . . . placing articles, open criminality, all together.'[43] According to another MP, 'In the 1930s we used to say Lithuania will only be safe when it transferred to Madagascar' – i.e. out of the reach of the Russians.[44] For another, Russia has already 'partially rebuilt the cultural memory of Soviet times . . . Russian propaganda doesn't cost much. It's cheaper to buy Lithuanians than Germans. Actually, we are paying for it ourselves by over-paying for Russian gas!'[45]

Belarus

Belarus was supposed to be Russia's ally, but is has always been a tricky partner under long-lasting dictator Alyaksandr Lukashenka, who, in summer 2014, celebrated twenty years in power. Lukashenka had no love of revolution, but the prospect of Russian invasion or destabilising influence was just as daunting. Belarus has faced Western sanctions since it rigged the 2010 elections and imprisoned most of the candidates afterwards. But in 2014, Lukashenka quietly began trying to rebuild a 'two-wing' foreign policy. His annual state of the nation address was dominated by the words 'state' and 'statehood': 'Thanks to the unity Belarus has been able to build an independent state over the past two decades. It is an achievement our ancestors dreamt about for centuries.' Lukashenka even defended the Belarusian language, which had not exactly been his number one priority in the past: 'If we lose the Russian language, we will lose our minds. If we stop speaking the Belarusian language, we will cease to be a nation.'[46]

Potentially, this would be an interesting shift. Lukashenka originally rose to power as a Soviet nostalgic and populist demoniser of Belarusian nationalism. But he defended and consolidated Belarusian statehood to preserve his own system of power (once he gave up the idea of a career in Russian politics); but a sense of Belarusian nationhood was still eclectic. After years of repression, actual Belarusian nationalists are now so marginal that Lukashenka thought he could bolster his system with a controlled dose of nationalism under strict control of state institutions. But nationalism is often something that develops a life of its own.

Anyway, in the short-term Lukashenka could pose as a defender of Belarusian statehood. The EU and the USA, torn as always between a normative and a geopolitical approach, seemed this time to have opted for the latter, as of 2014. 'Realists' in the West were happy to respond as a way of 'balancing' Russia. Lukashenka restarted the same old trading game over political prisoners that he had cynically exploited in the past. Belarus's most famous prisoner, Ales Bialiatski, who ran the Viasna NGO documenting local human rights abuses (a bitter irony), was released in June 2014 after three years in jail. But by most counts another nine prisoners remain. Belarus and the EU started on a visa liberalisation dialogue, and then a fantastically vague 'interim phase meeting on modernisation issues'.

Armenia and Azerbaijan

Armenia was supposed to be a Russian ally; Azerbaijan had enough energy to dream of becoming an energy superpower on its own. Russia has tried to control both, however, by constantly threatening to tip the balance between the two over the war over Nagorno-Karabakh that has remained frozen since the de facto ceasefire in 1994, but never quite following through.

Neither of the two is a proper democracy: Armenia has been since the late 1990s ruled by the men who were either from Nagorno-Karabakh or who had fought there in the early 1990s. Their power rested on a strong security state. One paradox has been that that state has coexisted with a strong opposition (or oppositions). It has never been allowed to take power, however, resulting in bitterly contested and fraudulent elections in 1996, 1998, 2003, 2008 and 2013. Ten were killed in March 2008. The other paradox is that this powerful local elite is so well integrated with the Russian oligarchy, both because of links with Armenian-origin oligarchs in Russia and because of the huge role of Russian capital in the Armenian economy. All of this has intermingled and been presided over by a diarchy of two presidents, Robert Kocharyan (1998–2008) and Serzh Sargsyan (2008–present), each of whom has controlled roughly half of the economy. Armenia is therefore normally Russia's most reliable ally, but Nagorno-Karabakh comes first. Russia has not been able to find a formula that combines its security support for Armenia with a free hand to operate in Azerbaijan, and with integrating Armenia into its Eurasian Union project (see Chapter 10).

Azerbaijan expanded the range of possible reactions to the crisis by using it to crack down harder on the local opposition, repressing NGO activists and the NIDA ('Exclamation!') youth group, and imposing long sentences on leaders of the two parties Musavat and Republican Alternative. Azerbaijan also received softer treatment after it became a major transit centre for US forces leaving Afghanistan; and possibly even softer if Europe grows serious about using the TANAP (trans-Anatolian, through Turkey) and TAP (trans-Adriatic, to Italy) pipelines as alternative gas supplies. Both are scheduled for completion by 2019, but could easily be fast-tracked by the crisis. There are also vague and more expensive plans for the AGRI project to supply LNG to Romania and Ukraine.

Russia still possesses considerable leverage over Azerbaijan. As always, it could threaten to side more obviously with Armenia over Nagorno-Karabakh, and the unresolved legal status of the Caspian Sea could always be used to threaten Azerbaijan's offshore energy interests. Russia could also stir up trouble among the Lezgin minority in the north, or disrupt the modus vivendi between Gazprom and the Azerbaijani national energy giant SOCAR.

Wider Ripples

In Central Asia, Russia may want to get in quick, because its position is in long-term decline in the region. The ethnic Russian population in post-Soviet Central Asia has almost halved, from 9.5 million in 1989 to 5.2 million in 2010. The largest communities are in Kazakhstan (3.8 million), Uzbekistan (650,000) and Kyrgyzstan (419,000). Fewer than 300,000 now live in Turkmenistan, and only 35,000 in Tajikistan. The Russian language is also in retreat, though Russia still has considerable influence in the mass media of Kazakhstan and Kyrgyzstan. Some 53 per cent of the population in Kyrgyzstan speaks Russian. Russia is also fighting a rearguard action against the rising influence of China, particularly in the energy and minerals sectors.

But many ageing autocrats in the region might bequeath their countries a succession crisis, which might give Russia the excuse to interfere in largely Russian-speaking northern Kazakhstan in particular. In August 2014 Putin stoked the fires by stating that Nazarbaev had 'done something unique – created a state on territory where a state has never been'.[47] Other potential 'Crimeas' include the mountainous Pamir region in south-eastern Tajikistan and Karakalpakstan in north-western Uzbekistan, whose language at least is closer to Kazakh than Uzbek.

All of Russia's other western neighbours are anxious to varying degrees. Norway is anxious about the high north and Arctic development rights. Sweden and Finland are again debating NATO membership, both for their own benefit and out of Baltic solidarity. Poland has seen its own Russia 'reset' collapse. Romania is anxious about maritime border agreements, now that Russia has claimed Crimea. And Turkey is anxious about a stronger Russian navy.

Conclusion

Russia's new expansive mood is not eternal. Putin manipulated the public mood when he spotted the chance after the Uprising in Kiev. So it could easily be set to one side once again if Russia gets bogged down in Ukraine. Only a couple of years ago, Russia was talking about its reluctance to take on a 'sphere of responsibility' rather than a sphere of influence, and about its preference for a 'lily-pad empire'. One of the agencies responsible for the 'near abroad' – the magnificently named Rossotrudnichestvo ('Russian Partnership', full name the Federal Agency for CIS Affairs, Compatriots Living Abroad and International Humanitarian Cooperation) – is planning a review of the operation of Russian 'soft power' abroad.[48] So look out. Not because Russia is planning to give up manipulating its neighbours, but because it wants to perfect the process.

CHAPTER 10

Russia versus the West

For Russia, the crisis was clearly about more than just Ukraine. This was also a crisis for the Russians themselves, although they were loath to admit it. First and foremost, it was about their addiction to self-justification. Russians liked to blame the crisis on anyone but themselves. For example, it was supposedly caused by 'the West's refusal to put an end de facto and de jure to the Cold War'.[1] Or by the fact that 'the international order after 1991 failed to guarantee the respect of national interests of a very large groups of states', including Russia. 'It left them no chance to influence the making of decisions on the most important world issues.' Or the crisis was only one symptom of a 'latent standoff between the West and the rest of humanity'.[2] Or, in terms of its decision-making, as one Russian sympathiser argued, 'in the crisis Moscow is responding', not deliberately making trouble. 'In 2008 it did that in Georgia and now in Ukraine. This is in concreto [sic]. But in grosso modo Russia is responding to the encroachment of the United States and its NATO allies closer and closer to the Russian borders.'[3] In the broadest terms, the crisis was due to Russia's alleged 'humiliation' in the 1990s.

This was classic displacement – never a good casus belli. It also failed to identify a proximate cause, as if what happened in 1989 or 1991 determined what happened in 2014, or as if Russia's grievances gave it good reason to destabilise another state or annex its territory. Russia only compounded the problem by mixing into these long-term theories implausible short-term propaganda about the 'fascist threat'. Russia has, in short, developed a dangerous and corrosive victim complex.

For the EU and its Member States, 2014 was potentially a great European moment, but without the solidarity of 1989. During the Maidan demonstrations there were protests and pickets of Ukrainian oligarchs' homes in London and Vienna – but unfortunately they were nearly all organised by local Ukrainians. Part of the reason for the 'unequal struggle' over Eastern Europe has been that the EU is unequally committed to projects like the Eastern Partnership, where the agenda has been set by the new Member States, particularly Poland (albeit ably supported by the likes of Sweden). Too many big EU Member States have been preoccupied with their own problems. The southern states have been largely absent from the debate, and France too. UK Prime Minister David Cameron was at the Vilnius Summit in 2013 to negotiate with Chancellor Merkel, but that was about keeping one lot of Eastern Europeans out (Bulgarians and Romanians), rather than inviting another lot in (Ukrainians).

For the US, the crisis has been a test of how far to take the era of retrenchment after Afghanistan and Iraq. Foreign policy hardly figured in either of Obama's election victories, except in so far as he promised to work to end the Bush wars. But it will likely be a factor in the 2016 election, and not just between the parties, as Hillary Clinton is hawkish and the Republicans have their own unresolved debates between neo-conservatives, isolationists and 'prudent conservative' realists like Rand Paul.

The Ukrainian demonstrators began by wrapping themselves in the European flag; they ended by castigating the West for not helping defend its own values and for facilitating the corruption of the Yanukovych elite. Then Germany in particular, with 'selective pacifism', has pressed Ukraine to lay down its arms in a conflict it thought it could win,[4] and to sign a bad peace deal putting it on an equal footing with Putin's proxies in the Donbas. The EU has flirted with moral disaster throughout the crisis. And the protestors have been right: Europe is not just about optimum bureaucracy and trade arrangements, but about the basic rights and freedoms we now take for granted in the West. Precisely because the West didn't care enough and its attention wandered too easily, it risked further humiliation. In academic terms, the West risked a 'soft power' disaster. In plainer language, why should the rest of the world even listen to Europe if it couldn't prevent disaster in its own neighbourhood? The crisis risked being a disaster for the EU's entire modus operandi, which is based on the assumption that its model is attractive to the rest of unfinished Europe.

What Did Putin Want?

The Maidan protestors wanted to change Ukraine. They may never have had much chance of changing Europe. But the one thing they apparently succeeded in changing was Putin. There were many interpretations of the new Putin, however. Most importantly, was Russia being opportunistic or was there a long-term revanchist plan?

According to the key Russian foreign policy analyst Fyodor Lukyanov, 'Putin is good at tactics. He has a vision. But there is no strategy in between.'[5] Putin's broader vision was clearer. In his victory speech after the annexation of Crimea in March 2014, he laid out his view of the world after 1991:

> the big country was gone. It was only when Crimea ended up as part of a different country that Russia realised that it was not simply robbed, it was plundered ... And what about the Russian state? What about Russia? It humbly accepted the situation. This country was going through such hard times then that realistically it was incapable of protecting its interests.[6]

So Putin wanted to restore the prestige of the 'big country'. His precise policy on Ukraine, however, was harder to make out. For good reason, as his policy was made up of a mixture of opportunism and flawed historical mythology, symbolised by one ex-political technologist's statement that 'all options are open, but there is no Plan A'.[7]

Most likely Putin was trying to make Ukraine a second Bosnia – a territory also with three parts: a west, centre and east, with the three in constant conflict and having different foreign policies. Novorossiya in the east would be the equivalent of Republika Srpska for Serbia, a Russian satellite state. Or some other dysfunctional arrangement, constantly weakening Ukraine until the West got tired of it.

Domestically, Putin had returned to the mode of permanent mobilisation that characterised the early 2000s. There was a show trial in Crimea against 'Right Sector terrorists' even after the annexation.[8] While this was not quite what another former political technologist called a 'putsch against his earlier self', it did make stopping and compromising unlikely. It 'would contradict the very logic' of distracting the Russian people with 'small victorious special operations'.[9] Though this one was far from small.

'Putin fatigue' turned into 'Putin forever': from a low point of 44 per cent approval in 2013,[10] his ratings climbed back over 80 per cent.[11] He reached 86 per cent in May, and, just as importantly, no longer lagged in Moscow and St Petersburg. The opposition, which had a broad front in 2011–12, was successfully split, although at the risk of pushing Putin to make commitments to his new nationalist supporters. The whole point of a high opinion poll rating in the past was to make Putin more independent, not suddenly beholden to public opinion.

Russian opposition activists were not capable of using the events in Ukraine to revisit their own 'Bolotnaya' protest movement (the demonstrations against Putin during the 2011–12 elections).[12] One made the obvious complaint that Bolotnaya was an elite phenomenon: Russia's 'main problem is a permanent false start' in which the leaders start the revolutionary race without their followers. In Ukraine there is the opposite problem: permanent catch-up revolution, when the whole stadium is already running and the athletes are trying to find out who starts in which lane.[13] However, the idea that the Russian opposition might eventually learn from its Ukrainian equivalent was severely hampered by the relative Russian consensus supporting Putin's stance on Ukraine. In 2004 there were Russian opposition politicians like Boris Nemtsov supporting the original Maidan. There was talk of a Russian version of the Maidan, a 'Maidan.ru', in Moscow in 2011–12. But there are few such supporters now. New Russian nationalists like Aleksey Navalny are often dismissive of Ukrainian nationhood:[14] nor do they want to support a Eurasian Union that is too (Central) Asian, without Ukraine. There may, however, be more tension between the Kremlin and its new acolytes in the longer run, as bailouts, military costs and the effect of sanctions kick in, at the same time as the general budget is being trimmed. As early as summer 2014, there were disappointed rumblings in Russian nationalist circles that Putin was not going far enough. Crimea was all very well, but Putin had not leveraged the annexation as expected, either to bring about the radical collapse of Ukraine or to bring about more radical changes in Russian domestic or foreign policy. Dugin contrasted 'lunar Putin' with 'solar Putin' – 'bad' (lunar) Putin having supposedly sold out the rebels in the Donbas and engineered Dugin's removal from his university post.[15] Currently quiescent liberal dissent could also easily resurface. Whatever was going to happen in Russia, it would now happen more quickly.

Blowback: The Russian Question

As even the short-term euphoria over Crimea faded away, there were many issues that appeared more problematic in the longer run. First and foremost, Putin had never previously been a Russian nationalist. He was what Russians call a 'statist' – a believer in a high and mighty state that takes precedence over national as well as individual 'rights'. Russia is a federal state, though it has never quite reconciled itself to the awkward federal structures it inherited in 1991. So-called 'asymmetrical federalism' is asymmetrical in many ways, the most important being the higher powers enjoyed by the ethnic republics like Tatarstan or Chechnya, compared to the ordinary Russian regions. Crimea, however, would be an ethnic Russian entity in all but name, sparking jealousies in other regions and questions about why other 'normal' Russian regions had no such privileges. And while Putin pushed hard for a federal Ukraine, he ruled out federation for the likes of Siberia at home.

More generally, once Putin lit the bonfire of ethnic rights, it made compromise difficult. Nationalists tend to be absolutists. Putin could easily abandon the Russian fighters if they were defeated – or before. He could also ignore protests if they were left in limbo. Russian nationalist circles have always been thoroughly infiltrated by the security services and successfully manipulated by political technologists. But there would be a price to pay. France's *Pieds-Noirs* caused huge disruptions in the 1960s, but they were disgruntled after ruling Algeria for 130 years. A potential wave of returning Russian fighters would be more like a combination of the Cuban adventurers in Florida after the failure of the Bay of Pigs invasion in 1961, or the disgruntled former military forces undermining inter-war Germany and neighbouring Central European states in the 1920s (west Ukraine, then under Poland, had quite a few).

Failure in Ukraine might also fatefully undermine some key overlapping pillars of Russian nationalism. One myth that could be discredited is the whole idea of a continuous, contiguous *Russkii mir* ('Russian world'), including, by definition, all those who speak Russian. Another was the idea of a common Orthodox world. In 2009 Kirill, chairman of the Russian Orthodox Church's Department for External Church Relations and a keen cigarette smuggler in the 1990s, was elected to be the new head of what is commonly mislabelled the 'Russian Orthodox Church'. His title is actually 'Patriarch of Muscovy and All Rus'. Less than half of the delegates who elected him were ethnic Russians, and a quarter were from Ukraine. The 'east Slavic' idea – of a holy trinity of three Rus nations, in tsarist times the *tri-edinyi Russkii narod*, the 'three-in-one Russian [or Rus] nation' – could also be fatally undermined.

The 'Moscow Patriarchate', which is still part of the broader Russian Church, used to be the biggest Church in Ukraine. Now it is caught falling between two stools: trying to maintain both its strong ties with Putin and its position in Ukraine. According to one poll in April 2014, the rival Kievan Patriarchate had leapt ahead: of the 70 per cent of Ukrainians who said they were of the Orthodox faith, 25 per cent associated themselves with the Moscow Patriarchate, 32 per cent with the Kievan Patriarchate and 40 per cent with Orthodoxy in general.[16] And where would Russian nationalism go next if it 'lost' Ukraine? Off into the wildlands of some new ethnic 'purity' myth? If it stayed with traditional myths, it would have to say that Ukraine had sold its soul to the West.

The Islamic Question

Crimea is, of course, not simply 'Russian' – hence the over-loud protests of the Russian nationalists who insist that it is. The Crimean Tatar problem threatens to become a broader Islamic problem for Russia if it is not solved, or if their organisations are repressed. The Crimean Tatars are Sunni, like the vast majority of Russia's Muslims, and so they have many potential allies, both in Russia and abroad. Tatarstan has proved unwilling to school them in the art of loyalty. Turkey has supported the Crimean Tatars, but not to the extent of upsetting its relationship with Russia. Ankara wants its aid agency TIKA to continue to play a role. The Diyanet (Presidency of Religious Affairs) has strong links with the main Crimean Tatar religious body, the Spiritual Directorate of Muslims of Crimea (DUMK). The Crimean Tatars may face pressure to conform to loyalist 'official Islam' in Russia, traditionally based in Tatarstan. But if the DUMK is forced to join Russian organisations, and a rival 'Tavrida Muftiat' was set up in August 2014, radical competitors will likely expand their foothold in Crimea.

The Crimean Tatars, especially the Nogay Tatar branch, are kin to the Circassians, who used the ill-timed 2014 Sochi Winter Olympics to draw attention to the 150th anniversary of their 'genocidal' deportation from the North Caucasus, which started in 1864. In July 2014, a bill (with little real chance of success) to recognise the Circassian genocide was laid before the Ukrainian parliament, which was suddenly friendly to the Crimean Tatar and broader issues.

Russia's reputation as a friend of Islam in the Middle East is also at risk. Ironically, after the fall of Gaddafi in Libya and Mubarak in Egypt, the non-fall of Assad in Syria, and the tottering of the Iraqi state, Russia has been gaining a reputation as a more reliable ally than the US in the region.

The Eurasian Union

One of the greatest ironies of Russia's actions in Ukraine was that Putin had put so much pressure on Yanukovych to join the proposed new Eurasian Union, and now that project looked to be under threat, even though it is still scheduled to launch in January 2015. Only Russia, Belarus and Kazakhstan are due to become full members. Armenia has been negotiating, but does not want to introduce a customs border with the occupied territory of Nagorno-Karabakh, still recognised internationally as part of Azerbaijan. Even Russia's closest allies in Central Asia have their doubts about the proposed Union. Kyrgyzstan has had a pro-Russian government since 2010 and received $1.2 billion in Russian loans and development funds in 2014, but is geographically a trade corridor between China and Russia. Re-export and drug smuggling are key elements of the local informal economy, and a tougher trade regime might lead to a 'third revolution' (after those in 2005 and 2010). Tajikistan is extremely poor. Its main concern is migrant labour, whose remittances provide more than half

(52 per cent) of its GDP,[17] and Russia is not as open as it was, with its economy stagnating.

Belarus and Kazakhstan were able in 2014 to negotiate subsidies and concessions as the price of their continued support. Minsk got a $2 billion loan from Russia's VTB Bank in June 2014 and the freedom to extract about $1.5 billion extra from refining Russian oil. Mention of a common parliament and potential common currency were dropped from the treaty.

The Eurasian Union has always faced structural and historical difficulties. All the talk of copying the EU was nonsense. Even if Russia adopts similarly worded technical laws, it has no rule of law. The major decisions in the proposed Union are to be made by politicians, and the Supreme Eurasian Economic Commission will have little power, despite being 'Supreme' – certainly not as much as the European Commission in Brussels. None of the states are democracies, and neither 'subsidiarity' (devolving power to the lowest practical level) nor trust in supranational institutions comes naturally to them. The EU's precursors from the 1950s were formed by states of similar size, but Russia is much bigger than its potential partners, even Kazakhstan. That is why Russia needs Ukraine; although even with Ukraine, Russia is still too big. There are no synergies between complementary economies, despite the rhetoric about restoring Soviet chains of production. Russia and Kazakhstan both sell energy and metals. Belarus is a special case, an 'offshore oil economy' based on refining Russian oil. In fact, Belarus is the world's third most oil-dependent economy – oil as a percentage of GDP was 0.5 per cent in 1993, but is expected to have risen to 13.9 per cent by 2018.[18] Trade between the Eurasian Union bloc and the rest of world has grown more quickly than has trade between the three constituent countries; and only Belarus trades more with the other two than it does with the rest of the world. Unlike Western Europe in the 1950s, there are few common values to bind the project together: the still common Russian language is form, not content. There is no big overarching idea to give the project drive. Franco-German reconciliation worked because both parties wanted it to. Russia (or more exactly Putin) may want to restore the great power glories of the USSR, but why would Kazakhstan? Despite Putin's anti-American rhetoric, there was no common enemy to unite the potential members of the Union, equivalent to the USSR itself for Western Europe after the war. On the contrary, many post-Soviet states see outside powers like the USA, China or Iran as allies or 'spoiler' powers. And why, ultimately, join a trade bloc with a country that is constantly imposing trade barriers on friend and foe? Russia's nonsensical 'health and safety' bans on carcinogenic chocolate (Ukraine) and fish (Latvia) could cost it dear in the end.

Internal Russian politics does not support a lopsided link with Central Asia. More than 4 million Russians have left Central Asia since 1991; perhaps three times that number of Central Asians work in Russia legally, illegally or semi-legally.

But the project will still go ahead, if mainly for political reasons – though more as a trade deal than as a political *grand projet*. But what to do with the former Soviet states that do not join? Russia's all-or-nothing approach to the Eurasian Union, and use of coercive pressure to persuade countries to join, means that it has no fall-back friendship policy. Instead Russian nationalists dominate the media, promoting all sorts of scary options. Many have openly sought the Balkanisation of the whole of the neighbourhood, including several states in the EU. This would include the re-Balkanisation of the Balkans, to create a 'Greater Balkans' down the centre of Europe from south to north, from Trieste to Murmansk. Some states have been targets because of their ethnic mix; others because of their political weakness and internal mafias.

Maximalists like Boris Mezhuev have claimed that 'now, after Crimea, the fate of "buffer" states has been called into question. For them, there are two scenarios. Either they are stored in a loose, neutral, federal-confederal status. Or they are divided into zones belonging to different civilisations – to the one that forms the Russian region, and to the one that creates the Euro-Atlantic region.'[19] 'The annexation of the Crimea is not only a reunion of the Russian nation, but it is also the beginning of the geopolitical division of Europe . . . In order to again unite Europe sometime in the future, she should now be properly divided.'[20]

Pivot to the East?

The Eurasian Union is supposed to be part of a bigger pivot to the East. It was therefore primarily a geopolitical move, which is why neither the economics nor the politics really adds up. Russia talks loudly of an alternative alliance with China, but it can feel Beijing's contempt for it as a declining power, even if that decline is one it shares with the West. With the Eurasian Union, Russia will be able to strike a balance against its two big neighbours, the EU and China. It could then define its relationship to a globalising world on its own terms. This is what lies behind statements like 'the EU has to recognise that its standard partnership approach is not applicable to . . . a regional economic bloc with 170 million people and a GDP of $2.4 trillion'.[21] Russia wants special status. It wants to be a dictator of terms, not a dictatee; and it wants to protect itself against Western leverage. Sanctions might make Russia seek out China as an alternative 'window on the world', via Hong Kong.

Nor does the bigger picture necessarily make sense. At the same time as Russia is rediscovering its Eurasian identity, Putin's conservative values project claims to reject the post-modern West, in the name of the real, 'traditional' West (i.e. a West so old-fashioned that it is basically the nineteenth-century England which Putin's hero Petr Stolypin, Tsar Nicholas II's reformist but authoritarian prime minister (1906–11) so greatly admired) – in other words, a stable, conservative Europe. Stolypin, incidentally, is buried in Kiev.

The Energy Non-Pivot

In fact, Gazprom was extraordinarily guilty of ignoring the rising East in favour of milking easy markets in Europe for so long. It should have built up relationships with, and constructed pipelines to, China many years ago. In late 2012 Putin woke up to the threat, but for geopolitical reasons. According to energy expert Mikhail Krutikhin, he ordered Gazprom management to 'go eastwards, regardless of cost'.[22] 'Putin is still obsessed with pipelines rather than LNG.' The 'Power of Siberia' pipeline to eastern China would be Russia's most expensive pipeline ever, at $8 million per kilometre (2011 prices) – so expensive it is nicknamed 'Goldstream'. 'Asia is not commercial, it is geopolitical . . . Russia paid too little attention to China for too long, and is now rushing the relationship. China will make them pay.'[23] 'Russia is playing the China card out of sheer necessity, but it doesn't control this card.'[21]

The much-trumpeted gas deal with China announced in May 2014, for $400 billion over thirty years, was no magic wand or real strategic alternative. Its real purposes were not good business: one reason was simply to claim that Russia no longer needed Europe. Another was to provide an alternative source of rake-offs for 'Putin's friends'. So everything was driven by foreign policy, not economics. The average price of $350 per 1,000 cubic metres was a hard bargain for Russia – China had many more options than Europe. The deal committed Russia to huge costs, primarily to develop the upstream fields and build the 'Power of Siberia' pipeline at an estimated $40 billion. Indeed that was probably the point: to create another gigantic mega-project for sub-contractors to gorge on. The list of extra side contracts nearly all went to 'Putin's friends': Yamal SPG, Novatek, Volga Group and Yamal LNG (Timchenko), Siberia Holding (Timchenko and friends), Rosneft (Sechin), Russian Railways (Yakunin), Inter RAO (the Kovalchuks), Gazprombank (Aleksey Miller), and En+ and Russian Machines (Oleg Deripaska). Putin had to suspend various taxes even to make this work. And, just to clarify who had the upper hand, Gazprom would be borrowing $25 billion from China, now that it was cut off from Western finance.

Hybrid War

The conflicts in Crimea and the Donbas were heralded as new types of war, albeit different types,[25] variously called 'hybrid war', 'non-contact war', or 'non-linear war'. Interestingly enough, none other than Igor Strelkov gave an unguarded interview on the subject in 2013, since unearthed and translated.[26] In it, he claimed the 'key to success in the new type of war is to carry out preventive special operations rather than large-scale military ones. With the timely elimination of selected leaders, be it by methods that are not always outwardly legal.' He seems to have been obsessed with the threat from radical Islam, against which the 'fight should be lawful but tough. It might perhaps even go beyond the framework of human rights.' Ukrainians would do just as well.

Hybrid war was the latest bastard offshoot of political technology, with the same ultra-cynical and often self-defeating methodology. Hybrid war did not look like old-fashioned war. Conventional armed forces hovered in the background as a controlling factor, creating fear but not being used for direct action. Well-prepared insurgency groups were front-stage instead. But even their role was shadowy. With 'plausible deniability', there was no responsibility-taking enemy – or any apparent enemy at all. The vast majority of conflict could therefore be information war, ideally without a shot being fired. Hybrid war would also transcend the old-fashioned idea of military blocs facing off against one another; shifting alliances of new actors would take the place of conventional alliances – manipulated media, NGOs, useful idiots and non-state actors.

According to Peter Pomerantsev, hybrid war was also a means whereby 'nominally "Western" companies' that did business with Russia could replace nation-state actors, which were in any case hollowed out by their willingness to accept, or even tout for, 'corrupt financial flows from the post-Soviet space'. 'Part of the rationale for fast-tracking Russia's inclusion into the global economy was that interconnection would be a check on aggression.'[27] 'Non-linear war is the means through which a geopolitical raider can leverage his relative weakness.'[28] It was foreign policy as *raidertsvo*, which in the cut-throat world of Russian *biznes* 'involves buying a minority share in a company, and then using any means at your disposal (false arrests, mafia threats, kidnapping, disinformation, blackmail) to acquire control. Russian elites sometimes refer to the country as a "minority shareholder in globalization," which, given Russia's experience with capitalism, implies it is the world's great "corporate raider".'[29]

Pomerantsev also quoted Vladislav Surkov (writing under his pseudonym) on 'non-linear war', in a rather chilling prediction of how the forces in the Donbas might be exploited and then dropped: 'In the primitive wars of the

19th and 20th centuries it was common for just two sides to fight'; but in future wars, 'a few provinces would join one side, a few others a different one. One town or generation or gender would join yet another. Then they could switch sides, sometimes mid-battle. Their aims were quite different.'

This was, in other words, 'a conflict of coercive communication – armed politics – in which actions are designed to send a political message, rather than militarily defeat an enemy'. 'Putin has encouraged the West to see his actions through a conventional war framework, which Western analysts accept each time they fixate on whether or not Russia will invade each time there is a fresh incident', leaving the West struggling to catch up. 'Over-reliance on Putin's framework harms Western interests by ensuring that its responses are too late: Moscow's goals can be achieved without a conventional invasion, the threat of which nonetheless functions as useful way [sic] of distracting opponents.'[30]

In Crimea, these tactics seemed to work. Few real, rather than warning, shots were fired, though plenty of Kalashnikovs were brandished. On the other hand, after the naïve use of communications by the Russian side in the 2008 Georgian war, Russian forces reverted to low-tech methods to escape detection, using couriers.

But despite the initial flush of commentary, hybrid war was not a new formula for success in the world after the Bush wars. In the Donbas, the longer the conflict went on, the more problems were apparent with the methodology. The length of the conflict led to a loss of control over proxies. It also meant that the quality of those proxies mattered more. The Crimean coup was over in days, before too much attention could be focused on who the proxies actually were. In the Donbas they were on the stage for too long. And plausible deniability became less and less plausible, as the same old grind reinforced the reality of who these people actually were. Russia found itself supplying more and more weapons in what looked more and more like a conventional war.

The Power of Bullshit

They say people come to believe their own myths. Maybe Putin does, as he reportedly only reads security briefs. But more likely than the idea that his virtual reality had developed a life of its own, was that cynicism and doublespeak had. Putin was perfectly capable of vehement defence of what he knew to be inventions, and of talking about defending the rights of Russian-speakers while simultaneously being busy manufacturing the threat in private.

But this was little noticed abroad. Russia initially reaped the benefits of the media network it had built up since the Orange Revolution. Russia Today, launched in 2005, claimed to be the world's third most popular TV channel (rebranded in 2009 as 'RT'), because it was 'alternative', and, just as significantly, the world's biggest supplier of news clips on YouTube. Up to 2.5 million people supposedly watch it in the UK alone.[31] In December 2013, the longstanding news agency RIA-Novosti was replaced and also renamed Russia Today. But the Kremlin line was also fed westwards by the traditional political technology troll army of bloggers, news posters and Facebook 'likers'.

Lenin is supposed to have talked of 'useful idiots', though there is controversy as to whether or not he really used the exact phrase. The original useful idiots in the middle of the twentieth century were literally fellow travellers on the left. They looked east, because they believed in some version of the Soviet project. In the 2010s, the West was solipsistic, not looking in any particular direction. But this actually gave Russia more scope. Putin could appeal to a variety of different audiences – some defined, some all the better for being undefined. There were still many on the left who thought in the anti-fascist frame. But Putin could also provide succour to some blood-and-soil nationalists on the right, whose greater hatred was for the EU. Indeed, the Kremlin's links with certain parties like Jobbik in Hungary or the National Front in France may have involved more than just inspiration or narrative manipulation.[32] Russia's cynicism also meant it was good at linking left and right and others, using a contradictory kaleidoscope of messages to build alliances with initially disparate discussion groups on the internet and in social media. There were also directly or discreetly pro-Russian groups on Twitter and the like.[33]

Russia's message was also pitched at broader groups. There were German intellectuals, for example, who still followed Thomas Mann's idea of a special connection between the Germans and the Russians, with their 'more mystical' souls.[34] Russia was also good at exploiting the mind-set of the old imperial states. Diplomacy between big states, if necessary over the heads of the likes of Ukraine, confirmed that France and the UK were still important. And then there were pro-Russian business interests, or just businesses with interests in Russia, which Russia thought could be relied on to undercut EU or Member State policies in the West (see above). 'Useful idiot' was clearly an outdated term, now that Russia had so many different types of sympathisers.

But Russian propaganda during the crisis also showed signs of domestic 'political technology' being too long in the tooth. Russia was subject to the same kinds of laziness abroad that had almost tripped up the system domestically in 2011. Russian propagandists may have assumed that Western public opinion would simply not fact-check on matters in Russia's backyard. Ukrainian journalists set up rebuttal units like www.stopfake.org to chronicle the most egregious and lazy propaganda. Russia 'cut and pasted' scenes both from Kosovo in 1999 and from a 2010 film made in Belarus about the 1941 Nazi invasion, in order to show 'refugees fleeing from Ukraine'.[35] A report showing Donetsk in flames was simply made with Photoshop.[36]

The crisis showed the power of Russian propaganda, especially in its early stages, when its tropes seemed plausible to some. But it also showed that Putin was a victim of his own propaganda. Ukraine was not full of fascists; nor was it a failed state or a tinderbox waiting to explode. It had become a stronger state, though it still had a long way to go, and survived terrible initial mistakes, like the civilian deaths in Odesa and Mariupol, when many in Kiev feared that just one such disaster would be all that Russian propaganda needed to gain decisive traction in the West.

The Return of Hard Power?

Paradoxically or not, Russia's perversion of soft power also led to more talk about the return of some hard power to the region. NATO was back on the agenda. Frontline states in Central Europe and the Baltic region were talking about spending more on defence. Latvia and Lithuania announced that they would increase defence spending to 2 per cent of GDP, as Estonia had done. Some politicians in Sweden and Finland wondered out loud whether to end the 'anomaly' that they were not members of NATO, beginning with more cooperation in Nordic Defence Cooperation (NORDEFCO). Or at least they argued that they should be free to debate the issue without Russian talk of a veto.

NATO was not likely to reverse the outflow of troops from Europe that had been going on since 1989; though the summit in September 2014 led to talk of a new rapid reaction force. The 'commitment' made in 1997 not to move men and materials into the new NATO member states in Central Europe, the Baltic and the Balkans came in for increasing scrutiny. The NATO–Russia 'Founding Act' signed in Paris in 1997 actually talked vaguely of 'further developing measures to prevent any potentially threatening build-up of conventional forces in agreed regions of Europe, to include Central and Eastern Europe'. But it also referred, rather more clearly, to 'the inviolability of borders' and to all parties 'refraining from the threat or use of force against each other as well as against any other state, its sovereignty, territorial integrity or political independence'.[37] So arguably the Agreement was void.

Poland asked NATO for two brigades, and 600 troops. The Baltic States got a few extra fighter planes. Obama asked Congress for $1 billion for new deployments to Poland and the Baltic States. But that left the 'NATO Partners', i.e. cooperative non-members like Ukraine, in limbo. NATO Partners had helped in Iraq, Afghanistan and elsewhere, so what would NATO do with them now?

A re-emphasis on Article 5 – an attack on one NATO member state is in attack on all – actually only emphasised the lack of security agreements for states in the 'Grey Zone'.

Ukraine dusted off the 1994 'Budapest Memorandum' during the crisis. It is often said that Ukraine 'gave up' nuclear weapons. But it did not. Soviet nuclear weapons were stationed on its soil when the Soviet Union collapsed. Actually, mobile weapons were moved back to Russia pretty quickly, but 179 intercontinental ballistic missiles (ICBMs) in silos weren't going anywhere. So 'location' was in Ukraine, but 'control' – Boris Yeltsin's trembling finger over the nuclear button – was firmly in Moscow. In 1992–93, some factions in Ukraine thought of asserting an intermediate category – 'ownership' – as the ICBMs were in Ukraine, but that was never formally established. Some even talked of working to gain 'control' via nuclear facilities at Kharkiv and elsewhere.

But the rest of the world leant on Ukraine pretty hard. The US in particular did not want to see Ukraine suddenly become a new nuclear state. All of Ukraine's other ambitions were on hold until it signed a trilateral agreement with Russia and the US in January 1994. In return for agreeing to the transfer and dismantlement of the missiles in Russia, Ukraine got a lot – including aid and diplomatic attention. It also got the Budapest Memorandum, signed in December 1994, in which three nuclear powers – the US, Russia and the UK – agreed to 'refrain from the threat or use of force against the territorial integrity or political independence of Ukraine' (Article 2) and to 'refrain from economic coercion' (Article 3). In Article 4 the parties promised 'to seek immediate United Nations Security Council action to provide assistance to Ukraine, as a non-nuclear-weapon State party to the Treaty on the Non-Proliferation of Nuclear Weapons, if Ukraine should become a victim of an act of aggression or an object of a threat of aggression in which nuclear weapons are used'. Article 6 promised that the parties would 'consult in the event a situation arises that raises a question concerning these commitments'.[38]

Unfortunately, Article 4 referred to nuclear attack, and Article 6 was vague. In 2014, the promises meant nothing, although Russia was clearly in breach of Article 2, and massively and consistently, Article 3. The one clear consequence, however, was the damage to non-proliferation. Why would other nuclear states and potential nuclear states give up their weapons or ambitions for similar worthless bits of paper?

But if the Budapest Memorandum was deemed not so relevant in the crisis, Ukraine and other non-NATO members clearly need something else. Europe has tried various ways of protecting its small states. The Treaty of Westphalia in 1648 introduced the idea of princely sovereignty, later interpreted as state sovereignty. The Congress of Vienna tried a concert of empires after 1815.

Post-war Europe was based on a stand-off between two blocs with superpower umbrellas. Many ideas were mooted in the years after 1989,[39] but incomplete NATO expansion without Ukraine or Russia became the new norm. Europe after the end of the 'post-' Cold War period has many unprotected states, and no real pan-European security architecture. Something will have to give.

Revisionism

Ironically, Russia also made the same point about gaps in the European security architecture, though it was obviously thinking of itself as the main gap. At the same time it was accused of tearing up the rules by annexing Crimea and staging a thinly disguised proxy war in the Donbas. Russia was indeed in breach of many rules and commitments, so it is worth listing a few, starting with the UN Charter from the 1940s and the OSCE commitments from the 1970s, as well as the 1994 Budapest Memorandum and the 1997 Friendship and Cooperation Treaty with Ukraine. Just to labour the point, the latter refers to 'sovereign equality, territorial integrity, inviolability of borders, peaceful settlement of disputes, the non-use of force or threat by force, including economic and different ways of pressure, the rights of the people freely to dispose of the destiny, non-interference to internal affairs . . .'[40]

Russia claimed it was somehow following the Kosovo 'precedent', which was nonsense. Between the NATO campaign against Yugoslavia in 1999 and Kosovo's declaration of independence in 2008, there were nine years filled with negotiations and followed by an International Court of Justice advisory opinion that the declaration did not violate international law, and a UN resolution leading to the 2013 Serbia–Kosovo Agreement.

Russian simply annexed Crimea. Regardless of whether each step in the Kosovo process was perfect, there was clearly more process. There was no Kosovo precedent. But there is now a Crimea precedent.

Russia is perhaps on stronger ground when it claims that others have broken the ill-defined norms of international law. Russians themselves like to make the joke that Russia has 'broken the West's monopoly on violating the bases of international law'.[41] But Russia spent more than twenty years after 1991 as a leading advocate of international law, because it thought that would restrain American primacy and power. In 2014 Putin twisted himself in knots, as he still had to pay lip-service to this. But in reality he had just done what he always accused America of doing, and driven a coach and horses through what passes for international law.

Russia is widely said to be a 'revisionist power'. But is it? More exactly, Russia has claimed that the post-Cold War rules were never agreed in the first place. Even the grand 'Paris Charter', a formal successor to the 1975 Helsinki Accords, was adopted in November 1990, before the end of the USSR (though the 1999 OSCE summit in Istanbul did include the signing of a Charter for European Security).

But Russia obviously wanted to change the status quo. Ironically, Russia's attitude was actually a combination of short-term rashness and long-term confidence. It thought that it could afford to wait and work with the 'next Europe', one more under the influence of traditional nation states and the likes of Marine Le Pen, and maybe Jobbik, too.

More generally, the annexation of Crimea pointed to the weakness of anything resembling global 'governance'. So long as Russia had a veto on the UN Security Council, votes like the General Assembly Resolution in March 2014 condemning the annexation were more useful for indicating the global line-up of sympathisers and opponents than actually forcing Russia to move back. Russia was temporarily excluded from the G8, but was actually a big fan of the G20, where many of what Moscow considered its fellow BRIC states were grouped (Russia's economy is actually too weak for it really to be considered a 'BRIC').

Energy

Many in Europe argued that it made no strategic sense to pick fights with Russia, as Russia was Europe's main energy supplier. Russia duly cut off the gas supply to Ukraine in June 2014, just after Poroshenko was elected president, in the middle of summer, when Ukraine's reserves were impressively high. But big bills still piled up. And any cut-off the following winter would, of course, be much more serious.

But the idea that Europe should be worried when it was Russia that needed the export income was at best always paradoxical. The January 2009 crisis was both the high point and the turning point in Gazprom's power. Even the idea of Russia as a monopoly was only a half-truth. Just before the 2008 crisis, Russia supplied 33 per cent of the EU's oil imports and 43 per cent of its gas imports (26 per cent of consumption). Six of the ten new Member States in Central and Eastern Europe import more than 80 per cent of their gas supply from Russia, though some don't use that much gas. Only Lithuania, Latvia, Hungary and Slovakia both use a lot of gas and mainly get it from Russia. Ronald Reagan's USA warned Europe that it would be a strategic mistake to hook up to the USSR's pipelines when they were built in the 1980s; but Europe went ahead, and supply was more or less reliable for twenty years. But in January 2006, Russia cut off the gas supply to punish the new Orange government in Ukraine. In January 2009, it engineered a much longer cut-off to repeat the message and to force then Prime Minister Yuliya Tymoshenko to pay a much higher price. And this wasn't the only occasion: even gas to Belarus was stopped in 2007, and to Moldova in 2005 (and 2009). The Baltic States frequently had the gas cut off in the 1990s and the oil in the 2000s.

Ironically, Russia's cut-offs were one reason why the North Stream pipeline under the Baltic Sea was built to Germany, opening in 2011. Germany now imports 36 per cent of its gas and 39 per cent of its oil from Russia.[42] Gazprom now also supplies gas through the NEL system to the Netherlands and Belgium (and maybe one day the UK), and OPAL down to the Czech Republic, plus potentially MEGAL from Bavaria to France. Gazprom Germania and WINGAS have a big role in gas storage. In August 2014, RWE sold its oil and gas section DEA to a Russian group for €5.1 billion. Gazprom also wants to expand in the Balkans. The South Stream project through the Black Sea and the Balkans to Central Europe ought to be killed by the crisis, especially as Russia is gleeful about $10 billion in potential savings from routeing the pipeline closer to, or across, Crimea. But Hungary and Austria are still keen – only Bulgaria has doubts. Serbia can usually be relied on to promote Russian interests, which is why Russia would actually like to see it join the EU.

Gazprom once dreamed of becoming a trillion-dollar company, with sales of 220 billion cubic metres. Its pipeline plans, if they all went ahead, would give it the capacity to supply between 250 billion cubic metres and 400 billion cubic metres. As a guide, the EU's total gas consumption in 2013 was 462 billion cubic metres. But Gazprom faces two massive problems. For its size, it is probably the most inefficient and corrupt company in the world, the embodiment of all the pathologies of the Russian state. Gazprom's share price has dropped by more than half from a high point of 387 roubles in May 2008 to 139 roubles at the end of 2013,[43] making it the poorest-value national energy company anywhere in the world. That made Gazprom's market value at the end of 2013 only $100.4 billion, down from $365 billion in May 2008.[44] In 'Europe' (minus the Baltic States)[45] Gazprom claimed sales of 139 billion cubic metres.[46] But this figure includes re-sales and gas of non-Russian origin. A more accurate picture can be obtained by looking at customs figures, to see exactly how much explicitly Russian gas crossed the border.[47] Using this methodology, Gazprom's European sales are actually down by a third from the 2008 peak of 154 billion cubic metres, to only 112 billion cubic metres in 2012, with the EU market likely to bottom out nearer to 100 billion cubic metres.[48]

Gazprom is woefully inefficient in all cost sectors. Anders Åslund estimates annual graft at $40 billion, effectively cancelling out the capital spend of $45 billion.[49] The net debt of the Gazprom group topped a trillion roubles by the end of 2012 (1.081 trillion, or $34 billion).[50] It is now the company with the highest foreign debt in Russia. Gazprom was also burdened with 'non-core spending' on special projects like the Olympics. At the same time, it was kept afloat by cross-subsidies, notably an extremely low gas extraction tax. But its own mega-projects were the real problem, and the key source of corruption. Gazprom's economic model was back to front. According to Andris Sprūds, 'In Russia money is made out of costs.'[51] Some of the biggest companies in Russia are actually Gazprom suppliers, such as Stroygazmontazh, created in 2008, and Stroygazkonsulting, creating 'a huge new profit centre, comparable to Gazprom itself'. And that 'profit centre is in construction, not in gas'.[52] 'Gazprom is a parasite, with other parasites on its back.'[53] Billions of dollars, up to half of total costs, have been raked off the North Stream project, with even more possible for South Stream, as it needs more connecting pipes on the Russian mainland. And all these companies are owned by 'Putin's friends'.

One other thing that changed after 2008 was the global energy market. Most obviously, demand was down, particularly in Europe. But a whole series of technological revolutions was transforming the market. The gas market isn't global, it's regional. And Europe was not developing its own shale gas potential. But it didn't have to do anything to reap the indirect benefits. The 'shale gale' in the US led to massive supply switching, as America became a net gas exporter. Liquefied natural gas from states like Qatar now came to Europe, as did cheap American coal that was no longer needed at home. Tight gas, deep water gas and 'Octopus drilling' (multiple vertical and horizontal drilling) for gas also increased supply. Huge additional supplies have also been explored or exploited in Canada, Australia, East Africa and China, with the eastern Mediterranean (Israel and Cyprus) a particular prospect for the EU. Once the US lifts its post-1970s ban on oil exports and gas restrictions dating back to the 1930s, a second wave of change might follow.

EU policy also made a difference after 2009, with two new programmes: the Baltic Energy Market Interconnection Plan (BEMIP), and the €4 billion European Energy Programme for Recovery 'to co-finance projects (fifty-nine so far), designed to make energy supplies more reliable and help reduce greenhouse emissions, while simultaneously boosting Europe's economic recovery'.[54] The Third Energy Package, which came into force in March 2011, sought to liberalise the market by unbundling production and supply from transmission. Most far-reaching of all was probably the case against Gazprom launched by the European Commission in 2012, whose three abuse-of-monopoly charges could potentially result in billions in fines. Already Gazprom has been forced to make a series of sweetener payments after the Italian company Edison brought a case against it in 2010, to head off charges of overpricing. In 2012, such payments amounted to around $3 billion; in 2013 Gazprom budgeted for $4.5 billion.

Russia's response to all these problems has been threefold. In Europe, it was a form of double-or-quits, pressing ahead with new pipelines. It doesn't need them all. With South Stream, Russia's supply capacity to Europe would be 400 billion cubic metres, more than three times its current level of business. At home, the rise of rivals like Novatek and Rosneft hinted at a 'temporary alliance . . . to establish a parallel gas industry in Russia, free of redundant geopolitical projects'.[55] But Rosneft was also another behemoth, with massive leverage and huge debts funding its shift from oil to gas and its takeover of TNK-BP for $55 billion in 2012 and of Itera in 2013. Because of the high burden, Rosneft was downgraded by the rating agency Fitch to BBB- in October 2013.[56] Novatek was at least a private company: 'it is not a Soviet giant taken over by an oligarch'.[57] Its costs were lower and it did not have the same social spending as Gazprom. But it was run by Gennadiy Timchenko, one of 'Putin's friends'. The third option was the 'pivot to the East' (see above).

In the 2000s, Russia's energy rents – the total income from oil and gas – exploded from around $100 billion to over $600 billion, which was 33 per cent of GDP. The impact of the 2008 recession showed how vulnerable Russia was, as they fell by a third to $400 billion, although by 2012 they were back above $600 billion, largely thanks to recovery in the oil price.[58] Russia would really be in trouble if the oil price collapsed, too: its huge foreign exchange reserves ($467 billion in May 2014), National Wealth Fund and Reserve Fund (both just over $87 billion) and low debt rate (2.6 per cent of GDP) could all disappear overnight.

The Sanctions Debate

A lot of time was wasted in the West during the crisis discussing whether sanctions 'work' or not. Sanctions involve a broad range of possible actions and reactions, so it is like asking whether the West is good at sports. Some types of sanctions work in some circumstances; some don't. Some might work only too well.

The West dragged its feet throughout the crisis, first proving reluctant to sanction Ukrainian leaders, then Russian. The shifting ground of counter-arguments gave away to underlying reluctance: 'sanctions don't work', 'the threat of sanctions is better than sanctions themselves', 'the threat of more sanctions is better than more sanctions', and so on. Ukrainian writer Irena Karpa raised a satirical sign in Germany: 'Your porn is harder than your sanctions.'

On Ukraine, the EU did not move until the morning of the sniper killings in Kiev, 20 February. Sanctions then instantly worked, by helping push over the tottering edifice of the Yanukovych regime. But the EU was rightly criticised for having taken so long to do what was so easy, given that so much of the regime's money was in plain sight.[59] Meanwhile, the EU had to cope with

Yanukovych officials petitioning against their places on the sanctions list: the Azarov family allegedly used a German law firm, Alber & Geiger.[60]

With respect to sanctions on Russia, Moscow was only likely to take the EU seriously once sanctions were significant enough to inflict damage on the EU itself. Unfortunately 2014 was exactly the wrong moment; with the eurozone economy flat-lining again, any serious measures could tip it back into formal recession – or at least that threat provided the perfect excuse not to act. The US was a different matter: its direct trade with Russia is low, but its indirect effect is massive, as it stands at the apex of the global financial system. America's hard power may be waning and its soft power easy to criticise, but it still has a massive comparative advantage in financial power and in intelligence. So the Obama administration has increasingly resorted to the 'smart power' of financial sanctions. The new cutting edges of US power are no longer just marines or drones, but agencies with long titles like the Securities and Exchange Commission and the Treasury Department Office of Foreign Assets Control (OFAC). The US may no longer want always to be the world's policeman, but it does want to be the world's private investigator.[61] So the US actually 'crossed the Rubicon' on 16 July, the day before the Malaysia Airlines tragedy. It finally hit the key companies – those owned by 'Putin's friends' and those that Russia depended on for energy export revenues: Rosneft, Novatek, Gazprombank and VEB. It also basically cut them off from foreign capital. Not only US firms, but European firms with US business interests would be forced not just away from new loans, but from holding existing debt or equity securities in the Russian companies targeted.

The damage to the Russian real economy would also be felt soon enough. Front-line companies like Rosneft demanded huge bailouts, in its case $42 billion. Most non-energy companies are dependent on the state banks. If their finance dries up, they will start laying people off and Russia's 'society of estates' (see Chapter 2) will seize up. Putin's counter-sanctions against EU food imports risk sending an already rising rate of inflation even higher – and rising real wages were more important to Putin's popularity than rising GDP in the 2000s. Oil and gas revenues make up 50 per cent of the Russian state budget, up from $17 billion in 2002 to $208 billion in 2012.

Ironically, in the longer run sanctions might be, if not too effective, then too extensive. Russia now joined a long list of other targeted countries (Belarus, Central African Republic, Ivory Coast, Democratic Republic of Congo, Iraq, Lebanon, Myanmar, Somalia, Sudan, Yemen and Zimbabwe). There are also 'secondary sanctions' (penalties on firms accused of helping others evade sanctions) on entities in China, Cyprus, Georgia, Liechtenstein, Switzerland, Ukraine and the United Arab Emirates. And 'there are now literally thousands of individuals and companies on the various sanctions lists drawn up and enforced by the US Treasury's Office of Foreign Assets Control.[62]

The near $9 billion fine against BNP Paribas in June 2014 for violating sanctions against Sudan, Iran and Cuba was highly symbolic. It guaranteed short-term compliance, but the US was starting to hit some important players. On 16 July, at a BRICS summit, Brazil, Russia, India, China and South Africa announced the formation of their own Bank (the New Development Bank), with $50 billion capital, and a $100 billion currency reserve arrangement, to be based in Shanghai by 2016. This bank was not set up just to support Russia, but it showed the direction in which Russia might try to move.

Russia could manage some of the short-term impact of sanctions. 'Putin's friends' were sheltered. Bank Rossiya got extra funds; Gennadiy Timchenko was thanked for giving up his stake in Gunvor. 'Putin's friends' might even grow more powerful in the short run: Kovalchuk consolidated control over the advertising industry, Sechin was nibbling away at Gazprom. Putin might have more power as distributor of a dwindling amount of funds. And only his rules would apply in a more isolated Russia.

But that was only for the very short term. In the longer term, Russia might prove to have a high pain threshold. But Putin and the masses are likely to have a different threshold from the oligarchs in between. Ultimately, both Surkov and Dugin are right: the 'offshore aristocracy' or 'sixth column' is the least patriotic part of the population.

The stock market and the rouble tended to fluctuate with the various phases of the crisis, but capital flight was sudden and heavy. According to the Central Bank of Russia, as of July net capital outflow was $62 billion in the first quarter of 2014, falling to $12.3 billion in the second. But that still made $74.5 billion, which was more than twice the already high level of $33.7 billion in the first half of 2013.[63] The Economic Development Ministry's estimate was $80 billion.[64]

Russia was also highly indebted. Not, that is, the state: Western loans were all paid off in the 2000s, and with the country's massive reserve funds, state borrowing and state debt are very low. But corporate debt is huge. Domestic rents not only corrupted the majority of Russian business, but they also under-pinned foreign borrowing, which had been all too easy for over a decade. As of 2014, Russian private debt was a massive $740 billion and growing. According to Reuters, 'Russian companies raised more than $46 billion on foreign markets in 2012.'[65] Bond sales dropped to less than $2 billion in March to May 2014, compared to $19 billion in the same period in 2013, and Russian banks and companies had $191 billion of foreign debt payments to make in 2014. Plus Russia needed FDI, both in general and an estimated $750 billion over twenty years to keep its energy exports going. A record $94 billion in FDI in 2013 could fall by half in 2014.[66] In recent years, inward FDI has roughly balanced outward capital flight; now Russia would be hit by money haemorrhaging on both sides of the equation.

Finally, it is fitting that Yukos also came back to bite Putin at this time. On 28 July, the international Permanent Court of Arbitration ruled in the long-running Yukos case that every stage in the break-up of the company had been illegitimate (an interim European Court of Human Rights ruling in 2011 is also expected to be finalised in 2014). Russia was ordered to pay $51.6 billion in compensation. The Court is based in The Hague and had actually reached its verdict the day after MH17 was shot down – presumably delaying it to avoid the two stories getting entangled. Russia will, of course, appeal and then almost certainly not pay – but the verdict raises the prospect of Russian assets being seized abroad.

Conclusion

The stakes in the crisis are high enough for Ukraine. But they are also high around Ukraine. Russia has put its entire economic future at stake, at the same time as challenging key pillars of the European and international security order. Other issues, such as European energy security, have been thrown into sharper relief by the crisis. The EU is torn between a foreign policy crisis with drastic repercussions and its own internal economic crisis. Russia's use of hard power in Crimea and the Donbas has had much more seismic consequences than its war with Georgia in 2008. But gains won with hard power are often fragile or themselves subject to revisionism. On the other hand, the crisis showed that not only was hard power not an option for the EU, but seemingly no longer part of its conceptual universe. The US placed its bets on the smart power of financial sanctions. The dichotomy of the West's ineffective soft power versus Russia's fragile hard power does not seem a recipe for stability.

Conclusions

When writing about Eastern Europe it is hard to resist quoting or mocking the British Prime Minister Neville Chamberlain's words about Czechoslovakia before the ill-fated Munich meeting with Hitler in 1938: 'a quarrel in a far-away country between people of whom we know nothing'. But just as the Czechoslovak crisis in 1938 could not in the end be isolated by the Western Powers, so whatever happens between Ukraine and Russia after 2014 will shape the future of Europe, at a time when Europe is anyway changing profoundly.

The original Crimean War in the 1850s sent shockwaves throughout Europe and beyond. It did not end the long peace of the 'long' nineteenth century, from 1815 to 1914; but it did begin many of the processes that would undermine it in the end. Piedmont, which had fought in Crimea, was emboldened to seek Italian unity; Prussia united Germany; Russia announced that it would no longer automatically defend any European monarchy; and the balance of power was profoundly destabilised. Russia upped its 'responsibility to protect' Orthodox Christians in the Balkans and continued to undermine the Ottoman Empire, at the same time as Britain and France sought to prop it up, and Russia grew bolder in challenging the Habsburgs in Central Europe. The effects even reached the US, where the slave interest was empowered by the threat of interference from victorious Britain and France. The war led to both victorious and defeated states launching vital internal reforms – Russia abolished serfdom and Britain modernised its lumbering imperial bureaucracy.[1]

The Ukraine crisis in 2014 might bring an immediate end to the post-Cold War order. Or, like the original Crimean War in the 1850s, it might mark the beginning of a transition to something else. At the time of writing, the crisis is far from over. The drama appears to have reached around the end of Act 4. The

Maidan protests went through their ups and downs. In early January it looked as if they might peter out. In February more effective repression would have had unpredictable effects. As it is, the Uprising was a success. An entire week of euphoria was then followed by the occupation and blitzkrieg annexation of Crimea. Then a planned general rebellion in the east and south became a local-ised revolt in the Donbas. That initially proved impossible to contain, but then the Ukrainians got their military act together. The tragedy of MH17 could have led to another pause on the ground, but in fact Ukraine continued its opera-tions. The tragedy happened because Russia was trying to increase its support for the rebels – which is why the rebels actually had the kind of missile to bring down an airliner in wheat fields in east Ukraine in the first place. After the deaths of 298 passengers and crew, Russia backed off, but not for long. As it looked like its proxies might be defeated within weeks, Russia resorted to increasing use of regular troops – making its 'hybrid war' look more and more like normal war. Ukraine even considered dropping the term 'anti-terrorist operation' – not because it was mellowing in its approach, but because it was fighting Russians.

Sanctions were taken to a higher level more quickly than had seemed likely before the tragedy of MH17, though the US actually announced its major measures the day before. As both sides keep recalibrating the balance of forces, it becomes difficult to predict where it will all end. If Ukraine actually re-establishes control in the Donbas, Putin's adventurism will suffer a severe blow. If it does not, Putin could continue destabilising Ukraine and other neighbours. In any case, change is the new norm. The Maidan Uprising was a self-limiting revolution: despite the hatred of the old regime, there was hardly any disorder in Kiev, but there was soon anarchy elsewhere in Ukraine. The Ukrainian army looked hopeless in March, but it appeared to be winning in July. At the start of August the separatists looked defeated, by the end of the month they were advancing again.

Formal invasion still seems unlikely – Russia's whole strategy has been based on avoiding the high costs of traditional attack. As of late summer 2014, Russia the aggressor was offering both 'humanitarian intervention' and mili-tary reinforcement. In fact, Putin got away with such a massive injection of men and weapons that the Ukrainians were beginning to think the West would do nothing to stop him doing even more. Which was the point – to persuade Kiev to sue for peace. And if the situation needed to be spun out further, Russia might switch to other tactics, with economic destabilisation most likely.

Germany is leading the push for a bad peace, based on two false premises. Berlin's first priority was simply that the fighting should stop, regardless of guilt. Its second was to allow Russia to negotiate from positions gained by subversion and 'hybrid war', rather than pressing for the status quo ante. The reasoning was that Russia would again be 'provoked' by too radical a defeat. Key limits were proposed to both Ukraine's foreign policy choices (no to NATO and even the EU) and its internal arrangements (far-reaching 'autonomy' for the Donbas, no return of Crimea), in which it was barely consulted. Many Ukrainians were therefore asking who put Germany in charge? The crisis showed that being Europe's pre-eminent economic power was no guarantee of being a successful foreign policy authority.

Meanwhile Russia and Ukraine have continued to lock horns, while simultaneously racing towards economic collapse. Neither side is likely to triumph from a position of strength; both have an interest in mobilising against the other if domestic problems remain strong. Both could spiral down together. The trick for the West is to get the balance of incentives right: to persuade Russia to back down, and to persuade Ukraine to reform.

And when (and if) it is all over, there will be an almighty task of post-war reconstruction. Both sides will have to deal with the legacy of artificially induced hatred and basic reconstruction work on the ground.

The picture may or may not be clearer by the time this book comes out, but I would guess not. Unlike the Orange Revolution in 2004, or even the war in Georgia in 2008, so many certainties, policies and predictions have been destabilised that the dust will not settle for a long time.

Notes

Introduction

1. 'Norman Stone: From Syria to Iraq, the mess of the first world war is with us still', *Spectator*, 14 December 2013; www.spectator.co.uk/features/9099222/wrong-track/
2. Interview with Rostyslav Pavlenko, 19 September 2012.

1 Unfinished Europe

1. Brussels Forum, 'A conversation with Herman Van Rompuy', 21 March 2014; http://brussels.gmfus.org/files/2014/03/A-Conversation-with-Herman-Van-Rompuy_ccedits.pdf, p. 21.
2. Roger Bootle, *The Trouble with Europe: Why the EU isn't working, how it can be reformed, what could take its place*, Nicholas Brealey, London, 2014.
3. Robert Cooper, *The Post-Modern State and the World Order*, Demos, London, 2000.
4. Robert Kagan, *Of Paradise and Power: America and Europe in the New World Order*, Alfred A. Knopf, New York, 2003, p. 3.
5. Dmitri Trenin, 'As Ukraine stares into the abyss, where is Europe's leadership?', *Observer*, 20 April 2014; www.theguardian.com/commentisfree/2014/apr/20/ukraine-stares-abyss-europe-leadership
6. Peter Pomerantsev, *Russia: A post-modern dictatorship?*, Legatum Institute, London, 2013; www.li.com/docs/default-source/default-document-library/2013-publications-russia-a-postmodern-dictatorship-.pdf
7. Ivan Krastev, *Democracy Disrupted: The politics of global protest*, University of Pennsylvania Press, Philadelphia, 2014.
8. Hans Kundnani, 'The Ostpolitik illusion', *IP Journal*, 17 October 2013; https://ip-journal.dgap.org/en/ip-journal/topics/ostpolitik-illusion
9. Serhii Plokhy, *The Last Empire: The final days of the Soviet Union*, Oneworld, London, 2014. See also Andrew Wilson and Taras Kuzio, *Ukraine: Perestroika to independence*, Macmillan, Basingstoke, 1994.
10. Tom Wallace and Farley Mesco, *The Odessa Network: Mapping facilitators of Russian and Ukrainian arms transfers*, C4ADS, Washington, DC, 2013; http://media.wix.com/ugd/e16b55_ab72c94c85c6e6c8e88865e93a1a0150.pdf
11. European Bank, 'Transition report 2012: Integration across borders', Chapter 2; http://tr.ebrd.com/tr12/index.php/chapter-2/vulnerability-of-transition-economies-to-their-external-environment

12. World Bank, 'Migration and remittance flows in Europe and Central Asia', 2 October 2013; www.worldbank.org/en/news/feature/2013/10/02/migration-and-remittance-flows-in-europe-and-central-asia-recent-trends-and-outlook-2013-2016
13. Interview with Gleb Pavlovsky, 18 December 2007.
14. Interview with Modest Kolerov, 20 October 2008.
15. Naazneen Barma, Ely Ratner and Steven Weber, 'A world without the West', *National Interest*, 90, July–August 2007.
16. Ahmet Davutoğlu, *Strategic Depth*, 2001.
17. Tadeusz Iwański, 'Ukraine, Belarus and Moldova and the Chinese economic expansion in Eastern Europe', OSW Commentary, 79, 2012; www.osw.waw.pl/sites/default/files/commentary_79.pdf
18. Lucy Hornby, 'China entrepreneur behind plans to build deepwater Crimean port', *Financial Times*, 5 December 2013.
19. Agnes Lovasz, 'Dashed Ikea dreams show decades lost to bribery in Ukraine', Bloomberg, 31 March 2014; www.bloomberg.com/news/2014-03-30/dashed-ikea-dreams-in-ukraine-show-decades-lost-to-corruption.html

2 Russia Putinesca

1. See http://cpj.org/killed/
2. Pomerantsev, *Russia: A post-modern dictatorship?*; interview with Pomerantsev, 25 June 2014.
3. Interview with Sergey Markov, 16 December 2007.
4. Interview with Gleb Pavlovsky, 18 December 2007.
5. Interview with Sergey Markov, 16 December 2007.
6. Interview with Gleb Pavlovsky, 18 December 2007.
7. Interview with Sergey Markov, 16 December 2007.
8. See Ben Judah, Jana Kobzova and Nicu Popescu, *Dealing with a Post-BRIC Russia*, ECFR Report no. 44, European Council on Foreign Relations, London, 2011; www.ecfr.eu/content/entry/dealing_with_a_post_bric_russia
9. Interview with Gleb Pavlovsky, Moscow, 4 February 2012.
10. Interview with Konstantin Sonin, Moscow, 7 February 2012.
11. Interview with Yevgeniy Gontmakher, Moscow, 6 February 2012.
12. David Hearst, 'Putin: We have lost Russia's trust', *Guardian*, 12 November 2011.
13. Interview with Simeon Kordonsky, 21 October 2008.
14. Remarks by Dmitri Trenin at the Royal Institute of International Affairs, 25 June 2014; www.chathamhouse.org/sites/files/chathamhouse/field/field_document/20140625RussiaUkraineWestINYT.pdf
15. Interview with Gleb Pavlovsky, 18 December 2007.
16. Interview with Gleb Pavlovsky, 18 December 2007.
17. Interview with Konstantin Sonin, 7 February 2012.
18. Stephen Holmes and Ivan Krastev, 'The sense of an ending: Putin and the decline of "no-choice" politics', Eurozine website, 17 February 2012; www.eurozine.com/articles/2012-02-17-krastev-en.html
19. Interview with Vladimir Milov, Moscow, 7 February 2012.
20. Nicu Popescu, 'Russia's liberal-nationalist cocktail: Elixir of life or toxic poison?', Open Democracy website, 3 February 2012; www.opendemocracy.net/od-russia/nicu-popescu/elixir-of-life-or-toxic-poison-russias-liberal-nationalist-cocktail
21. Interview with Konstantin Sonin, Moscow, 7 February 2012.
22. Robert Ortung and Christopher Walker, 'As Russia prepares for protests, new media battle the old', Freedom House blog, 2 February 2012; www.freedomhouse.org/blog/russia-prepares-protests-new-media-battle-old#.U5xE9_ldUmk
23. Konstantin von Eggert, 'Carnival spirit is not enough to change Russia', *Financial Times*, 1 March 2012.
24. Ekaterina Savina, 'Poll: Without TV airtime, opposition unknown and untrusted', Gazeta.ru website, 13 March 2012; http://en.gazeta.ru/news/2012/03/12/a_4087645.shtml

210 NOTES TO PP. 30–46

25. 'Number of internet users grows', Levada Centre press release, 20 March 2012; www.levada.ru/20-03-2012/chislo-polzovatelei-interneta-rastet
26. Paul Goble, 'Window on Eurasia: Dugin says Putin being undermined by insiders who don't back him all the way', Window on Eurasia website, 29 April 2014; http://windoweurasia2.blogspot.co.uk/2014/04/window-on-eurasia-dugin-says-putin.html
27. Kirill Rogov, 'The country has been set on the road to counter-modernisation', Vedomosti website, 25 February 2013; http://www.vedomosti.ru/opinion/news/9448152/vozvraschenie_v_nulevoj_cikl?utm_source=twitter&utm_media=post&utm_campaign=vedomosti&utm_content=link
28. Vladimir Putin, 'A new integration project for Eurasia: The future in the making', Izvestiya, 3 October 2011.
29. Patrick J. Buchanan, 'Is Putin one of us?', Patrick J. Buchanan website, 17 December 2013; http://buchanan.org/blog/putin-one-us-6071
30. Aleksandr Dugin, Osnovy geopolitiki: Geopoliticheskoe budushchee Rossii [The Bases of Geopolitics: The geopolitical future of Russia], Artogeya, Moscow, 1997.
31. 'Address by President of the Russian Federation', President of Russia website, 18 March 2014; http://eng.kremlin.ru/news/6889
32. Vadim Tsymbursky, Ostrov Rossiya: Geopoliticheskie i khronopoliticheskie raboty [Island Russia: Geopolitical and chronopolitical works], ROSSPEN, Moscow, 2007.
33. Interview with Vadim Tsimbursky, 21 October 2008.
34. 'Address by President of the Russian Federation', President of Russia website, 18 March 2014; http://eng.kremlin.ru/news/6889
35. Interview with Gleb Pavlovsky, 18 December 2007.
36. Interview with Modest Kolerov, 20 October 2008.
37. Interview with Sergey Markov, 16 December 2007.
38. Conversation with Rasa Juknevičienė, Lithuanian Minister of Defence, 2008–12, 12 January 2013.
39. Interview with Andris Sprūds, 12 January 2013.
40. Interview with Modest Kolerov, 20 October 2008.
41. There is even a website at www.infwar.ru
42. For example, Igor Panarin, Informatsionnaya voina i kommunikatsii [Information War and Communications], Goriachaya liniya – Telekom, Moscow, 2014.
43. Nerijus Maliukevicius, Russia's Information Policy in Lithuania: The spread of soft power or information geopolitics? FMSO, Fort Leavenworth, KS, 2010; http://fmso.leavenworth.army.mil/Collaboration/international/BalticDefenseCollege/InfoPolicy_final-high.pdf

3 Yanukovych's Ukraine

1. Mykola Ryabchuk, 'Bandera's controversy and Ukraine's future', Russkii Vopros website, 1, 2010; www.russkiivopros.com/index.php?pag=one&id=315&kat=9&csl=46
2. Mykola Ryabchuk, Postkolonial'nyi syndrom: Sposterezhennia [Post-Colonial Syndrome: Observations], Krytyka, Kiev, 2011.
3. Some of this section draws on Andrew Wilson, 'Ukraine', in Isobel Coleman and Terra Lawson-Remer (eds), Pathways to Freedom: Political and economic lessons from democratic transition, Council on Foreign Relations, New York, 2013, pp. 181–200.
4. Leonid Kravchuk, Mayemo te, shcho mayemo: Spohady i rozdumy [We Have What We Have: Memories and reflections], Stolittya, Kiev, 2002, pp. 227–29.
5. Interview with Oleh Rybachuk, 16 May 2013.
6. Interview with Rostyslav Pavlenko, 19 September 2012.
7. Interview with Oleh Rybachuk, 16 May 2013.
8. 'Has Yanukovych caused Ukraine much more damage than Tymoshenko is accused of?', Ukraïnska Pravda, 27 August 2011; www.pravda.com.ua/ukr/news/2011/08/27/6535301/
9. Interview with Oleh Rybachuk, 16 May 2013.
10. Ibid.

11. 'Firtash's mediator imposed Putin and close friends on Yushchenko?', *Ukraïnska Pravda*, 3 December 2010; www.pravda.com.ua/news/2010/12/3/5641201/
12. 'Mykhailo Doroshenko: Yushchenko with Firtash during the first meeting talked how to prevent a carve-up', *Ukraïnska Pravda*, 4 July 2006; www.pravda.com.ua/rus/articles/2006/07/4/4401731/
13. Interview with Oleh Rybachuk, 16 May 2013.
14. 'Yushchenko talked with Firtash at his cottage in the mountains and called him into a "narrow circle"', *Ukraïnska Pravda*, 3 December 2010; www.pravda.com.ua/rus/news/2010/12/3/5640987/
15. Andrew Rettman, 'Yushchenko urges EU to save Ukraine from Russia', EU Observer website, 7 June 2013; http://euobserver.com/foreign/120420
16. 'Yuliya Tymoshenko was transferred to the oppositional niche', *Ukraïnska Pravda*, 4 March 2010; www.pravda.com.ua/rus/articles/2010/03/4/4830315/
17. Leonid Aleksandrov, 'Getting ready to give "a Punch in the face"?', *Ukrainian Week*, 24 February 2012; http://ukrainianweek.com/Politics/43218
18. 'Anna German, "I wanted to get Yanukovych out of this prison"', *Novaya Gazeta*, 15 May 2014; www.novayagazeta.ru/politics/63613.html
19. 'Yanukovych's "family business" links him to Russia', East of Europe website, 28 January 2014; https://grahamstack.wordpress.com/2014/01/28/yanukovychs-family-business-links-him-to-russia/
20. Steven Woehrel, *Ukraine: Current issues and U.S. policy*, CRS Report for Congress, 10 May 2012; www.fas.org/sgp/crs/row/RL33460.pdf
21. Jaroslav Koshiw, *Beheaded: The killing of a journalist*, Artemia Press, Reading, 2003, p. 45.
22. Interview with Yuliya Mostova, editor of *Dzerkalo Tyzhnya*, 8 November 2011.
23. Interview with Mykhailo Honchar, 18 February 2014.
24. Leonid Kuchma, *Posle Maidana: Zapiski prezydenta 2005–2006 [After Maidan: Writings of the President 2005–2006]*, Dovira, Kiev, 2008, p. 635.
25. Interview with Rostyslav Pavlenko, 19 September 2012.
26. Anders Aslund, 'Payback time for the "Yanukovych Family"', Peterson Institute for International Economics website, 11 December 2013; http://blogs.piie.com/realtime/?p=4162
27. 'Billions received by Yanukovich government have disappeared: PM Yatseniuk', Reuters, 27 February 2014; www.reuters.com/article/2014/02/27/us-ukraine-crisis-money-idUSBREA1Q14Q20140227
28. Guy Faulconbridge, Anna Dabrowska and Stephen Grey, 'Toppled "mafia" president cost Ukraine up to $100 billion, prosecutor says', Reuters, 30 April 2014; www.reuters.com/article/2014/04/30/us-ukraine-crisis-yanukovich-idUSBREA3T0K820140430
29. Aslund, 'Payback time for the "Yanukovych Family"'.
30. 'Koroli ukraïns'koho hazu – 2', 17 August 2012; http://slidstvo.info/rozsliduvannia/5-2.html
31. Sławomir Matuszak, *The Oligarchic Democracy: The influence of business groups on Ukrainian politics*, OSW Studies, 42, September 2012; www.osw.waw.pl/sites/default/files/prace_42_en.pdf
32. Interview with Daria Kalenyuk, Executive Director of Ukraine's Anti-Corruption Action Centre, http://antac.org.ua, 9 June 2014.
33. Ibid.
34. See http://antac.org.ua/en/advocating/
35. Anna Babinets, 'How Kurchenko's offshores worked', Yanukovych Leaks website, 6 April 2014; http://stories.yanukovychleaks.org/how-kurchenkos-offshores-worked/
36. 'Due to corruption schemes in the sphere of state procurement the state lost billions of hryvnia – Oleg Mahnitsky', Ukraine General Procurator's Office website, 3 June 2014; www.gp.gov.ua/ua/news.html?_m=publications&_t=rec&id=139434&fp=10
37. Mark Franchetti and Hala Jaber, 'Ukraine leader's cronies "grab cash meant for Euro 2012"', *The Sunday Times*, 3 June 2012.

38. Carol Matlack, 'Poland, Ukraine suffer as Euro soccer hosts', *Bloomberg Business Week*, 8 June 2012; www.businessweek.com/articles/2012-06-08/poland-ukraine-suffer-as-euro-soccer-hosts
39. 'The best tournament money can buy', *The Economist*, 29 May 2012; www.economist.com/blogs/easternapproaches/2012/05/ukraine-and-euro-2012
40. Maria Danilova and Daniel Slatter, 'Nationwide pyramid scheme run by a Yanukovych crony squeezed $11 billion from Ukraine', *Business Insider*, 10 June 2014; www.businessinsider.com/pyramid-scheme-run-by-yanukovych-ally-2014-6
41. Ibid.
42. Oleg Savitsky, 'Yanukovich regime earns billions on illegal coal mining', 350.org website, undated; http://350.org/yanukovich-regime-earns-billions-on-illegal-coal-mining; Sergey Golovnev, 'This is how makeshift coalmine business is arranged in Ukraine', Antac website, 22 January 2014, translated from *Forbes*, 27 May 2013; http://antac.org.ua/en/2014/01/this-is-how-makeshift-coalmine-business-is-arranged-in-ukraine/
43. Nataliya Gumenyuk, Sébastien Gobert, Laurent Geslin, 'Digging for billions', *Ukrainian Week*, 15 March 2013; http://ukrainianweek.com/Society/74747
44. Interview with Daria Kalenyuk, Executive Director of Ukraine's Anti-Corruption Action Centre, 9 June 2014.
45. Interview with Oleksandr Danylyuk, 13 February 2014.
46. 'The Geography of Ukrainian business', delo.ua website, 5 February 2014; http://delo.ua/ukraine/geografija-ukrainskogo-biznesa-infografika-224243/
47. See http://yanukovich.info/oleksandr-yanukovych-assets/
48. 'Paper trail leads to massive corruption at heart of Ukraine', East of Europe website, 26 February 2014; https://grahamstack.wordpress.com/2014/02/26/paper-trail-leads-to-massive-corruption-at-heart-of-ukraine/
49. See the video at www.youtube.com/watch?v=KONhDdr3_nQ. Pshonka is the one with the white hair.
50. Shaun Walker, 'Viktor Yanukovych boasted of Ukraine corruption, says Mikheil Saakashvili', *Guardian*, 25 February 2014; www.theguardian.com/world/2014/feb/25/viktor-yanukovych-ukraine-corruption-mikheil-saakashvili
51. Interview with Hryhoriy Nemyriya, 15 January 2010.
52. 'Mass Media: Yushchenko gave Yanukovych a dacha with a secret decree', Korrespondent.net website, 28 February 2008; http://korrespondent.net/ukraine/politics/389202-smi-yushchenko-sekretnym-ukazom-podaril-yanukovichu-dachu
53. Sergii [Serhiy] Leshchenko, 'Yanukovych, the luxury residence and the money trail that leads to London', Open Democracy website, 8 June 2012; http://opendemocracy.net/od-russia/serhij-leschenko/yanukovych-luxury-residence-and-money-trail-that-leads-to-london
54. Max Seddon and Oleksandr Akymenko, '25 tales of corruption from documents found at the abandoned palace of Ukraine's ousted president', Buzzfeed News website, 1 April 2014; www.buzzfeed.com/maxseddon/25-tales-of-corruption-and-control-from-documents-found-at-t
55. Leshchenko, 'Yanukovych, the luxury residence and the money trail that leads to London'.
56. Matthew Luxmoore, 'Journalists gather for Mezhyhirya Fest investigative conference at fugitive ex-president's estate', *Kyiv Post*, 8 June 2014; www.kyivpost.com/content/ukraine/journalists-gather-for-mezhyhirya-fest-investigative-conference-at-fugitive-ex-presidents-estate-351131.html
57. Oleksandr Akimenko, Anna Babinets and Natalie Sedletska, '28 friends of the president', Yanukovych Leaks website, 26 April 2014; http://stories.yanukovychleaks.org/28-friends-of-the-president/; 'Where Yanukovych and his rich hunting buddies hung out', Yanukovych Leaks website, 26 April 2014; http://stories.yanukovychleaks.org/where-yanukovych-and-his-rich-hunting-buddies-hung-out/
58. 'Where Yanukovych and his rich hunting buddies hung out'.
59. Seddon and Akymenko, '25 tales of corruption'.

60. 'Where Yanukovych and his rich hunting buddies hung out'.
61. Viktoriya Rudenko, ' "Family" banks and money with tables: How Yanukovych's home accounting worked', Yanukovych Leaks website, 29 May 2014; http://yanukovychleaks. org/stories/family-banks-ua.html
62. Interview with Daria Kalenyuk, Executive Director of Ukraine's Anti-Corruption Action Centre, 9 June 2014.
63. 'Creative Yanukovych's creativity has dried up: The war against the "fascism" of the opposition 10 years ago', Tsenzor.net website, 2 June 2013; http://censor.net.ua/photo_ news/243346/kreativ_yanukovicha_issyak_voyina_s_fashizmom_oppozitsii_10_ let_nazad_fotoreportaj
64. In Russian, *tushka* means the corpse of a small animal – 'roadkill', basically.
65. See www.consilium.europa.eu/uedocs/cms_data/docs/pressdata/EN/foraff/134136.pdf
66. 'Before the EU–Ukraine summit Azarov is given eleven demands', *Ukraïnska Pravda*, 26 February 2013; www.pravda.com.ua/rus/news/2013/02/26/6984342/
67. 'Russia blocks Ukrainian export', Federation of Road Hauliers website, 14 August 2013; http://ua.fru.org.ua/rosiya-blokuye-ukrainskij-eksport
68. 'A trade war sputters as the tussle over Ukraine's future intensifies', *The Economist*, 22 August 2013; www.economist.com/news/europe/21583998-trade-war-sputters-tussle-over-ukraines-future-intensifies-trading-insults
69. 'The complex of measures to involve Ukraine in Eurasian integration process', *Dzerkalo Tyzhnya*, 16 August 2013; http://gazeta.zn.ua/internal/o-komplekse-mer-po-vovlech eniyu-ukrainy-v-evraziyskiy-integracionnyy-process-.html
70. 'The Eurasian project and its Ukrainian problem', Odnako website, undated; www. odnako.org/magazine/material/evraziyskiy-proekt-i-ego-ukrainskaya-problema/
71. 'EU offers Ukraine just one billion euros to modernize production – Azarov', Korrespondent.net website, 23 November 2013; http://korrespondent.net/business/ economics/3270649-es-predlahal-ukrayne-na-modernyzatsyui-proyzvodstva-vseho-myllyard-evro-azarov
72. 'Azarov called 1 billion euros from the EU "aid to the beggar on the porch" ', UNIAN website, 25 November 2013; http://economics.unian.net/finance/855447-azarov-nazval-1-mlrd-evro-ot-es-pomoschyu-nischemu-na-paperti.html
73. 'Arbuzov to lead Ukrainian delegation during talks in Brussels', *Kyiv Post*, 2 December 2013;www.kyivpost.com/content/ukraine/arbuzov-to-lead-ukrainian-delegation-during-talks-in-brussels-332857.html?flavour=obile
74. Roman Olearchyk and Peter Spiegel, 'Ukraine freezes talks on bilateral trade pact with EU', *Financial Times*, 21 November 2013; www.ft.com/cms/s/0/b90da798-5294-11e3-8586-00144feabdc0.html?siteedition=uk#axzz37Hdk7aZJ
75. 'With Yanukovych in charge, Ukraine leaves Vilnius empty-handed', *Kyiv Post*, 29 November 2013; www.kyivpost.com/opinion/op-ed/with-yanukovych-in-charge-ukraine-comes-away-empty-handed-in-vilnius-332637.html
76. 'Merkel to Yanukovych: "We expected more" ', *Kyiv Post*, 29 November 2013; www. kyivpost.com/content/politics/video-from-vilnius-gives-a-glimpse-at-how-yanukovych-turns-down-major-treaty-with-europe-332619.html. The video is at www.youtube. com/watch?v=2X2vmT7aOmM

4 Maidan 2.0

1. 'Revolutionary constructions', Kommersant website, 12 November 2013, www. kommersant.ua/doc/2341282
2. Ivan Krastev, *Democracy Disrupted: The politics of global protest*, University of Pennsylvania Press, Philadelphia, 2014.
3. See https://twitter.com/Yatsenyuk_AP/status/403453433648148481
4. Olga Onuch, 'Social networks and social media in Ukrainian "Euromaidan" protests', *Washington Post*, 2 January 2014; www.washingtonpost.com/blogs/monkey-cage/wp/2014/01/02/social-networks-and-social-media-in-ukrainian-euromaidan-protests-2/

5. 'A day and a night of Viktor Yanukovych', *Ukraïnska Pravda*, 8 December 2013; www.pravda.com.ua/rus/articles/2013/12/8/7005339/view_print/

6. 'Maidan-December and Maidan-February: What has changed?' Democratic Initiatives website, undated; http://dif.org.ua/en/events/vid-ma-zminilosj.htm

7. Anton Shekhovtsov, 'Provoking the Euromaidan', Open Democracy website, 3 December 2013; www.opendemocracy.net/od-russia/anton-shekhovtsov/provoking-euromaidan

8. See http://anton-shekhovtsov.blogspot.co.uk/2014/02/pro-russian-network-behind-anti.html

9. 'Ukraine's far-right Freedom Party hold torch-lit Kiev march', BBC News, 1 January 2014; www.bbc.co.uk/news/world-europe-25571805

10. See the interview with Yarosh in *Newsweek*, 12 March 2014; www.newsweek.com/2014/03/21/dmitry-yarosh-man-who-claims-victory-ukrainian-revolution-speaks-247987.html

11. Timothy Snyder, 'Putin's project', *Frankfurter Allgemeine Zeitung*, 16 April 2014; www.faz.net/aktuell/politik/ausland/timothy-snyder-about-europe-and-ukraine-putin-s-project-12898389.html

12. 'Yarosh should withdraw his candidacy and come with a confession', Espresso TV website, 1 April 2014; http://espreso.tv/article/2014/04/01/yarosh_povynen_znyaty_svoyu_kandydaturu_i_pryyty_z_povynnoyu

13. Halya Coynash, 'Right Sector's increasing problems with credibility', Human Rights in Ukraine website, 4 April 2014; http://khpg.org/en/index.php?id=1396527934

14. Halya Coynash, 'Russian propaganda must be challenged', Human Rights in Ukraine website, 3 March 2014; http://khpg.org/index.php?id=1393885654

15. 'A response to Cas Mudde's "A new (order) Ukraine"', Open Democracy website, 3 March 2014; www.opendemocracy.net/anton-shekhovtsov/response-to-cas-mudde%E2%80%99s-Ukraine-Far-RIght-How-Real-Russia

16. 'Expert: "Right Sector" is disintegrating', Deutsche Welle website, 2 April 2014; www.dw.de/%D1%8D%D0%BA%D1%81%D0%BF%D0%B5%D1%80%D1%82-%D0%BF%D1%80%D0%B0%D0%B2%D1%8B%D0%B9-%D1%81%D0%B5%D0%BA%D1%82%D0%BE%D1%80-%D1%80%D0%B0%D1%81%D0%BF%D0%B0%D0%B4%D0%B5%D1%82%D1%81%D1%8F/a-17537119

17. 'The Right Sector: An inside view', Euromaidan Press, 1 April 2014; http://euromaidanpr.com/2014/04/02/the-right-sector-an-inside-view/

18. Ibid.

19. Quoted in Valeria Burlakova, 'The chronicles of dignity', *Ukrainian Week*, 11 June 2014; http://ukrainianweek.com/Society/115466

20. 'Maidan-December and Maidan-February: What has changed?'

21. Anne Applebaum, 'Ukraine shows the "color revolution" model is dead', *Washington Post*, 25 January 2014; www.washingtonpost.com/opinions/anne-applebaum-ukraine-shows-the-color-revolution-model-is-dead/2014/01/24/c77d3ab0-8524-11e3-8099-9181471f7aaf_story.html

22. See https://www.facebook.com/pages/%D0%91%D0%B5%D1%80%D0%BA%D1%83%D1%82-%D0%A3%D0%BA%D1%80%D0%B0%D0%B8%D0%BD%D0%B0/1395559580688966?id=1395559580688966&sk=photos_stream

23. 'Jews in Ukraine outraged at "Berkut" anti-Semitic propaganda', Euro-Asian Jewish Congress website, 25 January 2014; http://eajc.org/page32/news43180.html

24. Interview with Taras Berezovets, 18 February 2014.

25. 'Zvit TSK shchodo podii 18-20 liutoho v Kyievi' ['Report of the Special Investigation Commission concerning the events on 18–20 February in Kiev'], 5 July 2014; http://moskal.in.ua/?categoty=news&news_id=1099

26. 'Maidan-December and Maidan-February: What has changed?'

27. 'Yanukovych's AutoMaidan "blacklist" of activists followed by kidnapping, harassment, arson', *Kyiv Post*, 26 March 2014; www.kyivpost.com/content/ukraine/yanukovychs-automaidan-blacklist-of-activists-followed-by-kidnapping-harassment-arsons-340886.html

28. See http://maidantranslations.com/tag/maidan-manifesto/
29. 'Maidan-December and Maidan-February: What has changed?'
30. See the selection of videos at http://globalvoicesonline.org/2013/11/30/videos-ukraines-police-surround-and-beat-euromaidan-protesters-to-clear-square/
31. 'Euromaidan: The dead, the missing, and the jailed', Radio Free Europe/Radio Liberty, 27 January 2014; www.rferl.org/content/ukraine-dead-missing-jailed/25244469.html
32. 'Interview: Revelations in the Yanukovych papers', Radio Free Europe/Radio Liberty, 4 March 2014; www.rferl.org/media/video/sedletska-yanukovych-documents/25285389.html. See also www.radiosvoboda.org/content/article/25281810.html
33. Interview with Rostyslav Pavlenko, 17 February 2014.
34. Interview with Jock Mendoza-Wilson, Akhmetov's CEO, 22 April 2014.
35. Interview with Rostyslav Pavlenko, 17 February 2014.
36. 'Anti-fascism & the Yanukovych regime', Ukrainian Week, 31 May 2013; http://ukrainianweek.com/Politics/81043
37. 'Titushki, the low-cost beastly thugs of the Yanukovich regime . . .', Historia Vivens website, undated; www.historiavivens.eu/2/titushki_the_low_cost_beastly_thugs_of_the_yanukovich_regime_1028900.html
38. 'What does it cost to hire a "titushka": Infographics', Ekonomichna Pravda, 1 December 2013; www.epravda.com.ua/publications/2013/12/5/407013/
39. 'Titushki paid $100 a day and working on "financial pyramid" scheme', Gazeta.ua website, 28 January 2014; http://gazeta.ua/articles/politics/_titushki-zaroblyayut-po-100-dolariv-v-den-ta-pracyuyut-za-shemoyu-finansovoyi-piramidi/538896
40. 'Kurchenko financed titushki and "Berkut" – Makhnitsky', IPress.ua website, 24 March 2014; http://ipress.ua/news/kurchenko_finansuvav_titushok__mahnitskyy_56152.html
41. 'Oleksandr Yanukovych finances Russian titushki – industrialists of Donetsk and Luhansk oblast', IPress.ua website, 8 March 2014; http://ipress.ua/news/oleksandr_yanukovych_finansuie_rosiyskyh_titushok__nardep_52967.html
42. 'Kharkiv AutoMaidan dealt with bank that financed "titushki"', IPress.ua website, 31 January 2014; http://gazeta.ua/articles/politics/_harkivskij-avtomajdan-poklav-bank-scho-finansuvav-titushok/539537
43. 'Siloviki and titushki wear the same yellow ribbons', Ukraïnska Pravda, 20 February 2014; www.pravda.com.ua/news/2014/02/20/7015152/
44. See www.youtube.com/watch?v=hcXC86FssTg
45. 'Yanukovych's secret diaries', Euromaidan Press, 12 March 2014; http://euromaidanpr.com/2014/03/12/yanukovychs-secret-diaries/
46. See the video at https://storify.com/MaximEristavi/maidanlaws
47. Oksana Forostyna, 'Bankers, hipsters, and housewives: A revolution of common people', Visegrad/Insight, 1, 2014, p. 14.
48. See the video at www.youtube.com/watch?v—jUWYKaVRAU
49. Oksana Forostyna, 'Bankers, hipsters, and housewives', p. 12.
50. Interview with Oleksandr Danylyuk, 25 March 2014.
51. Interview with Oleksandr Danylyuk, 13 February 2014.
52. Interview with Rostyslav Pavlenko, 17 February 2014.
53. Interview with Rostyslav Pavlenko, 17 February 2014.
54. See 'In Ukraine, fascists, oligarchs and western expansion are at the heart of the crisis', Guardian, 29 January 2014; www.theguardian.com/commentisfree/2014/jan/29/ukraine-fascists-oligarchs-eu-nato-expansion; and 'The Ukrainian nationalism at the heart of "Euromaidan"', Nation, 21 January 2014; www.thenation.com/article/178013/ukrainian-nationalism-heart-euromaidan
55. 'Paper trail leads to massive corruption at heart of Ukraine', East of Europe website, 26 February 2014; https://grahamstack.wordpress.com/2014/02/26/paper-trail-leads-to-massive-corruption-at-heart-of-ukraine/

5 The Uprising

1. 'Zvit TSK shchodo podii 18–20 liutoho v Kyievi' ['Report of the Special Investigation Commission concerning the events on 18–20 February in Kiev'], 5 July 2014; http://moskal.in.ua/?categoty=news&news_id=1099

2. See www.youtube.com/watch?v=9hYvM_aIc4Y

3. 'Avakov: The titushky received ammunition from Yuriy Enakyevskiy and the Ministry of the Interior', Evroua website, 3 April 2014; http://evroua.com/avakov-titushki-oderzhuvali-patroni-v-yuri-yenaki%D1%97vskogo-j-u-mvs/. See also the chilling video at http://espreso.tv/news/2014/02/18/titushky_zakydaly_hranatamy_ta_obstrilyaly_aktyvistiv__odyn_zahynuv

4. 'Ukraine President Yanukovych sacks army chief amid crisis', BBC News, 19 February 2014; www.bbc.co.uk/news/world-europe-26265808

5. Interview with Oleksandr Danylyuk, 25 March 2014.

6. See the video at www.youtube.com/watch?v=HcKv4iLdliE. Adam Taylor, 'What did Yanukovych take with him as he fled his mansion? Paintings, guns and a small dog, according to new video', Washington Post, 10 March 2014; www.washingtonpost.com/blogs/worldviews/wp/2014/03/12/what-did-yanukovych-take-with-him-as-he-fled-his-mansion-paintings-guns-and-a-small-dog-according-to-new-video/

7. 'Titushki shot two demonstrators – witnesses', Ukraïnska Pravda, 19 February 2014; www.pravda.com.ua/news/2014/02/19/7014579/

8. Mariya Lytvynova, ' "Right sector" does not want a truce with the Ukrainian authorities', Epoch Times website, 20 February 2014; www.epochtimes.com.ua/ukraine/society/praviy-sektor-ne-khoche-peremir-ya-z-ukrayinskoyu-vladoyu-114276.html; https://www.facebook.com/dyastrub/posts/598675630209325?stream_ref=10

9. Interview with Jock Mendoza-Wilson, Akhmetov's CEO, 22 April 2014.

10. 'Ukraine president warns force an option after bid to "seize power" ', Reuters, 19 February 2014; http://uk.reuters.com/article/2014/02/19/uk-ukraine-crisis-yanukovich-idUKBREA1I0OI20140219

11. 'Pshonka demands that Yanukovych introduce a state of emergency in Ukraine', Gordonua website, 24 February 2014; http://gordonua.com/news/politics/Pshonka-treboval-ot-YAnukovicha-vvesti-v-Ukraine-chrezvychaynoe-polozhenie-11279.html. See also Pshonka's posting on the Procuracy website, sometime on the afternoon of 18 February: www.gp.gov.ua/ua/news.html?_m=publications&_t=rec&id=134754

12. Jamie Dettner, 'Photographs expose Russian-trained killers in Kiev', Daily Beast, 30 March 2014; www.thedailybeast.com/articles/2014/03/30/exclusive-photographs-expose-russian-trained-killers-in-kiev.html#

13. 'Zvit TSK shchodo podii 18–20 liutoho v Kyievi' ['Report of the Special Investigation Commission concerning the events on 18–20 February in Kiev'].

14. See http://espreso.tv/article/2014/02/21/kyyivskyy_maydan_rozstrilyuvaly_krymski_snaypery

15. 'The organisers and those involved in the killings of people published: Plans and families', Ukraïnska Pravda, 24 February 2014; www.pravda.com.ua/rus/news/2014/02/24/7016050/

16. Mark Rachkevych, 'Putin's drive to destroy Ukraine: Accessory to murder?', Kyiv Post, 3 April 2014; www.kyivpost.com/content/ukraine/putins-drive-to-destroy-ukraine-accessory-to-murder-342033.html

17. 'Russia provided 5 tons of explosives and weapons to Yanukovych in January to disperse the Maidan', Ukrainian Week, 3 April 2014; http://ukrainianweek.com/News/106701

18. 'Ukrainian Security Service Chief: Twenty-six Russian security officers were involved in planning of the bloodshed on Maidan', Ukrainian Week, 3 April 2014; http://ukrainianweek.com/News/106691. See also http://alblogedup-investigative.blogspot.ca/2014/04/ukraine-crisis-russian-personnel.html

19. See http://maidantranslations.com/2014/04/05/dmitry-tymchuk-fsb-presence-in-ukraine-on-february-20-21/comment-page-1/

20. 'Zvit TSK shchodo podii 18–20 liutoho v Kyievi' ['Report of the Special Investigation
     Commission concerning the events on 18–20 February in Kiev'].
21. 'The Interior Ministry confirms there were snipers at the government building on
     20 February', *Ukraïnska Pravda*, 10 April 2014; www.pravda.com.ua/ukr/news/2014/
     04/10/7021997/
22. Interview with Oleksandr Danylyuk, 25 March 2014. See also his interview with
     the BBC, 25 January 2014, at: www.bbc.co.uk/ukrainian/politics/2014/01/140125_
     Danylyuk_interview_sx.shtml
23. Interview with Oleksandr Danylyuk, 25 March 2014.
24. See http://vk.com/video-62043361_167867050?list=d1107274d71482ba30
25. Ibid.
26. See 'Sixty militia captured on the Maidan fed and protected from mob justice', Prosport
     website, 20 February 2104; http://prosport.tsn.ua/politika/zahoplenih-na-maydani-
     60-vv-shnikiv-nagoduvali-i-ohoronyayut-vid-samosudu-335654.html   and   'Maidan
     Self-Defence states that it has freed captured internal forces militia', RBK website,
     www.rbc.ua/ukr/news/politics/samooborona-maydana-zayavlyaet-chto-osvobodila-
     zahvachennyh-21022014114700
27. See the interview with a Right Sector activist at www.youtube.com/watch?v–
     vdxIeI2cBM
28. 'Coordinator of the Medical Service of the Maidan: Seventy were killed today', *Ukraïnska
     Pravda*, 20 February 2014; http://life.pravda.com.ua/society/2014/02/20/152915/
29. '166 activists among those missing – VO Maidan', Liga Novosti website, 30 March 2014;
     http://news.liga.net/news/society/1191936-166_aktivistov_chislyatsya_propavshimi_
     bez_vesti_vo_maydan.htm
30. See Health Ministry press release, 22 February 2014; http://moz.gov.ua/ua/portal/
     pre_20140222_c.html
31. 'The Interior Ministry confirms there were snipers at the government building on
     20 February', *Ukraïnska Pravda*, 10 April 2014; www.pravda.com.ua/ukr/news/
     2014/04/10/7021997/
32. Christian Neef, 'Yanukovych's fall: The power of Ukraine's billionaires', *Der Spiegel*,
     25 February 2014; www.spiegel.de/international/europe/how-oligarchs-in-ukraine-
     prepared-for-the-fall-of-yanukovych-a-955328.html
33. Jaroslav Koshiw, 'Why President Yanukovych fled Ukraine', JV Kosiw blog, 23 April
     2014; www.jvkoshiw.com/#!Why-President-Yanukovych-fled-Ukraine/ck8a/F4D49016-
     F69F-45D6-AE4A-027C10E02B79
34. Michał Potocki and Zbigniew Parafianowicz, 'What he heard from sikorski: Sign your
     agreement or die: Oleksiy Haran reveals the backstage negotiations on Ukraine', *Gazeta
     Prawna*, 14 March 2014; www.gazetaprawna.pl/artykuly/783959,to-on-uslyszal-od-
     sikorskiego-podpiszecie-porozumienie-albo-zginiecie-oleksij-haran-ujawnia-kulisy-
     negocjacji-ws-ukrainy.html
35. 'Sikorski, arguing with the Maidan Council, said otherwise all will die', *Ukraïnska
     Pravda*, 21 February 2014; www.pravda.com.ua/news/2014/02/21/7015576/
36. 'Moskal names the leaders of the snipers who were on the Maidan', *Ukraïnska Pravda*,
     12 June 2014; www.pravda.com.ua/news/2014/06/12/7028836/
37. Roman Olearchyk and Neil Buckley, 'Papers reveal Yanukovich plans to turn army
     against protestors', *Financial Times*, 24 February 2014.
38. From the German Foreign Ministry's website; www.auswaertiges-amt.de/cae/servlet/
     contentblob/671350/publicationFile/190051/140221-UKR_Erklaerung.pdf
39. 'Media: Militia captured en masse by EuroMaidan activists', *Ukraïnska Pravda*,
     20 February 2014; www.pravda.com.ua/news/2014/02/20/7015081/
40. 'The cordon was urgently removed from outside parliament: the commander pushed
     fighters into buses', LB.ua website, 21 February 2014; http://lb.ua/news/2014/02/21/
     256477_izpod_radi_srochnom_poryadke_snyali.html
41. 'Seven buses of "Berkut" are travelling from Borispil [airport] to Kiev', LB.ua website,
     21 February 2014; http://lb.ua/news/2014/02/21/256494_borispolya_kiev_edut_sem.html

42. 'In place of the siloviki in Kiev come titushki with firearms', *Dzerkalo Tyzhnya*, 21 February 2014, story posted at 6.45 p.m., the same time as the agreement; http://zn.ua/UKRAINE/na-smenu-silovikam-v-kiev-pribyvayut-titushki-s-ognestrelnym-oruzhiem-139399_.html
43. See his speech at www.youtube.com/watch?v=C6cpyRwl-ZU; and the English version of his words at www.allreadable.com/32cd80Zp
44. See http://vk.com/video-62043361_167879081?list=d62f6e2f9fd3a0f0da
45. Dmitri Trenin, *The Ukraine Crisis and the Resumption of Great Power Rivalry*, Carnegie Center, Moscow, 2014, p. 6; http://carnegieendowment.org/files/ukraine_great_power_rivalry2014.pdf
46. Potocki and Parafianowicz, 'What he heard from Sikorski'.
47. Guy Faulconbridge, Anna Dabrowska and Stephen Grey, 'Toppled "mafia" president cost Ukraine up to $100 billion, prosecutor says', Reuters, 30 April 2014; www.reuters.com/article/2014/04/30/us-ukraine-crisis-yanukovich-idUSBREA3T0K820140430
48. See the video at www.youtube.com/watch?v=AxuIkpIrG9Q
49. Email from Rostyslav Pavlenko, 25 February 2014.
50. See 'Political legitimacy and international law in Crimea: Pushing the US and Russia apart', *Diplomatic Courier*, 8 May 2014; www.diplomaticourier.com/news/topics/politics/2187-political-legitimacy-and-international-law-in-crimea-pushing-the-u-s-and-russia-apart; and 'Here's what international law says about Russia's intervention in Ukraine', *New Republic*, 2 March 2014; www.newrepublic.com/article/116819/international-law-russias-ukraine-intervention
51. 'Cash, jewelry seized in ex-Ukrainian ministers' offices, apartments', *Kyiv Post*, 22 March 2014; www.kyivpost.com/content/ukraine/cash-jewelry-seized-in-ex-ukrainian-ministers-offices-apartments-340446.html
52. 'Belarus demands that Zakharchenko and Kurchenko leave the country by 1800', Khvylya website, 21 February 2014; http://hvylya.org/news/exclusive/belarus-potrebovala-ot-zaharchenko-i-kurchenko-do-18-00-pokinut-territoriyu-stranyi.html
53. Oliver Carroll, 'Why Ukraine's separatist movement failed in Kharkiv', *New Republic*, 22 June 2014; www.newrepublic.com/article/118301/kharkivs-kernes-returns-different-city-after-being-shot
54. Pavel Kozachenko, 'The public union "Ukrainian Front" was set up in Kharkiv: Details', Dozor website, 1 February 2014; http://dozor.kharkov.ua/events/politics/1147292.html
55. Interview with Jock Mendoza-Wilson, Akhmetov's CEO, 22 April 2014.
56. See www.youtube.com/watch?v=ltEvbum6LlE, for a spectacular mixture of swearing and incompetence.
57. Interview with Jock Mendoza-Wilson, Akhmetov's CEO, 22 April 2014.
58. 'How Yanukovich fled Ukraine – journalists' investigation', UNIAN website, 21 April 2014; www.unian.net/politics/910010-kak-yanukovich-ubegal-iz-ukrainyi-rassledo-vanie-jurnalistov.html
59. Koshiw, 'Why President Yanukovych fled Ukraine'.
60. Peter Ackerman, Maciej Bartkowski and Jack Duvall, 'Ukraine: A non-violent victory', Open Democracy website, 3 March 2014; www.opendemocracy.net/civilresistance/peter-ackerman-maciej-bartkowski-jack-duvall/ukraine-nonviolent-victory. See also http://maciejbartkowski.com/2014/03/22/understanding-civil-resistance-questions-i-am-asked-and-wrestle-with/
61. Roger Cohen, 'Gettysburg on the Maidan', *New York Times*, 19 May 2014; www.nytimes.com/2014/05/20/opinion/cohen-gettysburg-on-the-maidan.html?_r=0

6 Crimea

1. Interview with Petro Poroshenko, 28 November 2013.
2. 'Address by President of the Russian Federation', President of Russia website, 18 March 2014; http://eng.news.kremlin.ru/news/6889/print
3. Paul Robert Magocsi, *This Blessed Land: Crimea and the Crimean Tatars*, University of Toronto Press, Toronto, 2014, p. 126.

4.   Mara Kozelsky, *Christianizing Crimea: Shaping sacred space in the Russian Empire and beyond*, Northern Illinois University Press, DeKalb, IL, 2010.

5.   Ibid., p. 3.

6.   Aleksandr Prokhanov, 'Putin should get the Order of Nakhimov', *Izvestiya*, 10 March 2014; http://izvestia.ru/news/567223

7.   Alan Fisher, *The Crimean Tatars*, Hoover Institution Press, Stanford, 1978, p. 145.

8.   Brian Williams, *The Crimean Tatars: The Diaspora experience and the forging of a nation*, Brill, Leiden, 2001, p. 393.

9.   Ibid., p. 376; J. Otto Pohl, 'The false charges of treason against the Crimean Tatars', International Committee for Crimea, Washington, DC, 18 May 2010; www.iccrimea.org/scholarly/pohl20100518.pdf

10. B. Broshevan and P. Tygliiants, *Izgnanie i Vozvrashchenie* [*Exile and Return*], Tavrida, Simferopol, 1999, p. 34.

11. Süleyman Elik, 'The demographic engineering in Crimea: Soviet ethnic cleansing in Russia 1945–1953', BILGESAM analysis, 1122, March 2014; www.bilgesam.org/Images/Dokumanlar/0-75-20140318101122.pdf; J. Otto Pohl, 'The deportation and fate of the Crimean Tatars', International Committee for Crimea, Washington, DC, 2000; www.iccrimea.org/scholarly/jopohl.html

12. Edward Allworth, 'Renewing self awareness', in E. Allworth (ed.), *Tatars of the Crimea: Return to the homeland*, Duke University Press, Durham and London, 1998, p. 11.

13. Nikolai Fedorovich Bugai (ed.), *Iosif Stalin – Lavrentii Beriia: 'Ikh Nado deportirovat': Dokumenty, fakty, kommentarii* [Joseph Stalin – Lavrentiy Beria: They must be deported: Documents, facts, commentaries], Druzhba Narodov, Moscow, 1992.

14. Aleksandr M. Nekrich, *The Punished Peoples*, W.W. Norton and Co., New York, 1978.

15. See http://wikileaks.org/cable/2006/12/06KYIV4558.html

16. Valentina Samar, 'The division of Crimea', *Dzerkalo Tyzhnya*, 27 April 2014; http://gazeta.zn.ua/POLITICS/raspaevanie_kryma.html

17. See http://wikileaks.org/cable/2010/02/10MOSCOW317.html

18. 'Results for elections to Qurultay known', QHA Crimean News Agency, 19 June 2013; http://qha.com.ua/results-of-elections-for-qurultay-known-127731en.html

19. Interview with Mejlis leader Mustafa Dzhemilev, 17 January 2010.

20. 'Crimean Tatars dissatisfied with Yushchenko statement', Unrepresented Nations and Peoples Organization website, 31 May 2005; www.unpo.org/article/2565

21. Anatolii Mogilev [Mohylyov], 'In Crimea a conflict is brewing like the Kosovo scenario', *Krymskaya Pravda*, 24 January 2008.

22. Interview with Mustafa Dzhemilev, 15 May 2013.

23. 'In Crimea, the occupation authorities don't control what they created – Dzhemilev', RFE/RL Ukrainian Service website, 21 March 2014; www.radiosvoboda.org/content/article/25305246.html

24. 'Yanukovych reduced the composition of the Council of Representatives of the Crimean Tatar People by almost half', *Dzerkalo Tyzhnya*, 14 January 2011; http://dt.ua/POLITICS/yanukovich_skorotiv_sklad_radi_predstavnikiv_krimskotatarskogo_narodu_mayzhe_vdvichi.html

25. Anvar Derkach, 'A new Crimean front', *Ukrainian Week*, 7 March 2012; http://ukrainianweek.com/Politics/52392

26. See the video at www.youtube.com/watch?v=efii3FK9W7A

27. See the video at www.youtube.com/watch?v=atm0W5wA2y4

28. 'Moskal: The fighters of "Berkut" are rebelling in Crimea', *Dzerkalo Tyzhnya*, 27 February 2014; http://zn.ua/POLITICS/moskal-v-krymu-vzbuntovalis-boycy-berkuta-139917_.html

29. 'Moskal: The Crimean parliament has been taken by Berkut: The leader of the Sevastopol Berkut heads the operation', Espresso TV website, 21 February 2014; http://espreso.tv/new/2014/02/27/moskal_krymskyy_parlament_zakhopyv_berkut_operaciyeyu_keruye_kerivnyk_sevastopolskoho_berkutu; and 'Former commander of the Sevastopol "Berkut" that "cleaned up 40% of the Maidan" now blocks the entrance to

Crimea', Ekspres online website, 9 March 2014; http://expres.ua/video/2014/03/09/103171-eks-komandyr-sevastopolskogo-berkutu-zachystyv-40-maydanu-blokuye-vyizd

30. Dmitri Trenin, *The Ukraine Crisis and the Resumption of Great-Power Rivalry*, Carnegie Center, Moscow, 9 July 2014; http://carnegie.ru/2014/07/09/ukraine-crisis-and-resumption-of-great-power-rivalry/hfgs#

31. Oleg Kashin, 'From Crimea to the Donbas: The adventures of Igor Strelkov and Aleksandr Boroday', slon.ru website, 19 May 2014; http://slon.ru/russia/iz_kryma_v_donbass_priklyucheniya_igorya_strelkova_i_aleksandra_borodaya-1099696.xhtml

32. 'Patriarch Kirill "blessed" war against Ukraine', Newsru.ua website, 19 May 2014; www.newsru.ua/arch/ukraine/19may2014/kiril.html

33. 'Firms of Crimean parliament's head owe banks more than billion UAH', QHA Crimean News Agency, 7 March 2014; http://qha.com.ua/firms-of-crimean-parliament-s-head-owe-banks-more-than-billion-uah-130778en.html

34. Benjamin Bidder, 'Dossier of dubiousness: Did Putin's man in Crimea have mafia ties?', *Der Spiegel* website, 25 March 2014; www.spiegel.de/international/world/dossier-suggests-crimea-prime-minister-aksyonov-had-crime-ties-a-960644.html

35. Evan Ostryzniuk, 'Kremlin's leaders in Crimea deep in debt', *Kyiv Post*, 1 April 2014; www.kyivpost.com/content/business/kremlins-leaders-in-crimea-deep-in-debt-342973.html

36. See Michael Idov, 'The novel that predicts Russia's invasion of Crimea', *New Yorker* blog, 3 March 2014; www.newyorker.com/online/blogs/books/2014/03/the-great-1979-novel-that-predicts-russias-crimea-invasion.html

37. Lenor Yunusov, 'Crimea – holiday disobedience', *Ukraïnskyi Tyzhden*, 27 February 2014; http://tyzhden.ua/Politics/103420

38. 'There was no quorum at the extraordinary session of the Council of Crimea – MP', Liga.net website, 28 February 2014; http://news.liga.net/news/politics/991225-na_vneocherednoy_sessii_soveta_ark_ne_bylo_kvoruma_deputat.htm; Christopher J. Miller and Oksana Grytsenko, 'Putin's drive to destroy Ukraine: Crimean crimes', *Kyiv Post*, 3 April 2014; www.kyivpost.com/content/ukraine/putins-drive-to-destroy-ukraine-crimean-crimes-342034.html

39. 'The Supreme Council of Crimea took over the 45th Regiment Airborne special forces of the Russian Federation: These are the military "core strike force" for the assault on the East – Tymchuk', Tsenzor.net website, 18 April 2014; http://m.censor.net.ua/news/281675/verhovnyyi_sovet_kryma_zahvatyval_45yi_polk_spetsnaznacheniya_vdv_rf_eti_je_voennye_yavlyayutsya_udarnym

40. Andrei Vasiliev, 'The Crimean "Army" ', Open Democracy website, 14 March 2014; www.opendemocracy.net/od-russia/andrei-vasiliev/crimean-%E2%80%98army%E2%80%99

41. 'In Crimea, the Kuban Cossacks don't know who they are protecting and from whom', *Ukraïnska Pravda*, 14 March 2014; www.pravda.com.ua/rus/news/2014/03/14/7018794/?attempt=1

42. Maksym Bugriy, 'The Crimean Operation: Russian force and tactics', *Eurasia Daily Monitor*, 1 April 2014; www.jamestown.org/single/?tx_ttnews%5Btt_news%5D=42164&tx_ttnews%5BbackPid%5D=7

43. Vasiliev, 'The Crimean "Army" '.

44. 'Direct line with Vladimir Putin', President of Russia website, 17 April 2014; http://eng.kremlin.ru/news/7034

45. '10 days that lost Crimea: Crucial state organs defect to secessionists', Business New Europe website, 10 March 2014; www.bne.eu/content/10-days-lost-crimea-crucial-state-organs-defect-secessionists

46. 'Twenty two Russian artillery batteries were delivered to the Perekop district', Black Sea News website, 11 March 2014; www.blackseanews.net/read/77613

47. 'Mustafa Dzhemilev: We are being trapped', *Kyiv Weekly*, 16 May 2014.

48. 'Interview of President of the Republic of Belarus Alexander Lukashenko for the TV show Shuster Live', President of the Republic of Belarus website, 28 March 2014;

http://president.gov.by/en/news_en/view/interview-of-president-of-the-republic-of-belarus-alexander-lukashenko-for-the-tv-show-shuster-live-8402/
49. Vladimir Mukhin, 'In Ukraine they are breeding a mini-army', *Nezavisimaya Gazeta*, 16 April 2014; www.ng.ru/armies/2014-04-16/2_ukr_army.html
50. See Alexander J. Motyl, 'Yanukovych brings in Russian thugs for backup', *World Affairs*, 10 January 2012; www.worldaffairsjournal.org/blog/alexander-j-motyl/yanukovych-brings-russian-thugs-back; and 'Three appointments and five conclusions', *Den*, 15 January 2014; www.day.kiev.ua/en/article/topic-day/three-appointments-and-five-conclusions
51. 'Problems of the inhabitants of Crimea', Council under the President of the Russian Federation for Civil Society and Human Rights website, 21 April 2014; www.president-sovet.ru/structure/gruppa_po_migratsionnoy_politike/materialy/problemy_zhiteley_kryma.php
52. 'What relations between Ukraine and Russia should look like? Public opinion polls' results', Kiev International Institute of Sociology website, 4 March 2014; http://kiis.com.ua/?lang=eng&cat=reports&id=236&page=1
53. Interview with Rustam Temirgalyev and Refat Chubarov, *Novaya Gazeta*, 17 March 2014; www.novayagazeta.ru/politics/62756.html
54. 'Mustafa Jemilev: "In fact 34.2% of Crimean population took part in pseudo referendum on March 16" ', Mejlis of the Crimean Tatar People website, 25 March 2014; http://qtmm.org/en/news/4373-mustafa-jemilev-in-fact-34-2-of-crimean-population-took-part-in-pseudo-referendum-on-march-16. In a speech to the UN, Jemilev said 32 per cent; http://qtmm.org/en/news/4432-mustafa-jemilev-it-is-an-absurd-to-decide-issue-of-belonging-of-any-territory-region-or-settlement-to-any-state-on-referendum, 1 April 2014. It's a shame he was not more consistent on such an important matter.
55. 'Medvedev: Crimea became a headache for the Russian authorities', Novyi region website, 24 March 2014; www.nr2.ru/moskow/490519.html
56. Maksim Tovkailo and Margarita Liutova, 'Crimea could become one of the most sub-sidised regions', Vedomosti website, 11 July 2014; www.vedomosti.ru/companies/news/28853561/krym-prisoedinitsya-k-150-mlrd-rub
57. 'Russia struggling to pay for Kerch bridge to Crimea', *Moscow Times*, 14 July 2014; www.themoscowtimes.com/business/article/kerch-bridge-plan-faces-funding-dilemma/503384.html
58. Andriy Kireyev, 'Business under occupation', Ekonomichna Pravda website, 30 April 2014; www.epravda.com.ua/publications/2014/04/30/447045/
59. 'Report on the human rights situation in Ukraine', Office of the United Nations High Commissioner for Human Rights, 15 April 2014; www.ohchr.org/Documents/Countries/UA/Ukraine_Report_15April2014.doc
60. Unicef, 'Ukraine: Humanitarian situation report No. 17', 17 April 2014; http://reliefweb.int/sites/reliefweb.int/files/resources/UNICEF%20Ukraine%20SitRep%20No7%2017%20April%202014.pdf
61. 'Address by President of the Russian Federation', President of Russia website, 18 March 2014; http://eng.news.kremlin.ru/news/6889/print
62. 'Expert: The boycott of the referendum was a big mistake of the Crimean Tatar Mejlis', Natsionalny aktsent website, 16 April 2014; nazaccent.ru/content/10967-ekspert-bojkot-referenduma-byl-bolshoj-oshibkoj.html
63. 'Land under the infrastructure for the Crimean special economic zone will be taken away for three months', Vedomosti website, 29 May 2014; www.vedomosti.ru/realty/news/27105381/krymskie-zemli-zaberut-po-moskovski
64. 'The Crimean Tatars and Eurasianism', Geopolitika website, 6 August 2012; www.geopolitica.ru/Articles/1464/
65. Adam Klus, 'The new strategic reality in the Black Sea', New Eastern Europe website, 22 April 2014; www.neweasterneurope.eu/articles-and-commentary/1197-the-new-strategic-reality-in-the-black-sea
66. 'Heroes classified as "confidential" ', *Novaya Gazeta*, 16 June 2014; www.novayagazeta.ru/inquests/64030.html

67. See the commentary with videos, Max Seddon, 'This pro-Putin bike show is a trashy neo-Soviet "Triumph Of The Will" remake', BuzzFeed News website, 11 August 2014; www.buzzfeed.com/maxseddon/russian-motorbike-gang-tells-the-conflict-in-ukraine
68. Jacob W. Kipp and Roger McDermott, 'Putin's smart defense: Wars, rumors of war, and generations of wars (part two)', Eurasia Daily Monitor, 17 June 2014; www.jamestown. org/single/?tx_ttnews%5Btt_news%5D=42512&no_cache=1

7 The Eastern Imbroglio

1. 'Address by President of the Russian Federation', President of Russia website, 18 March 2014; http://eng.kremlin.ru/news/6889
2. 'Direct line with Vladimir Putin', President of Russia website, 17 April 2014; http://eng. kremlin.ru/news/7034
3. Hiroaki Kuromiya, Freedom and Terror in the Donbas: A Ukrainian–Russian border-land, 1870s–1990s, Cambridge University Press, Cambridge, 1998, p. 32.
4. 'Ukraine and the EU: Citizens' attitudes to Eurointegration', Yevroatlantika, 1–2, 2013, p. 42; http://dif.org.ua/modules/pages/files/1376400844_2627.pdf. 'East' Ukraine here meant the Donbas plus three neighbouring regions.
5. Kuromiya, Freedom and Terror in the Donbas, p. 116.
6. See http://2001.ukrcensus.gov.ua/eng/results/general/estimate/
7. Oleksandr Kramar, 'We were 52 million', Ukrainian Week, 14 March 2012; http:// ukrainianweek.com/Society/43071
8. Oleksandr Kramar, 'The price of the Donbas', Ukraïnskyi Tyzhden, 1 May 2014; http:// tyzhden.ua/Politics/108355
9. Lyubomyr Shavalyuk, 'Money of the Donbas', Ukrainian Week, 10 June 2014; http:// ukrainianweek.com/Economics/110350
10. Oleksandr Kramar, 'Breaking away from Eurasia', Ukrainian Week, 12 June 2014; http:// ukrainianweek.com/Economics/110351
11. Maksym Strykha, 'Ukraine and its Vendée: What next?', Ukraïnska Pravda, 11 May 2014; www.pravda.com.ua/rus/articles/2014/05/11/7024992/
12. Interview with the BBC, 15 August 2010; www.bbc.co.uk/ukrainian/ukraine/2010/08/100815_andrukhovych_friday_interview_sd.shtml. See also a May 2014 interview at http://zbruc.eu/node/22644
13. Strykha, 'Ukraine and its Vendée'; Volodymyr Dubrovsky, 'Think – for yourself, decide – for yourself: To have or have not?', Kritika website, 18 May 2014; http://krytyka.com/ua/community/blogs/dumayte-samy-reshayte-samy-ymet-yly-ne-ymet
14. Anna Nemtsova, 'Who will be the President of Novorossiya?', Foreign Policy, 29 April 2014; www.foreignpolicy.com/articles/2014/04/29/who_will_be_the_president_of_novorossiya
15. Vladimir Kornilov, Donetsko-Krivorozhskaya respublika: Rasstrelyannaya mechta [The Donetsk-Krivoi Rog Republic: An Assassinated Dream], Folio, 2011.
16. 'The views and opinions of residents of South-Eastern Ukraine: April 2014', Zn.ua website, 18 April 2014; http://zn.ua/UKRAINE/mneniya-i-vzglyady-zhiteley-yugo-vostoka-ukrainy-aprel-2014-143598_.html
17. Ibid.
18. 'Address by President of the Russian Federation', President of Russia website, 18 March 2014; http://eng.kremlin.ru/news/6889
19. Mark Rachkevych, 'Ukrainians form militias to defend nation against chaos', Kyiv Post, 7 May 2014; www.kyivpost.com/content/ukraine/ukrainians-form-militias-to-defend-nation-against-chaos-346813.html
20. 'Yanukovych's creative has dried up: The war against "fascism" of the opposition 10 years ago', Tsenzor.net website, 2 June 2014; http://censor.net.ua/photo_news/243346/kreativ_yanukovicha_issyak_voyina_s_fashizmom_oppozitsii_10_let_nazad_fotore-portaj
21. Thanks are due to Anton Shekhovtsov for help with this section.

22. 'Eurofascism', *Komsomol'skaya Pravda v Ukraine*, 12 May 2014; http://kp.ua/politics/452111-evrofashyzm
23. Anton Shekhovtsov, 'Extremism in south-eastern Ukraine', Open Democracy website, 7 May 2014; www.opendemocracy.net/od-russia/anton-shekhovtsov/dangers-of-extremism-in-southeastern-ukraine-far-right-eurasianism-slavic-unity
24. Andrey Petrov, 'Who is restricting the constitutional rights of the Don people', OstroV website, a local Donbas news site, 23 January 2014; www.ostro.org/donetsk/politics/articles/435874/
25. Interview with top Ukrainian security official, 16 May 2014.
26. 'Timchuk: In Slovyansk a part of the extremists are controlled by an oligrach', Zik.ua website, 13 April 2014; http://zik.ua/ua/news/2014/04/13/tymchuk_u_slovyansku_chastynoyu_ekstremistiv_keruie_oligarh_479114
27. Interviews with activists from the Donbas, 18 May 2014.
28. Interview with top Ukrainian security official, 16 May 2014.
29. Dmitriy Tymchuk, 'The police leadership in the east surrendered their buildings to separatists for a nice amount', Glavcom website, 6 May 2014; http://glavcom.ua/articles/19354.html
30. Interviews with activists from the Donbas, 18 May 2014.
31. 'Armen Sarkissian appeared as a leader of the titushki or the first time in Donetsk on 19 January: Media about Donetsk and Donbas', OstroV website, 7 April 2014; www.ostro.org/general/politics/articles/442003/
32. 'Yanukovych used bandits against the Maidan, proven in the 90s', Gazeta.ua, 6 April 2014; http://gazeta.ua/ru/articles/regions/_anukovich-ispolzoval-protiv-majdana-banditov-proverennyh-v-90h-godah/551088
33. Facebook messages from Donetsk activists, 1 June 2014.
34. Ibid.
35. 'Putin's neo-Nazi helpers', Human Rights in Ukraine website, 10 March 2014; http://khpg.org/index.php?id=1394442656
36. 'Russian neo-Nazi leader instructing separatists in Donetsk', Euroasian Jewish Congress website, 7 May 2014; http://eajc.org/page16/news44/49.html
37. 'Pro-Russian separatists in Eastern Ukraine were "nobodies" – until now', *Washington Post*, 30 April 2014; www.washingtonpost.com/world/europe/pro-russian-separatists-in-eastern-ukraine-were-nobodies—until-now/2014/04/30/c504e687-cc7a-40c3-a8bb-7c1b9cf718ac_story.html
38. Andrey Okara, 'Lumpens against Ukraine: Start of the third world [war]', Ekho Moskvy website, 6 May 2014; www.echo.msk.ru/blog/okara/1314908-echo/
39. Oliver Carroll, 'Why Ukraine's separatist movement failed in Kharkiv', *New Republic*, 22 June 2014; www.newrepublic.com/article/118301/kharkivs-kernes-returns-different-city-after-being-shot
40. 'How violent beating of protestors in Dnipropetrovsk was done', Worlds Apart website, 11 February 2014; http://vorobiov.wordpress.com/2014/02/11/how-violent-suppression-of-protests-in-dnipropetrovsk/
41. See Yarosh's press conference dated 23 April 2014 at www.youtube.com/watch?v=f5agYUQ5Zaw and www.youtube.com/watch?list=UUoy7rPE1lPVczP9y3gEJC7Q&v=7VV0uoOFB-g#t=93
42. 'Odessa 2nd May tragedy: Tentative narrative', HRWF International website, 6 June 2014; www.hrwf.net; 'Chronicle of events in Odesa on 2 May 2014 (part 1)', *Ukraïnska Pravda*, 26 June 2014; www.pravda.com.ua/articles/2014/06/26/7030205/
43. Denys Kazanksy, 'Who's behind separatism in the Donbas?', *Ukrainian Week*, 1 May 2014; http://ukrainianweek.com/Politics/108903
44. Paul Goble, 'Window on Eurasia: "Single command" prepared Donetsk, Luhansk and Crimean operations, Donetsk leader says', Window on Eurasia website, 17 May 2014; http://windowoneurasia2.blogspot.co.uk/2014/05/window-on-eurasia-single-command.html
45. 'Head of separatists from SBU recordings is a pro-Kremlin PR man', *Ukraïnska Pravda*, 14 April 2014; www.pravda.com.ua/news/2014/04/14/7022426/

46. 'Interview with GRU officer Igor Strelkov', translation of *Komsomol'skaya Pravda* article on https://storify.com/ystriya/interview-with-gru-officer-igor-strelkov; Oleg Kashin, 'From Crimea to the Donbas: The adventures of Igor Strelkov and Aleksandr Boroday', slon.ru website, 19 May 2014; http://slon.ru/russia/iz_kryma_v_donbass_priklyucheniya_igorya_strelkova_i_aleksandra_borodaya-1099696.xhtml
47. 'SBU: Yanukovych is controlled by Russian military intelligence', *Ukraïnska Pravda*, 16 April 2014; www.pravda.com.ua/news/2014/04/16/7022681/
48. Ibid.
49. 'Russian mercenaries in the Donbas', Ukrainian Winnipeg website, 13 May 2014; www.ukrainianwinnipeg.ca/russian-mercenaries-donbas/
50. Interviews with activists from the Donbas, 18 May 2014.
51. 'Why the Donetsk Republic is really fake', *Novaya Gazeta*, 30 April 2014; www.novayagazeta.ru/politics/63402.html
52. Interview with Gubarev, *Rossiiskaya Gazeta*, 12 May 2014; www.rg.ru/2014/05/12/gubarev.html
53. 'Source: The current situation in Donetsk is the result of Akhmetov's meeting with Putin', *Ukraïnskyi Tyzhden*, 7 April 2014; http://tyzhden.ua/News/106946; and 'Akhmetov went for talks with Putin – Media', Gazeta.ua website, 7 April 2014; http://gazeta.ua/ru/articles/politics/_ahmetov-s-ezdil-na-peregovory-k-putinu-smi/551172
54. Nina Mishchenko and Yuriy Vinnichuk, 'A "Friend of Putin" will manage the finances of Akhmetov and Novinsky', Forbes.ua website, 2 August 2013; http://forbes.ua/business/1356132-finansami-ahmetova-i-novinskogo-budet-upravlyat-menedzher-druga-putina
55. 'Yefremov going to Luhansk to discuss the possibility of the separation of the South-East – sources', lb.ua website, 20 February 2014; http://lb.ua/news/2014/02/20/256314_efremov_edet_lugansk_obsuzhdat.html
56. Kashin, 'From Crimea to the Donbas: The adventures of Igor Strelkov and Aleksandr Boroday'.
57. 'The views and opinions of residents of south-eastern Ukraine: April 2014', Zn.ua website, 18 April 2014; http://zn.ua/UKRAINE/mneniya-i-vzglyady-zhitcley-yugo-vostoka-ukrainy-aprel-2014-143598_.html
58. 'Attitudes to the situation in the East', Reiting Sociology Group, July 2014; www.rating-group.com.ua/upload/files/RG_East_072014.pdf
59. 'Turchynov: In the so-called "referendum" in the Luhansk region about 24% of the population took part, in Donetsk – more than 30%', UNIAN website, 12 May 2014; www.unian.net/politics/916842-turchinov-v-tak-nazyivaemom-referendume-v-luganskoy-oblasti-prinyali-uchastie-okolo-24-naseleniya-v-donetskoy-bolee-30.html
60. See www.youtube.com/watch?v=J18RziLIl30&feature=youtu.be
61. 'Fake image: PrivatBank advertising to pay 10,000 dollars for a "Moskal" ', Stopfake.org website, 17 April 2014; www.stopfake.org/en/fake-image-privatbank-advertising-to-pay-10-000-dollars-for-a-moskal/
62. Interviews with activists from the Donbas, 18 May 2014.
63. Interview with top Ukrainian security official, 16 May 2014.
64. 'About 4,500 Russian and Chechen mercenaries remain in eastern Ukraine – activist', UNIAN website, 31 May 2014; www.unian.net/politics/923988-okolo-45-tyisyach-rossiyskih-i-chechenskih-naemnikov-ostayutsya-na-vostoke-ukrainyi-aktivist.html
65. 'What makes up the DNR: A scheme of the hierarchy of the separatists is formed', *Dzerkalo Tyzhnya*, 27 June 2014; http://dt.ua/UKRAINE/z-chogo-skladayetsya-dnr-skladeno-shemu-iyerarhiyi-separatistiv-145934_.html
66. 'Slavyansk: Looting, shooting, curfew, Russian spies and manipulation', Novosti Donbassa website, 20 April 2014; http://novosti.dn.ua/details/223252/
67. Interviews with activists from the Donbas, 18 May 2014.
68. 'Militants quarrelled with the Kremlin propagandist because of "Strelkov" ', UNIAN website, 8 July 2014; www.unian.net/politics/937438-boeviki-peressorilis-s-kremlevskim-propagandistom-iz-za-strelkova.html

69. Amnesty International, 'Ukraine: Mounting evidence of abduction and torture', Amnesty International website, 11 July 2014; www.amnesty.org/en/news/ukraine-mounting-evidence-abduction-and-torture-2014-07-11
70. Denys Kasansky, 'Who's behind separatism in the Donbas?', *Ukrainian Week*, 1 May 2014; http://ukrainianweek.com/Politics/108903
71. Amnesty International, 'Ukraine: Mounting evidence of abduction and torture'.
72. 'Negotiator says hundreds of hostages held by separatists in eastern Ukraine', *Kyiv Post*, 16 July 2014; www.kyivpost.com/content/ukraine/negotiator-says-hundreds-of-hostages-held-by-the-separatists-in-the-east-356325.html
73. 'Soot-stained documents reveal firing squad executions in Ukraine', Mashable website, 10 July 2014; http://mashable.com/2014/07/10/evidence-of-execution-trial-discovered-in-the-rubble-of-rebel-headquarters-in-ukraine/
74. 'In Luhansk separatists and Chechens prepare to disrupt elections', *Ukraïnska Pravda*, 18 May 2014; http://ukr.pravda.com.ua/news/2014/05/18/7025701/
75. 'Fighting in the Donbass: Mercenaries from Chechnya earn $300 a day', Glavred website, 28 May 2014; http://glavred.info/politika/za-boi-na-donbasse-naemniki-iz-chechni-zarabatyvayut-po-300-dollarov-v-den-280912.html
76. Courtney Weaver, 'Chechens join pro-Russians in battle for east Ukraine', *Financial Times*, 27 May 2014; www.ft.com/cms/s/0/dcf5e16e-e5bc-11e3-aeef-00144feabdc0.html?siteedition=uk#axzz32wvizEVR
77. Claire Bigg, 'Vostok Battalion, a powerful new player in eastern Ukraine', Radio Free Europe/Radio Liberty website, 30 May 2014; www.rferl.org/content/vostok-battalion-a-powerful-new-player-in-eastern-ukraine/25404785.html
78. Interview with top Ukrainian security official, 16 May 2014.
79. Sean Walker and Howard Amos, 'Ukraine civil war fears mount as volunteer units take up arms', *Guardian*, 15 May 2014; www.theguardian.com/world/2014/may/15/ukraine-civil-war-fears-mount-volunteer-units-kiev-russia. For an early UN Human Rights Report, see www.ohchr.org/Documents/Countries/UA/HRMMUReport15May2014.pdf
80. Interview with top Ukrainian security official, 16 May 2014.
81. 'Right Sector – combat reconnaissance at Karlivka 10/07/2014', posted on 11 July 2014; www.youtube.com/watch?v=SadSxC-zgdc
82. See www.youtube.com/watch?v=tTb7efoe89I
83. See www.youtube.com/watch?v=H8lsaNXZnwM and www.youtube.com/watch?v=vrRTG14JPTU
84. See www.youtube.com/watch?v=AaKoVfDrKS4
85. 'Mustafa Naim acquaints Yarosh with Semenchenko', Hromadske TV, 9 July 2014; www.youtube.com/watch?v=nd65YwnqGg8
86. Oksana Grytsenko and Luke Harding, 'Ukrainians crowdfund to raise cash for "people's drone" to help outgunned army', *Guardian*, 29 June 2014; www.theguardian.com/world/2014/jun/29/outgunned-ukrainian-army-crowdfunding-people-drone
87. 'Joint declaration by the foreign ministers of Ukraine, Russia, France and Germany', German Federal Foreign Office press release, 2 July 2014; www.auswaertiges-amt.de/EN/Infoservice/Presse/Meldungen/2014/140702_Statement.html?nn=472730
88. Yuliya Latynina, 'A new view of war', *Ezhednevnyi zhurnal*, 23 April 2014; www.ej.ru/?a=note&id=24994
89. See http://eng.kremlin.ru/news/6889
90. 'Terrorists in the Donbass prepared to execute any of their comrades who want to surrender', Vostochny Dozor website, 27 June 2014; http://vostok.dozor.com.ua/news/teletype/ukraine/1158336.html
91. 'Russian border guards eliminate terrorists trying to break out from Ukraine into Russian Federation', Tsenzor.net website, 26 June 2014; http://censor.net.ua/news/291617/rossiyiskie_pogranichniki_unichtojayut_terroristov_kotorye_pytayutsya_prorvatsya_iz_ukrainy_v_rf_snbo
92. Max Seddon, 'Ukraine says new tapes prove Russia finances rebels who shot down Malaysian plane', Buzzfeed News website, 25 July 2014; www.buzzfeed.com/maxseddon/ukraine-says-new-tapes-prove-russia-finances-rebels-who-shot

93. Vladimir Socor, 'Donetsk "Republic" leaders' morale plummeting', *Eurasia Daily Monitor*, 1 August 2014; www.jamestown.org/single/?tx_ttnews%5Btt_news%5D=42703&tx_ttne ws%5BbackPid%5D=381&cHash=1b7be65002257ca40141e1007fa739f0

94. 'Terrorists have killed 181 people in the Donbas – General Prosecutor's Office', *Ukraïnska Pravda*, 3 June 2014; www.pravda.com.ua/news/2014/06/3/7027838/

95. Nick Cumming-Bruce, 'UN report details casualties in eastern Ukraine', *New York Times*, 18 June 2014; www.nytimes.com/2014/06/19/world/europe/un-report-details-casualties-in-eastern-ukraine.html

96. 'During the ATO 258 Ukrainian soldiers were killed, 922 injured – NSDC', TSN.ua website, 19 June 2014; http://tsn.ua/politika/za-chas-ato-zaginuli-258-ukrayinskih-viyskovih-922-poraneni-rnbo-359223.html

97. 'UN: In the east 423 people have been killed', BBC Ukrainian Service, 24 June 2014; www.bbc.co.uk/ukrainian/news_in_brief/2014/06/140624_dk_un_estimates_killed_people.shtml

98. Iryna Yeroshko and Olena Goncharova, 'At least 270 soldiers killed in Russia's war against Ukraine', *Kyiv Post*, 18 July 2014; www.kyivpost.com/content/ukraine/at-least-270-soldiers-killed-in-russias-war-against-ukraine-356572.html

99. 'Ukraine: UN report shows rising civilian deaths, ongoing rights abuses', UN News Centre, 29 August 2014; www.un.org/apps/news/story.asp?NewsID=48588

100. 'SSU [i.e. SBU], radio interception of conversations between terrorists, "Boeing-777" plane crash', YouTube, 17 July 2014; www.youtube.com/watch?v=BbyZYgSXdyw&feat ure=youtu.be

101. Seddon, 'Ukraine says new tapes prove Russia finances rebels who shot down Malaysian plane'.

102. 'Column with 100 pieces of equipment at night trying to break into Ukraine from Russia – NSDC', UNIAN website, 13 July 2014; www.unian.ua/politics/939080-kolona-zi-100-odinits-tehniki-vnochi-namagalasya-prorvatis-v-ukrajinu-z-rosiji-rnbo.html

103. 'Russia continues invasion – "green men" appear near Izvaryne', *Ukraïnska Pravda*, 17 July 2014; www.pravda.com.ua/news/2014/07/17/7032170/

104. Jeremy Bender, 'Ukraine separatists have shot down multiple aircraft over the past month', *Business Insider*, 17 July 2014; www.businessinsider.com/ukraine-separatists-have-shot-down-multiple-aircraft-over-the-past-month-2014-7

105. 'Ukrainians are fired on from the territory of the Russian Federation with Grads', Forbes.ua website, 19 July 2014; http://forbes.ua/ua/news/1375302-ukrayinciv-obstrilyuyut-z-teritoriyi-rf-gradom

106. Mark Rachkevych, 'Putin's attacks on Ukraine continue from Russian side', *Kyiv Post*, 24 July 2104; www.kyivpost.com/content/ukraine/putins-attacks-on-ukraine-continue-from-russian-side-357831.html

107. 'A "Tornado" has crossed the Ukrainian-Russian border – activist', *Novosti Donbassa*, 24 July 2014; http://novosti.dn.ua/details/230645/

108. Quoted in Vladimir Socor, 'Defining the Russia–Ukraine conflict: An uphill effort in Berlin', *Eurasia Daily Monitor*, 24 July 2014.

109. 'SSU [i.e. SBU], "Boeing-777" plane crash, "Buk-M1", 17.07.2014', YouTube, 18 July 2014; www.youtube.com/watch?v=MVAOTWPmMM4&list=UURxyjhmvBewJIRb2y ku5EuQ

110. 'SBU publishes telephone calls of terrorists two minutes before the shooting down of the "Boeing"', *Ukraïnska Pravda*, 25 July 2014; www.pravda.com.ua/news/2014/07/25/7032995/

111. 'SSU [i.e. SBU], radio interception of conversations between terrorists, "Boeing-777" plane crash'.

112. 'Strelkov rejoices in the death of nearly three hundred foreign citizens with Boeing 777', Espreso TV website, 17 July 2014; http://espreso.tv/news/2014/07/17/stryelkov_radiye_zahybeli_mayzhe_trokhsot_inozemnykh_hromadyan_z_boyinha_777

113. 'SSU [i.e. SBU], radio interception of conversations between terrorists, "Boeing-777" plane crash'.

114. 'Ukraine accuses Russian aid convoy of stealing factory equipment', Euronews website, 23 August 2014; www.euronews.com/2014/08/23/ukraine-accuses-russian-aid-convoy-of-stealing-factory-equipment/
115. Noah Barkin and Richard Balmforth, 'Insight – As Ukraine forces gain in east, focus of German diplomacy shifts', Reuters, 21 August 2014; http://in.reuters.com/article/2014/08/21/ukraine-crisis-diplomacy-idINKBN0GL1DZ20140821
116. 'Thousands of Russian soldiers sent to Ukraine, say rights groups', Guardian, 1 September 2014; www.theguardian.com/world/2014/sep/01/russian-soldiers-ukraine-rights-groups
117. Interview in Ukrainian Week, 1 June 2014; http://ukrainianweek.com/Society/110335

8 Ukraine's Unfinished Revolution, or a Revolution Barely Begun?

1. See the text of his speech at www.president.gov.ua/en/news/30488.html
2. See http://platforma-reform.org
3. Conversation with Anton Shekhovtsov, 8 May 2014.
4. 'Yarosh should withdraw his candidacy and come to confess', Espresso TV website, 1 April 2014; http://espreso.tv/article/2014/04/01/yarosh_povynen_znyaty_svoyu_kandydaturu_i_pryyty_z_povynnoyu
5. 'Regions decided to fully support the "Right Sector"', Espresso TV website, 2 April 2014; http://espreso.tv/new/2014/04/02/rehionaly_pryynyaly_rishennya_vsilyako_pidtrymuvaty_pravyy_sektor and 'Yuriy Enakievsky's guard wore the stripes of "Right Sector"' – Chornovol, Espresso TV website, 24 March 2014; http://espreso.tv/new/2014/03/24/okhorona_yury_yenakiyevskoho_odyahla_nashyvky_pravoho_sektora_chornovol
6. Anton Shekhovtsov, 'Look far right, and look right again', Open Democracy website, 11 July 2014; www.opendemocracy.net/od-russia/anton-shekhovtsov/look-far-right-and-look-right-again-avaz-batalion-neo-pagan-neo-nazi
7. Oleksandr Kramar, 'Linguistic discrimination in modern Ukraine', Ukrainian Week, 30 April 2013; http://ukrainianweek.com/Society/78764
8. Interview for Channel One, 4 September 2013; http://kremlin.ru/news/19143. For a proper English translation, see Alexander Motyl, 'Deconstructing Putin on Ukraine', World Affairs, 11 September 2013; www.worldaffairsjournal.org/blog/alexander-j-motyl/deconstructing-putin-ukraine
9. 'All-Russian Youth Forum "Seliger-2014"', President of Russia website, 29 August 2014; http://www.kremlin.ru/news/46507
10. 'What precisely Vladimir Putin said at Bucharest'; Dzerkalo Tyzhnya, 19 April 2008; www.mw.ua/1000/1600/62750. See also http://gazeta.dt.ua/POLITICS/to_scho_zh_skazav_volodimir_putin_u_buharesti.html
11. 'Address of the President of Ukraine during the ceremony of inauguration', Petro Poroshenko, President of Ukraine website, 7 June 2014; www.president.gov.ua/en/news/30488.html
12. 'Ukrainians' attitude to Russia's decision to send troops to Ukraine', Kiev International Institute of Sociology website, 16 March 2014; www.kiis.com.ua/?lang=rus&cat=repor ts&id=245&page=1
13. 'Public opinion survey: Residents of Ukraine – March 14–26, 2014', International Republican Institute, www.iri.org/sites/default/files/2014%20April%205%20IRI%20Public%20Opinion%20Survey%20of%20Ukraine%2C%20March%2014-26%2C%202014.pdf
14. See http://uacrisis.org/ru/putins-rating/
15. 'Ukrainians' attitude to Russia's decision to send troops to Ukraine'. See also Maria Snegovaya, 'Despite pro-Russian protests, majority of Ukrainians lean toward Europe', New Republic, 14 April 2014; www.newrepublic.com/article/117357/despite-pro-soviet-protests-majority-ukrainians-lean-toward-europe; Maria Snegovaya, 'The

Ukrainian nation has been born', *Moscow Times*, 1 June 2014; www.themoscowtimes. com/opinion/article/the-ukrainian-nation-has-been-born/501239.html

16. 'Attitudes to the situation in the East', Rating Sociology Group, July 2014; www.rating-group.com.ua/upload/files/RG_East_072014.pdf

17. Dmitriy Korneichuk, 'The Akhmetov–Tymoshenko pact, Dobkin and all'n'all', Glavcom website, 11 April 2014; http://glavcom.ua/articles/18848.html

18. From the official parliament site: http://w1.c1.rada.gov.ua/pls/site2/p_fractions

19. 'The head of the Lustration Committee Sobolev and activists block "elections" to the head of the Economic Court', Tsenzor.net website, 11 April 2014; http://censor.net.ua/news/280650/glava_lyustratsionnogo_komiteta_sobolev_i_aktivisty_ne_dopustili_vyborov_glavy_hozsuda

20. 'Electoral moods of the population of Ukraine: Elections to the Supreme Council of Ukraine', KIIS website, 25 July 2014; www.kiis.com.ua/?lang=ukr&cat=reports&id=383&page=1

21. 'The network obtained a telephone conversation of Kolomoisky and Kurchenko. AUDIO', VIKNA website, 9 March 2014; http://vikna.if.ua/news/category/ua/2014/03/09/16864/view

22. 'Why have Yeremeyev and Kolomoisky quarrelled?', theinsider.ua website, 11 April 2014; www.theinsider.ua/business/5346fd2930d4e/

23. Oliver Carroll, 'Why Ukraine's separatist movement failed in Kharkiv', *New Republic*, 22 June 2014; www.newrepublic.com/article/118301/kharkivs-kernes-returns-different-city-after-being-shot

24. 'In parliament they are trying to form a "Russian group" – expert', *Ukraïnska Pravda*, 7 June 2014; www.pravda.com.ua/news/2014/06/7/7028410/

25. 'Off the record: Grey cardinals of the new powers', *Ukraïnska Pravda*, 20 April 2014; www.pravda.com.ua/rus/photo-video/2014/04/20/7023122/

26. 'The director of UDAR Kovalchuk is a protégé of the Firtash group – the former head of the Ivano-Frankivsk UDAR', Tsenzor.net website, 28 April 2014; http://censor.net.ua/news/283063/rasporyaditel_udara_kovalchuk_stavlennik_gruppy_firtasha_eksglava_ivanofrankovskogo_udara_dokumenty

27. 'Serhiy Pashinsky – friend of Portnov and grey cardinal of Yuliya Tymoshenko', National Anti-Corruption Portal, 14 March 2014; http://antikor.com.ua/articles/3694-sergej_pashinskij__drug_portnova_i_seryj_kardinal_julii_timoshenko; 'Serhiy Pashinsky continues with reiderstvo and disorder', National Anti-Corruption Portal, 15 April 2014; http://antikor.com.ua/articles/5057-sergej_pashinskij_prodolhaet_zanimatjsja_rejderstvom_i_bespredelom

28. 'Putin's people write new constitution for Ukraine', Insider website, 17 April 2014; www.theinsider.ua/politics/534edb08add3e/

9 Other Hotspots

1. Mark Leonard, 'Why Crimea matters', Reuters, 9 April 2014; http://blogs.reuters.com/mark-leonard/2014/04/09/why-crimea-matters/

2. 'Address by President of the Russian Federation', President of Russia website, 18 March 2014; http://eng.news.kremlin.ru/news/6889/print

3. Interview with Iurie Muntean, leading Communist Party MP and rumoured eventual successor to Voronin, 10 April 2013.

4. Interview with Witold Rodkiewicz, 14 December 2011.

5. 'The talented Mr Plahotniuc', East of Europe website, 11 April 2011; http://graham-stack.wordpress.com/2011/04/11/the-talented-mr-plahotniuc/

6. See http://databank.worldbank.org/data/views/reports/tableview.aspx

7. See www.guardian.co.uk/world/2010/dec/02/wikileaks-cables-moldova-voronin-bribe and www.guardian.co.uk/world/us-embassy-cables-documents/224071

8. Interview with UK Ambassador to Moldova, 15 February 2012.

9. See the originally secret annexes to the agreement published at www.flux.md/editii/201142/articole/12545/ and www.hotnews.md/articles/view.hot?id=13579

10. See the accusations in 'Dossier of the Filat regime: Cigarette smuggling has increased considerably during the reign of Vladimir Filat', Omega website, 25 September 2012; http://omg.md/ru/105977/
11. Kamil Całus, 'Crimean Gagauzia?', New Eastern Europe website, 14 March 2014; www.neweasterneurope.eu/articles-and-commentary/1136-crimean-gagauzia
12. Kamil Całus, 'An aided economy: The characteristics of the Transnistrian economic model', OSW Commentary, 16 May 2013; http://www.osw.waw.pl/en/publikacje/osw-commentary/2013-05-16/aided-economy-characteristics-transnistrian-economic-model
13. Interview with George Balan, Moldovan Deputy Minister of Integration, 16 February 2012.
14. Interview with Shota Utiashvili, 27 September 2013.
15. Interview with Helen Khoshtaria, former State Minister for European and Euro-Atlantic Integration, 27 September 2013.
16. Interview with former Deputy Minister of Justice Otar Kakhidze, 27 September 2013.
17. Interview with Helen Khoshtaria, 27 September 2013.
18. Remarks by Tornike Gordadze, Deputy Foreign Minister, 4 November 2011.
19. Shota Utiashvili, 'Why should Russia hurry?', Tabula website, 18 March 2014; www.tabula.ge/en/story/81139-why-should-russia-hurry
20. See the statistics at http://data.worldbank.org/indicator/NY.GDP.PCAP.CD
21. See www.stat.gov.lt
22. 'Russia's policy towards compatriots in the former Soviet Union', Russia in Global Affairs, 2 March 2008; http://eng.globalaffairs.ru/number/n_10351
23. 'Money from Russia', Re:baltika website, undated; www.rebaltica.lv/en/investigations/money_from_russia
24. Luke Harding, 'Latvia: Russia's playground for business, politics – and crime', Guardian, 23 January 2013.
25. Council of Europe, Detecting Irregular Political Financing, 2014; www.coe.int/t/dghl/cooperation/economiccrime/corruption/Publications/EaP/Detecting%20Irregular%20Political%20Financing.pdf
26. Andis Kudors, 'Latvia between the centers of gravitation of soft power – the USA and Russia', in Ivars Indāns (ed.), Latvia and the United States: A new chapter in the partnership, Centre for East European Policy Studies, Riga, 2012, p. 105.
27. Ibid.
28. Interview with Andis Kudors, 12 January 2013.
29. Quoted in Rossiiskaya Gazeta, 4 October 2013.
30. 'Pro-Kremlin media showed inexplicable interest in Estonia's census – security police', Postimees website, 13 April 2013; http://news.postimees.ee/1201184/pro-kremlin-media-showed-inexplicable-interest-in-estonia-s-census-security-police
31. See the trio of books, supposedly based on archival research, Tragediia Litvi: 1941–1944 gody: Sbornik arkhivnykh dokumentov o prestupleniiakh litovskikh kollaboratsionistov v gody Vtoroi mirovoi voiny [Tragedy of Lithuania: 1941–1944], Evropa, Moscow, 2006; Latviia pod igom natsizma: Sbornik arkhivnykh dokumentov [Latvia Under the Nazi Yoke], Evropa, Moscow, 2006; Estoniia: Krovavyj sled natsizma: 1941–1944: Sbornik arkhivnykh dokumentov o prestupleniiakh estonskikh kollaboratsionistov v gody Vtoroi mirovoi voiny [Estonia: The bloody trail of Nazism: 1941–1944], Evropa, Moscow, 2006.
32. Aleksandr Gaponenko and Oleg Alants, Latgaliia: V poiskakh inogo bytiia [Latgalia in Search of a Different Life], Latvian Institute of European Research, Riga, 2012. The book can be found online at www.iarex.ru/books/book87.pdf. The 'think tank' is at www.esinstitute.org
33. Interview with Andis Kudors, 12 January 2013.
34. Remarks by Andrus Ansip at London meeting, 21 January 2013.
35. Interview with Nerijus Maliukevičius, 15 January 2014.
36. Dugin, Osnovy geopolitiki [The Bases of Geopolitics], p. 373.
37. Annual report of the Lithuanian Security Service (VSD) – see www.vsd.lt/vsd_ataskaita_20130607.pdf and www.vsd.lt/VSD_ataskaita_20120604.pdf
38. Interview with Lithuanian MP Mantas Adomėnas, 28 January 2014.

39. Calculations by Mantas Adomėnas.
40. Interview with Emanualis Zingeris, chair of the Foreign Affairs Committee in the Lithuanian Seimas, 12 January 2013.
41. Interview with Mindaugas Žičkus, foreign policy adviser to President Grybauskaitė, 11 January 2013.
42. Ibid.
43. Remarks by Dalia Grybauskaitė, 10 January 2013.
44. Interview with Emanualis Zingeris, chair of the Foreign Affairs Committee in the Lithuanian Seimas, 12 January 2013.
45. Remarks by Vilija Aleknaitė-Abramikienė, member of the Seimas since 1992, 12 January 2013.
46. 'State of the Nation Address to the Belarusian people and the National Assembly', President of the Republic of Belarus website, 22 April 2014; http://president.gov.by/en/news_en/view/alexander-lukashenko-to-deliver-state-of-the-nation-address-on-22-april-8550/
47. 'Another historical refinement by Putin: Kazakhstan has never been a state', Ekonomicheskie Izvestiya website, 29 August 2014; http://news.eizvestia.com/news_abroad/full/886-eshhe-odin-istoricheskij-izysk-putina-kazahstan-nikogda-ne-byl-gosudarstvom
48. 'Russia's image to get humanitarian aid', Gazeta Kommersant website, 10 July 2014; http://kommersant.ru/doc/2520474

10 Russia versus the West

1. Sergei Karaganov, 'Europe and Russia: Preventing a new Cold War', Russia in Global Affairs, 12:2 (April–June 2014), p. 9; http://eng.globalaffairs.ru/number/Europe-and-Russia-Preventing-a-New-Cold-War-16701
2. Both quotes are from Timofei Bordachev, 'Power, Morality and Justice', Russia in Global Affairs, 12:2 (April–June 2014), pp. 28 and 32; http://eng.globalaffairs.ru/number/Power-Morality-and-Justice-16703
3. Rein Müllerson, 'Two worlds – two kinds of international law?', Russia in Global Affairs, 12:2 (April–June 2014), p. 39; http://eng.globalaffairs.ru/number/Two-Worlds-Two-Kinds-of-International-Law-16704
4. Vladimir Socor, 'Ukraine determined to avoid the "frozen-conflict" paradigm', Eurasia Daily Monitor, 11 July 2014; www.jamestown.org/single/?tx_ttnews%5Btt_news%5D=42611&tx_ttnews%5BbackPid%5D=7
5. Interview with Fyodor Lukyanov, 12 June 2014.
6. 'Address by President of the Russian Federation', President of Russia website, 18 March 2014; http://eng.news.kremlin.ru/news/6889
7. Off-the-record comment.
8. Halya Coynash, 'Russia's FSB launches first Crimean show trial', Human Rights in Ukraine website, 2 June 2014; http://khpg.org/index.php?id=1401570936
9. 'Putin stages a putsch against his earlier self, Belkovsky says', Window on Eurasia website, 23 April 2014; http://windowoneurasia2.blogspot.co.uk/2014/04/window-on-eurasia-putin-stages-putsch.html
10. 'Russians less positive about Putin than 5 years ago – poll', RIA-Novosti website, 28 September 2013; http://en.ria.ru/russia/20130928/183796879/Russians-Less-Positive-About-Putin-Than-5-Years-Ago-Poll.html
11. 'Putin's approval rating rises to 80% – poll', RIA-Novosti website, 26 March 2014; http://en.ria.ru/russia/20140326/188776004/Putins-Approval-Rating-Rises-to-80—Poll.html
12. 'Russia's liberals are watching Ukraine's revolution very closely – and so is Putin', New Republic website, 2 December 2013; www.newrepublic.com/article/115796/kiev-protests-yanukovich-eu-deal-moscow-green-envy
13. Vladimir Pastukhov, 'Catch-up revolution', Polit.ru website, 24 January 2014; http://polit.ru/article/2014/01/26/ukraine/

14. Krzysztof Nieczypor, 'Ukraine in "big-time politics" of Alexey Navalny', Eastbook.eu website, 25 February 2012; http://eastbook.eu/en/2012/02/uncategorized-en/ukraine-in-big-time-politics-of-alexey-navalny/
15. 'Lunar Putin fired me from MGU', Gazeta.ru website, 1 July 2014; www.gazeta.ru/social/2014/07/01/6093433.shtml
16. Katarzyna Jarzyńska, 'Patriarch Kirill's game over Ukraine', OSW Commentary, 14 August 2014; www.osw.waw.pl/en/publikacje/osw-commentary/2014-08-14/patriarch-kirills-game-over-ukraine
17. 'Tajikistan: Migrant remittances now exceed half of GDP', Eurasianet.org website, 15 April 2014; www.eurasianet.org/node/68272
18. See www.bloomberg.com/visual-data/best-and-worst/most-oil-dependent-economies-countries
19. Andrey Polunin, 'The world after Crimea', Svobodnaya Pressa website, 19 March 2014; http://svpressa.ru/all/article/83997/
20. Boris Mezhuev, 'The separation of civilisations?', Izvestiya, 18 March 2014; http://izvestia.ru/news/567735
21. Evgeny Vinokurov, 'From Lisbon to Hanoi: The European Union and the Eurasian Economic Union in Greater Eurasia', in Kadri Liik (ed.), Russia's 'Pivot' to Eurasia, ECFR, 2014, p. 62.
22. Interview with Mikhail Krutikhin, 10 July 2013.
23. Ibid.
24. Interview with Ilian Vassilev, 9 July 2013.
25. Jolanta Darczewska, 'The anatomy of Russian information warfare: The Crimean operation, a case study', OSW Point of View, 42, Centre for Eastern Studies, Warsaw, 2014; www.osw.waw.pl/sites/default/files/the_anatomy_of_russian_information_warfare.pdf
26. See 'Igor Strelkov on war, Syria and the crushing of dissent'; https://storify.com/ystriya/waging-war-igor-girkin-aka-strelkov
27. Peter Pomerantsev, 'How Putin is reinventing warfare', Foreign Policy, 5 May 2014; www.foreignpolicy.com/articles/2014/05/05/how_putin_is_reinventing_warfare
28. Ibid.
29. Ibid.
30. Emile Simpson, 'It's not a Russian invasion of Ukraine we should be worried about', Foreign Policy, 30 May 2014; www.foreignpolicy.com/articles/2014/04/30/putin_russia_ukraine_war_invasion_framing
31. Oliver Bullough, 'Inside Russia Today: Counterweight to the mainstream media, or Putin's mouthpiece?', New Statesman, 10 May 2013; www.newstatesman.com/world-affairs/world-affairs/2013/05/inside-russia-today-counterweight-mainstream-media-or-putins-mou
32. 'The Russian Connection: The spread of pro-Russian policies on the European far right', Political Capital Institute, Budapest, 2014; www.riskandforecast.com/useruploads/files/pc_flash_report_russian_connection.pdf; Anton Shekhovtsov, 'Fascist vultures of the Hungarian Jobbik and the Russian connection', Anton Shekhovtsov blog, 12 April 2014; http://anton-shekhovtsov.blogspot.co.uk/2014/04/fascist-vultures-of-hungarian-jobbik.html; Katerina Safarikova, 'Putin and the European right: A love story', Transitions Online website, 16 April 2014; www.tol.org/client/article/24262-putin-and-the-european-right-a-love-story.html
33. See https://twitter.com/NOVORUSSIA2014
34. Heinrich August Winkler, 'Mit Russland gegen den Westen', Der Spiegel, 14 April 2014.
35. 'Fakes of Russian propaganda 2', EuroMaidan Press website, 17 June 2014; http://euromaidanpress.com/2014/06/17/fakes-of-russian-propaganda-2/
36. 'Russia's top lies about Ukraine: Part 1', Stopfake.org website, 10 July 2014; www.stopfake.org/en/russia-s-top-lies-about-ukraine-part-1/
37. The text is at www.nato.int/cps/en/natolive/official_texts_25468.htm
38. See the text at www.cfr.org/arms-control-disarmament-and-nonproliferation/budapest-memorandums-security-assurances-1994/p32484
39. Mary Elise Sarotte, 1989: The struggle to create post-Cold War Europe, revised edition, Princeton, Princeton University Press, 2014.

40. See http://cis-legislation.com/document.fwx?rgn=4181
41. From the Russian version of Timofey Bordachev, 'Strength, morality, justice', *Russia in Global Affairs*, 27 April 2014; www.globalaffairs.ru/number/Sila-moral-spravedlivost-16584
42. 'Germany's Russian energy dilemma', Deutsche Welle website, 29 March 2014; www.dw.de/germanys-russian-energy-dilemma/a-17529685
43. See www.gazprom.com/investors/stock/stocks/
44. See www.gazprom.com/investors/stock/
45. Gazprom still talks about the 'near abroad' and the 'far abroad'. The Baltic States are 'near', so are not normally included in 'European' sales figures.
46. See http://gazpromquestions.ru/?id=34
47. See http://customs.ru/index.php?option=com_newsfts&view=category&id=52&Itemid=1978
48. Interview with Vladimir Milov, 28 May 2013.
49. Anders Aslund, 'Why Gazprom resembles a crime syndicate', *Moscow Times*, 28 February 2012; Anders Aslund, 'How Putin is turning Russia into one big Enron', *Moscow Times*, 21 November 2012.
50. See http://en.rian.ru/business/20130430/180918044/Gazprom-2012-Net-Profit-Plunges-10-on-Lower-Sales.html
51. Remarks by Andris Sprūds, 4 July 2013.
52. Interview with Vladimir Milov, 28 May 2013.
53. Interview with Mikhail Krutikhin, 10 July 2013.
54. See http://ec.europa.eu/energy/eepr/
55. Interview with Mikhail Krutikhin, 10 July 2013.
56. See www.reuters.com/article/2013/10/18/fitch-downgrades-russias-rosneft-to-bbb-idUSFit67261920131018
57. Interview with James Mason, 27 May 2013.
58. Clifford G. Gaddy and Barry W. Ickes, *Caught in the Bear Trap*, Legatum Institute, London, 2013, pp. 6–7; www.li.com/docs/default-source/country-growth-reports/pid-2013-russia-caught-in-the-bear-trap.pdf?sfvrsn=4
59. Oliver Bullough, *Looting Ukraine: How East and West teamed up to steal a country*, Legatum Institute, London, 2014; www.li.com/docs/default-source/publications/ukraine_imr_a4_web.pdf
60. Andrew Rettman, 'Two more Ukrainians try to get off EU blacklist', EU Observer website, 8 April 2014; http://euobserver.com/foreign/123787
61. See the video 'Ian Bremmer on how US foreign policy is "becoming more Chinese" '; http://asiasociety.org/blog/asia/video-ian-bremmer-how-us-foreign-policy-becoming-more-chinese
62. John Kemp, 'US over-reaches with sanctions on Russian energy firms', Reuters, 18 July 2014; www.reuters.com/article/2014/07/18/us-usa-sanctions-policy-idUSKBN0FN26620140718
63. See www.cbr.ru/statistics/print.aspx?file=credit_statistics/bal_of_payments_est_new.htm&pid=svs&sid=itm_45297
64. 'Russian capital outflow in first half of 2014 exceeds entire 2013', *Moscow Times*, 9 July 2014; www.themoscowtimes.com/business/article/russian-capital-outflow-in-first-half-of-2014-exceeds-entire-2013/503225.html
65. 'Russian Eurobond delay risks missing sweet spot', Reuters, 1 February 2013; www.reuters.com/article/2013/02/01/russia-eurobonds-idUSL5N0B119H20130201
66. 'Why Putin is in trouble with 86% approval', Bloomberg website, 27 June 2014; www.bloomberg.com/news/2014-06-26/why-putin-is-in-trouble-with-86-approval.html

Conclusions

1. Brendan Simms, *Europe: The struggle for supremacy, 1453 to the present*, Penguin, London, 2013, pp. 222–7.

Index

Abkhazia 89, 113, 116, 170
Adjara 126, 170
Afghanistan viii, 2, 9, 27, 76, 181, 184, 195
Akhmetov, Rinat 47, 54, 61, 74, 88, 95,
  96, 106, 119, 121, 122, 126, 127, 129,
  130–1, 133, 134, 136, 138, 145, 152,
  153, 157, 160
Aksyonov, Sergey 109, 110, 114, 116, 123,
  124, 135
Aksyonov, Vasiliy 109, 115
Andrukhovych, Yuriy 123
anti-fascism 78, 125–6 passim, 194
Antyufeyev, Vladimir 140
Applebaum, Anne 74
Arbuzov, Serhiy 85
Armenia 2, 4, 15, 17, 100, 102, 104, 105,
  161, 170, 180–1, 188
AutoMaidan 75–7 passim, 81, 88, 115
Azarov, Mykola 48, 58, 65, 85, 126, 202
Azerbaijan 2, 13, 20, 161, 171, 180–1, 188

Baltic States viii, ix, 4, 8, 11, 12, 35, 47, 65,
  69, 145, 159, 164, 168, 171–9, 195, 199,
  232 n. 45
Bandera, Stepan 40, 49, 69
Belarus 2, 15, 16, 20, 68, 80, 94, 99, 101,
  112, 122, 161, 179–80, 188, 189, 194, 199,
  202
Berkut vi, 74–5, 78, 84, 85, 88–92, 94, 97,
  108, 110, 111, 127, 152
Bezler 134–5, 141
Black Sea Fleet 99, 101, 108, 111–12, 116,
  117
Bolotnaya (anti-Putin protests, 2011–12)
  28–30, 185–6

Boroday, Aleksandr 130
Budapest Memorandum (1994) 196–7
Bush, George H.W. 11
Bush, George W. viii, 9, 125, 149, 184, 193

Chaly, Aleksey 108, 109
Chechnya, Chechens 104, 105, 111, 114–15,
  134, 136, 186
Chersonesus 99, 101, 102
China 9, 16, 25, 36, 57, 91, 161, 181, 188–91
  passim, 200, 202
Chornovol, Tetyana 71, 77, 147, 155, 160
Christianity, Orthodox religion 3, 31, 77,
  99, 101–2, 109, 130, 148, 167, 171, 178,
  187, 205, 219 n. 4
Chubarov, Refat 107, 116
Clinton, Hillary 184
conservative values project (Putin) vii, 3,
  18, 21, 30–2 passim, 79, 177, 191
Cooper, Robert 5
Crimea vi, vii, 1, 2, 3, 16, 19, 33, 36, 42, 72,
  75, 94, 95, 96, 99–117 passim, 118–21,
  123–6, 128, 130, 131, 135, 136, 137, 139,
  142, 147, 148–51, 153, 154, 157, 161, 162,
  170, 181, 182, 185, 186–8, 190, 192, 193,
  197, 198, 199, 204, 205, 206, 207
Crimean Tatars 100, 101, 102, 103–4
  passim, 105, 106, 107, 110, 112, 113, 115,
  116, 188, 218 n. 3
Crimean War (1853–56) 100, 101, 102,
  103, 205

Danylyuk, Oleksandr 57, 83
Dnipropetrovsk 42, 70, 84, 120, 121, 122,
  124, 125, 128, 133, 134, 154, 157, 158

Donbas vii, 2, 36, 42, 43, 53, 56, 72, 75, 89, 95, 115, 118–43 *passim*, 144–8, 150–2, 154–7, 160, 162, 167, 170, 184, 186, 192–3, 197, 204, 206–7
Donetsk 34, 55, 58, 79, 95, 107, 118, 119, 120–4, 126, 127–40 *passim*, 151, 195
Donetsk-Kryvy-Rih Republic 124
Doroshenko, Mykhailo 47
Dugin, Aleksandr 32, 33, 64, 123, 139, 177–8, 186, 203
Dzhankoy 111, 115
Dzharty, Vasyl 107
Dzhemilev, Mustafa 107, 112, 113, 116

Eastern Partnership 2, 13, 14, 16, 17, 63, 164, 175, 184
Eastern Slavs 79, 101, 173, 187
Estonia 5, 48, 112, 172, 174–7, 195
Eurasia, Eurasian Union vii, 14, 17, 32, 64, 101, 116, 117, 119, 123, 125, 171, 177, 180, 186, 188–90 *passim*, 191
euro, euro crisis 1, 7–8 *passim*
European Union (EU) viii, 1–6 *passim*, 7–8 *passim*, 9–11, 13–14, 15, 16–18 *passim*, 34–7, 44, 53, 63–95 *passim*, 66–9, 73–4, 79, 85, 88, 91–3 *passim*, 121–3, 125, 141, 142, 150, 152, 159–61, 164, 166, 167, 168, 170–1, 175, 176, 178, 180, 183–4 *passim*, 189, 190–4, 198–204 *passim*

'Family' (interests around Yanukovych) 51–8, 60, 61, 63, 64, 67, 72, 73, 75, 78, 79, 85, 94, 126–8 *passim*, 129, 131, 132, 146, 157, 168
Fatherland Party 61, 83, 94, 135, 147, 155, 156
Filat, Vlad 163–5
Firtash, Dmytro 47, 54, 61, 72, 106, 109, 157–8
France viii, 4, 5, 11, 31, 39, 61, 91, 117, 152, 184, 187, 194, 199, 205
Freedom Party 41, 61, 62, 70, 71, 82, 83, 84, 138, 147, 152

Gazprom 35, 46, 166, 175, 176, 178, 181, 191, 198, 199–203
Gelman, Marat 74
geopolitics 32–3 *passim*, 36, 151
Georgia ix, 2, 3, 4, 5, 6, 10, 12, 14, 16, 26–7, 34, 35, 47, 58, 104, 108, 112, 113, 116, 117, 126, 132, 149, 151, 159, 161, 162, 164, 167, 168–71 *passim*, 183, 193, 202, 204, 207

Germany 194, 199, 201, 202, 205, 206–7
Glazyev, Sergey 125
Gongadze, Heorhiy 43, 45, 51, 68
Gubarev, Pavel 128, 130

Haran, Oleksiy 217 n. 34
Herman, Hanna 50
Hetman Sahaidachny 116
Horlivka 126, 127, 134, 135
hybrid war 117, 129, 139–40 *passim*, 141, 192–3 *passim*, 206, 207

Ilovaisk 142–3
information war 36, 192, 210 n. 42
Iraq viii, 2, 9, 11, 184, 188, 195, 202
Islam 15, 101, 102, 187–8 *passim*, 192
Italy viii, 7, 8 10, 40, 125, 152, 181
Ivanishvili, Bidzina 169–71
Ivanyushchenko, Yuriy 79, 127

Kadyrov, Ramzan 114
Kagan, Robert 5
Kazakhstan 13, 20, 113, 122, 171, 181, 188, 189
Kerch 99, 111, 113, 114, 130
Kharkiv 42, 55, 72, 79, 93, 94–5 *passim*, 98, 108, 117, 120, 121, 128, 132, 151, 157, 196, 223 n. 39
Khodorkovsky, Mikhail 22, 26, 38
Khomutynnik, Vitaliy 52, 55, 157
Khrushchev 99, 100, 104, 120
Kiev vi, 1, 2, 8, 38, 40, 43, 44, 49, 55, 58, 59, 65, 66–98, 101, 103, 105, 108, 110, 112, 122, 124, 126, 127, 128, 130, 136, 144, 145, 148, 151, 154, 157, 158, 159, 191, 201, 206
Klitschko, Vitaliy 61, 82, 93, 147
Klyuyev, Andriy 68, 72, 84, 91, 106
Klyuyev, Serhey 59, 106
Kobzar, Konstantin 77, 96
Kolerov, Modest 34, 35, 174
Kolomoisky, Ihor 72, 73, 128, 129, 133, 134, 155–8, 160
Konstantinov, Vladimir 108–9
Korchynsky, Dmytro 69, 71
Kordonsky, Simeon 26
Kostyantynivka 134
Krasny Luch 134
Krasny Lyman 121, 138
Kravchuk, Leonid 41, 42, 154
Kuchma, Leonid 15, 40–5, 48, 51–4, 63, 71, 94, 99, 105, 113, 126, 138
Kurchenko, Serhiy 52–4, 56, 64, 78, 94, 129, 157
Kyrgyzstan 27, 34, 38, 126, 181, 188

Latgalia 176, 229 n. 32
Latvia 35, 38, 48, 140, 172, 174–8 *passim*, 189, 195, 198
Leshchenko, Sergii 59, 212 n. 53
Libya 11, 188
Lithuania 11, 65, 101, 172, 175–9 *passim*, 195, 198
Lovochkin, Serhiy 72, 84, 157, 158
Luhansk 56, 79, 94, 121, 122, 124, 131–6, 138, 139, 140, 142, 151
Lukashenka, Alyaksandr 16, 94, 112, 161, 179–80 *passim*
Lviv 40, 55, 90, 93, 108, 151
Lyashko, Oleh 137, 138, 146, 152, 153, 156, 158

Maidan ix, 38, 39, 44, 49, 53, 57, 62, 65, 66–98 *passim*, 108, 110, 115, 124, 127–9, 137, 139, 144–6 *passim*, 147, 149, 152, 155, 160, 168, 183, 184, 186, 206, 214 n. 6
Maidan Public Council 76, 93, 145, 146
Makhno, Nestor 134
Makiyivka 107, 126
Malofeev, Konstantin 31, 109, 130
Mariupol 96, 109, 121, 132, 138, 142, 195
Markov, Sergey 23–5 *passim*, 34, 176
Medvedchuk, Viktor 69, 126, 138, 139
Medvedev, Dmitriy 2, 3, 11, 21, 26–7 *passim*, 29, 31, 32, 46, 114
Meshkov, Yuriy 105
Mezhyhirya 58–60 *passim*, 75, 77, 81, 85, 88, 93, 106, 126
MH17 (Malaysia Airlines tragedy) vii, 140–2 *passim*, 143, 204, 206
Milli Firka 107, 116
Mohylyov, Anatoliy 107
Moldova ix, 2, 6, 14, 15, 16, 35, 60, 96, 114, 117, 140, 161, 162–8 *passim*, 171, 199
Moskal, Hennadiy 90, 108, 111
Mostova, Yuliya 52
Mozgovoy, Oleksiy 135

Naim, Mustafa 68
Naryshkin, Sergey 164
NATO vii, 2, 4, 5, 9, 10, 12, 13, 15, 27, 60, 108, 113, 125, 129, 142, 149 150, 170, 171, 178, 182, 183, 195–7 *passim*, 207
Navalny, Aleksey 30, 31, 186, 231 n. 14
Novatek 191, 201, 202
Novorossiya 120, 124, 140, 185
Novynsky, Vadym 75

Obama, Barack viii, 2, 8, 9, 11, 12, 27, 184, 195, 202

Odesa 12, 42, 54, 113, 116, 117, 120, 129, 132–4, 151, 157, 195
oligarchs vii, 1, 11, 18, 19, 20, 21, 22, 24, 26, 31, 39, 42–3 *passim*, 44, 45, 47, 48, 49, 52–4 *passim*, 56, 57, 61, 62, 64, 67, 69, 72–5, 78–80, 90, 94, 106, 109, 112, 114, 119, 122–4, 126–8, 130, 131–3 *passim*, 136, 137, 146, 152, 153, 155, 156, 157–8 *passim*, 160, 163, 167, 168, 174–6, 180, 184, 201, 203, 211 n. 31
Oplot 79, 95, 134, 135
Orange Revolution (2004) 13, 23, 35, 38, 39, 44, 45, 46, 46, 66, 94, 125, 149, 154, 161, 174, 193, 207

Party of Regions 48, 50, 60, 61, 72, 87, 90, 91, 109, 129, 147, 152, 153, 155, 156, 157
Parubiy, Andriy 71, 73, 147
Paul, Rand 184
Pavlenko, Pavlenko 45
Pavlovsky, Gleb 13, 23–5, 28, 34, 176
Pinchuk, Viktor 133
Plahotniuc, Vladimir 163–6
Plokhy, Serhii 11
Poland 5, 6, 9, 10, 16, 40, 45, 55, 91, 152, 177, 182, 184, 187, 195
political technology 20–4 *passim*, 27, 32, 34, 35, 36, 37, 42, 61, 62, 71, 74, 84, 108, 110, 125, 132, 146, 192, 194
Pomerantsev, Peter 192, 208 n. 6, 209 n. 2, 231 n. 27
Ponomaryov, Vyacheslav 135
Poroshenko, Petro 45, 64, 69, 72, 99, 139, 142, 143, 144, 150, 151–3 *passim*, 154, 156, 158, 198
Portnov, Andrey 91, 158–9
Pshonka, Viktor 54, 58, 85, 88, 95, 126
Pushilin, Denis 128, 130
Putin, Vladimir vii, viii, ix, 1, 2, 3, 10, 11, 17, 18, 19–37 *passim*, 38, 46, 52, 61, 64, 69, 74, 79, 81, 91, 98–100, 108, 111, 113–18, 120, 125, 128–33, 138, 139, 141, 142, 145, 147–50 *passim*, 160, 162, 164, 167, 170, 176, 177, 181, 182, 184–6 *passim*, 187–9, 191, 193–5, 197, 200–4, 206
'Putin's friends' vii, 20, 26, 32, 38, 114, 131, 176, 191, 200–3

Right Sector 69–72 *passim*, 76, 88, 90, 91, 94, 96, 109, 125, 129, 137, 138, 146–7 *passim*, 152, 185
Romania 4, 40, 92, 117, 163, 166, 181, 182, 184
Rosneft 176, 191, 201, 202
RosUkrEnergo 35, 46, 54, 64

236

INDEX

Russian nationalism 25, 29, 120, 123, 187
Russian neighbourhood policy 13–14,
  33–6 *passim*, 173–9 *passim*, 190
Russkii mir ('Russian world') 35,
  174–5, 187
Ryabchuk, Mykola 124
Rybachuk, Oleh 46–7

Saakashvili, Mikheil 15, 26, 58, 159, 168–71
  passim
sanctions 85, 93, 115, 141, 152, 170, 179,
  186, 190, 201–4 *passim*, 205–7
Sarkisian, Armen 126–7
Semenchenko, Semen 138, 143
Sevastopol 75, 96, 99, 106, 108–14, 116,
  117, 124, 152
Severodonetsk 94, 121
Shufrych, Nestor 138
Simferopol 106, 109–12, 117
Slovyansk 121, 126, 130–2, 134, 135,
  137–9
'soft power' 10, 14, 18, 34, 36, 132, 182, 184,
  195, 202, 204
South Ossetia 89, 113, 170
Sprūds, Andris 35, 200
Stakhanov, Aleksey 118
Stone, Norman vii
Strelkov, Igor (Girkin) 130, 134, 135,
  139–41, 192
Sukhodolsk 141
Surkov, Vladislav 19, 22, 23, 31, 33, 108–10
  passim, 192, 203
Symonenko, Petro 63
Syria 11, 52, 161, 188

Taruta, Serhiy 133, 136
Temirgalyev, Rustam 107, 109, 116
Tihipko, Serhiy 153, 158
Timchenko, Gennadiy 131, 191, 201, 203
titushki vi, 78–9 *passim*, 84, 87, 88, 92,
  95, 127
Titushko, Vadym 78
Transnistria 105, 114, 140, 143, 167–8
  passim
Trenin, Dmitri (Dmitriy) 5
Tsaryov, Oleh 127, 140
Tsymbursky, Vadym 33

Turchynov, Oleksandr 94, 124, 133, 147
Turkey 13, 15, 60, 104, 117, 122, 160, 181,
  182, 188
tushki 61
Tyahnybok, Oleh 63, 71, 152, 153
Tymchuk, Dmytro 125, 137
Tymoshenko, Yuliya 17, 48, 43, 44, 46–51
  passim, 58, 59, 61, 63, 91, 92, 94, 96, 106,
  147, 152, 153, 158, 199

UDAR (Ukrainian Democratic Alliance for
  Reform – Klitschko's party) 61, 77, 82,
  83, 84, 147, 155, 156, 158
US, American policy viii, 7, 8, 9, 11, 14, 15,
  20, 33, 36, 93, 117, 121, 125, 141, 180,
  184, 188, 189, 196, 198, 200, 202–6
Uzbekistan 20, 181

Vilnius Summit (November 2013) 14, 16,
  17, 63, 65, 68, 184
Vradiyivka 57, 72

Yanukovych, Okeksandr 52, 53, 56, 58, 79,
  89, 106, 111, 126, 127
Yanukovych, Viktor viii, ix, 2, 15, 16, 27,
  38–65 *passim*, 66–81, 83–98 *passim*, 107,
  109, 112, 113, 116, 121–2, 124, 126,
  136–7, 147, 149, 151, 153–60, 184, 188,
  201, 202
Yarosh, Dmytro 70, 72, 137, 138, 152, 153
Yatsenyuk, Arseniy 46, 53, 61, 68, 80,
  141, 156
Yefremov, Serhiy 56, 127, 131
Yekhanurov, Yuriy 48
Yeltsin, Boris vii, 11, 19, 20–2, 24, 34, 38,
  105, 148, 196
Yenakiyeve 126
Yeremeyev, Ihor 155, 157, 158
Yukos affair (2003) 20, 22, 26, 34, 38, 204
Yushchenko, Andriy 45
Yushchenko, Petro 47
Yushchenko, Viktor ix, 15, 39, 43–50
  passim, 53, 58–60, 71, 79, 94, 106, 125,
  131, 136

Zakharchenko, Vitaliy 79, 84, 90, 92, 94
Zaporizhzhya 84, 119, 133